50% OFF ACCUPLACER Pre

Dear Customer,

We consider it an honor and a privilege that you chose our ACCUPLACER Study Guide. As a way of showing our appreciation and to help us better serve you, we have partnered with Mometrix Test Prep to offer you **50% off their online ACCUPLACER Test Prep Course.** Many ACCUPLACER courses are needlessly expensive and don't deliver enough value. With their course, you get access to the best ACCUPLACER prep material, and you only pay half price.

Mometrix has structured their online course to perfectly complement your printed study guide. The ACCUPLACER Online Course contains **in-depth lessons** that cover all the most important topics, **200+ video reviews** that explain difficult concepts, over **850 practice questions** to ensure you feel prepared, and more than **300 flashcards** so you can study on the go.

Online ACCUPLACER Test Prep Course

Topics Include:

- Reading
  - o Information and Ideas
  - o Rhetoric
  - o Vocabulary
- Writing
  - o Foundations of Grammar
  - o Word Usage and Confusion
  - o Punctuation
- Mathematics
  - o Arithmetic
  - o Quantitative Reasoning, Algebra, and Statistics
  - o Advanced Algebra and Functions

Course Features:

- ACCUPLACER Study Guide
  - o Get content that complements our best-selling study guide.
- Full-Length Practice Tests
  - o With over 850 practice questions, you can test yourself again and again.
- Mobile Friendly
  - o If you need to study on the go, the course is easily accessible from your mobile device.
- ACCUPLACER Flashcards
  - o Their course includes a flashcard mode consisting of over 300 content cards to help you study.

To receive this discount, visit their website at mometrix.com/university/accuplacer or simply scan this QR code with your smartphone. At the checkout page, enter the discount code: **APEXACCU50**

If you have any questions or concerns, please contact them at universityhelp@mometrix.com.

Sincerely,

   in partnership with

FREE

Free Study Tips Videos/DVD

In addition to this guide, we have created a FREE set of videos with helpful study tips. **These FREE videos provide you with top-notch tips to conquer your exam and reach your goals.**

Our simple request is that you give us feedback about the book in exchange for these strategy-packed videos. We would love to hear what you thought about the book, whether positive, negative, or neutral. It is our #1 goal to provide you with quality products and customer service.

To receive your **FREE Study Tips Videos**, scan the QR code or email freevideos@apexprep.com. Please put "FREE Videos" in the subject line and include the following in the email:

    a. The title of the book

    b. Your rating of the book on a scale of 1-5, with 5 being the highest score

    c. Any thoughts or feedback about the book

Thank you!

ACCUPLACER
Study Guide 2023-2024
ACCUPLACER Math, Reading, Writing, and Essay
Prep Book with Practice Test Questions
for the College Board Exam [5th Edition]

J. M. Lefort

Written and edited by APEX Publishing.

ISBN 13: 9781637751343
ISBN 10: 1637751346

APEX Publishing is not connected with or endorsed by any official testing organization. APEX Publishing creates and publishes unofficial educational products. All test and organization names are trademarks of their respective owners.

The material in this publication is included for utilitarian purposes only and does not constitute an endorsement by APEX Publishing of any particular point of view.

For additional information or for bulk orders, contact info@apexprep.com.

Table of Contents

Test Taking Strategies

1. Reading the Whole Question

A popular assumption in Western culture is the idea that we don't have enough time for anything. We speed while driving to work, we want to read an assignment for class as quickly as possible, or we want the line in the supermarket to dwindle faster. However, speeding through such events robs us from being able to thoroughly appreciate and understand what's happening around us. While taking a timed test, the feeling one might have while reading a question is to find the correct answer as quickly as possible. Although pace is important, don't let it deter you from reading the whole question. Test writers know how to subtly change a test question toward the end in various ways, such as adding a negative or changing focus. If the question has a passage, carefully read the whole passage as well before moving on to the questions. This will help you process the information in the passage rather than worrying about the questions you've just read and where to find them. A thorough understanding of the passage or question is an important way for test takers to be able to succeed on an exam.

2. Examining Every Answer Choice

Let's say we're at the market buying apples. The first apple we see on top of the heap may *look* like the best apple, but if we turn it over we can see bruising on the skin. We must examine several apples before deciding which apple is the best. Finding the correct answer choice is like finding the best apple. Although it's tempting to choose an answer that seems correct at first without reading the others, it's important to read each answer choice thoroughly before making a final decision on the answer. The aim of a test writer might be to get as close as possible to the correct answer, so watch out for subtle words that may indicate an answer is incorrect. Once the correct answer choice is selected, read the question again and the answer in response to make sure all your bases are covered.

3. Eliminating Wrong Answer Choices

Sometimes we become paralyzed when we are confronted with too many choices. Which frozen yogurt flavor is the tastiest? Which pair of shoes look the best with this outfit? What type of car will fill my needs as a consumer? If you are unsure of which answer would be the best to choose, it may help to use process of elimination. We use "filtering" all the time on sites such as eBay® or Craigslist® to eliminate the ads that are not right for us. We can do the same thing on an exam. Process of elimination is crossing out the answer choices we know for sure are wrong and leaving the ones that might be correct. It may help to cover up the incorrect answer choice. Covering incorrect choices is a psychological act that alleviates stress due to the brain being exposed to a smaller amount of information. Choosing between two answer choices is much easier than choosing between all of them, and you have a better chance of selecting the correct answer if you have less to focus on.

4. Sticking to the World of the Question

When we are attempting to answer questions, our minds will often wander away from the question and what it is asking. We begin to see answer choices that are true in the real world instead of true in the world of the question. It may be helpful to think of each test question as its own little world. This world may be different from ours. This world may know as a truth that the chicken came before the egg or may assert that two plus two equals five. Remember that, no matter what hypothetical nonsense may be in the question, assume it to be true. If the question states that the chicken came before the egg, then choose

1

your answer based on that truth. Sticking to the world of the question means placing all of our biases and assumptions aside and relying on the question to guide us to the correct answer. If we are simply looking for answers that are correct based on our own judgment, then we may choose incorrectly. Remember an answer that is true does not necessarily answer the question.

5. Key Words

If you come across a complex test question that you have to read over and over again, try pulling out some key words from the question in order to understand what exactly it is asking. Key words may be words that surround the question, such as *main idea, analogous, parallel, resembles, structured,* or *defines.* The question may be asking for the main idea, or it may be asking you to define something. Deconstructing the sentence may also be helpful in making the question simpler before trying to answer it. This means taking the sentence apart and obtaining meaning in pieces, or separating the question from the foundation of the question. For example, let's look at this question:

> Given the author's description of the content of paleontology in the first paragraph, which of the following is most parallel to what it taught?

The question asks which one of the answers most *parallels* the following information: The *description* of paleontology in the first paragraph. The first step would be to see *how* paleontology is described in the first paragraph. Then, we would find an answer choice that parallels that description. The question seems complex at first, but after we deconstruct it, the answer becomes much more attainable.

6. Subtle Negatives

Negative words in question stems will be words such as *not, but, neither,* or *except.* Test writers often use these words in order to trick unsuspecting test takers into selecting the wrong answer—or, at least, to test their reading comprehension of the question. Many exams will feature the negative words in all caps (*which of the following is NOT an example*), but some questions will add the negative word seamlessly into the sentence. The following is an example of a subtle negative used in a question stem:

> According to the passage, which of the following is *not* considered to be an example of paleontology?

If we rush through the exam, we might skip that tiny word, *not,* inside the question, and choose an answer that is opposite of the correct choice. Again, it's important to read the question fully, and double check for any words that may negate the statement in any way.

7. Spotting the Hedges

The word "hedging" refers to language that remains vague or avoids absolute terminology. Absolute terminology consists of words like *always, never, all, every, just, only, none,* and *must.* Hedging refers to words like *seem, tend, might, most, some, sometimes, perhaps, possibly, probability,* and *often.* In some cases, we want to choose answer choices that use hedging and avoid answer choices that use absolute terminology. It's important to pay attention to what subject you are on and adjust your response accordingly.

2

8. Restating to Understand

Every now and then we come across questions that we don't understand. The language may be too complex, or the question is structured in a way that is meant to confuse the test taker. When you come across a question like this, it may be worth your time to rewrite or restate the question in your own words in order to understand it better. For example, let's look at the following complicated question:

> Which of the following words, if substituted for the word *parochial* in the first paragraph, would LEAST change the meaning of the sentence?

Let's restate the question in order to understand it better. We know that they want the word *parochial* replaced. We also know that this new word would "least" or "not" change the meaning of the sentence. Now let's try the sentence again:

> Which word could we replace with *parochial,* and it would not change the meaning?

Restating it this way, we see that the question is asking for a synonym. Now, let's restate the question so we can answer it better:

> Which word is a synonym for the word *parochial*?

Before we even look at the answer choices, we have a simpler, restated version of a complicated question.

9. Predicting the Answer

After you read the question, try predicting the answer *before* reading the answer choices. By formulating an answer in your mind, you will be less likely to be distracted by any wrong answer choices. Using predictions will also help you feel more confident in the answer choice you select. Once you've chosen your answer, go back and reread the question and answer choices to make sure you have the best fit. If you have no idea what the answer may be for a particular question, forego using this strategy.

10. Avoiding Patterns

One popular myth in grade school relating to standardized testing is that test writers will often put multiple-choice answers in patterns. A runoff example of this kind of thinking is that the most common answer choice is "C," with "B" following close behind. Or, some will advocate certain made-up word patterns that simply do not exist. Test writers do not arrange their correct answer choices in any kind of pattern; their choices are randomized. There may even be times where the correct answer choice will be the same letter for two or three questions in a row, but we have no way of knowing when or if this might happen. Instead of trying to figure out what choice the test writer probably set as being correct, focus on what the *best answer choice* would be out of the answers you are presented with. Use the tips above, general knowledge, and reading comprehension skills in order to best answer the question, rather than looking for patterns that do not exist.

FREE Videos/DVD OFFER

Achieving a high score on your exam depends on both understanding the content and applying your knowledge. **Because your success is our primary goal, we offer FREE Study Tips Videos, which provide top-notch test taking strategies to help optimize your testing experience.**

Our simple request is that you email us feedback about our book in exchange for the strategy-packed videos.

To receive your **FREE Study Tips Videos**, scan the QR code or email freevideos@apexprep.com. Please put "FREE Videos" in the subject line and include the following in the email:

    a. The title of the book

    b. Your rating of the book on a scale of 1-5, with 5 being the highest score

    c. Any thoughts or feedback about the book

Thank you!

Introduction to the ACCUPLACER

Function of the Test

The ACCUPLACER is a computer assessment exam that tests reading, writing, and math skills for students hoping to enter secondary or postsecondary institutions. The exam has three integrated components built into it: placement assessments for the purpose of the test-taker finding a placement in an institution to align with course requirements, diagnostic assessments in the topics to see areas where they succeed or have knowledge gaps, and skill-building support in the topics used to improve skills in the topics and improve preparedness for college.

The exam tests preparedness for that specific institution in the three core subjects and is given by The College Board for the purposes of measuring where students are at academically in their studies. Schools that assess ACCUPLACER scores are community colleges, technical school, four-year universities, and high schools that use the scores for placement in their institutions. Over 2,000 institutions administer over 8.5 million exams each year to students.

Test Administration

The ACCUPLACER is typically given by appointment through the college or institution's advising and counseling office, though they offer testing alternatives if you live far away from a school or university. Those who do poorly on the exam have the option to retest seven days after the first exam is complete, although they may not exceed five retests in a year's time. Disability accommodations will be handled by the institution's testing center.

Test Format

The test will be given at a local college campus or school, so each testing environment for the ACCUPLACER will be different. Bring a photo ID and any other materials suggested by your institution. If the school you want to attend is located in a different area, your school should have remote options available to you.

The testing format is multiple-choice with no time limit. Keep in mind that with the computer-based assessment, each test question you answer correctly will make the next question more difficult, and each question you answer incorrectly will make the next question easier. With that said, do not rush through this exam, but give each question your undivided attention. The following bullet points show each section of the test and the types of questions in each. Each section has at least 12 questions but no more than 40.

- Arithmetic: Operations with whole numbers and fractions, operations with decimals and percents, and number comparisons and equivalents.

- Quantitative Reasoning, Algebra, and Statistics: Ratios and proportional relationships, exponents, basic algebra, solutions of equations and inequalities, geometry, probability, and statistics.

- Advanced Algebra and Functions: Linear equations and systems, quadratics, factoring, trigonometry, functions, polynomials

- Reading: Understanding what's been read, making inferences, identifying main ideas, and distinguishing between direct statements or supporting ideas

- Writing: Sentence structure, development, organization, usage, logic of a sentence, relationships between sentences

- Writeplacer section: Measures ability to write effectively, specifically looking at focus, organization, development and support, sentence structure, and mechanical conventions

Scoring

As soon as you are finished with the ACCUPLACER exam, the score reporting is instantly reported back to you. The ACCUPLACER Math and English sections are graded on scales that range from 20 to 120 points. The Writeplacer is scored between 0 and 8 points. The scores are used by college counselors to place you in the appropriate college courses, or by the admissions office for admission purposes. Score results are available to you for four years.

Study Prep Plan for the ACCUPLACER

 Breathe

Reducing stress is key when preparing for your test.

 Build

Create a study plan to help you stay on track.

 Begin

Stick with your study plan. You've got this!

1 Week Study Plan

Day 1	Day 2	Day 3	Day 4	Day 5	Day 6	Day 7
Arithmetic	Descriptive Statistics	Advanced Algebra and Functions	Reading	Practice Tests #1 & #2	Practice Test #3	Take Your Exam!

2 Week Study Plan

Day 1	Day 2	Day 3	Day 4	Day 5	Day 6	Day 7
Arithmetic	Quantitative Reasoning, Algebra, and Statistics	Linear Applications and Graphs	Geometry Concepts	Advanced Algebra and Functions	Reading	Writing

Day 8	Day 9	Day 10	Day 11	Day 12	Day 13	Day 14
Practice Test #1	Answer Explanations	Practice Test #2	Answer Explanations	Practice Test #3	Answer Explanations	Take Your Exam!

30 Day Study Plan

Day 1	Day 2	Day 3	Day 4	Day 5	Day 6	Day 7
Arithmetic	Decimal Operations	Practice Quiz	Quantitative Reasoning, Algebra, and Statistics	Exponents	Linear Equations	Probability Sets

Day 8	Day 9	Day 10	Day 11	Day 12	Day 13	Day 14
Descriptive Statistics	Geometry Concepts	Geometric Measurements	Plane Geometry	Practice Quiz	Advanced Algebra and Functions	Radical and Rational Equations

Day 15	Day 16	Day 17	Day 18	Day 19	Day 20	Day 21
Practice Quiz	Reading	Synthesis	Vocabulary	Practice Quiz	Writing	Standard English Conventions

Day 22	Day 23	Day 24	Day 25	Day 26	Day 27	Day 28
Practice Quiz	Write Placer	Practice Test #1	Answer Explanations	Practice Test #2	Answer Explanations	Practice Test #3

Day 29	Day 30
Answer Explanations	Take Your Exam!

Arithmetic

Whole Number Operations

Addition, Subtraction, Multiplication, and Division With Whole Numbers

The four basic operations include addition, subtraction, multiplication, and division. The result of addition is a sum, the result of subtraction is a difference, the result of multiplication is a product, and the result of division is a quotient. Each type of operation can be used when working with rational numbers; however, the basic operations need to be understood first while using simpler numbers before working with fractions and decimals.

These operations should first be learned using whole numbers. Addition needs to be done column by column. To add two whole numbers, add the ones column first, then the tens columns, then the hundreds, etc. If the sum of any column is greater than 9, a one must be carried over to the next column. For example, the following is the result of $482 + 924$:

$$
\begin{array}{r}
{}^{1} \\
482 \\
+924 \\
\hline
1406
\end{array}
$$

Notice that the sum of the tens column was 10, so a one was carried over to the hundreds column. Subtraction is also performed column by column. Subtraction is performed in the ones column first, then the tens, etc. If the number on top is less than the number below, a one must be borrowed from the column to the left. For example, the following is the result of $5,424 - 756$:

$$
\begin{array}{r}
4\ 13\ 11\ 14 \\
\cancel{5}\ \cancel{4}\ \cancel{2}\ \cancel{4} \\
-\ \ 7\ \ 5\ \ 6 \\
\hline
4\ \ 6\ \ 6\ \ 8
\end{array}
$$

Notice that a one is borrowed from the tens, hundreds, and thousands place. After subtraction, the answer can be checked through addition. A check of this problem would be to show that $756 + 4,668 = 5,424$.

In multiplication, the number on top is known as the multiplicand, and the number below is the multiplier. Complete the problem by multiplying the multiplicand by each digit of the multiplier. Make sure to place the ones value of each result under the multiplying digit in the multiplier. The final product is found by adding each partial product. The following example shows the process of multiplying 46 times 37:

Finally, division can be performed using long division. When dividing, the first number is known as the **dividend,** and the second is the **divisor**. For example, with $a \div b = c$, a is the dividend, b is the divisor, and c is the quotient. For long division, place the dividend within the division bar and the divisor on the outside. For example, with $8{,}764 \div 4$, refer to the first problem in the diagram below. First, there are two 4's in the first digit, 8. This number 2 gets written above the 8. Then, multiply 4 times 2 to get 8, and that product goes below the 8. Subtract to get 0, and then carry down the second digit, 7. Continue the same steps.

$$7 \div 4 = 1\,R\,3$$

So, 1 is written above the 7. Multiply 4 times 1 to get 4 and write it below the 7. Subtract to get 3 and carry the 6 down next to the 3. The resulting steps give a 9 and a 1. The final subtraction results in a 0, which means that 8,764 is evenly divisible by 4 with no remaining numbers.

The second example shows that:

$$4{,}536 \div 216 = 21$$

The steps are a little different because 216 cannot be contained in 4 or 5, so the first step is placing a 2 above the 3 because there are two 216's in 453. Finally, the third example shows that $546 \div 31 = 17\,R\,19$. The 19 is a remainder. Notice that the final subtraction does not result in a 0, which means that 546 is not divisible by 31.

The remainder can also be written as a fraction over the divisor to say that:

$$546 \div 31 = 17\frac{19}{31}$$

```
    2 1 9 1              2 1               1 7  r  19
  4 8 7 6 4          216 4 5 3 6         31 5 4 6
    8                    4 3 2              3 1
    0 7                    2 1 6            2 3 6
      4                    2 1 6            2 1 7
      3 6                      0              1 9
      3 6
        0 4
          4
          0
```

A remainder can have meaning in a division problem with real-world application. For example, consider the third example:

$$546 \div 31 = 17 \, R \, 19$$

Let's say that we had $546 to spend on calculators that cost $31 each, and we wanted to know how many we could buy. The division problem would answer this question. The result states that 17 calculators could be purchased, with $19 left over. Notice that the remainder will never be greater than or equal to the divisor.

Interpreting Remainders in Division Problems

Understanding remainders begins with understanding the division problem. The problem $24 \div 7$ can be read as "twenty-four divided by seven." The problem is asking how many groups of 7 will fit into 24. Counting by seven, the multiples are 7, 14, 21, 28. Twenty-one, which is three groups of 7, is the closest to 24. The difference between 21 and 24 is 3, which is called the remainder. This is a remainder because it is the number that is left out after the three groups of seven are taken from 24. The answer to this division problem can be written as 3 with a remainder 3, or $3\frac{3}{7}$.

The fraction $\frac{3}{7}$ can be used because it shows the part of the whole left when the division is complete. Another division problem may have the following numbers: $36 \div 5$. This problem is asking how many groups of 5 will fit evenly into 36. When counting by multiples of 5, the following list is generated: 5, 10, 15, 20, 25, 30, 35, 40. As seen in the list, there are seven groups of five that make 35. To get to the total of 36, there needs to be one additional number. The answer to the division problem would be:

$$36 \div 5 = 7 \, R \, 1 = 7\frac{1}{5}$$

The fractional part represents the number that cannot make up a whole group of five.

Addition, Subtraction, Multiplication, and Division with Integers

Once the operations are understood with whole numbers, they can be used with negative numbers. There are many rules surrounding operations with negative numbers. First, consider addition with integers. The sum of two numbers can first be shown using a number line. For example, to add $-5 + (-6)$, plot the point -5 on the number line. Adding a negative number is the same as subtracting, so move 6 units to the left. This process results in landing on -11 on the number line, which is the sum of -5 and -6. If adding a positive number, move to the right. While visualizing this process using a number line is useful for understanding, it is more efficient to learn the rules of operations. When adding two numbers with the same sign, add the absolute values of both numbers, and use the common sign of both numbers as the sign of the sum. For example, to add:

$$-5 + (-6)$$

Add their absolute values:

$$5 + 6 = 11$$

Then, introduce a negative number because both addends are negative. The result is -11. To add two integers with unlike signs, subtract the lesser absolute value from the greater absolute value, and apply the sign of the number with the greater absolute value to the result. For example, the sum $-7 + 4$ can be computed by finding the difference $7 - 4 = 3$ and then applying a negative because the value with the larger absolute value is negative. The result is -3. Similarly, the sum $-4 + 7$ can be found by computing the same difference but leaving it as a positive result because the addend with the larger absolute value is positive. Also, recall that any number plus 0 equals that number. This is known as the **Addition Property of 0.**

Subtracting two integers with opposite signs can be computed by changing to addition to avoid confusion. The rule is to add the first number to the opposite of the second number. The opposite of a number is the number with the same value on the other side of 0 on the number line. For example, -2 and 2 are opposites. Consider $4 - 8$. Change this to adding the opposite as follows: $4 + (-8)$. Then, follow the rules of addition of integers to obtain -4. Secondly, consider $-8 - (-2)$. Change this problem to adding the opposite as $-8 + 2$, which equals -6. Notice that subtracting a negative number functions the same as adding a positive number.

Multiplication and division of integers are actually less confusing than addition and subtraction because the rules are simpler to understand. If two factors in a multiplication problem have the same sign, the result is positive. If one factor is positive and one factor is negative, the result, known as the **product,** is negative. For example, $(-9)(-3) = 27$ and $9(-3) = -27$. Also, any number times 0 always results in 0.

If a problem consists of several multipliers, the result is negative if it contains an odd number of negative factors, and the result is positive if it contains an even number of negative factors. For example:

$$(-1)(-1)(-1)(-1) = 1$$

and

$$(-1)(-1)(-1)(-1)(-1) = -1$$

Similar rules apply within division. First, consider some vocabulary. When dividing 14 by 2, it can be written in the following ways:

$$14 \div 2 = 7$$

or

$$\frac{14}{2} = 7$$

14 is the **dividend,** 2 is the **divisor,** and 7 is the **quotient.** If two numbers in a division problem have the same sign, the quotient is positive. If two numbers in a division problem have different signs, the quotient is negative. For example,

$$14 \div (-2) = -7$$

and

$$-14 \div (-2) = 7$$

To check division, multiply the quotient times the divisor to obtain the dividend. Also, remember that 0 divided by any number is equal to 0. However, any number divided by 0 is undefined. It just does not make sense to divide a number by 0 parts.

The Order of Operations

If more than one operation is to be completed in a problem, follow the **Order of Operations**. The mnemonic device, **PEMDAS**, states the order in which addition, subtraction, multiplication, and division need to be done. It also includes when to evaluate operations within grouping symbols and when to incorporate exponents. PEMDAS, which some remember by thinking "please excuse my dear Aunt Sally," refers to parentheses, exponents, multiplication, division, addition, and subtraction.

First, complete any operation within parentheses or any other grouping symbol like brackets, braces, or absolute value symbols. Note that this does not refer to when parentheses are used to represent multiplication like $(2)(5)$. An operation is not within parentheses like it is in (2×5). Then, any exponents must be computed. Next, multiplication and division are performed from left to right. Finally, addition and subtraction are performed from left to right. The following is an example in which the operations within the parentheses need to be performed first, so the order of operations must be applied to the exponent, subtraction, addition, and multiplication within the grouping symbol:

$$9-3(3^2-3+4\cdot3)$$

$$9-3(3^2-3+4\cdot3)$$ Work within the parentheses first

$$=9-3(9-3+12)$$

$$=9-3(18)$$

$$=9-54$$

$$=-45$$

Estimating

Sometimes it is helpful to find an estimated answer to a problem rather than working out an exact answer. An estimation might be much quicker to find, and it might be all that is required given the scenario. For example, if Aria goes grocery shopping and has only a $100 bill to cover all of her purchases, it might be appropriate for her to estimate the total of the items she is purchasing to determine if she has enough money to cover them. Also, an estimation can help determine if an answer makes sense. For instance, if you estimate that an answer should be in the 100s, but your result is a fraction less than 1, something is probably wrong in the calculation.

The first type of estimation involves rounding. **Rounding** consists of expressing a number in terms of the nearest decimal place like the tenth, hundredth, or thousandth place, or in terms of the nearest whole number unit like tens, hundreds, or thousands place. When rounding to a specific place value, look at the digit to the right of the place. If it is 5 or higher, round the number to its left up to the next value, and if it is 4 or lower, keep that number at the same value. For instance, 1,654.2674 rounded to the nearest thousand is 2,000, and the same number rounded to the nearest thousandth is 1,654.267. Rounding can make it easier to estimate totals at the store. Items can be rounded to the nearest dollar. For example, a can of corn that costs $0.79 can be rounded to $1.00, and then all other items can be rounded in a similar manner and added together.

When working with larger numbers, it might make more sense to round to higher place values. For example, when estimating the total value of a dealership's car inventory, it would make sense to round the car values to the nearest thousands place. The price of a car that is on sale for $15,654 can be estimated at $16,000. All other cars on the lot could be rounded in the same manner and then added together. Depending on the situation, it might make sense to calculate an over-estimate. For example, to make sure Aria has enough money at the grocery store, rounding up for each item would ensure that she will have enough money when it comes time to pay. A $0.40 item rounded up to $1.00 would ensure that there is a dollar to cover that item. Traditional rounding rules would round $0.40 to $0, which does not make sense in this particular real-world setting. Aria might not have a dollar available at checkout to pay for that item if she uses traditional rounding. It is up to the customer to decide the best approach when estimating.

Estimating is also very helpful when working with measurements. Bryan is updating his kitchen and wants to retile the floor. Again, an over-measurement might be useful. Also, rounding to nearest half-unit might be helpful. For instance, one side of the kitchen might have an exact measurement of 14.32 feet, and the most useful measurement needed to buy tile could be estimating this quantity to be 14.5 feet. If the kitchen was rectangular and the other side measured 10.9 feet, Bryan might round the other side to 11 feet. Therefore, Bryan would find the total tile necessary according to the following area calculation:

$$14.5 \times 11 = 159.5 \text{ square feet}$$

To make sure he purchases enough tile, Bryan would probably want to purchase at least 160 square feet of tile. This is a scenario in which an estimation might be more useful than an exact calculation. Having more tile than necessary is better than having an exact amount, in case any tiles are broken or otherwise unusable.

Finally, estimation is helpful when exact answers are necessary. Consider a situation in which Sabina has many operations to perform on numbers with decimals, and she is allowed a calculator to find the result. Even though an exact result can be obtained with a calculator, there is always a possibility that Sabina could make an error while inputting the data. For example, she could miss a decimal place, or misuse a parenthesis, causing a problem with the actual order of operations. A quick estimation at the beginning could help ensure that her final answer is within the correct range.

Sabina has to find the exact total of 10 cars listed for sale at the dealership. Each price has two decimal places included to account for both dollars and cents. If one car is listed at $21,234.43 but Sabina incorrectly inputs into the calculator the price of $2,123.443, this error would throw off the final sum by almost $20,000. A quick estimation at the beginning, by rounding each price to the nearest thousands place and finding the sum of the prices, would give Sabina an amount to compare the exact amount to. This comparison would let Sabina see if an error was made in her exact calculation.

Fraction Operations

Distribution of a Quantity into its Fractional Parts

Fractions are ratios of whole numbers and their negatives. Fractions represent parts of wholes, whether they be pies, or money, or work. The number on top, or numerator, represents the part, and the bottom number, or denominator, represents the whole. The number $\frac{1}{2}$ represents half of a whole. Other ways to represent one-half are $\frac{2}{4}, \frac{3}{6}$, and $\frac{5}{10}$. These are fractions not written in simplest form, but the numerators are all halves of the denominators. The fraction $\frac{1}{4}$ represents 1 part to a whole of 4 parts. This can be modeled by the quarter's value in relation to the dollar.

One quarter is $\frac{1}{4}$ of a dollar. In the same way, 2 quarters make up $\frac{1}{2}$ of a dollar, so 2 fractions of $\frac{1}{4}$ make up a fraction of $\frac{1}{2}$. Three quarters make up three-fourths of a dollar.

Consider the following:

$$\frac{1}{4} + \frac{1}{4} + \frac{1}{4}$$

The three fractions are equal to $\frac{3}{4}$ of a whole. This illustration can be seen using the bars below divided into one whole, then two halves, then three sections of one-third, then four sections of one-fourth. Based on the size of the fraction, different numbers of each fraction are needed to make up a whole.

A **unit fraction** is a fraction where the numerator has a value of one. The fractions one-half, one-third, one-seventh, and one-tenth are all examples of unit fractions. Non-examples of unit fractions include three-fourths, four-fifths, and seven-twelfths. The value of unit fractions changes as the denominator changes because the numerator is always one. The unit fraction one-half requires two parts to make a whole. The unit fraction one-third requires three parts to make a whole. In the same way, if the unit fraction changes to one-thirteenth, then the number of parts required to make a whole becomes thirteen. An illustration of this is seen in the figure below. As the denominator increases, the size of the parts for each fraction decreases. As the bar goes from one-fourth to one-fifth, the size of the bars decreases, but the size of the denominator increases to five. This pattern continues down the diagram, and as the bars, or value of the fraction, get smaller, the denominator gets larger.

Addition, Subtraction, Multiplication, and Division with Fractions

A **rational number** is a number that can be written in the form $\frac{a}{b}$, where a and b are integers, and b is not equal to zero. In other words, rational numbers can be written in a fraction form. The value a is the **numerator,** and b is the **denominator**. If the numerator is equal to zero, the entire fraction is equal to zero. Non-negative fractions can be less than 1, equal to 1, or greater than 1. Fractions are less than 1 if the numerator is smaller (less than) than the denominator. For example, $\frac{3}{4}$ is less than 1. A fraction is equal to 1 if the numerator is equal to the denominator. For instance, $\frac{4}{4}$ is equal to 1. Finally, a fraction is greater than 1 if the numerator is greater than the denominator: the fraction $\frac{11}{4}$ is greater than 1.

When the numerator is greater than the denominator, the fraction is called an **improper fraction**. An improper fraction can be converted to a **mixed number,** a combination of both a whole number and a fraction. To convert an improper fraction to a mixed number, divide the numerator by the denominator. Write down the whole number portion, and then write any remainder over the original denominator. For example, $\frac{11}{4}$ is equivalent to $2\frac{3}{4}$. Conversely, a mixed number can be converted to an improper fraction by multiplying the denominator times the whole number and adding that result to the numerator.

If a rational number is in fraction form, performing addition, subtraction, multiplication, and division is more complicated than when working with integers. First, consider addition. To add two fractions having the same denominator, add the numerators and then reduce the fraction. When an answer is a fraction, it should always be in lowest terms. **Lowest terms** means that every common factor, other than 1, between the numerator and denominator is divided out. For example,

$$\frac{2}{8} + \frac{4}{8} = \frac{6}{8} = \frac{6 \div 2}{8 \div 2} = \frac{3}{4}$$

Both the numerator and denominator of $\frac{6}{8}$ have a common factor of 2, so 2 is divided out of each number to put the fraction in lowest terms. If denominators are different in an addition problem, the fractions must be converted to have common denominators. The **least common denominator (LCD)** of all the given denominators must be found, and this value is equal to the **least common multiple (LCM)** of the denominators. This non-zero value is the smallest number that is a multiple of both denominators. Then, each original fraction can be written as an equivalent fraction using the new denominator. Once in this form, process of adding with like denominators is completed. For example, consider:

$$\frac{1}{3} + \frac{4}{9}$$

The LCD is 9 because 9 is the smallest multiple of both 3 and 9. The fraction $\frac{1}{3}$ must be rewritten with 9 as its denominator. Therefore, multiply both the numerator and denominator by 3. Multiplying by $\frac{3}{3}$ is the same as multiplying times 1, which does not change the value of the fraction. Therefore, an equivalent fraction is $\frac{3}{9}$, so:

$$\frac{1}{3} + \frac{4}{9} = \frac{3}{9} + \frac{4}{9} = \frac{7}{9}$$

$\frac{7}{9}$ is in lowest terms. Subtraction is performed in a similar manner; once the denominators are equal, the numerators are then subtracted. The following is an example of addition of a positive and a negative fraction:

$$-\frac{5}{12}+\frac{5}{9}=-\frac{5\times3}{12\times3}+\frac{5\times4}{9\times4}$$

$$-\frac{15}{36}+\frac{20}{36}=\frac{5}{36}$$

Common denominators are not used in multiplication and division. To multiply two fractions, multiply the numerators together and the denominators together. Then, write the result in lowest terms.

For example,

$$\frac{2}{3}\times\frac{9}{4}=\frac{18}{12}=\frac{3}{2}$$

Alternatively, the fractions could be factored first to cancel out any common factors before performing the multiplication. For example,

$$\frac{2}{3}\times\frac{9}{4}=\frac{2}{3}\times\frac{3\times3}{2\times2}=\frac{3}{2}$$

This second approach is helpful when working with larger numbers, as common factors might not be obvious. Multiplication and division of fractions are related because the division of two fractions is changed into a multiplication problem. This means that dividing a fraction by another fraction is the same as multiplying the first fraction by the **reciprocal** of the second fraction, so that second fraction must be inverted, or "flipped," to be in reciprocal form. For example:

$$\frac{11}{15}\div\frac{3}{5}=\frac{11}{15}\times\frac{5}{3}=\frac{55}{45}=\frac{11}{9}$$

The fraction $\frac{5}{3}$ is the reciprocal of $\frac{3}{5}$. It is possible to multiply and divide numbers containing a mix of integers and fractions. In this case, convert the integer to a fraction by placing it over a denominator of 1. For example, a division problem involving an integer and a fraction is:

$$3\div\frac{1}{2}=\frac{3}{1}\times\frac{2}{1}=\frac{6}{1}=6$$

Comparing Fractions

Comparing fractions requires the use of a common denominator. This necessity can be seen by the two pies below. The first pie has a shaded value of $\frac{2}{10}$ because two pieces are shaded out of the total of ten equal pieces. The second pie has a shaded value of $\frac{2}{7}$ because two pieces are shaded out of a total of seven equal pieces. These two fractions, two-tenths and two-sevenths, have the same numerator, and so a misconception may be that they are equal. By looking at the shaded region in each pie, it is apparent that the fractions are not equal.

The numerators are the same, but the denominators are not. Two parts of a whole are not equivalent unless the whole is broken into the same number of parts. To compare the shaded regions, the denominators seven and ten must be made equal. The lowest number that the two denominators will both divide evenly into is 70, so this is the lowest common denominator. Then the numerators must be converted by multiplying by the opposite denominator. These operations result in the two fractions $\frac{14}{70}$ and $\frac{20}{70}$. Now that these two have the same denominator, the conclusion can be made that $\frac{2}{7}$ represents a larger portion of the pie, as seen in the figure below.

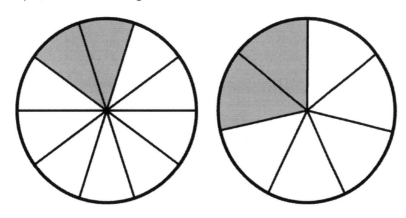

Decimal Operations

Recognition of Decimals

A **decimal** is a number that uses a decimal point and numbers to the right of the decimal point representing the part of the number that is less than 1. For example, 3.5 is a decimal and is equivalent to the fraction $\frac{7}{2}$ or the mixed number $3\frac{1}{2}$. The decimal is found by dividing 2 into 7. Other examples of decimals are 15.8, 0.75, and -10.2158.

Fractions can be converted to decimals. With a calculator, a fraction is converted to a decimal by dividing the numerator by the denominator. For example:

$$\frac{2}{5} = 2 \div 5 = 0.4$$

Sometimes, rounding might be necessary. Consider:

$$\frac{2}{7} = 2 \div 7 = 0.28571429$$

This decimal could be rounded for ease of use, and if it needed to be rounded to the nearest thousandth, the result would be 0.286. If a calculator is not available, a fraction can be converted to a decimal manually.

First, find a number that, when multiplied by the denominator, has a value equal to 10, 100, 1,000, etc. Then, multiply both the numerator and denominator times that number. The decimal form of the fraction is equal to the new numerator with a decimal point placed as many place values to the left as there are zeros in the denominator. For example, to convert $\frac{3}{5}$ to a decimal, multiply both the numerator and denominator times 2, which results in $\frac{6}{10}$. The decimal is equal to 0.6 because there is one zero in the denominator, and so the decimal place in the numerator is moved one unit to the left.

In the case where rounding would be necessary while working without a calculator, an approximation must be found. A number close to 10, 100, 1,000, etc. can be used. For example, to convert $\frac{1}{3}$ to a decimal, the numerator and denominator can be multiplied by 33 to turn the denominator into approximately 100, which makes for an easier conversion to the equivalent decimal. This process results in $\frac{33}{99}$ and an approximate decimal of 0.33. Once in decimal form, the number can be converted to a percentage. Multiply the decimal by 100 and then place a percent sign after the number. For example, 0.614 is equal to 61.4%. In other words, move the decimal place two units to the right and add the percentage symbol.

Addition, Subtraction, Multiplication, and Division with Decimals

Operations can be performed on rational numbers in decimal form. Recall that to write a fraction as an equivalent decimal expression, divide the numerator by the denominator. For example:

$$\frac{1}{8} = 1 \div 8 = 0.125$$

With the case of decimals, it is important to keep track of place value. To add decimals, make sure the decimal places are in alignment and add vertically. If the numbers do not line up because there are extra or missing place values in one of the numbers, then zeros may be used as placeholders.

For example, $0.123 + 0.23$ becomes:

$$\begin{array}{r} 0.123 \\ \underline{0.230} \\ 0.353 \end{array}$$

Subtraction is done the same way. Multiplication and division are more complicated. To multiply two decimals, place one on top of the other as in a regular multiplication process and do not worry about lining up the decimal points. Then, multiply as with whole numbers, ignoring the decimals. Finally, in the solution, insert the decimal point as many places to the left as there are total decimal values in the original problem. Here is an example of a decimal multiplication problem:

$$\begin{array}{r} 0.52 \quad \textit{2 decimal places} \\ \times \ 0.2 \quad \textit{1 decimal place} \\ \hline 0.104 \quad \textit{3 decimal places} \end{array}$$

The answer to 52 times 2 is 104, and because there are three decimal values in the problem, the decimal point is positioned three units to the left in the answer.

The decimal point plays an integral role throughout the whole problem when dividing with decimals. First, set up the problem in a long division format. If the divisor is not an integer, move the decimal to the right

20

as many units as needed to make it an integer. The decimal in the dividend must be moved to the right the same number of places to maintain equality. Then, complete division normally. Here is an example of long division with decimals:

**Long division
with decimals**

$$
\begin{array}{r}
2\,1\,2 \\
6\,\overline{\smash{)}\,1\,2\,7\,2} \\
1\,2 \\
\overline{0\,7} \\
6 \\
\overline{1\,2}
\end{array}
$$

The decimal point in 0.06 needed to move two units to the right to turn it into an integer (6), so it also needed to move two units to the right in 12.72 to make it 1,272. The quotient is 212. To check a division problem, multiply the answer by the divisor to see if the result is equal to the dividend.

Sometimes it is helpful to round answers that are in decimal form. First, find the place to which the rounding needs to be done. Then, look at the digit to the right of it. If that digit is 4 or less, the number in the place value to its left stays the same, and everything to its right becomes a 0. This process is known as *rounding down*. If that digit is 5 or higher, the number in the place value to its left increases by 1, and every number to its right becomes a 0. This is called rounding up. Excess 0s at the end of a decimal can be dropped. For example, 0.145 rounded to the nearest hundredth place would be rounded up to 0.15, and 0.145 rounded to the nearest tenth place would be rounded down to 0.1.

Percent

Percent Problems

Percentages are defined as parts per one hundred. To convert a decimal to a percentage, move the decimal point two units to the right and place the percent sign after the number. Percentages appear in many scenarios in the real world. It is important to make sure the statement containing the percentage is translated to a correct mathematical expression. Be aware that it is extremely common to make a mistake when working with percentages within word problems.

An example of a word problem containing a percentage is the following: 35% of people speed when driving to work. In a group of 5,600 commuters, how many would be expected to speed on the way to their place of employment? The answer to this problem is found by finding 35% of 5,600. First, change the percentage to the decimal 0.35. Then compute the product: $0.35 \times 5,600 = 1,960$. Therefore, it would be expected that 1,960 of those commuters would speed on their way to work based on the data given. In this situation, the word "of" signals to use multiplication to find the answer. Another way percentages are used is in the following problem: Teachers work 8 months out of the year. What percent of the year do they work? To answer this problem, find what percent of 12 the number 8 is, because there are 12 months in a year. Therefore, divide 8 by 12, and convert that number to a percentage:

$$\frac{8}{12} = \frac{2}{3} = 0.66\overline{6}$$

The percentage rounded to the nearest tenth place tells us that teachers work 66.7% of the year. Percentage problems can also find missing quantities like in the following question: 60% of what number is 75? To find the missing quantity, turn the question into an equation. Let x be equal to the missing quantity. Therefore:

$$0.60x = 75$$

Divide each side by 0.60 to obtain 125. Therefore, 60% of 125 is equal to 75.

Sales tax is an important application relating to percentages because tax rates are usually given as percentages. For example, a city might have an 8% sales tax rate. Therefore, when an item is purchased with that tax rate, the real cost to the customer is 1.08 times the price in the store. For example, a $25 pair of jeans costs the customer:

$$\$25 \times 1.08 = \$27$$

If the sales tax rate is unknown, it can be determined after an item is purchased. If a customer visits a store and purchases an item for $21.44, but the price in the store was $19, they can find the tax rate by first subtracting $21.44 − $19 to obtain $2.44, the sales tax amount. The sales tax is a percentage of the in-store price. Therefore, the tax rate is:

$$\frac{2.44}{19} = 0.128$$

This has been rounded to the nearest thousandths place. In this scenario, the actual sales tax rate given as a percentage is 12.8%.

Number Comparisons and Equivalents

Comparing and Ordering Numbers

Ordering rational numbers is a way to compare two or more different numerical values. Determining whether two amounts are equal, less than, or greater than is the basis for comparing both positive and negative numbers. Also, a group of numbers can be compared by ordering them from the smallest amount to the largest amount. A few symbols are necessary to use when ordering rational numbers. The equals sign, =, shows that the two quantities on either side of the symbol have the same value. For example, $\frac{12}{3} = 4$ because both values are equivalent. Another symbol that is used to compare numbers is <, which represents "less than."

With this symbol, the smaller number is placed on the left and the larger number is placed on the right. Always remember that the symbol's "mouth" opens up to the larger number. When comparing negative and positive numbers, it is important to remember that the number occurring to the left on the number line is always smaller and is placed to the left of the symbol. This idea might seem confusing because some values could appear at first glance to be larger, even though they are not. For example, $-5 < 4$ is read "negative 5 is less than 4." Here is an image of a number line to help:

The symbol $\leq$ represents "less than or equal to," and it joins $<$ with equality. Therefore, both $-5 \leq 4$ and $-5 \leq -5$ are true statements and "-5 is less than or equal to both 4 and -5." Other symbols are $>$ and $\geq$, which represent "greater than" and "greater than or equal to." Both $4 \geq -1$ and $-1 \geq -1$ are correct ways to use these symbols.

Here is a chart of these four inequality symbols:

Symbol	Definition
$<$	less than
$\leq$	less than or equal to
$>$	greater than
$\geq$	greater than or equal to

Comparing integers is a straightforward process, especially when using the number line, but the comparison of decimals and fractions is not as obvious. When comparing two non-negative decimals, compare digit by digit, starting from the left. The larger value contains the first larger digit. For example, 0.1456 is larger than 0.1234 because the value 4 in the hundredths place in the first decimal is larger than the value 2 in the hundredths place in the second decimal. When comparing a fraction with a decimal, convert the fraction to a decimal and then compare in the same manner. Finally, there are a few options when comparing fractions. If two non-negative fractions have the same denominator, the fraction with the larger numerator is the larger value.

If they have different denominators, they can be converted to equivalent fractions with a common denominator to be compared, or they can be converted to decimals to be compared. When comparing two negative decimals or fractions, a different approach must be used. It is important to remember that the smaller number exists to the left on the number line. Therefore, when comparing two negative decimals by place value, the number with the larger first place value is smaller due to the negative sign. Whichever value is closer to 0 is larger. For instance, -0.456 is larger than -0.498 because of the values in the hundredth places. If two negative fractions have the same denominator, the fraction with the larger numerator is smaller because of the negative sign.

Using Number Lines to Compare Numbers

As mentioned, a **number line** is a tool used to compare numbers by showing where they fall in relation to one another. Labeling a number line with integers is simple because they have no fractional component, and the values are easier to understand. The number line may start at -3 and go up to -2, then -1, then 0, and 1, 2, 3. This order shows that number 2 is larger than -1 because it falls further to the right on the number line. When positioning rational numbers, the process may take more time because it requires that they all be in the same form. If they are percentages, fractions, and decimals, then conversions will have to be made to put them in the same form. For example, if the numbers $\frac{5}{4}$, 45%, and 2.38 need to be put in order on a number line, the numbers must first be transformed into one single form. Decimal form is an easy common ground because fractions can be changed by simply dividing, and percentages can be changed by moving the decimal point. After conversions are made, the list becomes 1.25, 0.45, and 2.38 respectively. Now the list is easier to arrange.

The number line with the list in order is shown in the top half of the graphic below in the order 0.45, 1.25, and 2.38:

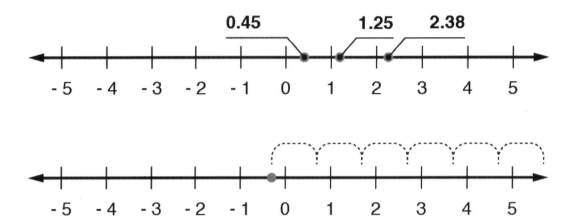

The sums and differences of rational numbers can be found using a number line after the rational numbers are put into the same form. This method is especially helpful when understanding the addition and subtraction of negative numbers. For example, the rational number six can be added to negative one-half using the number line. The following expression represents the problem:

$$-\frac{1}{2} + 6$$

First, the original number $-\frac{1}{2}$ can be plotted by a dot on the number line, as shown in the lower half of the graphic above. Then 6 can be added by counting by whole numbers on the number line. The arcs on the graph represent the addition. The final answer is positive $5\frac{1}{2}$.

Practice Quiz

1. Joey and Sandy wanted to sell lemonade and cookies to earn some extra money. They sold cookies for $1 and lemonade for $0.50. At the end of the first day, they sold 24 cookies. The total money that they collected was $35.50. How many cups of lemonade did they sell?
   a. 11
   b. 21
   c. 22
   d. 23

2. Carla is starting a cake-decorating business and wants to know how long it will take her to start making a profit. She knows the original investment is $100. After that investment, she can begin making cakes and selling them for $20 each. How many cakes will she need to sell to break even on her investment?
   a. 5
   b. 100
   c. 10
   d. 2

3. If the ratio of x to y is 1:8, what is the product of x and y when $y = 48$?
   a. 6
   b. 183
   c. 98
   d. 288

4. The percent increase from 8 to 18 is equivalent to the percent increase from 234 to what number?
   a. 468
   b. 526
   c. 526.5
   d. 125

5. A box is filled with blue, purple, and red stickers. If $\frac{1}{5}$ of the stickers are blue and $\frac{2}{3}$ are purple, what fraction of the stickers are red?
   a. $\frac{1}{3}$

   b. $\frac{2}{15}$

   c. $\frac{4}{5}$

   d. $\frac{4}{15}$

See answers on next page.

Answer Explanations

1. D: The following equation can be used to model how much money they collect for their sale: $M = 1c + 0.5l$, where M is money collected, c is cookies, and l is lemonade. By substituting 35.50 in for the variable M and 24 for the variable c, the equation can be solved for l, which is found to be 23 cups of lemonade. If there were 11 lemonades sold, the money collected would be $29.50. If 21 lemonades were sold, the money collected would be $34.50. If 22 lemonades were sold, the money collected would be $35.

2. A: The equation used to model this situation is $y = 20x - 100$, where 20 is price of each cake and 100 is the original investment. The value of x is the number of cakes and y is the money she makes. If this line is plotted on the graph, the x-intercept will be the number of cakes she needs to make in order to recoup her investment and break even. The x-intercept occurs when the y-value is zero. For this equation, setting $y = 0$ and solving for x gives a value of 5 cakes. 100 cakes would yield a profit of $1,900, ten cakes would yield a profit of $100, and 2 cakes would still leave her in the negative (-$10).

3. D: The ratio gives the proportion $\frac{x}{y} = \frac{1}{8}$. If $y = 48$, then $\frac{x}{48} = \frac{1}{8}$ means that $x = 6$. The product of x and y is therefore:

$$(6)(48) = 288$$

4. C: First, calculate the percent increase from 8 to 18 as:

$$\frac{18 - 8}{8} = 1.25 = 125\%$$

Then, add 125% of 234 onto 234 to obtain:

$$292.5 + 234 = 526.5$$

5. B: The total fraction of blue and purple stickers is:

$$\frac{1}{5} + \frac{2}{3} = \frac{3}{15} + \frac{10}{15} = \frac{13}{15}$$

Therefore, the total fraction of red stickers is:

$$\frac{15}{15} - \frac{13}{15} = \frac{2}{15}$$

Quantitative Reasoning, Algebra, and Statistics

Rational Numbers

Computation With Rational Numbers

Rational numbers are any numbers that can be written as a fraction of integers. Operations to be performed on rational numbers include adding, subtracting, multiplying, and dividing. Essentially, this refers to performing these operations on fractions. For the denominators to become 35, the first fraction must be multiplied by 7 and the second by 5. For example, the problem:

$$\frac{3}{5} + \frac{6}{7}$$

requires that the common multiple be found between 5 and 7. The smallest number that divides evenly by 5 and 7 is 35. For the denominators to become 35, the first fraction must be multiplied by 7 and the second by 5. The fraction $\frac{3}{5}$ can be multiplied by 7 on the top and bottom to yield the fraction $\frac{21}{35}$. The fraction $\frac{6}{7}$ can be multiplied by 5 to yield the fraction $\frac{30}{35}$.

Now that the fractions have the same denominator, the numerators can be added. The answer to the addition problem becomes:

$$\frac{3}{5} + \frac{6}{7} = \frac{21}{35} + \frac{30}{35} = \frac{51}{35}$$

The same technique can be used to subtract fractions. Multiplication and division may seem easier to perform because finding common denominators is unnecessary. If the problem reads:

$$\frac{1}{3} \times \frac{4}{5}$$

then the numerators and denominators are multiplied by each other and the answer is found to be $\frac{4}{15}$. For division, the problem must be changed to multiplication before performing operations. To complete a fraction division problem, you need to leave, change, and flip before multiplying. If the problem reads:

$$\frac{3}{7} \div \frac{3}{4}$$

then the first fraction is *left* alone, the operation is *changed* to multiplication, and then the last fraction is *flipped*. The problem becomes:

$$\frac{3}{7} \times \frac{4}{3} = \frac{12}{21}$$

Rational numbers can also be negative. When two negative numbers are added, the result is a negative number with an even greater magnitude. When a negative number is added to a positive number, the result depends on the value of each addend. For example,

$$-4 + 8 = 4$$

Because the positive number is larger than the negative number.

For multiplying two negative numbers, the result is positive. For example,

$$-4 \times -3 = 12$$

The negatives cancel out and yield a positive answer.

Rational numbers can be whole or negative numbers, fractions, or repeating decimals because these numbers can all be written as fractions. Whole numbers can be written as fractions by putting the number itself as the numerator and 1 as the denominator; for example, 25 and 17 can be written as $\frac{25}{1}$ and $\frac{17}{1}$, respectively. One way of interpreting these fractions is to say that they are *ratios*, or comparisons of two quantities. The fractions given may represent 25 students to 1 classroom, or 17 desks to 1 computer lab. Repeating decimals can also be written as fractions; 0.3333 and 0.6666667 can be written as $\frac{1}{3}$ and $\frac{2}{3}$.

Fractions can be described as having a part-to-whole relationship. The fraction $\frac{1}{3}$ may represent 1 piece of pizza out of the whole cut into 3 pieces. The fraction $\frac{2}{3}$ may represent 2 pieces of the same whole pizza. Adding the fractions $\frac{1}{3}$ and $\frac{2}{3}$ is as simple as adding the numerators, 1 and 2, because the denominator on both fractions is 3. This means the numbers in the numerators are referring to multiples of the same size piece of pizza. When adding these fractions, the result is $\frac{3}{3}$, or 1. Both of these numbers are rational and represent a whole, or in this problem, a whole pizza.

In addition to fractions, rational numbers also include whole numbers and negative integers. When whole numbers are added, the result is always greater than the addends (unless 0 is added to the number, in which case its value would remain the same). For example, the equation $4 + 18 = 22$ shows 4 increased by 18, with a result of 22.

When subtracting rational numbers, sometimes the result is a negative number. For example, the equation $5 - 12 = -7$ shows that taking 12 away from 5 results in a negative answer (-7) because the starting number (5) is smaller than the number taken away (12). For multiplication and division, similar results are found.

Multiplying rational numbers may look like the following equation:

$$5 \times 7 = 35$$

Both numbers are positive and whole, and the result is a larger number than the factors. The number 5 is counted 7 times, which results in a total of 35. Sometimes, the equation looks like:

$$-4 \times 3 = -12$$

So, the result is negative because a positive number times a negative number gives a negative answer. The rule is that any time a negative number and a positive number are multiplied or divided, the result is negative.

Absolute Values

The **absolute value** of any real number is the distance from that number to 0 on the number line. The absolute value of a number can never be negative. For example, the absolute value of both 8 and −8 is 8 because they are both 8 units away from 0 on the number line. This is written as:

$$|8| = |-8| = 8$$

Ratio and Proportional Relationships

Rate, Percent, and Measurement Problems

Real-world problems frequently involve proportions. For example, consider the following problem: If 2 out of 50 pizzas are usually delivered late from a local Italian restaurant, how many would be late out of 235 orders? The following proportion would be solved with x as the unknown quantity of late pizzas:

$$\frac{2}{50} = \frac{x}{235}$$

Cross multiplying results in:

$$470 = 50x$$

Divide both sides by 50 to obtain:

$$x = \frac{470}{50}$$

In lowest terms, this is equal to $\frac{47}{5}$. In decimal form, this improper fraction is equal to 9.4. Because it does not make sense to answer this question with decimals (portions of pizzas do not get delivered) the answer must be rounded. Traditional rounding rules would say that 9 pizzas would be expected to be delivered late. However, to be safe, rounding up to 10 pizzas out of 235 would probably make more sense.

Recall that a ratio is the comparison of two different quantities. Comparing 2 apples to 3 oranges results in the ratio 2 : 3, which can be expressed as the fraction $\frac{2}{5}$. Note that order is important when discussing ratios. The number mentioned first is the antecedent, and the number mentioned second is the consequent. Note that the consequent of the ratio and the denominator of the fraction are *not* the same. When there are 2 apples to 3 oranges, there are five fruit total; two fifths of the fruit are apples, while three fifths are oranges.

The ratio 2 : 3 represents a different relationship than the ratio 3 : 2. Also, it is important to make sure that when discussing ratios that have units attached to them, the two quantities use the same units. For example, to think of 8 feet to 4 yards, it would make sense to convert 4 yards to feet by multiplying by 3.

Therefore, the ratio would be 8 feet to 12 feet, which can be expressed as the fraction $\frac{8}{20}$. Also, note that it is proper to refer to ratios in lowest terms. Therefore, the ratio of 8 feet to 4 yards is equivalent to the fraction $\frac{2}{5}$.

Many real-world problems involve ratios. Often, problems with ratios involve proportions, as when two ratios are set equal to find the missing amount. However, some problems involve deciphering single ratios. For example, consider an amusement park that sold 345 tickets last Saturday. If 145 tickets were sold to adults and the rest of the tickets were sold to children, what would the ratio of the number of adult tickets to children's tickets be? A common mistake would be to say the ratio is 145 : 345. However, 345 is the total number of tickets sold, not the number of children's tickets. There were $345 - 145 = 200$ tickets sold to children. The correct ratio of adult to children's tickets is 145 : 200. As a fraction, this expression is written as $\frac{145}{345}$, which can be reduced to $\frac{29}{69}$.

While a ratio compares two measurements using the same units, rates compare two measurements with different units. Examples of rates would be $200 for 8 hours of work, or 500 miles traveled per 20 gallons. Because the units are different, it is important to always include the units when discussing rates. Key words in rate problems include for, per, on, from, and in. Just as with ratios, it is important to write rates in lowest terms. A common rate in real-life situations is cost per unit, which describes how much one item/unit costs. When evaluating the cost of an item that comes in several sizes, the cost per unit rate can help buyers determine the best deal. For example, if 2 quarts of soup was sold for $3.50 and 3 quarts was sold for $4.60, to determine the best buy, the cost per quart should be found.

$$\frac{\$3.50}{2 \text{ qt}} = \$1.75 \text{ per quart}$$

and

$$\frac{\$4.60}{3 \text{ qt}} = \$1.53 \text{ per quart}$$

Therefore, the better deal would be the 3-quart option.

Rate of change problems involve calculating a quantity per some unit of measurement. Usually, the unit of measurement is time. For example, meters per second is a common rate of change. To calculate this measurement, find the amount traveled in meters and divide by total time traveled. The result is the average speed over the entire time interval. Another common rate of change used in the real world is miles per hour. Consider the following problem that involves calculating an average rate of change in temperature. Last Saturday, the temperature at 1:00 a.m. was 34 degrees Fahrenheit, and at noon, the temperature had increased to 75 degrees Fahrenheit. What was the average rate of change over that time interval? The average rate of change is calculated by finding the change in temperature and dividing by the total hours elapsed. Therefore, the rate of change was equal to:

$$\frac{75 - 34}{12 - 1} = \frac{41}{11} \text{ degrees per hour}$$

This quantity rounded to two decimal places is equal to 3.73 degrees per hour.

A common rate of change that appears in algebra is the slope calculation. Given a linear equation in one variable, $y = mx + b$, the **slope**, m, is equal to:

$$\frac{rise}{run} = \frac{change\ in\ y}{change\ in\ x}$$

In other words, slope is equivalent to the ratio of the vertical and horizontal changes between any two points on a line. The vertical change is known as the *rise*, and the horizontal change is known as the *run*. Given any two points on a line (x_1, y_1) and (x_2, y_2), slope can be calculated with the formula:

$$m = \frac{y_2 - y_1}{x_2 - x_1} = \frac{\Delta y}{\Delta x}$$

Common real-world applications of slope include determining how steep a staircase should be, calculating how steep a road is, and determining how to build a wheelchair ramp.

Many times, problems involving rates and ratios involve proportions. A proportion states that two ratios (or rates) are equal. The property of cross products can be used to determine if a proportion is true, meaning both ratios are equivalent. If $\frac{a}{b} = \frac{c}{d}$, then to clear the fractions, multiply both sides by the least common denominator, bd. This results in $ad = bc$, which is equal to the result of multiplying along both diagonals. For example, $\frac{4}{40} = \frac{1}{10}$ grants the cross product:

$$4 \times 10 = 40 \times 1$$

This is equivalent to $40 = 40$ and shows that this proportion is true. Cross products are used when proportions are involved in real-world problems. Consider the following: If 3 pounds of fertilizer will cover 75 square feet of grass, how many pounds are needed for 375 square feet? To solve this problem, set up a proportion using two ratios. Let x equal the unknown quantity, pounds needed for 375 feet. Setting the two ratios equal to one another yields the equation:

$$\frac{3}{75} = \frac{x}{375}$$

Cross-multiplication gives:

$$3 \times 375 = 75x$$

Therefore,

$$1,125 = 75x$$

Divide both sides by 75 to get $x = 15$. Therefore, 15 pounds of fertilizer are needed to cover 375 square feet of grass.

Proportional Relationships

Fractions appear in everyday situations, and in many scenarios, they appear in the real-world as ratios and in proportions. A **ratio** is formed when two different quantities are compared. For example, in a group of 50 people, if there are 33 females and 17 males, the ratio of females to males is 33 to 17. This expression can be written in the fraction form as $\frac{33}{50}$, where the denominator is the sum of females and males, or by using the ratio symbol, $33 : 17$. The order of the number matters when forming ratios. In the same setting, the ratio of males to females is 17 to 33, which is equivalent to $\frac{17}{50}$ or $17 : 33$. A **proportion** is an equation involving two ratios. The equation:

$$\frac{a}{b} = \frac{c}{d}$$

or

$$a : b = c : d$$

This is a proportion, for real numbers a, b, c, and d. Usually, in one ratio, one of the quantities is unknown, and cross-multiplication is used to solve for the unknown. Consider: $\frac{1}{4} = \frac{x}{5}$. To solve for x, cross-multiply to obtain $5 = 4x$. Divide each side by 4 to obtain the solution $x = \frac{5}{4}$. It is also true that percentages are ratios in which the second term is 100 minus the first term. For example, 65% is 65:35 or $\frac{65}{100}$. Therefore, when working with percentages, one is also working with ratios.

Real-world problems frequently involve proportions. For example, consider the following problem: If 2 out of 50 pizzas are usually delivered late from a local Italian restaurant, how many would be late out of 235 orders? The following proportion would be solved with x as the unknown quantity of late pizzas:

$$\frac{2}{50} = \frac{x}{235}$$

Cross multiplying results in:

$$470 = 50x$$

Divide both sides by 50 to obtain:

$$x = \frac{470}{50}$$

In lowest terms, this is equal to $\frac{47}{5}$. In decimal form, this improper fraction is equal to 9.4. Because it does not make sense to answer this question with decimals (portions of pizzas do not get delivered) the answer must be rounded. Traditional rounding rules would say that 9 pizzas would be expected to be delivered late. However, to be safe, rounding up to 10 pizzas out of 235 would probably make more sense.

Solving Unit Rate Problems

A **unit rate** is a rate with a denominator of one. It is a comparison of two values with different units where one value is equal to one. Examples of unit rates include 60 miles per hour and 200 words per minute. Problems involving unit rates may require some work to find the unit rate. For example, if Mary travels 360 miles in 5 hours, what is her speed, expressed as a unit rate? The rate can be expressed as the following fraction:

$$\frac{360 \text{ miles}}{5 \text{ hours}}$$

The denominator can be changed to one by dividing by five. The numerator will also need to be divided by five to follow the rules of equality. This division turns the fraction into:

$$\frac{72 \text{ miles}}{1 \text{ hour}}$$

This can now be labeled as a unit rate because one unit has a value of one. Another type question involves the use of unit rates to solve problems. For example, if Trey needs to read 300 pages and his average speed is 75 pages per hour, will he be able to finish the reading in 5 hours? The unit rate is 75 pages per hour, so the total of 300 pages can be divided by 75 to find the time. After the division, the time it takes to read is four hours. The answer to the question is yes, Trey will finish the reading within 5 hours.

Unit Conversions

When working with dimensions, sometimes the given units don't match the formula, and conversions must be made. When performing operations with rational numbers, it might be helpful to round the numbers in the original problem to get a rough idea of what the answer should be. This system expands to three places above the base unit and three places below. These places correspond to prefixes that each signify a specific base of 10.

The following table shows the conversions:

kilo-	hecto-	deka-	base	deci-	centi-	milli-
1,000 times the base	100 times the base	10 times the base		1/10 times the base	1/100 times the base	1/1000 times the base

To convert between units within the metric system, values with a base ten can be multiplied. The decimal can also be moved in the direction of the new unit by the same number of zeros on the number. For example, 3 meters is equivalent to 0.003 kilometers. The decimal moved three places (the same number of zeros for kilo-) to the left (the same direction from base to kilo-). Three meters is also equivalent to 3,000 millimeters. The decimal is moved three places to the right because the prefix milli- is three places to the right of the base unit.

The English Standard system, which is used in the United States, uses the base units of foot for length, pound for weight, and gallon for liquid volume. Conversions within the English Standard system are not as easy as those within the metric system because the former does not use a base ten model.

The following table shows the conversions within this system.

Length	Weight	Capacity
1 foot (ft) = 12 inches (in) 1 yard (yd) = 3 feet 1 mile (mi) = 5,280 feet 1 mile = 1,760 yards	1 pound (lb) = 16 ounces (oz) 1 ton = 2,000 pounds	1 tablespoon (tbsp) = 3 teaspoons (tsp) 1 cup (c) = 16 tablespoons 1 cup = 8 fluid ounces (oz) 1 pint (pt) = 2 cups 1 quart (qt) = 2 pints 1 gallon (gal) = 4 quarts

When converting within the English Standard system, most calculations include a conversion to the base unit and then another to the desired unit. For example, take the following problem: 3 qt = ___ c. There is no straight conversion from quarts to cups, so the first conversion is from quarts to pints. There are 2 pints in 1 quart, so there are 6 pints in 3 quarts. This conversion can be solved as a proportion:

$$\frac{3 \text{ qt}}{x} = \frac{1 \text{ qt}}{2 \text{ pt}}$$

It can also be observed as a ratio 2 : 1, expanded to 6 : 3. Then the 6 pints must be converted to cups. The ratio of pints to cups is 1 : 2, so the expanded ratio is 6 : 12. For 6 pints, the measurement is 12 cups. This problem can also be set up as one set of fractions to cancel out units. It begins with the given information and cancels out matching units on top and bottom to yield the answer. Consider the following expression:

$$\frac{3 \text{ qt}}{1} \times \frac{2 \text{ pt}}{1 \text{ qt}} \times \frac{2 \text{ c}}{1 \text{ pt}}$$

It's set up so that units on the top and bottom cancel each other out:

$$\frac{3 \text{ qt}}{1} \times \frac{2 \text{ pt}}{1 \text{ qt}} \times \frac{2 \text{ c}}{1 \text{ pt}}$$

The numbers can be calculated as 3 × 2 × 2 on the top and 1 on the bottom. It still yields an answer of 12 cups.

This process of setting up fractions and canceling out matching units can be used to convert between standard and metric systems. A few common equivalent conversions are:

$$2.54 \text{ cm} = 1 \text{ in}$$

$$3.28 \text{ ft} = 1 \text{ m}$$

$$2.205 \text{ lb} = 1 \text{ kg}$$

Writing these as fractions allows them to be used in conversions. For the problem 5 meters = ___ ft, use the feet-to-meter conversion and start with the expression $\frac{5 \text{ m}}{1} \times \frac{3.28 \text{ ft}}{1 \text{ m}}$. The "meters" will cancel each other out, leaving "feet" as the final unit. Calculating the numbers yields 16.4 feet. This problem only required two fractions. Others may require longer expressions, but the underlying rule stays the same. When a unit in the numerator of a fraction matches a unit in the denominator, then they cancel each other out. Using this logic and the conversions given above, many units can be converted between and within the different systems.

The conversion between Fahrenheit and Celsius is found in a formula:

$$°C = (°F - 32) \times \frac{5}{9}$$

For example, to convert 78°F to Celsius, the given temperature would be entered into the formula:

$$°C = (78 - 32) \times \frac{5}{9}$$

Solving the equation, the temperature comes out to be 25.56°C. To convert in the other direction, the formula becomes:

$$°F = °C \times \frac{9}{5} + 32$$

Remember the order of operations when calculating these conversions.

Exponents

Evaluating Positive Rational Roots and Exponents

A **rational number** is any number that can be written as a fraction of two integers. Examples of rational numbers include $\frac{1}{2}, \frac{5}{4}$, 2.75 and 8. The number 8 is rational because it can be expressed as a fraction: $\frac{8}{1} = 8$.

Rational exponents are used to express the root of a number raised to a specific power. For example, $3^{\frac{1}{2}}$ has a base of 3 and rational exponent of $\frac{1}{2}$. The square root of 3 raised to the first power can be written as $\sqrt[2]{3^1}$. Any number with a rational exponent can be written this way.

The **numerator**, or number on top of the fraction, becomes the whole number exponent and the **denominator**, or bottom number of the fraction, becomes the root. Another example is $4^{\frac{3}{2}}$. It can be rewritten as the square root of four to the third power, or $\sqrt[2]{4^3}$. To simplify this, first solve for 4 to the third power: $4^3 = 4 \times 4 \times 4 = 64$. Then take the square root of 64, written as $\sqrt[2]{64}$, which yields an answer of 8. Another way of stating the answer would be 4 to power of $\frac{3}{2}$ is eight, or that 4 to the power of $\frac{3}{2}$ is the square root of 4 cubed:

$$\sqrt[2]{4}^3 = 2^3 = 2 \times 2 \times 2 = 8$$

When performing operations with exponents, one must make sure that the **order of operations** is followed. Therefore, once all operations within any parentheses or grouping symbols are performed, all exponents must be evaluated before any other operation is completed. For example, to evaluate:

$$(3 - 5)^2 + 4 - 5^3$$

The subtraction in parentheses is done first. Then the exponents are evaluated to obtain:

$$(-2)^2 + 4 - 5^3$$

or

$$4 + 4 - 125$$

This is equivalent to -117. A common mistake involves negative signs combined with exponents. Note that -4^2 is not equal to $(-4)^2$. The negative sign is in front of the first exponential expression, so the result is:

$$-(4 \times 4) = -16$$

However, the negative sign is inside the parentheses in the second expression, so the result is:

$$(-4 \times -4) = 16$$

Laws of exponents can also help when performing operations with exponents. If two exponential expressions have the same base and are being multiplied, just add the exponents. For example,

$$2^5 \times 2^7 = 2^{5+7} = 2^{12}$$

If two exponential expressions have the same base and are being divided, subtract the exponents. For example,

$$\frac{4^{30}}{4^2} = 4^{30-2} = 4^{28}$$

If an exponential expression is being raised to another exponent, multiply the exponents together. For example,

$$(3^2)^5 = 3^{2 \times 5} = 3^{10}$$

Manipulating Roots and Exponents

Numbers can also be written using exponents. The number 7,000 can be written as $7 \times 1,000$, because 7 is in the thousands place. It can also be written as 7×10^3, because $1,000 = 10^3$.

Another number that can use this notation is 500. It can be written as 5×100, or 5×10^2, because $100 = 10^2$. The number 30 can be written as 3×10, or 3×10^1, because $10 = 10^1$. Notice that each one of the exponents of 10 is equal to the number of zeros in the number. Seven is in the thousands place, with three zeros, and the exponent on ten is 3. The five is in the hundreds place, with two zeros, and the exponent on the ten is 2. A question may give the number 40,000 and ask for it to be rewritten using exponents with a base of ten. Because the number has a four in the ten-thousands place and four zeros, it can be written using an exponent of four:

$$4 \times 10^4$$

The nth root of a is given as $\sqrt[n]{a}$, which is called a **radical**. Typical values for n are 2 and 3, which represent the square and cube roots. In this form, n represents an integer greater than or equal to 2, and a is a real number. If n is even, a must be nonnegative, and if n is odd, a can be any real number. This radical can be written in exponential form as $a^{\frac{1}{n}}$.

Therefore, $\sqrt[4]{15}$ is the same as $15^{\frac{1}{4}}$ and $\sqrt[3]{-5}$ is the same as $(-5)^{\frac{1}{3}}$.

In a similar fashion, the nth root of a can be raised to a power m, which is written as:

$$\left(\sqrt[n]{a}\right)^m$$

This expression is the same as $\sqrt[n]{a^m}$. For example,

$$\sqrt[2]{4^3} = \sqrt[2]{64} = 8 = \left(\sqrt[2]{4}\right)^3 = 2^3$$

Because $\sqrt[n]{a} = a^{\frac{1}{n}}$, both sides can be raised to an exponent of m, resulting in:

$$\left(\sqrt[n]{a}\right)^m = \sqrt[n]{a^m} = a^{\frac{m}{n}}$$

This rule allows:

$$\sqrt[2]{4^3} = \left(\sqrt[2]{4}\right)^3 = 4^{\frac{3}{2}}$$

$$(2^2)^{\frac{3}{2}} = 2^{\frac{6}{2}} = 2^3 = 8$$

Negative exponents can also be incorporated into these rules. Any time an exponent is negative, the base expression must be flipped to the other side of the fraction bar and rewritten with a positive exponent. For instance:

$$2^{-3} = \frac{1}{2^3} = \frac{1}{8}$$

Therefore, two more relationships between radical and exponential expressions are:

$$a^{-\frac{1}{n}} = \frac{1}{\sqrt[n]{a}}$$

$$a^{-\frac{m}{n}} = \frac{1}{\sqrt[n]{a^m}} = \frac{1}{\left(\sqrt[n]{a}\right)^m}$$

Thus,

$$8^{-\frac{1}{3}} = \frac{1}{\sqrt[3]{8}} = \frac{1}{2}$$

All of these relationships are very useful when simplifying complicated radical and exponential expressions. If an expression contains both forms, use one of these rules to change the expression to contain either all radicals or all exponential expressions. This process makes the entire expression much easier to work with, especially if the expressions are contained within equations.

Consider the following example:

$$\sqrt{x} \times \sqrt[4]{x}$$

It is written in radical form; however, it can be simplified into one radical by using exponential expressions first. The expression can be written as:

$$x^{\frac{1}{2}} \times x^{\frac{1}{4}}$$

It can be combined into one base by adding the exponents as:

$$x^{\frac{1}{2}+\frac{1}{4}} = x^{\frac{3}{4}}$$

Writing this back in radical form, the result is $\sqrt[4]{x^3}$.

Creating Equivalent Expressions Involving Rational Exponents and Radicals

Re-writing complex radical expressions as equivalent forms with rational exponents can help to simplify them. The rule that helps this conversion is:

$$\sqrt[n]{x^m} = x^{\frac{m}{n}}$$

If $m = 1$, the rule is simply:

$$\sqrt[n]{x} = x^{\frac{1}{n}}$$

For instance, consider the following expression:

$$\sqrt[4]{x}\sqrt{y}$$

This can be written as one radical expression, but first it needs to be converted to an equivalent expression. The equivalent expression is:

$$x^{\frac{1}{4}}y^{\frac{1}{2}}$$

The goal is to have one radical, which means one index n, so a common denominator of the exponents must be found. The common denominator is 4, so an equivalent expression is $x^{\frac{1}{4}}y^{\frac{2}{4}}$. The exponential rule $a^m b^m = (ab)^m$ can be used to factor $\frac{1}{4}$ out of both variables. This process results in the expression:

$$(xy^2)^{\frac{1}{4}}$$

Its equivalent radical form is:

$$\sqrt[4]{xy^2}$$

Converting to rational exponents has allowed the entire expression to be written as one radical.

Another type of problem could involve going in the opposite direction: starting with rational exponents and using an equivalent radical form to simplify the expression. For instance, $32^{\frac{1}{5}}$ might not appear equal

38

to 2, but putting it in its equivalent radical form $\sqrt[5]{32}$ shows that it is equivalent to the fifth root of 32, which is 2.

Algebraic Expressions

An **algebraic expression** is a mathematical phrase that may contain numbers, variables, and mathematical operations. An expression represents a single quantity. For example, $3x + 2$ is an algebraic expression.

An **algebraic equation** is a mathematical sentence with two expressions that are equal to each other. That is, an equation must contain an equals sign, as in $3x + 2 = 17$. This statement says that the value of the expression on the left side of the equals sign is equivalent to the value of the expression on the right side. In an expression, there are not two sides because there is no equals sign. The equals sign ($=$) is the difference between an expression and an equation.

To distinguish an expression from an equation, just look for the equals sign.

Example: Determine whether each of these is an expression or an equation.

$16 + 4x = 9x - 7$	Solution: Equation
$-27x - 42 + 19y$	Solution: Expression
$4 = x + 3$	Solution: Equation

Using Mathematical Terms to Identify Parts of Expressions and Describe Expressions

A **variable** is a symbol used to represent a number. Letters, like x, y, and z, are often used as variables in algebra.

A **constant** is a number that cannot change its value. For example, 18 is a constant.   3

A **term** is a constant, variable, or the product of constants and variables. In an expression, terms are separated by $+$ and $-$ signs. Examples of terms are $24x$, -32, and $15xyz$.

Like terms are terms that contain the same variables. For example, $6z$ and $-8z$ are like terms, and $9xy$ and $17xy$ are like terms. Constants, like 23 and 51, are like terms as well.

A **factor** is something that is multiplied by something else. A factor may be a constant, a variable, or a sum of constants or variables.

A **coefficient** is the numerical factor in a term that has a variable. In the term $16x$, the coefficient is 16.

Example: Given the expression: $6x - 12y + 18$ answer the following questions.

- How many terms are in the expression?
  - ○ Solution: 3
- Name the terms.
  - ○ Solution: $6x$, $-12y$, and 18 (Notice that the minus sign preceding the 12 is interpreted to represent negative 12)

- Name the factors.
  - Solution: $6, x, -12, y$
- What are the coefficients in this expression?
  - Solution: 6 and -12
- What is the constant in this expression?
  - Solution: 18

Translating Written Phrases into Algebraic Expressions

When presented with a real-world problem, the first step is to determine what unknown quantity must be solved for. Use a variable, such as x or t, to represent that unknown quantity. Sometimes there can be two or more unknown quantities. In this case, either choose an additional variable, or if a relationship exists between the unknown quantities, express the other quantities in terms of the original variable. After choosing the variables, form algebraic expressions and/or equations that represent the verbal statement in the problem. The following table shows examples of vocabulary used to represent the different operations.

Addition	Sum, plus, total, increase, more than, combined, in all
Subtraction	Difference, less than, subtract, reduce, decrease, fewer, remain
Multiplication	Product, multiply, times, part of, twice, triple
Division	Quotient, divide, split, each, equal parts, per, average, shared

The combination of operations and variables form both mathematical expression and equations. The differences between expressions and equations are that there is no equals sign in an expression, and that expressions are **evaluated** to find an unknown quantity, while equations are *solved* to find an unknown quantity. Also, inequalities can exist within verbal mathematical statements. Instead of a statement of equality, expressions state quantities are *less than*, *less than or equal to*, *greater than*, or *greater than or equal to*. Another type of inequality is when a quantity is said to be not equal to another quantity ($\neq$).

The steps for solving inequalities in one variable are the same steps for solving equations in one variable. The addition and multiplication principles are used. However, to maintain a true statement when using the $<, \leq, >$, and $\geq$ symbols, if a negative number is either multiplied times both sides of an inequality or divided from both sides of an inequality, the sign must be flipped. For instance, consider the following inequality: $3 - 5x \leq 8$. First, 3 is subtracted from each side to obtain $-5x \leq 5$. Then, both sides are divided by -5, while flipping the sign, to obtain $x \geq -1$. Therefore, any real number greater than or equal to -1 satisfies the original inequality.

Adding and Subtracting Linear Algebraic Expressions

To add and subtract linear algebraic expressions, you must combine like terms. Like terms are terms that have the same variable with the same exponent. In the following example, the x-terms can be added because the variable and exponent are the same. These terms add to be $9x$. Terms without a variable component are called constants. These terms will add to be nine.

Example: Add $(3x - 5) + (6x + 14)$

$3x - 5 + 6x + 14$ Rewrite without parentheses

$3x + 6x - 5 + 14$ Commutative property of addition

40

$$9x + 9 \qquad \text{Combine like terms}$$

When subtracting linear expressions, be careful to add the opposite when combining like terms. Do this by distributing -1, which is multiplying each term inside the second parenthesis by negative one. Remember that distributing -1 changes the sign of each term.

Example: Subtract $\quad (17x + 3) - (27x - 8)$

$$17x + 3 - 27x + 8 \qquad \text{Distributive Property}$$

$$17x - 27x + 3 + 8 \qquad \text{Commutative property of addition}$$

$$-10x + 11 \qquad \text{Combine like terms}$$

Example: Simplify by adding or subtracting:

$$(6m + 28z - 9) + (14m + 13) - (-4z + 8m + 12)$$

$$6m + 28z - 9 + 14m + 13 + 4z - 8m - 12 \quad \text{Distributive Property}$$

$$6m + 14m - 8m + 28z + 4z - 9 + 13 - 12 \quad \text{Commutative Property of Addition}$$

$$12m + 32z - 8 \qquad \text{Combine like terms}$$

Creating an Equivalent Form of an Algebraic Expression

Two algebraic expressions are equivalent if they represent the same value, even if they look different. To obtain an equivalent form of an algebraic expression, follow the laws of algebra. For instance, addition and multiplication are both commutative and associative. Therefore, terms in an algebraic expression can be added in any order and multiplied in any order. For instance, $4x + 2y$ is equivalent to $2y + 4x$ and $y \times 2 + x \times 4$.

Also, the **distributive property** allows a number to be distributed throughout parentheses, as in the following:

$$a(b + c) = ab + ac$$

The distributive property is a way of taking a factor and multiplying it through a given expression in parentheses. Each term inside the parentheses is multiplied by the outside factor, eliminating the parentheses. The following example shows how to distribute the number 3 to all the terms inside the parentheses.

Example: Use the distributive property to write an equivalent algebraic expression:

$$3(2x + 7y + 6)$$

$$3(2x) + 3(7y) + 3(6) \qquad \text{Distributive property}$$

$$6x + 21y + 18 \qquad \text{Simplify}$$

Because $a - b$ can be written $a + (-b)$, the distributive property can be applied in the example below.

Example: Use the distributive property to write an equivalent algebraic expression.

$7(5m - 8)$

$7[5m + (-8)]$ Rewrite subtraction as addition of -8

$7(5m) + 7(-8)$ Distributive property

$35m - 56$ Simplify

In the following example, note that the factor of 2 is written to the right of the parentheses but is still distributed as before.

Example: Use the distributive property to write an equivalent algebraic expression:

$(3m + 4x - 10)2$

$(3m)2 + (4x)2 + (-10)2$ Distributive property

$6m + 8x - 20$ Simplify

Example: $-(-2m + 6x)$

In this example, the negative sign in front of the parentheses can be interpreted as $-1(-2m + 6x)$

$-1(-2m + 6x)$

$-1(-2m) + (-1)(6x)$ Distributive property

$2m - 6x$ Simplify

Note that an expression is not an equation, and therefore expressions cannot be multiplied times numbers, divided by numbers, or have numbers added to them or subtracted from them and still have equivalent expressions. These processes can only happen in equations when the same step is performed on both sides of the equals sign.

Evaluating Simple Algebraic Expressions for Given Values of Variables

To evaluate an algebra expression for a given value of a variable, replace the variable with the given value. Then perform the given operations to simplify the expression.

Example: Evaluate $12 + x$ for $x = 9$

$12 + (9)$ Replace x with the value of 9 as given in the problem. It is a good idea to always use parentheses when substituting this value. This will be particularly important in the following examples.

21 Add

Now see that when x is 9, the value of the given expression is 21.

Example: Evaluate $4x + 7$ for $x = 3$

$$4(3) + 7 \qquad \text{Replace the } x \text{ in the expression with 3}$$

$$12 + 7 \qquad \text{Multiply (remember order of operations)}$$

$$19 \qquad \text{Add}$$

Therefore, when x is 3, the value of the given expression is 19.

Example: Evaluate $-7m - 3r - 18$ for $m = 2$ and $r = -1$

$$-7(2) - 3(-1) - 18 \qquad \text{Replace } m \text{ with 2 and } r \text{ with } -1$$

$$-14 + 3 - 18 \qquad \text{Multiply}$$

$$-29 \qquad \text{Add}$$

So, when m is 2 and r is -1, the value of the given expression is -29.

Simplifying Rational Algebraic Expressions

When given a problem, it is necessary to determine the best form of an expression or equation to use, given the context. Usually this involves some algebraic manipulation. If an equation is given, the simplest form of the equation is best. Simplifying involves using the distributive property, collecting like terms, etc. If an equation is needed to be solved, properties involving performing the same operation on both sides of the equation must be used. For instance, if a number is added to one side of the equals sign, it must be added to the other side as well. This maintains a true equation.

If an expression is given, simplifying can only involve properties allowing to rewrite the expression as an equivalent form. If there is no equals sign, mathematical operations cannot be performed on the expression, unless it is a rational expression. A **rational expression** can be written in the form of a fraction, in which the numerator and denominator are both polynomials and the denominator is not equal to zero. Rational expressions can always be multiplied times a form of 1. For example, consider the following rational expression involving radicals: $\frac{2}{\sqrt{2}}$. It is incorrect to write a fraction with a root in the denominator, and therefore the expression must be rationalized. Multiply the fraction times $\frac{\sqrt{2}}{\sqrt{2}}$, a form of 1. This results in:

$$\frac{2}{\sqrt{2}} \times \frac{\sqrt{2}}{\sqrt{2}} = \frac{2\sqrt{2}}{\sqrt{4}} = \frac{2\sqrt{2}}{2} = \sqrt{2}$$

This is the most suitable form of the expression.

A polynomial is a mathematical expression containing addition, subtraction, or multiplication of one or more constants multiplied by variables raised to positive powers. Here are some examples of rational expressions: $\frac{2x^2+6x}{x}$, $\frac{x-2}{x^2-6x+8}$, and $\frac{x^3-1}{x+2}$. Such expressions can be simplified using different forms of division. The first example can be simplified in two ways. Then, cancelling out an x in each numerator and the x in each denominator results in $2x + 6$. It also can be simplified using factoring and then crossing out common factors in the numerator and denominator. For instance, it can be written as:

$$\frac{2x(x + 3)}{x} = 2(x + 3) = 2x + 6$$

The second expression above can also be simplified using factoring. It can be written as:

$$\frac{x - 2}{(x - 2)(x - 4)} = \frac{1}{x - 4}$$

Finally, the third example can only be simplified using long division, as there are no common factors in the numerator and denominator. First, divide the first term of the numerator by the first term of the denominator, then write the result in the quotient. Then, multiply the divisor by that number and write it below the dividend. Subtract and continue the process until each term in the divisor is accounted for. Here is the actual long division:

Simplifying Expressions Using Long Division

$$
\begin{array}{r}
x^2 - 2x + 4 \\
x + 2 \enclose{longdiv}{x^3 \qquad\qquad - 1} \\
\underline{x^3 + 2x^2 \qquad\qquad} \\
-2x^2 \qquad - 1 \\
\underline{-2x^2 - 4x \qquad} \\
4x - 1 \\
\underline{4x + 8} \\
-9
\end{array}
$$

Linear Equations

Solving Linear Equations and Inequalities

Solving Linear Equations

An **equation in one variable** is a mathematical statement where two algebraic expressions in one variable, usually x, are set equal. To solve the equation, the variable must be isolated on one side of the equals sign. The addition and multiplication principles of equality are used to isolate the variable. The **addition principle of equality** states that the same number can be added to or subtracted from both sides of an equation. Because the same value is being used on both sides of the equals sign, equality is maintained.

For example, the equation:

$$2x = 5x$$

This is equivalent to both:

$$2x + 3 = 5x + 3$$

$$2x - 5 = 5x - 5$$

This principle can be used to solve the following equation:

$$x + 5 = 4$$

The variable x must be isolated, so to move the 5 from the left side, subtract 5 from both sides of the equals sign. Therefore:

$$x + 5 - 5 = 4 - 5$$

So, the solution is $x = -1$. This process illustrates the idea of an **additive inverse** because subtracting 5 is the same as adding -5.

Basically, add the opposite of the number that must be removed to both sides of the equals sign. The multiplication principle of equality states that equality is maintained when both sides of an equation are multiplied or divided by the same number. For example,

$$4x = 5$$

This is equivalent to both:

$$16x = 20$$

$$x = \frac{5}{4}$$

Multiplying both sides times 4 and dividing both sides by 4 maintains equality. Solving the equation:

$$6x - 18 = 5$$

This requires the use of both principles. First, apply the addition principle to add 18 to both sides of the equals sign, which results in:

$$6x = 23$$

Then use the multiplication principle to divide both sides by 6, giving the solution $x = \frac{23}{6}$. Using the multiplication principle in the solving process is the same as involving a multiplicative inverse. A **multiplicative inverse** is a value that, when multiplied by a given number, results in 1. Dividing by 6 is the same as multiplying by $\frac{1}{6}$, which is both the reciprocal and multiplicative inverse of 6.

When solving linear equations, check the answer by plugging the solution back into the original equation. If the result is a false statement, something was done incorrectly during the solution procedure. Checking the example above gives the following:

$$6 \times \frac{23}{6} - 18 = 23 - 18 = 5$$

Therefore, the solution is correct.

Some equations in one variable involve fractions or the use of the distributive property. In either case, the goal is to obtain only one variable term and then use the addition and multiplication principles to isolate that variable. Consider the equation:

$$\frac{2}{3}x = 6$$

To solve for x, multiply each side of the equation by the reciprocal of $\frac{2}{3}$, which is $\frac{3}{2}$. This step results in:

$$\frac{3}{2} \times \frac{2}{3}x = \frac{3}{2} \times 6$$

This simplifies into the solution $x = 9$. Now consider the equation:

$$3(x + 2) - 5x = 4x + 1$$

Use the distributive property to clear the parentheses. Therefore, multiply each term inside the parentheses by 3. This step results in:

$$3x + 6 - 5x = 4x + 1$$

Next, collect like terms on the left-hand side. **Like terms** are terms with the same variable or variables raised to the same exponent(s). Only like terms can be combined through addition or subtraction. After collecting like terms, the equation is:

$$-2x + 6 = 4x + 1$$

Finally, apply the addition and multiplication principles. Add $2x$ to both sides to obtain:

$$6 = 6x + 1$$

Then, subtract 1 from both sides to obtain $5 = 6x$. Finally, divide both sides by 6 to obtain the solution $\frac{5}{6} = x$.

Two other types of solutions can be obtained when solving an equation in one variable. There could be no solution, or the solution set could contain all real numbers. Consider the equation:

$$4x = 6x + 5 - 2x$$

First, the like terms can be combined on the right to obtain:

$$4x = 4x + 5$$

Next, subtract $4x$ from both sides. This step results in the false statement $0 = 5$. There is no value that can be plugged into x that will ever make this equation true. Therefore, there is no solution. The solution procedure contained correct steps, but the result of a false statement means that no value satisfies the equation. The symbolic way to denote that no solution exists is $\emptyset$. Next, consider the equation:

$$5x + 4 + 2x = 9 + 7x - 5$$

Combining the like terms on both sides results in:

$$7x + 4 = 7x + 4$$

The left-hand side is exactly the same as the right-hand side. Using the addition principle to move terms, the result is $0 = 0$, which is always true. Therefore, the original equation is true for any number, and the solution set is all real numbers. The symbolic way to denote such a solution set is $\mathbb{R}$, or in interval notation, $(-\infty, \infty)$.

One-step problems take only one mathematical step to solve. For example, solve the equation:

$$5x = 45$$

This is a one-step problem because the one step of dividing both sides of the equation by 5 is the only step necessary to obtain the solution $x = 9$. The multiplication principle of equality is the one step used to isolate the variable. The equation is of the form $ax = b$, where a and b are rational numbers. Similarly, the addition principle of equality could be the one step needed to solve a problem. In this case, the equation would be of the following form for real numbers a and b:

$$x + a = b$$

or

$$x - a = b$$

A multi-step problem involves more than one step to find the solution, or it could consist of solving more than one equation. An equation that involves both the addition principle and the multiplication principle is a two-step problem, and an example of such an equation is:

$$2x - 4 = 5$$

To solve, add 4 to both sides and then divide both sides by 2. An example of a two-step problem involving two separate equations is:

$$y = 3x$$

$$2x + y = 4$$

The two equations form a system that must be solved together in two variables. The system can be solved by the substitution method. Since y is already solved for in terms of x, replace y with $3x$ in the equation $2x + y = 4$, resulting in $2x + 3x = 4$. Therefore, $5x = 4$ and $x = \frac{4}{5}$. Because there are two variables, the solution consists of a value for both x and for y. Substitute $x = \frac{4}{5}$ into either original equation to find y. The easiest choice is $y = 3x$. Therefore,

$$y = 3 \times \frac{4}{5} = \frac{12}{5}$$

The solution can be written as the ordered pair $\left(\frac{4}{5}, \frac{12}{5}\right)$.

Real-world problems can be translated into both one-step and multi-step problems. In either case, the word problem must be translated from the verbal form into mathematical expressions and equations that can be solved using algebra. An example of a one-step real-world problem is the following: A cat weighs half as much as a dog living in the same house. If the dog weighs 14.5 pounds, how much does the cat weigh? To solve this problem, an equation can be used. In any word problem, the first step must be defining variables that represent the unknown quantities. For this problem, let x be equal to the unknown weight of the cat. Because two times the weight of the cat equals 14.5 pounds, the equation to be solved is:

$$2x = 14.5$$

Use the multiplication principle to divide both sides by 2. Therefore, $x = 7.25$, and the cat weighs 7.25 pounds.

Most of the time, real-world problems require multiple steps. The following is an example of a multi-step problem: The sum of two consecutive page numbers is equal to 437. What are those page numbers? First, define the unknown quantities. If x is equal to the first page number, then $x + 1$ is equal to the next page number because they are consecutive integers. The sum is equal to 437. Putting this information together results in the equation:

$$x + x + 1 = 437$$

To solve, first collect like terms to obtain:

$$2x + 1 = 437$$

Then, subtract 1 from both sides and then divide by 2. The solution to the equation is $x = 218$. Therefore, the two consecutive page numbers that satisfy the problem are 218 and 219.

It is always important to make sure that answers to real-world problems make sense. For instance, it should be a red flag if the solution to this same problem resulted in decimals, which would indicate the need to check the work. Page numbers are whole numbers; therefore, if decimals are found to be answers, the solution process should be double-checked for mistakes.

Solving Inequalities

Inequalities can be solved in a similar method as equations. Basically, the goal is to isolate the variable, and this process can be completed by adding numbers onto both sides, subtracting numbers off of both sides, multiplying numbers onto both sides, and dividing numbers off of both sides of the inequality.

Basically, if something is done to one side, it has to be done to the other side, just like when solving equations.

However, there is one important difference, and that difference occurs when multiplying times negative numbers and dividing by negative numbers. If either one of these steps must be performed in the solution process, the inequality symbol must be reversed. Consider the following inequality:

$$2 - 3x < 11$$

The goal is to isolate the variable x, so first subtract 2 off both sides to obtain:

$$-3x < 9$$

Then divide both sides by -3, making sure to "*flip the sign.*" This results in $x > -3$, which is the solution set. This solution set means that all numbers greater than -3 satisfy the original inequality, and therefore any number larger than -3 is a solution. In **set-builder notation**, this set can be written as $\{x | x > -3\}$, which is read "all x values such that x is greater than -3." In addition to the inequality form of the solution, solutions of inequalities can be expressed by using both a number line and interval notation. Here is a chart that highlights all three types of expressing the solutions:

Interval Notation	Number Line Sketch	Set-builder Notation
(a, b)		$\{ x \mid a < x < b \}$
$(a, b]$		$\{ x \mid a < x \leq b \}$
$[a, b)$		$\{ x \mid a \leq x < b \}$
$[a, b]$		$\{ x \mid a \leq x \leq b \}$
(a, ∞)		$\{ x \mid x > a \}$
$(-\infty, b)$		$\{ x \mid x < b \}$
$[a, \infty)$		$\{ x \mid x \geq a \}$
$(-\infty, b]$		$\{ x \mid x \leq b \}$
$(-\infty, \infty)$		$\mathbb{R}$

Equation Systems

Simultaneous equations, otherwise known as a **system of equations**, can be solved in a variety of ways. If the system consists of two linear equations, they can be solved by graphing, substitution, or elimination.

When graphing, the solution of a system of equations is the point of intersection. If the two lines are parallel, they will never intersect, and there is no solution. If the two lines are the same, there are infinitely many solutions, and the solution set is equal to the entire line. Here are the three cases:

Consistent	**Inconsistent**	**Dependent**
One solution	No solution	Infinite number of solutions
Lines intersect	Lines are parallel	Coincide/Same line

There are two algebraic methods to finding solutions. The first is **substitution**. This is better suited when one of the equations is already solved for one variable, or it is easy to do so. Then this equation gets substituted into the other equation for that variable, resulting in an equation in one variable. Solve for the given variable and plug that value into one of the original equations to find the other variable. This last step is known as **back-substitution**.

Here is an example of solving a system with the substitution method:

$$y = x + 1 \qquad 2y = 3x$$

$$2y = 3x$$
$$2(x + 1) = 3x$$
$$2x + 2 = 3x$$
$$\underline{-2x \qquad\quad -2x}$$
$$2 = x$$

$$y = x + 1$$
$$y = 2 + 1 = 3$$
$$\text{Solution: } (2 , 3)$$

The other method is known as **elimination**, or the **addition method**. This is better suited when the equations are in standard form:

$$Ax + By = C$$

The goal in this method is to multiply one or both equations times numbers that result in opposite coefficients. Then add the equations together to obtain an equation in one variable. Solve for the given variable, and then take that value and back-substitute to obtain the other part of the ordered pair solution. Here is an example of elimination:

$$\begin{cases} -x + 5y = 8 \\ 3x + 7y = -2 \end{cases} \xrightarrow{\times 3} \begin{cases} -3x + 15y = 24 \\ 3x + 7y = -2 \end{cases}$$

$$\begin{aligned} -3x + 15y &= 24 \\ 3x + 7y &= -2 \\ \hline 22y &= 22 \\ \frac{22y}{22} &= \frac{22}{22} \\ y &= 1 \end{aligned}$$

Note that in order to check an answer when solving a system of equations, the solution must be checked in both original equations to show that it solves both equations.

Systems of Linear Inequalities in Two Variables

A **system of linear inequalities in two variables** consists of two inequalities in two variables, x and y. For example, the following is a system of linear inequalities in two variables:

$$\begin{cases} 4x + 2y < 1 \\ 2x - y \leq 0 \end{cases}$$

The curly brace on the left side shows that the two inequalities are grouped together. A solution of a single inequality in two variables is an ordered pair that satisfies the inequality. For example, $(1, 3)$ is a solution of the linear inequality:

$$y \geq x + 1$$

because when plugged in, it results in a true statement. The graph of an inequality in two variables consists of all ordered pairs that make the solution true. Therefore, the entire solution set of a single inequality contains many ordered pairs, and the set can be graphed by using a half plane.

A **half plane** consists of the set of all points on one side of a line. If the inequality consists of $>$ or $<$, the line is dashed because no solutions actually exist on the line shown. If the inequality consists of $\geq$ or $\leq$, the line is solid and solutions are on the line shown. To graph a linear inequality, graph the corresponding equation found by replacing the inequality symbol with an equals sign. Then pick a test point that exists on either side of the line. If that point results in a true statement when plugged into the original inequality, shade in the side containing the test point. If it results in a false statement, shade in the opposite side.

Solving a system of linear inequalities must be done graphically. Follow the process as described above for both given inequalities. The solution set to the entire system is the region that is in common to every graph in the system. For example, here is the solution to the following system:

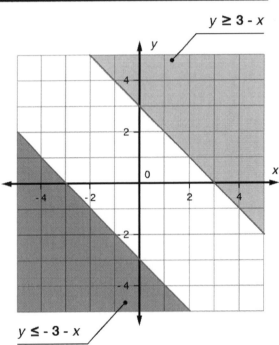

Note that there is no region in common, so this system has no solution.

Systems of Two Linear Equations in Two Variables

An example of a *system of two linear equations in two variables* is the following:

$$2x + 5y = 8$$

$$5x + 48y = 9$$

A solution to a **system of two linear equations** is an ordered pair that satisfies both the equations in the system. A system can have one solution, no solution, or infinitely many solutions. The solution can be found through a graphing technique. The solution to a system of equations is actually equal to the point where both lines intersects. If the lines intersect at one point, there is one solution and the system is said to be **consistent**. However, if the two lines are parallel, they will never intersect and there is no solution. In this case, the system is said to be **inconsistent**. Third, if the two lines are actually the same line, there are infinitely many solutions and the solution set is equal to the entire line. The lines are **dependent**. Here is a summary of the three cases that was previously shown:

Solving Systems by Graphing

Consistent	Inconsistent	Dependent
One solution	No solution	Infinite number of solutions
Lines intersect	*Lines are parallel*	*Coincide: same line*

Consider the following system of equations:

$$y + x = 3$$

$$y - x = 1$$

To find the solution graphically, graph both lines on the same xy-plane. Graph each line using either a table of ordered pairs, the x- and y-intercepts, or slope and the y-intercept. Then, locate the point of intersection.

The graph is shown here:

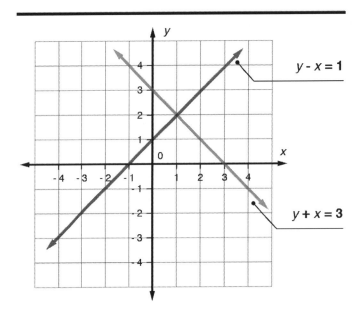

The System of Equations
$$\begin{cases} y + x = 3 \\ y - x = 1 \end{cases}$$

It can be seen that the point of intersection is the ordered pair $(1, 2)$. This solution can be checked by plugging it back into both original equations to make sure it results in true statements. This process results in:

$$2 + 1 = 3$$

$$2 - 1 = 1$$

Both equations are true, so the solution is correct.

The following system has no solution:

$$y = 4x + 1$$

$$y = 4x - 1$$

Both lines have the same slope and different y-intercepts, so they are parallel, meaning that they run alongside each other and never intersect.

Finally, the following solution has infinitely many solutions:

$$2x - 7y = 12$$

$$4x - 14y = 24$$

Note that the second equation is equal to the first equation times 2. Therefore, they are the same line. The solution set can be written in set notation as:

$$\{(x, y)|2x - 7y = 12\}$$

This represents the entire line.

Algebraically Solving Linear Equations or Inequalities in One Variable

A *linear equation in one variable* can be solved using the following steps:

1. Simplify both sides of the equation by removing all parentheses, using the distributive property, and collecting all like terms.

2. Collect all variable terms on one side of the equation and all constant terms on the other side by adding the same quantity to or subtracting the same quantity from both sides.

3. Isolate the variable by either multiplying or dividing both sides of the equation by the same number.

4. Check the answer.

The only difference between solving linear inequalities versus equations is that when multiplying by a negative number or dividing by a negative number, the direction of the inequality symbol must be reversed.

If an equation contains multiple fractions, it might make sense to clear the equation of fractions first by multiplying all terms by the least common denominator. Also, if an equation contains several decimals, it might make sense to clear the decimals as well by multiplying times a factor of 10. If the equation has decimals in the hundredths place, multiply every term in the equation by 100.

Linear Applications and Graphs

The Connection Between Proportional Relationships and Linear Equations

Linear growth involves a quantity, the **dependent variable**, increasing or decreasing at a constant rate as another quantity, the **independent variable**, increases as well. The graph of linear growth is a straight line. Linear growth is represented as the following equation: $y = mx + b$, where m is the **slope** of the line, also known as the **rate of change**, and b is the **y-intercept**. If the y-intercept is 0, then the linear growth is actually known as **direct variation**. If the slope is positive, the dependent variable increases as the independent variable increases, and if the slope is negative, the dependent variable decreases as the independent variable increases.

A linear function that models a linear relationship between two quantities is of the form $y = mx + b$, or in function form:

$$f(x) = mx + b$$

In a linear function, the value of y depends on the value of x and y increases or decreases at a constant rate as x increases. Therefore, the independent variable is x, and the dependent variable is y. The graph of a linear function is a line, and the constant rate can be seen by looking at the steepness, or slope, of the line. If the line increases from left to right, the slope is positive. If the line slopes downward from left to right, the slope is negative. In the function, m represents slope. Each point on the line is an **ordered pair** (x, y), where x represents the x-coordinate of the point and y represents the y-coordinate of the point. The point where $x = 0$ is known as the y-intercept, and it is the place where the line crosses the y-axis. If $x = 0$ is plugged into:

$$f(x) = mx + b$$

The result is $f(0) = b$, so therefore, the point $(0, b)$ is the y-intercept of the line. The derivative of a linear function is its slope.

Consider the following situation. A taxicab driver charges a flat fee of $2 per ride and $3 a mile. This statement can be modeled by the function $f(x) = 3x + 2$ where x represents the number of miles and $f(x) = y$ represents the total cost of the ride. The total cost increases at a constant rate of $2 per mile, and that is why this situation is a linear relationship. The slope $m = 3$ is equivalent to this rate of change. The flat fee of $2 is the y-intercept. It is the place where the graph crosses the x-axis, and it represents the cost when $x = 0$, or when no miles have been traveled in the cab. The y-intercept in this situation represents the flat fee.

Probability Sets

Permutations and Combinations

A probability experiment is a repeated action that has a specific set of possible results. The result of such an experiment is known as an **outcome**, and the set of all potential outcomes is known as the **sample space**. An **event** consists of one or more of those outcomes. For example, consider the probability experiment of tossing a coin and rolling a six-sided die. The coin has two possible outcomes—a heads or a tails—and the die has six possible outcomes—rolling each number 1–6. Therefore, the sample space has twelve possible outcomes: a heads or a tails paired with each roll of the die.

A **simple event** is an event that consists of a single outcome. For instance, selecting a queen of hearts from a standard fifty-two-card deck is a simple event; however, selecting a queen is not a simple event because there are four possibilities.

Classical, or **theoretical, probability** is when each outcome in a sample space has the same chance to occur. The probability for an event is equal to the number of outcomes in that event divided by the total number of outcomes in the sample space. For example, consider rolling a six-sided die. The probability of rolling a 2 is $\frac{1}{6}$, and the probability of rolling an even number is $\frac{3}{6}$, or $\frac{1}{2}$, because there are three even numbers on the die. This type of probability is based on what should happen in theory but not what actually happens in real life.

Empirical probability is based on actual experiments or observations. For example, if a die is rolled eight times, and a 1 is rolled two times, the empirical probability of rolling a 1 is $\frac{2}{8} = \frac{1}{4}$, which is higher than the theoretical probability. The Law of Large Numbers states that as an experiment is completed repeatedly, the empirical probability of an event should get closer to the theoretical probability of an event.

Probabilities range from 0 to 1. The closer the probability of an event occurring is to 0, the less likely it will occur. The closer it is to 1, the more likely it is to occur.

The **addition rule** is necessary to find the probability of event A or event B occurring, or both occurring at the same time. If events A and B are **mutually exclusive** or **disjoint**, which means they cannot occur at the same time:

$$P(A \text{ or } B) = P(A) + P(B)$$

If events A and B are not mutually exclusive:

$$P(A \text{ or } B) = P(A) + P(B) - P(A \text{ and } B)$$

$P(A \text{ and } B)$ represents the probability of event A and B both occurring at the same time. An example of two events that are mutually exclusive are rolling a 6 on a die and rolling an odd number on a die. The probability of rolling a 6 or rolling an odd number is:

$$\frac{1}{6} + \frac{3}{6} = \frac{4}{6} = \frac{2}{3}$$

Rolling a 6 and rolling an even number are not mutually exclusive because there is some overlap. The probability of rolling a 6 or rolling an even number is:

$$\frac{1}{6} + \frac{3}{6} - \frac{1}{6} = \frac{3}{6} = \frac{1}{2}$$

Conditional Probability

The **multiplication rule** is necessary when finding the probability that event A occurs in a first trial and event B occurs in a second trial, which is written as $P(A \text{ and } B)$. This rule differs if the events are independent or dependent. Two events A and B are **independent** if the occurrence of one event does not affect the probability that the other will occur. If A and B are not independent, they are **dependent**, and the outcome of the first event somehow affects the outcome of the second. If events A and B are independent:

$$P(A \text{ and } B) = P(A)P(B)$$

If events A and B are dependent, then:

$$P(A \text{ and } B) = P(A)P(B|A)$$

$P(B|A)$ represents the probability event B occurs given that event A has already occurred.

$P(B|A)$ represents **conditional probability**, or the probability of event B occurring given that event A has already occurred. $P(B|A)$ can be found by dividing the probability of events A and B both occurring by the probability of event A occurring using the formula:

$$P(B|A) = \frac{P(A \text{ and } B)}{P(A)}$$

57

This represents the total number of outcomes remaining for B to occur after A occurs. This formula is derived from the multiplication rule with dependent events by dividing both sides by $P(A)$. Note that $P(B|A)$ and $P(A|B)$ are not the same. The first quantity shows that event B has occurred after event A, and the second quantity shows that event A has occurred after event B. Incorrectly interchanging these ideas is known as **confusing the inverse**.

Consider the case of drawing two cards from a deck of fifty-two cards. The probability of pulling two queens would vary based on whether the initial card was placed back in the deck for the second pull. If the card is placed back in, the probability of pulling two queens is:

$$\frac{4}{52} \times \frac{4}{52} = 0.00592$$

If the card is not placed back in, the probability of pulling two queens is:

$$\frac{4}{52} \times \frac{3}{51} = 0.00452$$

When the card is not placed back in, both the numerator and denominator of the second probability decrease by 1. This is due to the fact that, theoretically, there is one less queen in the deck, and there is one less total card in the deck as well.

Conditional probability is used frequently when probabilities are calculated from tables. Two-way frequency tables display data with two variables and highlight the relationships between those two variables. They are often used to summarize survey results and are also known as **contingency tables**. Each cell shows a count pertaining to that individual variable pairing, known as a **joint frequency**, and the totals of each row and column also are in the tables. Consider the following two-way frequency table:

	70 or older	69 or younger	Totals
Women	20	40	60
Men	5	35	40
Total	25	75	100

This table shows the breakdown of ages and sexes of 100 people in a particular village. Consider a randomly selected villager. The probability of selecting a male 69 years old or younger is $\frac{35}{100}$ because there are 35 males under the age of 70 and 100 total villagers.

Probability Distributions

A **discrete random variable** is a set of values that is either finite or countably infinite. If there are infinitely many values, being **countable** means that each individual value can be paired with a natural number. For example, the number of coin tosses before getting heads could potentially be infinite, but the total number of tosses is countable. Each toss refers to a number, like the first toss, second toss, etc. A **continuous random variable** has infinitely many values that are not countable. The individual items cannot be enumerated; an example of such a set is any type of measurement. There are infinitely many heights of human beings due to decimals that exist within each inch, centimeter, millimeter, etc.

Each type of variable has its own **probability distribution**, which calculates the probability for each potential value of the random variable. Probability distributions exist in tables, formulas, or graphs. The expected value of a random variable represents what the mean value should be in either a large sample

58

size or after many trials. According to the Law of Large Numbers, after many trials, the actual mean and that of the probability distribution should be very close to the expected value. The **expected value** is a weighted average that is calculated as:

$$E(X) = \sum x_i p_i$$

x_i represents the value of each outcome, and p_i represents the probability of each outcome. The expected value if all of the probabilities are equal is:

$$E(X) = \frac{x_1 + x_2 + \cdots + x_n}{n}$$

Expected value is often called the **mean of the random variable** and is known as a **measure of central tendency** like mean and mode.

A binomial probability distribution adheres to some important criteria: it must consist of a fixed number of trials where all trials are independent, each trial must have an outcome classified as either success or failure, and the probability of a success must be the same in each trial. Within any binomial experiment, x is the number of resulting successes, n is the number of trials, P is the probability of success within each trial, and $Q = 1 - P$ is the probability of failure within each trial. The probability of obtaining x successes within n trials is:

$$\binom{n}{x} P^x (1 - P)^{n-x} \text{, where } \binom{n}{x} = \frac{n!}{x! (n - x)!}$$

This is called the **binomial coefficient**. A binomial probability distribution could be used to find the probability of obtaining exactly two heads on five tosses of a coin. In the formula, $x = 2$, $n = 5$, $P = 0.5$, and $Q = 0.5$.

A **uniform probability distribution** exists when there is constant probability. Each random variable has equal probability, and its graph looks a rectangle because the height, representing the probability, is constant.

Finally, a **normal probability distribution** has a graph that is symmetric and bell-shaped; an example using body weight is shown here:

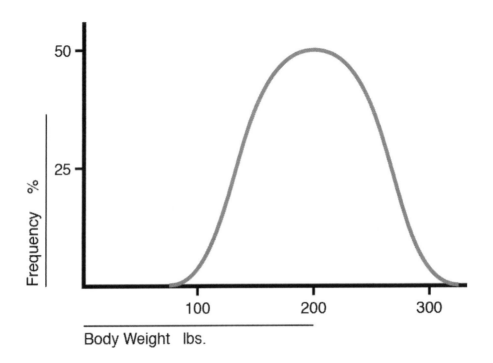

Population percentages can be estimated using normal distributions. For example, the probability that a data point will be less than the mean is 50 percent. The Empirical Rule states that 68 percent of the data falls within 1 standard deviation of the mean, 95 percent falls within 2 standard deviations of the mean, and 99.7 percent falls within 3 standard deviations of the mean. A **standard normal distribution** is a normal distribution with a mean equal to 0 and standard deviation equal to 1. The area under the entire curve of a standard normal distribution is equal to 1.

Counting Methods

The total number of events in the sample space must be known to solve probability problems. Different methods can be used to count the number of possible outcomes, depending on whether different arrangements of the same items are counted only once or separately. **Permutations** are arrangements in which different sequences are counted separately. Therefore, order matters in permutations. **Combinations** are arrangements in which different sequences are not counted separately. Therefore, order does not matter in combinations. Permutations would consider 123 different from 321; combinations, on the other hand, consider 123 the same as 321.

If the sample space contains n different permutations of n different items and all of them must be selected, there are $n!$ different possibilities. For example, five different books can be rearranged $5! = 120$ times. The probability of one person randomly ordering those five books in the same way as another person is $\frac{1}{120}$. A different calculation is necessary if a number less than n is to be selected or if order does not matter. In general, the notation $P(n, r)$ represents the number of ways to arrange r objects from a set of n if order does matter, and:

$$P(n, r) = \frac{n!}{(n-r)!}$$

Therefore, in order to calculate the number of ways five books can be arranged in three slots if order matters, plug $n = 5$ and $r = 3$ in the formula to obtain:

$$P(5, 3) = \frac{5!}{(5-3)!} = \frac{5!}{2!} = 60$$

Secondly, $C(n, r)$ represents the total number of r combinations selected out of n items when order does not matter, and:

$$C(n, r) = \frac{n!}{(n-r)! \; r!}$$

Therefore, the number of ways five books can be arranged in three slots if order does not matter is:

$$C(5, 3) = \frac{5!}{(5-3)! \; 3!} = 10$$

The following relationship exists between permutations and combinations:

$$C(n, r) = \frac{P(n, r)}{r!}$$

Sets of numbers and other similarly organized data can also be represented graphically. Venn diagrams are a common way to do so. A Venn diagram represents each set of data as a circle. The circles overlap, showing that each set of data is overlapping. A Venn diagram is also known as a **logic diagram** because it visualizes all possible logical combinations between two sets. Common elements of two sets are represented by the area of overlap. The following is an example of a Venn diagram of two sets A and B:

Parts of the Venn Diagram

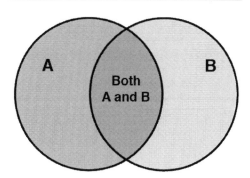

Another name for the area of overlap is the **intersection**. The intersection of A and B, $A \cap B$, contains all elements that are in both sets A and B. The union of A and B, $A \cup B$, contains all elements in both sets A

and B. Finally, the complement of $A \cup B$ is equal to all elements that are not in either set A or set B. These elements are placed outside of the circles.

The following is an example of a Venn diagram in which 24 students were surveyed asking if they had brothers or sisters or both. Ten students only had brothers, 7 students only had sisters, and 5 had both brothers and sisters. This number 5 is the intersection and is placed where the circles overlap. Two students did not have a cat or a dog. Two is therefore the complement and is placed outside of the circles.

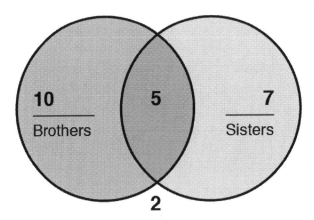

Venn diagrams can have more than two sets of data. The more circles, the more logical combinations are represented by the overlapping. The following is a Venn diagram that represents students who like the colors green, pink, or blue. There were 30 students surveyed. The innermost region represents those students that like green, pink, and blue. Therefore, 2 students like all three. In this example, all students like at least one of the colors, so no one exists in the complement.

30 students

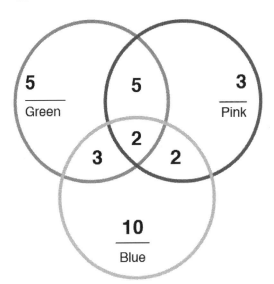

Venn diagrams are typically not drawn to scale; however, if they are, and if each circle's area is proportional to the amount of data it represents, then it is called an area-proportional Venn diagram.

Descriptive Statistics

Interpreting Categorical and Quantitative Data

They all organize, categorize, and compare data, and they come in different shapes and sizes. Each type has its own way of showing information, whether through a column, shape, or picture. To answer a question relating to a table, chart, or graph, some steps should be followed. First, the problem should be read thoroughly to determine what is being asked to determine what quantity is unknown. Then, the title of the table, chart, or graph should be read. The title should clarify what data is actually being summarized in the table. Next, look at the key and labels for both the horizontal and vertical axes, if they are given. These items will provide information about how the data is organized. Finally, look to see if there is any more labeling inside the table. Taking the time to get a good idea of what the table is summarizing will be helpful as it is used to interpret information.

Tables are a good way of showing a lot of information in a small space. The information in a table is organized in columns and rows. For example, a table may be used to show the number of votes each candidate received in an election. By interpreting the table, one may observe which candidate won the election and which candidates came in second and third. In using a bar chart to display monthly rainfall amounts in different countries, rainfall can be compared between countries at different times of the year. Graphs are also a useful way to show change in variables over time, as in a line graph, or percentages of a whole, as in a pie graph.

The table below relates the number of items to the total cost. The table shows that one item costs $5. By looking at the table further, five items cost $25, ten items cost $50, and fifty items cost $250. This cost can be extended for any number of items. Since one item costs $5, then two items would cost $10. Though this information is not in the table, the given price can be used to calculate unknown information.

Number of Items	1	5	10	50
Cost ($)	5	25	50	250

A **bar graph** is a graph that summarizes data using bars of different heights. It is useful when comparing two or more items or when seeing how a quantity changes over time. It has both a horizontal and vertical axis. To interpret bar graphs, recognize what each bar represents and connect that to the two variables. The bar graph below shows the scores for six people during three different games. The different colors of the bars distinguish between the three games, and the height of the bar indicates their score for that game. William scored 25 on game 3, and Abigail scored 38 on game 3. By comparing the bars, it is obvious that Williams scored lower than Abigail.

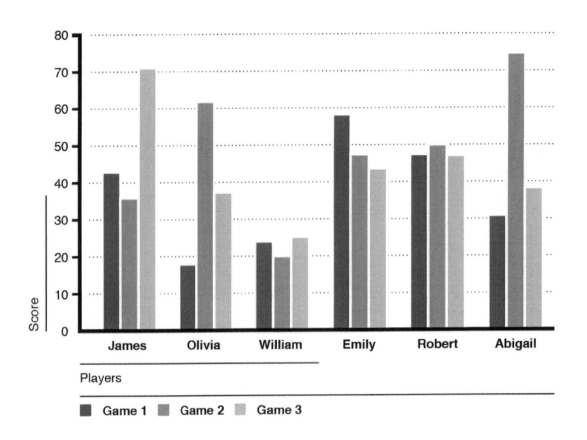

A line graph is a way to compare two variables that are plotted on opposite axes of a graph. The line indicates a continuous change as it rises or falls. The line's rate of change is known as its slope. The horizontal axis often represents a variable of time. Readers can quickly see if an amount has grown or decreased over time. The bottom of the graph, or the x-axis, shows the units for time, such as days, hours, months, etc. If there are multiple lines, a comparison can be made between what the two lines represent. For example, the following line graph, shown previously, displays the change in temperature over five days.

The top line represents the high, and the bottom line represents the low for each day. Looking at the top line alone, the high decreases for a day, then increases on Wednesday. Then it decreases on Thursday and increases again on Friday. The low temperatures have a similar trend, shown in the bottom line. The range in temperatures each day can also be calculated by finding the difference between the top line and bottom line on a particular day. On Wednesday, the range was 14 degrees, from 62 to 76°F.

Pie charts show percentages of a whole; they are circular representations of data used to highlight numerical proportions. Each category represents a piece of the pie, and together, all of the pieces make up a whole. The size of each pie slice is proportional to the amount it represents; therefore, a reader can quickly make comparisons by visualizing the sizes of the pieces. They can be useful for comparison between different categories. The following pie chart is a simple example of three different categories shown in comparison to each other.

Light gray represents cats, dark gray represents dogs, and the medium shade of gray represents other pets. These three equal pieces each represent just more than 33 percent, or $\frac{1}{3}$ of the whole. Values 1 and 2 may be combined to represent $\frac{2}{3}$ of the whole. In an example where the total pie represents 75,000 animals, then cats would be equal to $\frac{1}{3}$ of the total, or 25,000. Dogs would equal 25,000 and other pets also equal 25,000.

Since circles have 360 degrees, they are used to create pie charts. Because each piece of the pie is a percentage of a whole, that percentage is multiplied times 360 to get the number of degrees each piece represents. In the example above, each piece is $\frac{1}{3}$ of the whole, so each piece is equivalent to 120 degrees. Together, all three pieces add up to 360 degrees.

Stacked bar graphs are also used fairly frequently when comparing multiple variables at one time. They combine some elements of both pie charts and bar graphs, using the organization of bar graphs and the proportionality aspect of pie charts. The following is an example of a stacked bar graph that represents the number of students in a band playing drums, flute, trombone, and clarinet. Each bar graph is broken up further into girls and boys.

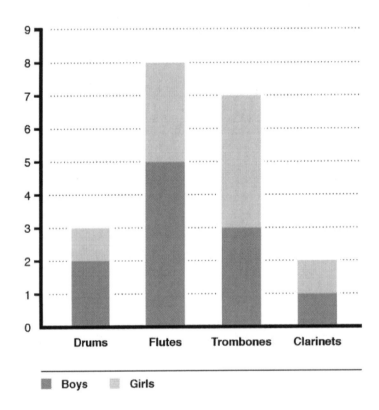

To determine how many boys play trombone, refer to the darker portion of the trombone bar, which indicates three boys.

As mentioned, a **scatterplot** is another way to represent paired data. It uses Cartesian coordinates, like a line graph, meaning it has both a horizontal and vertical axis. Each data point is represented as a dot on the graph. The dots are never connected with a line. For example, the following is a scatterplot showing the connection between people's ages and heights.

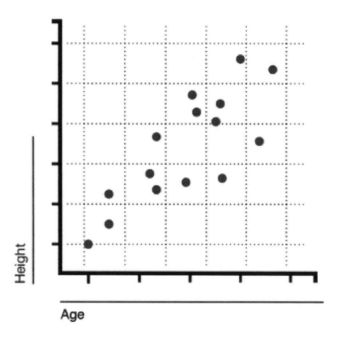

A scatterplot, also known as a **scattergram**, can be used to predict another value and to see if a correlation exists between two variables in a set of data. If the data resembles a straight line, then it is associated, or correlated. The following is an example of a scatterplot in which the data does not seem to have an association:

Describing Distributions

One way information can be interpreted from tables, charts, and graphs is through statistics. The three most common calculations for a set of data are the mean, median, and mode. These three are called **measures of central tendency**, which are helpful in comparing two or more different sets of data. The **mean** refers to the average and is found by adding up all values and dividing the total by the number of values. In other words, the mean is equal to the sum of all values divided by the number of data entries. For example, if you bowled a total of 532 points in 4 bowling games, your mean score was $\frac{532}{4} = 133$ points per game. Students can apply the concept of mean to calculate what score they need on a final exam to earn a desired grade in a class.

The **median** is found by lining up values from least to greatest and choosing the middle value. If there is an even number of values, then calculate the mean of the two middle amounts to find the median. For example, the median of the set of dollar amounts $5, $6, $9, $12, and $13 is $9. The median of the set of dollar amounts $1, $5, $6, $8, $9, $10 is $7, which is the mean of $6 and $8. The **mode** is the value that occurs the most. The mode of the data set {1, 3, 1, 5, 5, 8, 10} actually refers to two numbers: 1 and 5. In this case, the data set is **bimodal** because it has two modes. A data set can have no mode if no amount is repeated. Another useful statistic is range. The **range** for a set of data refers to the difference between the highest and lowest value.

In some cases, numbers in a list of data might have weights attached to them. In that case, a **weighted mean** can be calculated. A common application of a weighted mean is GPA. In a semester, each class is assigned a number of credit hours, its weight, and at the end of the semester each student receives a grade. To compute GPA, an A is a 4, a B is a 3, a C is a 2, a D is a 1, and an F is a 0. Consider a student that takes a 4-hour English class, a 3-hour math class, and a 4-hour history class and receives all B's. The weighted mean, GPA, is found by multiplying each grade times its weight, number of credit hours, and dividing by the total number of credit hours. Therefore, the student's GPA is:

$$\frac{3 \times 4 + 3 \times 3 + 3 \times 4}{11} = \frac{33}{11} = 3.0.$$

The following bar chart shows how many students attend a cycle class on each day of the week. To find the mean attendance for the week, add each day's attendance together:

$$10 + 7 + 6 + 9 + 8 + 14 + 4 = 58$$

Then divide the total by the number of days:

$$58 \div 7 = 8.3.$$

The mean attendance for the week was 8.3 people. The median attendance can be found by putting the attendance numbers in order from least to greatest: 4, 6, 7, 8, 9, 10, 14, and choosing the middle number:

8 people. This set of data has no mode because no numbers repeat. The range is 10, which is found by finding the difference between the lowest number, 4, and the highest number, 14.

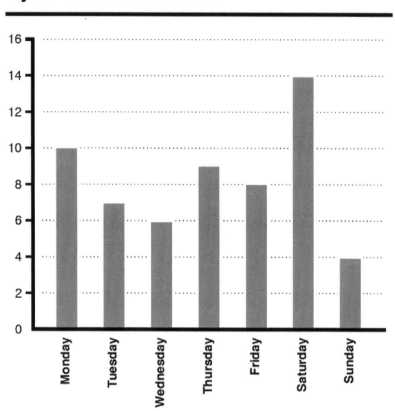

A **histogram** is a bar graph used to group data into "bins" that cover a range on the horizontal, or x-axis. Histograms consist of rectangles whose heights are equal to the frequency of a specific category. The horizontal axis represents the specific categories. Because they cover a range of data, these bins have no gaps between bars, unlike the bar graph above. In a histogram showing the heights of adult golden retrievers, the bottom axis would be groups of heights, and the y-axis would be the number of dogs in each range. Evaluating this histogram would show the height of most golden retrievers as falling within a certain range. It also provides information to find the average height and range for how tall golden retrievers may grow.

The following is a histogram that represents exam grades in a given class. The horizontal axis represents ranges of the number of points scored, and the vertical axis represents the number of students. For example, approximately 33 students scored in the 60 to 70 range.

Results of the exam

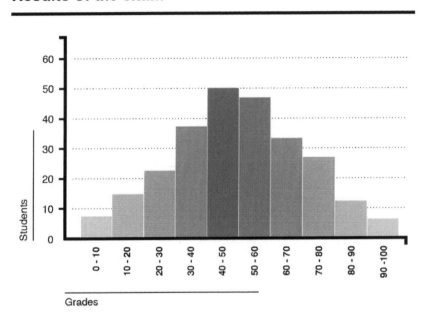

Certain measures of central tendency can be easily visualized with a histogram. If the points scored were shown with individual rectangles, the tallest rectangle would represent the mode. A bimodal set of data would have two peaks of equal height. Histograms can be classified as having data skewed to the left, skewed to the right, or **normally distributed**, which is also known as **bell-shaped**.

These three classifications can be seen in the following chart:

Measures of central tendency images

70

When the data is normal, the mean, median, and mode are very similar because they all represent the most typical value in the data set. In this case, the mean is typically considered the best measure of central tendency because it includes all data points. However, if the data is skewed, the mean becomes less meaningful because it is dragged in the direction of the skew. Therefore, the median becomes the best measure because it is not affected by any outliers.

The measures of central tendency and the range may also be found by evaluating information on a line graph.

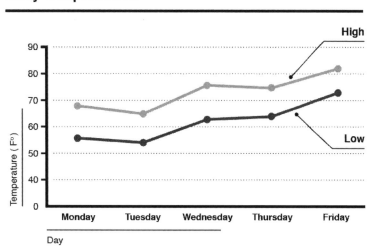

Daily Temperatures

In the line graph above that shows the daily high and low temperatures, the average high temperature can be found by gathering data from each day on the triangle line. The days' highs are 69, 65, 75, 74, and 81. To find the average, add them together to get 364, then divide by 5 (because there are 5 temperatures). The average high for the five days is 72.8. If 72.8 degrees is found on the graph, it will fall in the middle of all the values. The average low temperature can be found in the same way.

Given a set of data, the **correlation coefficient**, r, measures the association between all the data points. If two values are **correlated**, there is an association between them. However, correlation does not necessarily mean causation, or that one value causes the other. There is a common mistake made that assumes correlation implies causation. Average daily temperature and number of sunbathers are both correlated and have causation. If the temperature increases, that change in weather causes more people to want to catch some rays. However, wearing plus-size clothing and having heart disease are two variables that are correlated but do not have causation. The larger someone is, the more likely he or she is to have heart disease. However, being overweight does not cause someone to have the disease.

The value of the correlation coefficient is between -1 and 1, where -1 represents a perfect negative linear relationship, 0 represents no relationship between the two data sets, and 1 represents a perfect positive linear relationship. A negative linear relationship means that as x-values increase, y-values decrease. A positive linear relationship means that as x-values increase, y-values increase. The formula for computing the correlation coefficient is:

$$r = \frac{n \sum xy - (\sum x)(\sum y)}{\sqrt{n(\sum x^2) - (\sum x)^2}\sqrt{n(\sum y^2) - (y)^2}}$$

where n is the number of data points. The closer r is to 1 or -1, the stronger the correlation. A correlation can be seen when plotting data. If the graph resembles a straight line, there is a correlation.

Solving Problems Involving Measures of Center and Range

As mentioned, a data set can be described by calculating the mean, median, and mode. These values allow the data to be described with a single value that is representative of the data set.

The most common measure of center is the **mean**, also referred to as the **average.**

To calculate the mean:

- Add all data values together
- Divide by the sample size (the number of data points in the set)

The **median** is middle data value, so that half of the data lies below this value and half lies below the data value.

To calculate the median:

- Order the data from least to greatest
- The point in the middle of the set is the median
- If there is an even number of data points, add the two middle points and divide by 2

The **mode** is the data value that occurs most often.

To calculate the mode:

- Order the data from least to greatest
- Find the value that occurs most often

Example: Amelia is a leading scorer on the school's basketball team. The following data set represents the number of points that Amelia has scored in each game this season. Use the mean, median, and mode to describe the data.

> 16, 12, 26, 14, 28, 14, 12, 15, 25

Solution:

Mean:

$$16 + 12 + 26 + 14 + 28 + 14 + 12 + 15 + 25 = 162$$

$$162 \div 9 = 18$$

Amelia averages 18 points per game.

Median:

> 12, 12, 14, 14, **15**, 16, 25, 26, 28

Amelia's median score is 15.

Mode:

12, 12, 14, 14, 15, 16, 25, 26, 28

The numbers 12 and 14 each occur twice, so this data set has 2 modes: 12 and 14.

The **range** is the difference between the largest and smallest values in the set. In the example above, the range is $28 - 12 = 16$.

Determining How Changes in Data Affect Measures of Center or Range

An **outlier** is a data point that lies an unusual distance from other points in the data set. Removing an outlier from a data set will change the measures of central tendency. Removing a large outlier (a high number) from a data set will decrease both the mean and the median. Removing a small outlier (a number much lower than most in the data set) from a data set will increase both the mean and the median. For example, in data set {3, 6, 8, 12, 13, 14, 60}, the data point 60, is an outlier because it is unusually far from the other points. In this data set, the mean is 16.6. Notice that this mean number is even larger than all other data points in the set except for 60. Removing the outlier changes the mean to 9.3, and the median goes from 12 to 10. Removing an outlier will also decrease the range. In the data set above, the range is 57 when the outlier is included, but it decreases to 11 when the outlier is removed.

Adding an outlier to a data set will also affect the measures of central tendency. When a larger outlier is added to a data set, the mean and median increase. When a small outlier is added to a data set, the mean and median decrease. Adding an outlier to a data set will increase the range.

This does not seem to provide an appropriate measure of center when considering this data set. What will happen if that outlier is removed? Removing the extremely large data point, 60, is going to reduce the mean to 9.3. The mean decreased dramatically because 60 was much larger than any of the other data values. What would happen with an extremely low value in a data set like this one, {12, 87, 90, 95, 98, 100}? The mean of the given set is 80. When the outlier, 12, is removed, the mean should increase and fit more closely to the other data points. Removing 12 and recalculating the mean show that this is correct. After removing the outlier, the mean is 94. So, removing a large outlier will decrease the mean while removing a small outlier will increase the mean.

Statistical Measures

Statistics is the branch of mathematics that deals with the collection, organization, and analysis of data. Statistical questions can be answered by compiling and analyzing data. When collecting data, expect variability. For example, "How many pets does Yanni own?" is not a statistical question because it can be answered in one way. "How many pets do the people in a certain neighborhood own?" is a statistical question because, to determine this answer, one would need to collect data from each person in the neighborhood, and it is reasonable to expect the answers to vary.

Identify these as statistical or not statistical:

- How old are you?
- What is the average age of the people in your class?
- How tall are the students in Mrs. Jones' sixth grade class?
- Do you like Brussels sprouts?

The first and last questions are not statistical, but the two middle questions are.

Data collection can be done through surveys, experiments, observations, and interviews. A **census** is a type of survey that is done with a whole population. Because it can be difficult to collect data for an entire population, sometimes a **sample** is used. In this case, one would survey only a fraction of the population and make inferences about the data. Sample surveys are not as accurate as a census, but they are an easier and less expensive method of collecting data. An **experiment** is used when a researcher wants to explain how one variable causes changes in another variable. For example, if a researcher wanted to know if a particular drug affects weight loss, he or she would choose a **treatment group** that would take the drug, and another group, the **control group**, that would not take the drug.

Special care must be taken when choosing these groups to ensure that bias is not a factor. **Bias** occurs when an outside factor influences the outcome of the research. In observational studies, the researcher does not try to influence either variable but simply observes the behavior of the subjects. Interviews are sometimes used to collect data as well. The researcher will ask questions that focus on her area of interest in order to gain insight from the participants. When gathering data through observation or interviews, it is important that the researcher is well trained so that he or she does not influence the results and the study remains reliable. A study is reliable if it can be repeated under the same conditions and the same results are received each time.

The Random Processes Underlying Statistical Experiments

For researchers to make valid conclusions about population characteristics and parameters, the sample used to compare must be random. In a **random sample**, every member of the population must have an equal chance of being selected. In this situation, the sample is **unbiased** and is said to be a good representation of the population. If a sample is selected in an inappropriate manner, it is said to be **biased.** A sample can be biased if, for example, some subjects were more likely to be chosen than others. In order to have unbiased samples, the four main sampling methods used tend to be random, systematic, stratified, and cluster sampling.

Random sampling occurs when, given a sample size n, all possible samples of that size are equally likely to be chosen. Random numbers from calculators are typically used in this setting. Each member of a population is paired with a number, and then a set of random numbers is generated. Each person paired with one of those random numbers is selected. A **systematic sample** is when every fourth, seventh, tenth, etc., person from a population is selected to be in a sample. A **stratified sample** is when the population is divided into subgroups, or **strata**, using a characteristic, and then members from each stratum are randomly selected. For example, university students could be divided into age groups and then selected from each age group. Finally, a **cluster sample** is when a sample is used from an already selected group, like city block or zip code. These four methods are used most frequently because they are most likely to yield unbiased results.

Once an unbiased sample is obtained, data need to be collected. Common data collection methods include surveys with questions that are unbiased, contain clear language, avoid double negatives, and do not contain compound sentences that ask two questions at once. When formulating these questions, the simpler verbiage, the better.

Using Random Sampling to Draw Inferences About a Population

In statistics, a **population** contains all subjects being studied. For example, a population could be every student at a university or all males in the United States. A **sample** consists of a group of subjects from an entire population. A sample would be 100 students at a university or 100,000 males in the United States.

Inferential statistics is the process of using a sample to generalize information concerning populations. Hypothesis testing is the actual process used when evaluating claims made about a population based on a sample.

A **statistic** is a measure obtained from a sample, and a **parameter** is a measure obtained from a population. For example, the mean SAT score of the 100 students at a university would be a statistic, and the mean SAT score of all university students would be a parameter.

The beginning stages of hypothesis testing starts with formulating a **hypothesis**, a statement made concerning a population parameter. The hypothesis may be true, or it may not be true. The test will answer that question. In each setting, there are two different types of hypotheses: the **null hypothesis**, written as H_0, and the **alternative hypothesis**, written as H_1. The null hypothesis represents verbally when there is not a difference between two parameters, and the alternative hypothesis represents verbally when there is a difference between two parameters.

Consider the following experiment: A researcher wants to see if a new brand of allergy medication has any effect on drowsiness of the patients who take the medication. He wants to know if the average hours spent sleeping per day increases. The mean for the population under study is 8 hours, so $\mu = 8$. In other words, the population parameter is μ, the mean. The null hypothesis is $\mu = 8$ and the alternative hypothesis is $\mu > 8$. When using a smaller sample of a population, the **null hypothesis** represents the situation when the mean remains unaffected, and the **alternative hypothesis** represents the situation when the mean increases. The chosen statistical test will apply the data from the sample to actually decide whether the null hypothesis should or should not be rejected.

Geometry Concepts

Shapes and Solids

Shapes are defined by their angles and number of sides. A shape with one continuous side, where all points on that side are equidistant from a center point is called a **circle**. A shape made with three straight line segments is a **triangle**. A shape with four sides is called a **quadrilateral**, but more specifically a **square**, **rectangle**, **parallelogram**, or **trapezoid**, depending on the interior angles. These shapes are two-dimensional and only made of straight lines and angles.

Solids can be formed by combining these shapes and forming three-dimensional figures. While two-dimensional figures have only length and height, three-dimensional figures also have depth. Examples of solids may be prisms or spheres. The four figures below have different names based on their sides and dimensions. Figure 1 is a **cone**, a three-dimensional solid formed by a circle at its base and the sides combining to one point at the top. Figure 2 is a **triangle**, a shape with two dimensions and three line segments. Figure 3 is a **cylinder** made up of two base circles and a rectangle to connect them in three dimensions. Figure 4 is an **oval** formed by one continuous line in two dimensions; it differs from a circle because not all points are equidistant from the center.

Shapes and Solids

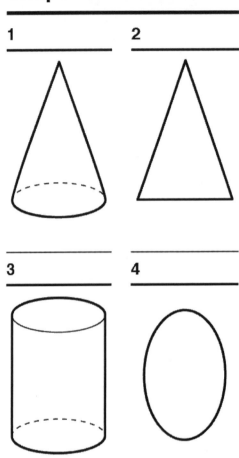

The **cube** in Figure 5 below is a three-dimensional solid made up of squares. Figure 6 is a **rectangle** because it has four sides that intersect at right angles. More specifically, it is a square because the four sides are equal in length. Figure 7 is a **pyramid** because the bottom shape is a square and the sides are all triangles. These triangles intersect at a point above the square. Figure 8 is a **circle** because it is made up of one continuous line where the points are all equidistant from one center point.

Shapes and Solids

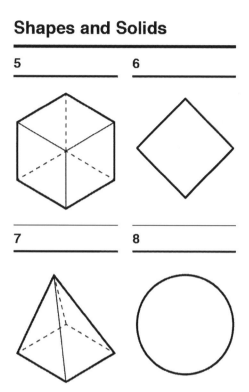

Basic shapes are those polygons that are made up of straight lines and angles and can be described by their number of sides and concavity. Some examples of those shapes are rectangles, triangles, hexagons, and pentagons. These shapes have identifying characteristics on their own, but they can also be decomposed into other shapes. For example, the following can be described as one hexagon, as seen in the first figure.

It can also be decomposed into six equilateral triangles. The last figure shows how the hexagon can be decomposed into three rhombuses.

Decomposing a Hexagon

More complex shapes can be formed by combining basic shapes or lining them up side by side. Below is an example of a house. This house is one figure all together but can be decomposed into seven different shapes. The chimney is a parallelogram, and the roof is made up of two triangles. The bottom of the

77

house is a square alongside three triangles. There are many other ways of decomposing this house. Different shapes can be used to line up together and form one larger shape. The area for the house can be calculated by finding the individual areas for each shape, then adding them all together. For this house, there would be the area of four triangles, one square, and one parallelogram. Adding these all together would result in the area of the house as a whole. Decomposing and composing shapes is commonly done with a set of tangrams. A **tangram** is a set of shapes that includes different size triangles, rectangles, and parallelograms.

A Tangram of a House

Lines and Angles

Straight Lines

Geometric figures can be identified by matching the definition with the object. For example, a line segment is made up of two connected endpoints. A **ray** is made up of one endpoint and one extending side that goes on forever. A line has no endpoints and two sides that extend forever. These three geometric figures are shown below. What happens at A and B determines the name of each figure.

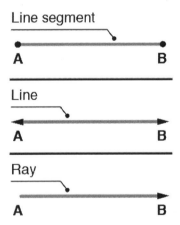

A set of lines can be parallel, perpendicular, or neither, depending on how the two lines interact. Parallel lines run alongside each other but never intersect. **Perpendicular** lines intersect at a 90-degree, or a right, angle. The image below shows both an example and a non-example of each set of lines. Because the first set of lines, in the top left corner, will eventually intersect if they continue, they are not parallel. In the second set, the lines run in the same direction and will never intersect, making them parallel. The third set, in the bottom left corner, intersect at an angle that is not right, or not 90 degrees. The fourth set is perpendicular because the lines intersect at exactly a right angle.

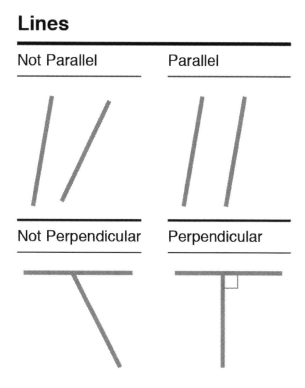

Lines

| Not Parallel | Parallel |
| Not Perpendicular | Perpendicular |

Angles

When two rays join together at their endpoints, they form an angle. Angles can be described based on their measure. An angle whose measure is ninety degrees is a right angle. Ninety degrees is a standard to which other angles are compared. If an angle is less than ninety degrees, it is an **acute angle**. If it is greater than ninety degrees, it is an **obtuse angle**. If an angle is equal to twice a right angle, or 180 degrees, it is a **straight angle**.

Examples of these types of angles are shown below:

Acute Angle

Less than 90°

Right Angle

Exactly 90°

Obtuse Angle

Greater than 90° but less than 180°

Straight Angle

Exactly 180°

A **straight angle** is equal to 180 degrees, or a straight line. If the line continues through the **vertex**, or point where the rays meet, and does not change direction, then the angle is straight. This is shown in Figure 1 below. The second figure shows an obtuse angle. Its measure is greater than ninety degrees, but less than that of a straight angle. An estimate for its measure may be 175 degrees. Figure 3 shows an acute angle because it is just less than that of a right angle. Its measure may be estimated to be 80 degrees.

The last image, Figure 4, shows another acute angle. This measure is much smaller, at approximately 35 degrees, but it is still classified as acute because it is between zero and 90 degrees.

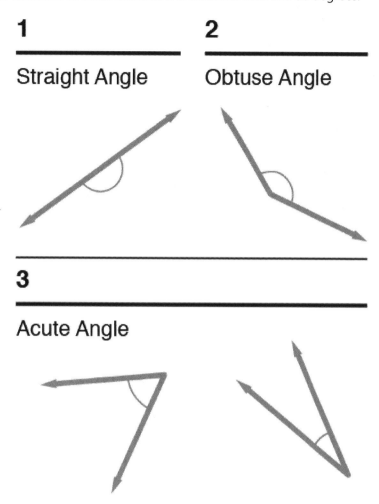

1

Straight Angle

2

Obtuse Angle

3

Acute Angle

Geometric Measurements

Area

Area is the two-dimensional space covered by an object. These problems may include the area of a rectangle, a yard, or a wall to be painted. Finding the area may require a simple formula or multiple formulas used together. The units for area are square units, such as square meters, square inches, and square miles. Given a square with side length s, the formula for its area is $A = s^2$.

Some other formulas for common shapes are shown below.

Shape	Formula	Graphic
Rectangle	$Area = length \times width$	
Triangle	$Area = \dfrac{1}{2} \times base \times height$	
Circle	$Area = \pi \times radius^2$	

The following formula, not as widely used as those shown above, but very important, is the area of a trapezoid:

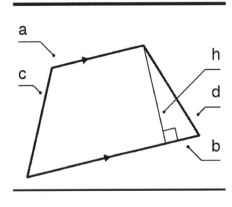

Area of a Trapezoid

$$A = \frac{1}{2}(a+b)h$$

To find the area of the shapes above, use the given dimensions of the shape in the formula. Complex shapes might require more than one formula. To find the area of the figure below, break the figure into two shapes. The rectangle has dimensions 11 cm by 6 cm. The triangle has dimensions 3 cm by 6 cm. Plug the dimensions into the rectangle formula:

$$A = 11 \times 6$$

Multiplication yields an area of 66 cm². The triangle's area can be found using the formula:

$$A = \frac{1}{2} \times 4 \times 6$$

Multiplication yields an area of 12 cm². Add the two areas to find the total area of the figure, which is 78 cm².

Instead of combining areas, some problems may require subtracting them, or finding the difference.

To find the area of the shaded region in the figure below, determine the area of the whole figure. Then subtract the area of the circle from the whole.

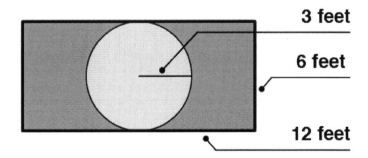

The following formula shows the area of the outside rectangle:

$$A = 12 \times 6 = 72 \text{ ft}^2$$

The area of the inside circle can be found by the following formula:

$$A = \pi(3)^2 = 9\pi = 28.3 \text{ ft}^2$$

As the shaded area is outside the circle, the area for the circle can be subtracted from the area of the rectangle to yield an area of 43.7 ft^2.

Perimeter

Perimeter is the distance around an object. The perimeter of an object can be found by adding the lengths of all sides. Perimeter may be used in problems dealing with lengths around objects such as fences or borders. It may also be used in finding missing lengths or working backwards. If the perimeter is given, but a length is missing, use subtraction to find the missing length.

Given a square with side length s, the formula for perimeter is $P = 4s$. Given a rectangle with length l and width w, the formula for perimeter is:

$$P = 2l + 2w$$

The perimeter of a triangle is found by adding the three side lengths, and the perimeter of a trapezoid is found by adding the four side lengths. The units for perimeter are always the original units of length, such as meters, inches, miles, etc. When discussing a circle, the distance around the object is referred to as its **circumference**, not perimeter. The formula for the circumference of a circle is $C = 2\pi r$, where r represents the radius of the circle. This formula can also be written as $C = d\pi$, where d represents the diameter of the circle.

Volume

Volume is three-dimensional and describes the amount of space that an object occupies, but it's different from area because it has three dimensions instead of two. The units for volume are cubic units, such as cubic meters, cubic inches, and cubic millimeters. Volume can be found by using formulas for common objects such as cylinders and boxes.

The following chart shows a diagram and formula for the volume of two objects.

Shape	Formula	Diagram
Rectangular Prism (box)	$V = length \times width \times height$	length, height, width
Cylinder	$V = \pi \times radius^2 \times height$	radius, height

Volume formulas of these two objects are derived by finding the area of the bottom two-dimensional shape, such as the circle or rectangle, and then multiplying times the height of the three-dimensional shape. Other volume formulas include the volume of a cube with side length s: $V = s^3$; the volume of a sphere with radius r: $V = \frac{4}{3}\pi r^3$; and the volume of a cone with radius r and height h:

$$V = \frac{1}{3}\pi r^2 h$$

If a soda can has a height of 5 inches and a radius on the top of 1.5 inches, the volume can be found using one of the given formulas. A soda can is a cylinder. Knowing the given dimensions, the formula can be completed as follows:

$$V = \pi(radius)^2 \times height$$

$$\pi(1.5 \text{ in})^2 \times 5 \text{ in} = 35.325 \text{ in}^3$$

Notice that the units for volume are inches cubed because it refers to the number of cubic inches required to fill the can.

Surface Area

Surface area is defined as the area of the surface of a figure. A pyramid has a surface made up of four triangles and one square. To calculate the surface area of a pyramid, the areas of each individual shape are calculated. Then the areas are added together. This method of decomposing the shape into two-dimensional figures to find area, then adding the areas, can be used to find surface area for any figure. Once these measurements are found, the area is described with square units. For example, the following figure shows a rectangular prism. The figure beside it shows the rectangular prism broken down into two-dimensional shapes, or rectangles. The area of each rectangle can be calculated by multiplying the length by the width. The area for the six rectangles can be represented by the following expression:

$$5 \times 6 + 5 \times 10 + 5 \times 6 + 6 \times 10 + 5 \times 10 + 6 \times 10$$

The total for all these areas added together is 280 cm^2, or 280 centimeters squared. This measurement represents the surface area because it is the area of all six surfaces of the rectangular prism.

The Net of a Rectangular Prism

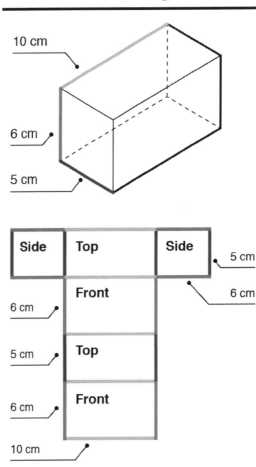

Another shape that has a surface area is a cylinder. The shapes used to make up the cylinder are two circles and a rectangle wrapped around between the two circles. A common example of a cylinder is a can. The two circles that make up the bases are obvious shapes. The rectangle can be more difficult to see, but the label on a can will help illustrate it. When the label is removed from a can and laid flat, the shape is a rectangle. When the areas for each shape are needed, there will be two formulas. The first is the area for the circles on the bases. This area is given by the formula $A = \pi r^2$.

There will be two of these areas—one for the top and one for the bottom if the can (cylinder) is standing upright on a shelf. Then the area of the rectangle must be determined. The width of the rectangle is equal to the height of the can, h. The length of the rectangle is equal to the circumference of the base circle, $2\pi r$. The area for the rectangle can be found by using the formula $A = 2\pi r \times h$. By adding the two areas for the bases and the area of the rectangle, the surface area of the cylinder can be found, described in units squared.

Using Nets to Determine the Surface Area of Three-Dimensional Figures

The surface area of a three-dimensional figure is the total area of each of the figure's faces. Because nets lay out each face of an object, they make it easier to visualize and measure surface area. The following figure shows a triangular prism. The bases are triangles and the sides are rectangles. The second figure shows the net for this triangular prism. The dimensions are labeled for each of the faces of the prism. To determine the area for the two triangles, use the following formula:

$$A = \frac{1}{2}bh = \frac{1}{2} \times 8 \times 9 = 36 \text{ cm}^2$$

The rectangles' areas can be described by the equation:

$$A = lw = 8 \times 5 + 9 \times 5 + 10 \times 5$$

$$40 + 45 + 50 = 135 \text{ cm}^2$$

The area for the triangles can be multiplied by two, then added to the rectangle areas to yield a total surface area of 207 cm².

A Triangular Prism and Its Net

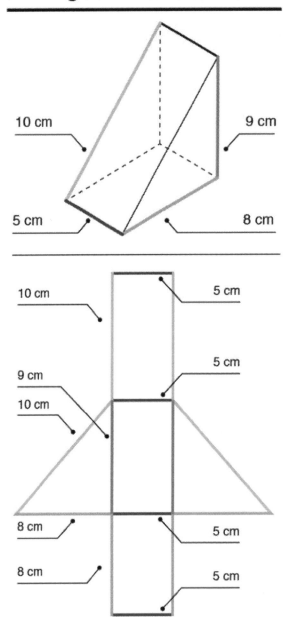

10 cm   9 cm

5 cm   8 cm

10 cm   5 cm

5 cm

9 cm

10 cm

8 cm   5 cm

8 cm   5 cm

$$SA = 2 \times (\frac{1}{2} bh) + lw$$

$$= 2 \times (\frac{1}{2} \times 8 \times 9) + (8 \times 5 + 9 \times 5 + 10 \times 5)$$

$$= 207 cm^2$$

Other figures that have rectangles or triangles in their nets include pyramids, rectangular prisms, and cylinders. When the shapes of these three-dimensional objects are found, and areas are calculated, the sum will result in the surface area. The following picture shows the net for a rectangular prism and the dimensions for each shape making up the prism. As a formula, the surface area is the sum of each shape added together. The following equation shows the formula:

$$SA = 5 \times 10 + 5 \times 6 + 6 \times 10 + 5 \times 6 + 5 \times 10 + 6 \times 10$$

$$SA = 50 + 30 + 60 + 30 + 50 + 60 = 280 \text{ m}^2$$

A Rectangular Prism and its Net

SA = 5×10 + 5×6 + 6×10 + 5×6 + 5×10 + 6×10

= 50 + 30 + 60 + 30 + 50 + 60

= 280cm²

Solving for Missing Values in Triangles, Circles, and Other Figures

Solving for missing values in shapes requires knowledge of the shape and its characteristics. For example, a triangle has three sides and three angles that add up to 180 degrees. If two angle measurements are given, the third can be calculated. For the triangle below, the one given angle has a measure of 55 degrees. The missing angle is x. The third angle is labeled with a square, which indicates a measure of 90 degrees. Because all angles must add up to 180 degrees, the following equation can be used to find the missing x-value:

$$55° + 90° + x = 180°$$

Adding the two given angles and subtracting the total from 180 gives an answer of 35 degrees.

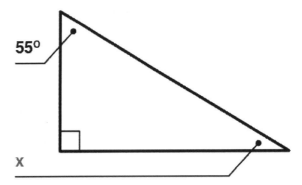

A similar problem can be solved with circles. If the radius is given but the circumference is unknown, the circumference can be calculated based on the formula $C = 2\pi r$. This example can be used in the figure below. The radius can be substituted for r in the formula. Then the circumference can be found as:

$$C = 2\pi \times 8 = 16\pi = 50.24 \text{ cm}$$

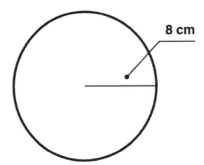

Other figures that may have missing values could be the length of a square, given the area, or the perimeter of a rectangle, given the length and width. All of the missing values can be found by first identifying all the characteristics that are known about the shape, then looking for ways to connect the missing value to the given information.

Determining How Changes to Dimensions Change Area and Volume

When the dimensions of an object change, the area and volume are also subject to change. For example, the following rectangle has an area of 98 square centimeters:

$$A = 7 \times 14 = 98 \text{ cm}^2$$

If the length is increased by 2, becoming 16 cm, then the area becomes:

$$A = 7 \times 16 = 112 \text{ cm}^2$$

The area increased by 14 cm, or twice the width because there were two more widths of 7 cm.

For the volume of an object, there are three dimensions. The given prism has a volume of:

$$V = 4 \times 12 \times 3 = 144 \text{ m}^3$$

If the height is increased by 3, the volume becomes $V = 4 \times 12 \times 6 = 288 \text{ m}^3$. When the height increased by 3, it doubled, which also resulted in the volume doubling. From the original, if the width was doubled, the volume would be:

$$V = 8 \times 12 \times 3 = 288 \text{ m}^3$$

The rectangle's dimensions are 6 cm by 7 cm. The same increase in volume would result if the length was doubled.

Plane Geometry

The coordinate plane is a way of identifying the position of a point in relation to two axes. The **coordinate plane** is made up of two intersecting lines, the x-axis and the y-axis. These lines intersect at a right angle, and their intersection point is called the **origin**. The points on the coordinate plane are labeled based on their position in relation to the origin. If a point is found 4 units to the right and 2 units up from the origin, the location is described as $(4, 2)$. These numbers are the x- and y-coordinates, always written in the order (x, y). This point is also described as lying in the first quadrant. Every point in the first quadrant has a location that is positive in the x and y directions.

The following figure shows the coordinate plane with examples of points that lie in each quadrant.

The Coordinate Plane

Point B lies in the first quadrant, described with positive x- and y-values, above the x-axis and to the right of the y-axis. Point A lies in the second quadrant, where the x-value is negative and the y-value is positive. This quadrant is above the x-axis and to the left of the y-axis. Point D lies in the third quadrant, where both the x- and y-values are negative. Points in this quadrant are described as being below the x-axis and to the left of the y-axis. Point C is in the fourth quadrant, where the x-value is positive and the y-value is negative.

Coordinate geometry is the intersection of algebra and geometry. Within this system, the points in a geometric shape are defined using ordered pairs. In the two-dimensional coordinate system, an x- and y-axis form the ***xy*-plane**. The x-axis is a horizontal scale, and the y-axis is a vertical scale. The ordered pair where the axes cross is known as the **origin**. To the right of the origin, the x-values are positive, and to the left of the origin, the x-values are negative. The y-values above the origin are positive, and y-values below the origin are negative. The axes split the plane into four quadrants, and the first quadrant is where both x- and y-values are positive. To plot an ordered pair means to locate the point corresponding to the x- and y-coordinates. For example, plotting $(4, 3)$ means moving to the right 4 units from 0 in the x direction and then moving up 3 units in the y direction.

Here is a picture of the xy-plane, also known as the **rectangular** or **Cartesian coordinate system**:

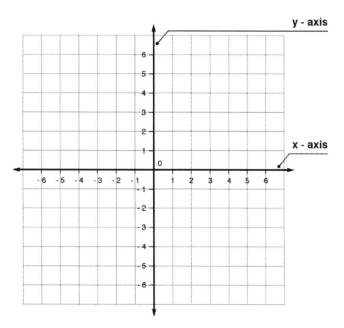

The coordinate system allows us to visualize relationships between equations and geometric figures. For instance, an equation in two variables, x and y, is represented as a straight line on the xy-coordinate plane. A solution of an equation in two variables is an ordered pair that satisfies the equation. A graph of an equation can be found by plotting several ordered pairs that are solutions of the equation and then connecting those points with a straight line or smooth curve. Here is the graph of:

$$4x + y = 8$$

Three ordered pairs that are solutions to the equation were found and plotted. Those points are $(-2, 16)$, $(0, 8)$, and $(2, 0)$. The points were connected using a straight line. Note that the point $(0, 8)$ is where the line crosses the y-axis. This point is known as the **y-intercept**. The y-intercept can always be found by plugging $x = 0$ into the equation. Also, the point $(2, 0)$ is where the line crosses the x-axis. This point is known as the **x-intercept**, and it can always be found for any equation of a line by plugging $y = 0$ into the equation. The equation above is written in standard form:

$$Ax + By = C$$

Often an equation is written in slope-intercept form, $y = mx + b$, where m represents the slope of the line, and b represents the y-intercept. The above equation can be solved for y to obtain:

$$y = -4x + 8$$

This shows a slope of -4 and a y-intercept of 8, meaning the point $(0, 8)$.

The slope of a line is the measure of steepness of a line, and it compares the vertical change of the line, the **rise**, to the horizontal change of the line, the **run**. The formula for slope of a line through two distinct points (x_1, y_1) and (x_2, y_2) is:

$$m = \frac{y_2 - y_1}{x_2 - x_1}$$

If the line increases from left to right, the slope is positive, and if the line decreases from left to right, as shown above, the slope is negative. If a line is horizontal, like the line representing the equation $y = 5$, the slope is 0. If a line is vertical, like the line representing the equation $x = 2$, the line has undefined slope.

In order to graph a function, it can be done the same way as equations. The $f(x)$ represents the dependent variable y in the equation, so replace $f(x)$ with y and plot some points. For example, the same graph above would be found for the function:

$$f(x) = -4x + 8$$

Graphs other than straight lines also exist. For example, here are the graphs of $f(x) = x^2$ and $f(x) = x^3$, the squaring and cubic functions:

If the equals sign is changed to an inequality symbol such as $<$, $>$, $\leq$, or $\geq$ in an equation, the result is an inequality. If it is changed to a linear equation in two variables, the result is a linear inequality in two variables. A solution of an inequality in two variables is an ordered pair that satisfies the inequality. For example, $(1, 3)$ is a solution of the linear inequality $y \geq x + 1$ because when plugged in, it results in a true statement. The graph of an inequality in two variables consists of all ordered pairs that make the solution true.

A half-plane consists of the set of all points on one side of a line in the xy-plane, and the solution to a linear inequality is a half-plane. If the inequality consists of $>$ or $<$, the line is dashed, and no solutions actually exist on the line shown. If the inequality consists of $\geq$ or $\leq$, the line is solid, and solutions do exist on the line shown. In order to graph a linear inequality, graph the corresponding equation found by replacing the inequality symbol with an equals sign. Then pick a test point on either side of the line. If that point results in a true statement when plugged into the original inequality, shade in the side containing the test point. If it results in a false statement, shade in the opposite side. Here is the graph of the inequality:

$$y < x + 1$$

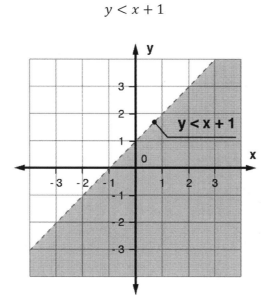

Transformations of a Plane

Two figures are **congruent** if they have the same shape and same size, meaning same angle measurements and equal side lengths. Two figures are similar if they have the same angle measurements but not side lengths. Basically, angles are congruent in similar triangles and their side lengths are constant multiples of each other. Proving two shapes are similar involves showing that all angles are the same; proving two shapes are congruent involves showing that all angles are the same *and* that all sides are the same. If two pairs of angles are congruent in two triangles, then those triangles are similar because their third angles have to be equal due to the fact that all three angles add up to 180 degrees.

There are five main theorems that are used to prove congruence in triangles. Each theorem involves showing that different combinations of sides and angles are the same in two triangles, which proves the triangles are congruent. The side-side-side (SSS) theorem states that if all sides are equal in two triangles, the triangles are congruent. The side-angle-side (SAS) theorem states that if two pairs of sides and the included angles are equal in two triangles then the triangles are congruent. Similarly, the angle-side-angle

(ASA) theorem states that if two pairs of angles and the included side lengths are equal in two triangles, the triangles are similar. The angle-angle-side (AAS) theorem states that two triangles are congruent if they have two pairs of congruent angles and a pair of corresponding equal side lengths that are not included. Finally, the hypotenuse-leg (HL) theorem states that if two right triangles have equal hypotenuses and an equal pair of shorter sides, the triangles are congruent. An important item to note is that angle-angle-angle (AAA) is not enough information to prove congruence because the three angles could be equal in two triangles, but their sides could be different lengths.

Sets of Points in the Plane

A figure can also be reflected, or flipped, over a given line known as the **line of reflection**. The original triangle (called the preimage) is seen in the figure below in the first quadrant. The reflection of this triangle is in the second quadrant. A reflection across the y-axis can be found by determining each point's distance to the y-axis and moving it that same distance on the opposite side. For example, the point C is located at $(4, 1)$. The reflection of this point moves to $(-4, 1)$ when reflected across the y-axis. The original point A The original point A is located at $(1, 3)$, and the reflection across the y-axis is located at $(-1, 3)$. It is evident that the reflection across the y-axis changes the sign of the x-coordinate. A reflection across the x-axis changes the sign of the y-coordinate instead.

Circles in the Coordinate Plane

Recall that a circle is the set of all points the same distance, known as radius r, from a single point C, known as the center of the circle. The center has coordinates (h, k) and any point on the circle is an ordered pair with coordinates (x, y). A right triangle with hypotenuse r can be formed with these two points as seen here:

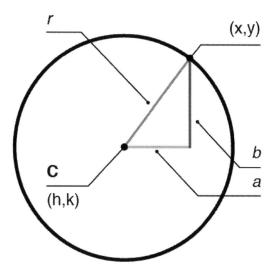

The other side lengths are a and b. The Pythagorean Theorem states that:

$$a^2 + b^2 = r^2$$

However, a can be replaced by $|x - h|$ and b can be replaced by $|y - k|$ because the distance between any two coordinates in the coordinate plane is the absolute value of their difference. That substitution gives:

$$(x - h)^2 + (y - k)^2 = r^2$$

This is the formula used to find the equation of any circle with center (h, k) and radius r. Therefore, if any problem gives the coordinates of the center of a circle and its radius length, this is the equation in two variables that allows any other point on the circle to be found.

Oftentimes, the center or the radius of a circle are not easily seen in the given equation of the circle. If the equation is in standard form of a polynomial equation:

$$ax^2 + ay^2 + cx + dy + e = 0$$

The algebraic technique of completing the square must be used to find the coordinates of the center and the radius. Completing the square must be done within both variables x and y. First, the constant term needs to be subtracted off of both sides of the equation, and then the x- and y-terms need to be grouped together. Then, the entire equation needs to be divided by a. Then, divide the coefficient of the x-term by 2, square it, and add that value to both sides of the equation. This value should be grouped with the x-terms. Next, divide the coefficient of the y-term by 2, square it, and add it to both sides of the equation, grouping it with the y-terms. The trinomial in both x and y are now perfect square trinomials and can be factored into squares of a binomial. This process results in:

$$(x - h)^2 + (y - k)^2 = r^2$$

This shows the radius and coordinates of the center.

The formula for area of a circle is $A = \pi r^2$ and therefore, formula for area of a **sector** is:

$$\pi r^2 \frac{A}{360}$$

A fraction of the entire area of the circle. If the radius of a circle and arc length is known, the central angle measurement in degrees can be found by using the formula:

$$\frac{360 \times arc\ length}{2\pi r}$$

If the desired central angle measurement is in radians, the formula for the central angle measurement is much simpler as:

$$\frac{arc\ length}{r}$$

The Center, Radius, Central Angle, a Sector, and an Arc of a Circle

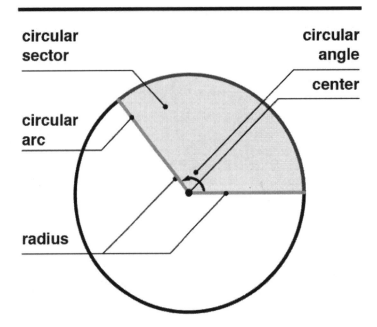

A **chord** of a circle is a straight-line segment that connects any two points on a circle. The line segment does not have to travel through the center, as the diameter does. Also, note that the chord stops at the circumference of the circle. If it did not stop and extended toward infinity, it would be known as a **secant**

line. The following shows a diagram of a circle with a chord shown by the dotted line. The radius is r and the central angle is A:

A Circle with a Chord

$$\text{Chord Length} = 2\,r\,\sin\frac{A}{2}$$

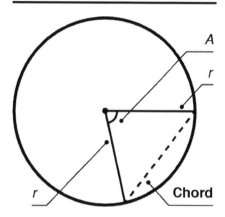

One formula for chord length can be seen in the diagram and is equal to $2r\sin\frac{A}{2}$, where A is the central angle. Another formula for chord length is:

$$chord\ length = 2\sqrt{r^2 - D^2}$$

D is equal to the distance from the chord to the center of the circle. This formula is basically a version of the Pythagorean Theorem.

Formulas for chord lengths vary based on what type of information is known. If the radius and central angle are known, the first formula listed above should be used by plugging the radius and angle in directly. If the radius and the distance from the center to the chord are known, the second formula listed previously ($chord\ length = 2\sqrt{r^2 - D^2}$) should be used.

Many theorems exist between arc lengths, angle measures, chord lengths, and areas of sectors. For instance, when two chords intersect in a circle, the product of the lengths of the individual line segments are equal. For instance, in the following diagram, $A \times B = C \times D$.

A x B = C x D

Conics

The intersection of a plane and a double right circular cone is called a **conic section**. There are four basic types of conic sections, a circle, a parabola, a hyperbola, and an ellipse. The equation of a circle is given by: $(x - h)^2 + (y - k)^2 = r^2$, where the center of the circle is given by (h, k) and the radius of the circle is r. A parabola that opens up or down has a horizontal axis. The equation of a parabola with a horizontal axis is given by $(y - k)^2 = 4p(x - h)$, where $p \neq 0$ and the vertex is given by (h, k). A parabola that opens to the left or right has a vertical axis. The equation of the parabola with a vertical axis is given by $(x - h)^2 = 4p(y - k)$, where $p \neq 0$ and the vertex is given by (h, k). The equation of an ellipse with a horizontal major axis and center (h, k) is given by:

$$\frac{(x - h)^2}{a^2} + \frac{(y - k)^2}{b^2} = 1$$

The distance between center and either focus is c with $c^2 = a^2 - b^2$, when $a > b > 0$. The major axis has length $2a$ and the minor axis has length $2b$. For an ellipse with a vertical major axis and center (h, k), where $a > b > 0$, the a and b switch places so the equation is given by:

$$\frac{(x - h)^2}{b^2} + \frac{(y - k)^2}{a^2} = 1$$

The major axis still has length $2a$ and the minor axis still has length $2b$, and the distance between center and either focus is $c^2 = a^2 - b^2$, where $a > b > 0$.

A hyperbola has an equation similar to the ellipse except that there is a minus in place of the plus sign. A hyperbola with a vertical transverse axis has equation:

$$\frac{(x - h)^2}{a^2} - \frac{(y - k)^2}{b^2} = 1$$

A hyperbola with a horizontal transverse axis has equation:

$$\frac{(y - k)^2}{a^2} - \frac{(x - h)^2}{b^2} = 1$$

For each of these, the center is given by (h, k) and distance between the vertices $2a$.

Practice Quiz

1. Which of the following is the correct factorization of the polynomial $625x^8 - 25y^4$?
   a. $25(5x^4 + y^2)(5x^2 - y)(x^2 + y)$
   b. $25(5x^4 + y^2)(5x^4 - y^2)$
   c. $(25x^4 + 5y^2)(25x^4 - 5y^2)$
   d. $(25x^4 - y^2)(5x^4 - 5y^2)$

2. If $4^x = 1024$, what is the value of $9x^4$?
   a. 5
   b. 5,625
   c. 45
   d. 625

3. Which of the following represents the equation $z = \frac{xy-4}{x-y}$ when solved for y?
   a. $y = \frac{xz+4}{z+x}$
   b. $y = \frac{z+x}{xz+4}$
   c. $y = \frac{x-y}{xy-4}$
   d. $y = (xz + 4)(z + x)$

4. A set of cards contains n numbers, one of which is an odd number. If one card is randomly selected from the set, what is the probability that the card is even?
   a. $\frac{1}{n}$
   b. $\frac{1}{n-1}$
   c. $\frac{n-2}{n-1}$
   d. $\frac{n-1}{n}$

5. Jimmy is designing a play parachute for his PE class. The equation for the parachute to be graphed on a coordinate plane is $(x - 3)^2 + (y + 1)^2 = 16$. If modeled on a graph, what point would be the center of the parachute, and what would be the radius?
   a. $(3, -1)$ and $r = 16$
   b. $(3, -1)$ and $r = 4$
   c. $(-3, 1)$ and $r = 4$
   d. $(-3, 1)$ and $r = 16$

See answers on next page.

Answer Explanations

1. B: First factor out the common factor of 25, resulting in:

$$25(25x^8 - y^4)$$

The resulting polynomial in parentheses is a difference of squares, and therefore, the entire polynomial factors into:

$$25(5x^4 + y^2)(5x^4 - y^2)$$

This can be checked by multiplication.

2. B: First, solve for x in the given equation. Because $4^5 = 1024$, we know that $x = 5$. Then, plug 5 in for x in the given expression. Following order of operations:

$$9 \times 5^4 = 9 \times 625 = 5{,}625$$

3. A: First, multiply both sides of the equation times the quantity $(x - y)$. This results in:

$$z(x - y) = xy - 4$$

The goal is to get all y-terms isolated onto one side of the equals sign. Distributing results in:

$$zx - zy = xy - 4$$

Moving the y-terms to the right side and the 4 to the left side results in:

$$zx + 4 = xy + zy$$

Factoring out a y on the right side gives:

$$zx + 4 = y(x + z)$$

Finally, dividing both sides by the quantity $(x + z)$ gives:

$$y = \frac{zx + 4}{x + z}$$

4. D: There are n total cards, which means that the denominator needs to be n (the total number of outcomes). If there is only 1 odd number, then the rest are even. There are $n - 1$ even cards. Therefore, the probability of selecting an even card is $\frac{n-1}{n}$.

5. B: The general form for the equation of a circle is:

$$(x - h)^2 + (y - k)^2 = r^2$$

The radius of the circle is the value of r and the center of the circle has coordinates (h, k). For the given equation $(x - 3)^2 + (y + 1)^2 = 16$, the value for the radius is:

$$\sqrt{16} = 4 = r$$

The center of the circle has coordinates $(3, -1)$.

Advanced Algebra and Functions

Linear Equations

Understanding Linear Equations and Functions in Context

A **linear function of the form $f(x) = mx + b$** has two important quantities: m and b. The quantity m represents the slope of the line, and the quantity b represents the y-intercept of the line. When the function represents a real-life situation or a mathematical model, these two quantities are very meaningful. The slope, m, represents the rate of change, or the amount y increases or decreases given an increase in x. If m is positive, the rate of change is positive, and if m is negative, the rate of change is negative. The y-intercept, b, represents the amount of quantity y when x is 0. In many applications, if the x-variable is never a negative quantity, the y-intercept represents the initial amount of the quantity y. The x-variable often represents time, so it makes sense that it would not be negative.

Consider the following example. These two equations represent the cost, C, of t-shirts, x, at two different printing companies:

$$C(x) = 7x$$

$$C(x) = 5x + 25$$

The first equation represents a scenario in which each t-shirt costs \$7. In this equation, x varies directly with y. There is no y-intercept, which means that there is no initial cost for using that printing company. The rate of change is 7, which is price per shirt. The second equation represents a scenario that has both an initial cost and a cost per t-shirt. The slope of 5 shows that each shirt is \$5. The y-intercept of 25 shows that there is an initial cost of using that company. Therefore, it makes sense to use the first company at \$7 per shirt when only purchasing a small number of t-shirts. However, any large orders would be cheaper from the second company because eventually that initial cost would become negligible.

The Solution of Linear Equations and Inequalities

Multistep one-variable equations involve the use of one variable in an equation with many operations. For example, the equation:

$$2x + 4 = 10$$

This involves one variable, x, and multiple steps to solve for the value of x. The first step is to move the four to the opposite side of the equation by subtracting 4. The next step is to divide by 2. The final answer yields a value of 3 for the variable x. The steps for this process are shown below.

$$
\begin{aligned}
2x + 4 &= 10 \\
\underline{-4 \quad -4} & \qquad \text{Subtract 4 on both sides} \\
2x &= 6 \\
\underline{\div 2 \quad \div 2} & \qquad \text{Divide by 2 on both sides} \\
x &= 3
\end{aligned}
$$

When the result is found, the value of the variable must be interpreted. For this problem, a value of 3 can be understood as the number that can be doubled and then increased by 4 to yield a value of 10.

Inequalities can also be interpreted in much the same way. The following inequality can be solved to find the value of b:

$$\frac{b}{7} - 8 \geq 7$$

This inequality models the amount of money a group of friends earned for cleaning up a neighbor's yard, b. There were 7 friends, so the money had to be split seven times. Then $8 was taken away from each friend to pay for materials they bought to help clean the yard. All these things needed to be less than or equal to seven for the friends to each receive at least $7. The first step is to add 8 to both sides of the inequality. Then, both sides can be multiplied by 7 to get rid of the denominator on the left side. The resulting inequality is $b \geq 105$. Because the answer is not only an equals sign, the value for b is not a single number. In this problem, the answer communicates that the value of b must be greater than or equal to $105 in order for each friend to make at least $7 for their work. The number for b, what they are paid, can be more than 105 because that would mean they earned more money. They do not want it to be less than 105 because their profit will drop below $7 a piece.

Creating, Solving, or Interpreting a Linear Inequality in One Variable

A linear equation in x can be written in the form $ax + b = 0$. A linear inequality is very similar, although the equals sign is replaced by an inequality symbol such as $<$, $>$, $\leq$, or $\geq$. In any case, a can never be 0. Some examples of linear inequalities in one variable are:

$$2x + 3 < 0$$

$$4x - 2 \leq 0$$

Solving an inequality involves finding the set of numbers that, when plugged into the variable, makes the inequality a true statement. These numbers are known as the solution set of the inequality. To solve an inequality, use the same properties that are necessary in solving equations. First, add or subtract variable terms and/or constants to obtain all variable terms on one side of the equals sign and all constant terms on the other side. Then, either multiply or divide both sides by the same number to obtain an inequality that gives the solution set. When multiplying or dividing by a negative number, change the direction of the inequality symbol. The solution set can be graphed on a number line. Consider the linear inequality:

$$-2x - 5 > x + 6$$

First, add 5 to both sides and subtract x from both sides to obtain $-3x > 11$. Then, divide both sides by -3, making sure to change the direction of the inequality symbol. These steps result in the solution $x < -\frac{11}{3}$. Therefore, any number less than $-\frac{11}{3}$ satisfies this inequality.

Linear Applications and Graphs

Using Linear Relationships Represented by Graphs, Equations, and Tables, to Solve Problems

Graphs, equations, and tables are three different ways to represent linear relationships. The following graph shows a linear relationship because the relationship between the two variables is constant. Each time the distance increases by 25 miles, 1 hour passes. This pattern continues for the rest of the graph. The line represents a constant rate of 25 miles per hour.

This graph can also be used to solve problems involving predictions for a future time. After 8 hours of travel, the rate can be used to predict the distance covered. Eight hours of travel at 25 miles per hour covers a distance of 200 miles. The equation at the top of the graph corresponds to this rate also. The same prediction of distance in a given time can be found using the equation. For a time of 10 hours, the distance would be 250 miles, as the equation yields $d = 25 \times 10 = 250$.

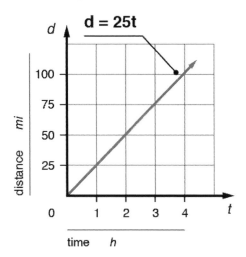

Another representation of a linear relationship can be seen in a table. In the table below, the y-values increase by 3 as the x-values increase by 1. This pattern shows that the relationship is linear. If this table shows the money earned, y-value, for the hours worked, x-value, then it can be used to predict how much money will be earned for future hours. If 6 hours are worked, then the pay would be $19. For further hours and money to be determined, it would be helpful to have an equation that models this table of values. The equation will show the relationship between x and y. The y-value can be determined by multiplying the x-value by 3, then adding 1. The following equation models this relationship:

$$y = 3x + 1$$

Now that there is an equation, any number of hours, x, can be substituted into the equation to find the amount of money earned, y.

y = 3x + 1	
x	y
0	1
1	4
2	7
4	13
5	16

Factoring

Factoring

Factorization is the process of breaking up a mathematical quantity, such as a number or polynomial, into a product of two or more factors. For example, a factorization of the number 16 is $16 = 8 \times 2$. If multiplied out, the factorization results in the original number. A **prime factorization** is a specific factorization when the number is factored completely using prime numbers only. For example, the prime factorization of 16 is:

$$16 = 2 \times 2 \times 2 \times 2$$

A factor tree can be used to find the prime factorization of any number. Within a factor tree, pairs of factors are found until no other factors can be used, as in the following factor tree of the number 84:

A factor tree

84

4   21

2   2   3   7

84 = 2 x 2 x 3 x 7

It first breaks 84 into 21 × 4, which is not a prime factorization. Then, both 21 and 4 are factored into their primes. The final numbers on each branch consist of the numbers within the prime factorization. Therefore,

$$84 = 2 \times 2 \times 3 \times 7$$

Factorization can be helpful in finding greatest common divisors and least common denominators.

Also, a factorization of an algebraic expression can be found. Throughout the process, a more complicated expression can be decomposed into products of simpler expressions. To factor a polynomial, first determine if there is a greatest common factor. If there is, factor it out. For example, $2x^2 + 8x$ has a greatest common factor of $2x$ and can be written as:

$$2x(x + 4)$$

Once the greatest common monomial factor is factored out, if applicable, count the number of terms in the polynomial. If there are two terms, is it a difference of squares, a sum of cubes, or a difference of cubes?

If so, the following rules can be used:

$$a^2 - b^2 = (a + b)(a - b)$$

$$a^3 + b^3 = (a + b)(a^2 - ab + b^2)$$

$$a^3 - b^3 = (a - b)(a^2 + ab + b^2)$$

If there are three terms, and if the trinomial is a perfect square trinomial, it can be factored into the following:

$$a^2 + 2ab + b^2 = (a + b)^2$$

$$a^2 - 2ab + b^2 = (a - b)^2$$

If not, try factoring into a product of two binomials in the form of $(x + p)(x + q)$. For example, to factor:

$$x^2 + 6x + 8$$

Determine what two numbers have a product of 8 and a sum of 6. Those numbers are 4 and 2, so the trinomial factors into:

$$(x + 2)(x + 4)$$

Finally, if there are four terms, try factoring by grouping. First, group terms together that have a common monomial factor. Then, factor out the common monomial factor from the first two terms. Next, look to see if a common factor can be factored out of the second set of two terms that results in a common binomial factor. Finally, factor out the common binomial factor of each expression, for example:

$$xy - x + 5y - 5$$

$$x(y - 1) + 5(y - 1) = (y - 1)(x + 5)$$

After the expression is completely factored, check the factorization by multiplying it out; if this results in the original expression, then the factoring is correct. Factorizations are helpful in solving equations that consist of a polynomial set equal to zero. If the product of two algebraic expressions equals zero, then at least one of the factors is equal to zero. Therefore, factor the polynomial within the equation, set each factor equal to zero, and solve. For example:

$$x^2 + 7x - 18 = 0$$

This can be solved by factoring into:

$$(x + 9)(x - 2) = 0$$

Set each factor equal to zero, and solve to obtain $x = -9$ and $x = 2$.

Quadratics

Quadratic Functions

When given data in ordered pairs, choosing an appropriate function or equation to model the data is important. Besides linear relationships, other common relationships that exist are quadratic and exponential. A helpful way to determine what type of function to use is to find the difference between consecutive dependent variables. Basically, find pairs of ordered pairs where the x-values increase by 1, and take the difference of the y-values. If the differences in the y-values are always the same value, then the function is **linear**. If the differences in the y-values when the x-values increase by 1 are not the same, the function could be quadratic or exponential. If the differences are not the same, find differences of those differences. If consecutive differences are the same, then the function is **quadratic**. If consecutive differences are not the same, try taking ratios of consecutive y-values. If the ratios are the same, the data have an **exponential** relationship and an exponential function should be used.

For example, the ordered pairs $(1, 4)$, $(2, 6)$, $(3, 8)$, and $(4, 10)$ have a linear relationship because the difference in y-values is 2 for every increase in x of 1. The ordered pairs $(1, 0)$, $(2, 3)$, $(3, 10)$, and $(4, 21)$ have a nonlinear relationship. The first differences in y-values are 3, 7, and 11; however, consecutive second differences are both 4, which means this is a quadratic relationship. Lastly, the ordered pairs $(1, 10)$, $(2, 30)$, $(3, 90)$, and $(4, 270)$ have an exponential relationship. Taking ratios of consecutive y-values leads to a common ratio of 4.

The general form of a **quadratic equation** is $y = ax^2 + bx + c$, and its vertex form is:

$$y = a(x - h)^2 + k \text{ with vertex } (h, k)$$

If the vertex and one other point are known, the vertex form should be used to solve for a. If three points, not the vertex, are known, the general form should be used. The three points create a system of three equations in three unknowns that can be solved for.

Solving Quadratic Equations

A **quadratic equation** in standard form, $ax^2 + bx + c = 0$, can have either two solutions, one solution, or two complex solutions (no real solutions). This is determined using the determinant $b^2 - 4ac$. If the

108

determinant is positive, there are two real solutions. If the determinant is negative, there are no real solutions. If the determinant is equal to 0, there is one real solution. For example, given the quadratic equation:

$$4x^2 - 2x + 1 = 0$$

Its determinant is:

$$(-2)^2 - 4(4)(1) = 4 - 16 = -12$$

So, it has two complex solutions, meaning no real solutions.

There are quite a few ways to solve a quadratic equation. The first is by **factoring**. If the equation is in standard form and the polynomial can be factored, set each factor equal to 0, and solve using the Principle of Zero Products. For example:

$$x^2 - 4x + 3 = (x - 3)(x - 1)$$

Therefore, the solutions of:

$$x^2 - 4x + 3 = 0$$

They have to satisfy both:

$$x - 3 = 0$$

$$x - 1 = 0$$

$$x = 3$$

$$x = 1$$

This is the simplest method to solve quadratic equations; however, not all polynomials inside the quadratic equations can be factored.

Another method is **completing the square**. For example,

$$x^2 + 10x - 9$$

The polynomial cannot be factored, so the next option is to complete the square in the equation to find its solutions:

$$x^2 + 10x - 9 = 0$$

The first step is to add 9 to both sides, moving the constant over to the right side, resulting in:

$$x^2 + 10x = 9$$

Then, the coefficient of x is divided by 2 and squared. This result is then added to both sides of the equation. In this example, $\left(\frac{10}{2}\right)^2 = 25$ is added to both sides of the equation to obtain:

$$x^2 + 10x + 25 = 9 + 25 = 34$$

The left-hand side can then be factored into:

$$(x + 5)^2 = 34$$

Solving for x then involves taking the square root of both sides and subtracting 5. This leads to the two solutions:

$$x = \pm\sqrt{34} - 5$$

The third method is the **quadratic formula**. Given a quadratic equation in standard form, $ax^2 + bx + c = 0$, its solutions always can be found using the formula:

$$x = \frac{-b \pm \sqrt{b^2 - 4ac}}{2a}$$

Systems of Linear and Quadratic Equations

The graph of a linear equation is a line, and the graph of a quadratic equation is a parabola. Together, they form a system of a linear and quadratic equation. Here is an example of such a system:

$$\begin{cases} y = -2x + 3 \\ y = x^2 - 6x + 3 \end{cases}$$

Its solution consists of the points in which the two graphs intersect. Therefore, systems of equations involving a linear and quadratic equation can be solved graphically by physically locating those points, as in the following graphic:

The Graph of the System has Two Solutions:
$$\begin{cases} y = -2x + 3 \\ y = x^2 - 6x + 3 \end{cases}$$

In this example, there are two points at which the graphs intersect, so there are two solutions. However, there could also be only one solution, as seen in the following example:

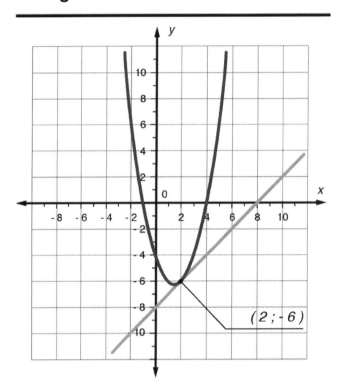

A System of Equations with a Single Solution

Third, it could be true that the graphs do not intersect, and in this case, there is no solution.

The solutions can also be found algebraically. In this case, solve for y in both equations and then set them equal to one another, as an equation in one variable, x. Then, put it in **standard form**, meaning move all terms to one side of the equals sign so that 0 is on the other side. This results in a quadratic equation that needs to be solved. It can be solved using factoring, completing the square, or by applying the quadratic formula. This results in either one solution (one point of intersection), two solutions (two points of intersection), or complex number solutions (no solution, no points of intersection). Then, substitute the x-values back into the linear equation to find the corresponding y-values. This results in the entire ordered pair solutions of the system.

The system above already has both equations equal to y, so they can be set equal to one another as:

$$x^2 - 6x + 3 = -2x + 3$$

Moving all terms to the left side results in $x^2 - 4x = 0$. Factoring the expression on the left gives:

$$x(x - 4) = 0$$

112

Setting both factors equal to 0 results in $x = 0$ and $x = 4$. Plugging both x-values into the linear equation results in $y = 3$ and $y = -5$, respectively. Therefore, the ordered pair solutions are $(0, 3)$ and $(4, -5)$. Both of these ordered pairs satisfy both equations in the original system.

Functions

Relations and Functions

In math, a **relation** is a relationship between two sets of numbers. By using a rule, it takes a number from the first set and matches it to a number in the second set. A relation consists of a set of inputs, known as the **domain**, and a set of outputs, known as the **range**. A **function** is a relation in which each member of the domain is paired to only one other member of the range. In other words, each input has only one output.

Here is an example of a relation that is not a function:

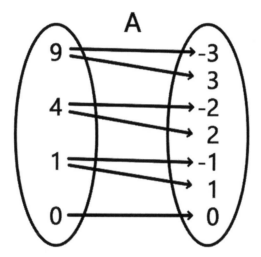

Every member of the first set, the domain, is mapped to two members of the second set, the range. Therefore, this relation is not a function.

A function can also be represented by a table of ordered pairs, a graph of ordered pairs (a scatterplot), or a set of ordered pairs as shown in the following:

Mapping

Domain   Range
inputs   outputs

Table

x	y
0	2
1	3
2	4
3	5

Graph

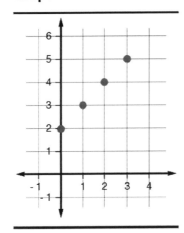

Ordered Pairs

$\{(0,2),(1,3),(2,4),(3,5)\}$

Note that this relation is a function because every member of the domain is mapped to exactly one member of the range.

An **equation** occurs when two algebraic expressions are set equal to one another. Functions can be represented in equation form. Given an equation in two variables, x and y, it can be expressed in function form if solved for y. For example, the linear equation:

$$2x + y = 5$$

This can be solved for y to obtain:

$$y = -2x + 5$$

otherwise known as **slope-intercept** form. To place the equation in function form, replace y with $f(x)$, which is read "f of x." Therefore,

$$f(x) = -2x + 5$$

This notation clarifies the input–output relationship of the function. The function f is a function of x, so an x-value can be plugged into the function to obtain an output. For example:

$$f(2) = -2 \times 2 + 5 = 1$$

Therefore, an input of 2 corresponds to an output of 1.

A function can be graphed by plotting ordered pairs in the xy-plane in the same way that the equation form is graphed. The graph of a function always passes the **Vertical Line Test**. Basically, for any graph, if a vertical line can be drawn through any part of the graph and it hits the graph in more than one place, the graph is not a function. For example, the graph of a circle is not a function. The Vertical Line Test shows that with these relationships, the same x-value has more than one y-value, which goes against the definition of a function.

Inequalities look like equations, but instead of an equals sign, $<, >, \leq, \geq$, or $\neq$ are used. Here are some examples of inequalities:

$$2x + 7 < y$$

$$3x^2 \geq 5$$

and

$$x \neq 4$$

Inequalities show relationships between algebraic expressions when the quantities are different. Inequalities can also be expressed in function form if they are solved for y. For instance, the first inequality listed above can be written as:

$$2x + y < f(x)$$

Even and Odd Functions

A function is considered **even** when $f(x) = f(-x)$ for all values of x. This relationship means that the graph of an even function is perfectly symmetrical about the y-axis. In other words, the graph is reflected over the y-axis. The term "even" describes these functions because functions like x^2, x^4, x^6, and so on display this characteristic. That said, there are some functions that are even that don't involve x raised to an even exponent. For example, the graph of $f(x) = cos(x)$ is also symmetrical over the y-axis. There are also functions that *do* have an even exponent that are *not* even functions; although $f(x) = x^2 + 3$ is an even function, $f(x) = (x + 3)^2$ is not because $f(x) \neq f(-x)$ for all values of x.

A function is considered **odd** when $-f(x) = f(-x)$ for all values of x. This relationship means that the graph of an odd function is perfectly symmetrical about the origin. The term "odd" describes these functions because functions like x, x^3, x^5, x^7, and so on display this characteristic. As with even functions, exceptions to these exponential values exist. For example, the graph of:

$$f(x) = sin(x)$$

This also has origin symmetry. There are also function that *do* have an odd exponent that are *not* odd functions; while $f(x) = x^3 - 3x$ is an odd function $f(x) = x^3 - 1$ is not because $-f(x) \neq f(-x)$ for all values of x.

The majority of functions do not display these unique relationships and are thus neither even nor odd. Essentially, to algebraically determine if a function is even, odd, or neither, various values need to be plugged in for $f(x)$ and $f(-x)$. If all values of x yield the same output for $f(x)$ and $f(-x)$, the function is even. If all values of x yield the same output for $-f(x)$ and $f(-x)$, the function is odd. Any other situation indicates the function is neither even nor odd. To graphically determine if a function is even, odd, or neither, symmetry needs to be evaluated. If the function is perfectly symmetrical across the y-axis, it is an even function. If it is symmetrical about the origin, it is odd. Any other situation indicates that the function is neither even nor odd.

It should be noted that there is one function that is both even *and* odd: $f(x) = 0$.

Piecewise Functions

A **piecewise function** is basically a function that is defined in pieces. The graph of the function behaves differently over different intervals along the x-axis, or different intervals of its domain. Therefore, the function is defined using different mathematical expressions over these intervals. The function is not defined by only one equation. In a piecewise function, the function is actually defined by two or more equations, where each equation is used over a specific interval of the domain.

Here is a graph of a piecewise function:

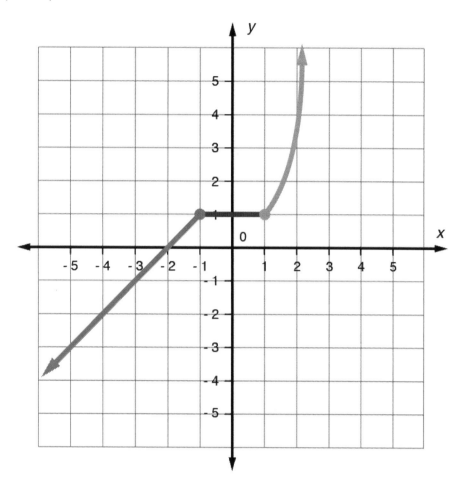

Notice that from $(-\infty, -1]$, the graph is a line with a positive slope. From $[-1, 1]$ the graph is a horizontal line. Finally, from $[1, \infty)$ the graph is a nonlinear curve. Both the domain and range of this piecewise defined function are all real numbers, which is expressed as $(-\infty, \infty)$.

Piecewise functions can also have discontinuities, which are jumps in the graph. When drawing a graph, if the pencil must be picked up at any point to continue drawing, the graph has a discontinuity.

Here is the graph of a piecewise function with discontinuities at $x = 1$ and $x = 2$:

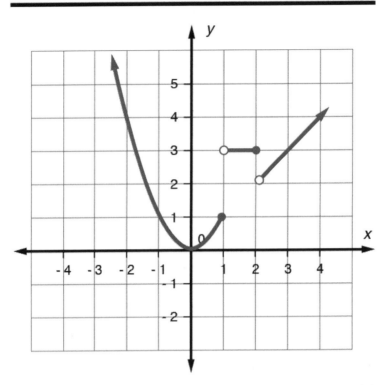

A Piecewise Function

The open circle at a point indicates that the endpoint is not included in that part of the graph, and the closed circle indicates that the endpoint is included. The domain of this function is all real numbers; however, the range is all nonnegative real numbers $[0, \infty)$.

Radical and Rational Equations

Radical Functions

Recall that a **radical expression** is an expression involving a square root, a cube root, or a higher order root such as fourth root, fifth root, etc. The expression underneath the radical is known as the **radicand,** and the **index** is the number corresponding to the root. An index of 2 corresponds to a square root. A radical function is a function that involves a radical expression. For instance, $\sqrt{x + 1}$ is a radical expression, $x + 1$ is the radicand, and the corresponding function is $y = \sqrt{x + 1}$. It can also be written in function notation as:

$$f(x) = \sqrt{x + 1}$$

If the root is even, meaning a square root, fourth root, etc., the radicand must be positive. Therefore, in order to find the domain of a radical function with an even index, set the radicand greater than or equal to zero and find the set of numbers that satisfies that inequality. The domain of $f(x) = \sqrt{x + 1}$ is all numbers greater than or equal to -1. The range of this function is all non-negative real numbers because

118

the square root, or any even root, can never output a negative number. The domain of an odd root is all real numbers because the radicand can be negative in an odd root.

Simplifying Radical Equations

A **radical equation** is an equation that contains a variable in the **radicand**, which is the expression under the root. The radical can be a square root, a cube root, or a higher root. To solve an equation containing a root, arrange the terms so that one radical is by itself on one side of the equals sign. Then raise both sides of the equation to the value of the root. For example, square both sides if the root contains a square root, and cube both sides if the root contains a cube root. Then, solve the resulting equation. If the equation still contains a radical, those steps must be completed again to remove the equation of all radicals. Finally, it is crucial that all solutions are checked in the original equation. Some solutions to this equation, once the radicals are removed, might not be solutions to the original radical equation. Consider the following radical equation:

$$\sqrt{3x + 1} - \sqrt{x + 4} = 1$$

Add the second radical to both sides, and then square both sides to obtain:

$$3x + 1 = x + 4 + 2\sqrt{x + 4} + 1$$

Next, collect like terms and isolate the radical to obtain:

$$4x^2 - 16x + 16 = 4(x + 4)$$

This simplifies into the quadratic equation $4x^2 - 20x$, which can be solved using factoring:

$$4x(x - 5) = 0$$

So, it has solutions, $x = 0$ and $x = 5$. Both values must be checked into the original radical equation. because $x = 0$ does not check, it is not a real solution and is called an **extraneous solution**. However, $x = 5$ is a solution.

If an equation contains a variable in the denominator of a fraction, it is known as a **rational equation**. Anything that when plugged into the equation contains a zero denominator cannot be a solution of the equation. To solve a rational equation, multiply both sides of the equation by the LCD (least common denominator) of all of the terms in the equation. Then, solve the resulting equation, making sure that the solutions do not cause any term to have a zero denominator in the original equation. Here is an example of solving the rational equation:

$$\frac{5}{x} - \frac{1}{3} = \frac{1}{x}$$

$$3x \times \left(\frac{5}{x} - \frac{1}{3}\right) = 3x \times \left(\frac{1}{x}\right)$$ — Multiply both sides by the LCD

$$3x \times \frac{5}{x} - 3x \times \frac{1}{3} = 3x \times \frac{1}{x}$$ — Distribute

$$15 - x = 3$$ — Simplify, and then solve

$$-x = -12$$

$$x = 12$$

Both sides of the equation were initially multiplied times the LCD, $3x$. Note that the only number that could cause a problem as a solution would be $x = 0$, because it would create a 0 in the denominator.

Polynomial Equations

Polynomial Equations and Functions

A **polynomial equation** is an equation containing a polynomial expression, which is an expression containing constants and variables combined using the four mathematical operations. The degree of a polynomial depends on the largest exponent in the expression. Typical polynomial equations or functions are **quartic**, with a degree of 4, **cubic**, with a degree of 3, and **quadratic**, with a degree of 2. Note that the exponents on the variables can only be nonnegative integers. The domain of any polynomial function is all real numbers because any number plugged into a polynomial expression grants a real number output. An example of a quartic polynomial equation is:

$$y = x^4 + 3x^3 - 2x + 1$$

The zeros of a polynomial function are the points where its graph crosses the y-axis. In order to find the number of real zeros of a polynomial function, use **Descartes' Rule of Signs**, which states that the number of possible positive real zeros is equal to the number of sign changes in the coefficients. If there is only one sign change, there is only one positive real zero. In the example above, the signs of the coefficients are positive, positive, negative, and positive. The sign changes twice; therefore, there are at most two positive real zeros. The number of possible negative real zeros is equal to the number of sign changes in the coefficients when plugging $-x$ into the equation. Again, if there is only one sign change, there is only one negative real zero. The polynomial result when plugging $-x$ into the equation is:

$$y = (-x)^4 + 3(-x)^3 - 2(-x) + 1$$

$$y = x^4 - 3x^3 + 2x + 1$$

The sign changes two times, so there are at most two negative real zeros. Another polynomial equation this rule can be applied to is:

$$y = x^3 + 2x - x - 5$$

There is only one sign change in the terms of the polynomial, so there is exactly one real zero. When plugging $-x$ into the equation, the polynomial result is:

$$-x^3 - 2x - x - 5$$

There are no sign changes in this polynomial, so there are no possible negative zeros.

Expanding Polynomials

A polynomial is a mathematical expression containing addition, subtraction, or multiplication of one or more constants multiplied by variables raised to positive powers. A polynomial is considered expanded when there are no variables contained within parentheses, the distributive property has been carried out for any terms that were within parentheses, and like terms have been collected.

Recall that the **distributive property** is a way of taking a factor and multiplying it through a given expression in parentheses. Each term inside the parentheses is multiplied by the outside factor, eliminating the parentheses. In simple terms, the distributive property is:

$$a(b + c) = ab + ac$$

To exemplify how to use the distributive property and expand a polynomial, consider the equation:

$$3(x + 2) - 5x = 4x + 1$$

Use the distributive property to clear the parentheses. Therefore, multiply each term inside the parentheses by 3. This step results in:

$$3x + 6 - 5x = 4x + 1$$

Next, collect like terms on the left-hand side. **Like terms** are terms with the same variable or variables raised to the same exponent(s). Only like terms can be combined through addition or subtraction. After collecting like terms, the equation is:

$$-2x + 6 = 4x + 1$$

Finally, apply the addition and multiplication principles. Add $2x$ to both sides to obtain:

$$6 = 6x + 1$$

Then, subtract 1 from both sides to obtain $5 = 6x$. Finally, divide both sides by 6 to obtain the solution $\frac{5}{6} = x$.

Adding and Subtracting Monomials and Polynomials

When working with polynomials, **like terms** are terms that contain the same variables with the same powers. For example, x^4y^5 and $9x^4y^5$ are like terms. The coefficients are different, but the same variables are raised to the same powers. When adding polynomials, only terms that are like can be added. When adding two like terms, just add the coefficients and leave the variables alone. This process uses the distributive property. For example,

$$x^4y^5 + 9x^4y^5 = (1+9)x^4y^5 = 10x^4y^5$$

Therefore, when adding two polynomials, simply add the like terms together. Unlike terms cannot be combined.

Subtracting polynomials involves adding the opposite of the polynomial being subtracted. Basically, the sign of each term in the polynomial being subtracted is changed, and then the like terms are combined because it is now an addition problem. For example, consider the following:

$$6x^2 - 4x + 2 - (4x^2 - 8x + 1)$$

Add the opposite of the second polynomial to obtain:

$$6x^2 - 4x + 2 + (-4x^2 + 8x - 1)$$

Then, collect like terms to obtain:

$$2x^2 + 4x + 1$$

Multiplying and Dividing Monomials and Polynomials

Multiplying polynomials involves using the product rule for exponents that:

$$b^m b^n = b^{m+n}$$

Basically, when multiplying expressions with the same base, just add the exponents. Multiplying a monomial times a monomial involves multiplying the coefficients together and then multiplying the variables together using the product rule for exponents. For example:

$$8x^2y \times 4x^4y^2 = 32x^6y^3$$

When multiplying a monomial times a polynomial that is not a monomial, use the distributive property to multiply each term of the polynomial times the monomial. For example:

$$3x(x^2 + 3x - 4) = 3x^3 + 9x^2 - 12x$$

Finally, multiplying two polynomials when neither one is a monomial involves multiplying each term of the first polynomial times each term of the second polynomial. There are some shortcuts, given certain scenarios. For example, a binomial times a binomial can be found by using the *FOIL (Firsts, Outers, Inners, Lasts)* method shown here.

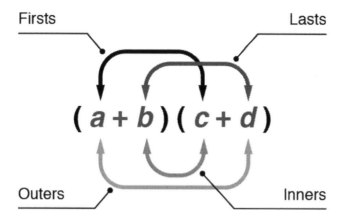

Finding the product of a sum and difference of the same two terms is simple because if it was to be foiled out, the outer and inner terms would cancel out. For instance:

$$(x + y)(x - y) = x^2 + xy - xy - y^2$$

Finally, the square of a binomial can be found using the following formula:

$$(a \pm b)^2 = a^2 \pm 2ab + b^2$$

The Relationship Between Zeros and Factors of Polynomials

A polynomial is a mathematical expression containing addition, subtraction, or multiplication of one or more constants multiplied by variables raised to positive powers. A **polynomial equation** is a polynomial set equal to another polynomial, or in standard form, a polynomial is set equal to 0. A **polynomial function** is a polynomial set equal to y. For instance,

This is a polynomial:

$$x^2 + 2x - 8$$

This is a polynomial equation:

$$x^2 + 2x - 8 = 0$$

This is the corresponding polynomial function:

$$y = x^2 + 2x - 8$$

To solve a polynomial equation, the x-values in which the graph of the corresponding polynomial function crosses the x-axis are sought. These coordinates are known as the **zeros** of the polynomial function because they are the coordinates in which the y-coordinates are 0. One way to find the zeros of a polynomial is to find its factors, then set each individual factor equal to 0, and solve each equation to find the zeros. A **factor** is a linear expression, and to completely factor a polynomial, the polynomial must be rewritten as a product of individual linear factors. The polynomial listed above can be factored as $(x + 4)(x - 2)$. Setting each factor equal to zero results in the zeros $x = -4$ and $x = 2$.

Here is the graph of the zeros of the polynomial:

The Graph of the Zeros of x² + 2x - 8 = 0

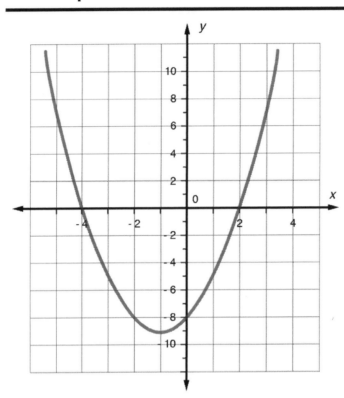

Exponential and Logarithmic Equations

Exponential Equations

An **exponential equation** is used to model something with exponential growth or decay. If something grows exponentially, such as compound interest, the amount is multiplied times a growth factor for every increase in x. If something decays exponentially, the amount is multiplied times a factor between 0 and 1 for every increase in x. When a population is declining, an exponential decay equation can be used to represent the situation. The general form of an exponential function is $y = b \times a^x$, where a is the base and b is the y-intercept.

Exponential growth involves the dependent variable changing by a common ratio every unit increase. The equation of exponential growth is $y = a^x$ for $a > 0$, $a \neq 1$. The value a is known as the **base**. Consider the exponential equation $y = 2^x$. When x equals 1, y equals 2, and when x equals 2, y equals 4. For every unit increase in x, the value of the output variable doubles. Here is the graph of $y = 2^x$. Notice that as the dependent variable, y, gets very large, x increases slightly. This characteristic of this graph is why sometimes a quantity is said to be blowing up exponentially.

$y = 2^x$

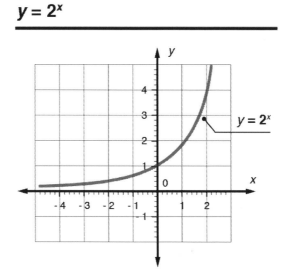

Logarithmic Functions

For $x > 0, b > 0, b \neq 1$, the function:

$$f(x) = \log_b x$$

This is known as the **logarithmic function** with base b. With $y = \log_b x$ its exponential equivalent is $b^y = x$. In either case, the exponent is y and the base is b. Therefore,

$$3 = \log_2 8$$

This is the same as $2^2 = 8$. So, in order to find the logarithm with base 2 of 8, find the exponent that when 2 is raised to that value results in 8. Similarly,

$$\log_3 243 = 5$$

In order to do this mentally, ask the question, what exponent does 3 need to be raised to so that it results in 243? The answer is 5. Most logarithms do not have whole number results. In this case, a calculator can be used. A calculator typically has buttons with base 10 and base e, so the change of base formula can be used to calculate these logs. For instance,

$$\log_3 55 = \frac{\log 55}{\log 3} = 3.64$$

Similarly, the natural logarithm with base e could be used to obtain the same result.

$$\log_3 55 = \frac{\ln 55}{\ln 3} = 3.64$$

The domain of a logarithmic function $f(x) = \log_b x$ is all positive real numbers. This is because the exponent must be a positive number. The range of a logarithmic function $f(x) = \log_b x$ is all real numbers. The graphs of all logarithmic functions of the form $f(x) = \log_b x$ always pass through the point

125

(1, 0) because anything raised to the power of 0 is 1. Therefore, such a function always has an x-intercept at 1. If the base is greater than 1, the graph increases from the left to the right along the x-axis. If the base is between 0 and 1, the graph decreases from the left to the right along the x-axis. In both situations, the y-axis is a vertical asymptote. The graph will never touch the y-axis, but it does approach it closely. Here are the graphs of the two cases of logarithmic functions:

Trigonometry

Trigonometric Functions

Within right triangles, trigonometric ratios can be defined for the acute angle within the triangle. Consider the following right triangle. The side across from the right angle is known as the **hypotenuse**, the acute angle being discussed is labeled θ, the side across from the acute angle is known as the *opposite* side, and the other side is known as the **adjacent** side.

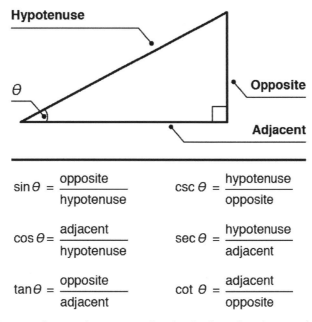

$$\sin \theta = \frac{\text{opposite}}{\text{hypotenuse}} \qquad \csc \theta = \frac{\text{hypotenuse}}{\text{opposite}}$$

$$\cos \theta = \frac{\text{adjacent}}{\text{hypotenuse}} \qquad \sec \theta = \frac{\text{hypotenuse}}{\text{adjacent}}$$

$$\tan \theta = \frac{\text{opposite}}{\text{adjacent}} \qquad \cot \theta = \frac{\text{adjacent}}{\text{opposite}}$$

The six trigonometric ratios are shown above as well. "Sin" is short for sine, "cos" is short for cosine, "tan" is short for tangent, "csc" is short for cosecant, "sec" is short for secant, and "cot" is short for cotangent. A mnemonic device exists that is helpful to remember the ratios. SOHCAHTOA stands for Sine = Opposite/Hypotenuse, Cosine = Adjacent/Hypotenuse, and Tangent = Opposite/Adjacent. The other three trigonometric ratios are reciprocals of sine, cosine, and tangent because:

$$\csc \theta = \frac{1}{\sin \theta}$$

$$\sec \theta = \frac{1}{\cos \theta}$$

$$\cot \theta = \frac{1}{\tan \theta}.$$

The **Pythagorean Theorem** expresses an important relationship between the three sides of a right triangle. It states that the square of the hypotenuse is equal to the sum of the squares of the other two sides. When using the Pythagorean Theorem, the hypotenuse is labeled as side c, the opposite is labeled as side a, and the adjacent side is side b. The theorem can be seen in the following diagram:

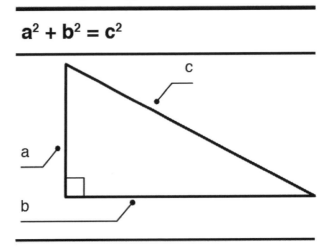

The Pythagorean Theorem

$a^2 + b^2 = c^2$

Both the trigonometric ratios and Pythagorean Theorem can be used in problems that involve finding either a missing side or missing angle of a right triangle. Look to see what sides and angles are given and select the correct relationship that will assist in finding the missing value. These relationships can also be used to solve application problems involving right triangles. Often, it is helpful to draw a figure to represent the problem to see what is missing.

Using the Relationship Between Similarity, Right Triangles, and Trigonometric Ratios

Within two similar triangles, corresponding side lengths are proportional, and angles are equal. In other words, regarding corresponding sides in two similar triangles, the ratio of side lengths is the same. Recall that the SAS theorem for similarity states that if an angle in one triangle is congruent to an angle in a second triangle, and the lengths of the sides in both triangles are proportional, then the triangles are similar. Also, because the ratio of two sides in two similar right triangles is the same, the trigonometric ratios in similar right triangles are always going to be equal.

If two triangles are similar, and one is a right triangle, the other is a right triangle. The definition of similarity ensures that each triangle has a 90-degree angle. In a similar sense, if two triangles are right triangles containing a pair of equal acute angles, the triangles are similar because the third pair of angles must be equal as well. However, right triangles are not necessarily always similar.

The following triangles are similar:

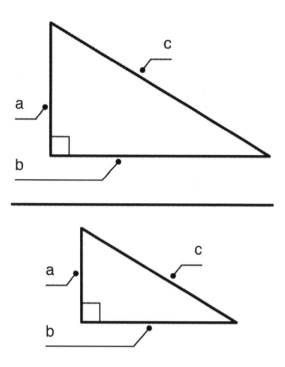

This similarity is not apparent at first glance; however, theorems can be used to show similarity. The Pythagorean Theorem can be used to find the missing side lengths in both triangles. In the larger triangle, the missing side is the hypotenuse, c. Therefore,

$$9^2 + 12^2 = c^2$$

This equation is equivalent to $225 = c^2$, so taking the square root of both sides results in the positive root $c = 15$. In the other triangle, the Pythagorean theorem can be used to find the missing side length b. The theorem shows that:

$$6^2 + b^2 = 10^2$$

b is then solved for to obtain $b = 8$. The ratio of the sides in the larger triangle to the sides in the smaller triangle is the same value, 1.5. Therefore, the sides are proportional. Because they are both right triangles, they have a congruent angle. The SAS theorem for similarity can be used to show that these two triangles are similar.

Using the Relationship Between Sine and Cosine of Complementary Angles

Two **complementary angles** add up to 90 degrees, or π radians. Within a right triangle, the sine of an angle is equal to the ratio of the side opposite the angle to the hypotenuse and the cosine of an angle is equal to the ratio of the side adjacent to the angle to the hypotenuse. Within a right triangle, there is a right angle, and because the sum of all angles in a triangle is 180 degrees, the two other angles add up to

90 degrees, and are therefore complementary. Consider the following right triangle with angles A, B, and C, and sides a, b, and c.

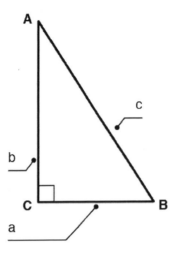

It is true by using such ratios described above that:

$$\sin B = \frac{b}{c}$$

and

$$\cos B = \frac{a}{c}$$

Also, it is true that

$$\cos A = \frac{b}{c}$$

and

$$\sin A = \frac{a}{c}$$

Therefore, $\sin B = \cos A$ and $\cos B = \sin A$.

A and B are complementary angles, so given two complementary angles, the sine of one equals the cosine of the other, and the cosine of one equals the sine of the other. Given the two complementary angles 30 degrees and 60 degrees:

$$\sin 30 = \frac{1}{2}$$

$$\cos 60 = \frac{1}{2}$$

$$\cos 30 = \frac{\sqrt{3}}{2}$$

$$\sin 60 = \frac{\sqrt{3}}{2}$$

Either a calculator set in degrees mode, a unit circle, or the Pythagorean Theorem could be used to find all of these values.

Using Trigonometric Functions of Radian Measure

When inputting values into trigonometric functions, the values can either be in degrees or radians. It is important when using calculators to evaluate trigonometric functions that the calculator is in the correct mode: degrees or radians. If a calculator is in the mode in which it is supposed to use degrees, and a value in radians is plugged into a trig function, the result will be incorrect.

Another way to evaluate trig functions in degrees and radians is to use the **unit circle**. When using radians, the degree measure used should be the one in radians, which would contain a multiple of π. Here is a unit circle:

The Unit Circle

Notice that each angle measure is given in both radians and degrees. The **sine** of an angle is the y-coordinate of the corresponding ordered pair. For instance, $\sin \pi = 0$. The **cosine** of any angle is the x-coordinate of the corresponding ordered pair, and therefore, $\cos \pi = -1$. The **tangent** of any angle is the ratio of the y-coordinate over the x-coordinate, and therefore $\tan \pi = \frac{0}{-1} = 0$. **Cosecant**, **secant**, and **cotangent** of any angles are the corresponding reciprocals of sine, cosine, and tangent. In this case, $\csc \pi$ is undefined, $\sec \pi = -1$, and $\cot \pi$ is undefined.

Practice Quiz

1. Simplify $\left[\dfrac{2vw^3}{-4w}\right]^2$.

   a. $\dfrac{v^2w^3}{8}$

   b. $\dfrac{v^2w^2}{16}$

   c. $\dfrac{v^2w^4}{8}$

   d. $\dfrac{v^2w^4}{4}$

2. Solve: $\dfrac{x-3}{2x+10} = \dfrac{1}{x-1}$.

   a. $x = 7, -1$
   b. $x = 3, 1$
   c. $x = -7, 1$
   d. $x = 6, 7$

3. Simplify: $\dfrac{x^3+4x^2y-5xy^2}{x^2-xy}$.

   a. $x - y$
   b. $x^2 + 5xy$
   c. $x + 5y$
   d. $x^2 - xy$

4. Solve for r: $A = P(1 + rt)$

   a. $r = \dfrac{A}{Pt} - \dfrac{1}{t}$

   b. $r = \dfrac{At}{P} - t$

   c. $r = \dfrac{A}{P} - t$

   d. $r = AP - \dfrac{1}{t}$

5. What is the equation of a straight line through $(0, 3)$ and $(4, 8)$?

   a. $y = \dfrac{5}{3}x + 3$

   b. $y = 5x + 3$

   c. $y = \dfrac{5}{4}x + 3$

   d. $y = 4x + 3$

See answers on next page.

Answer Explanations

1. D: Choice D is the simplified expression by using the order of operations. The expression $\left[\frac{2vw^3}{-4w}\right]^2$ can be simplified by first distributing the exponent to each term inside the brackets. The expression then becomes $\frac{4v^2w^6}{16w^2}$. By simplifying the fraction at the front and canceling out the common variables on top and bottom, the expression becomes $\frac{v^2w^4}{4}$.

2. A: Choice A gives the two correct values for x. The first step in this process to solve for x would be multiplying by the denominator on both sides. This will eliminate the fractions. The new expression becomes:

$$(x - 3)(x - 1) = 2x + 10$$

From here, the two binomials on the left side can be combined to form the equation:

$$x^2 - 4x + 3 = 2x + 10$$

Now, the terms can be collected to one side to form the equation:

$$x^2 - 6x - 7 = 0$$

From this point, to find the value of x, the left side of the equation can be factored into two binomials:

$$(x - 7)(x + 1) = 0$$

Since one term must be zero for this equation to be correct, there are two answers for x: $x = 7$ and $x = -1$.

3. C: In order to simplify this expression, a common factor can be taken out of the numerator and denominator. The expression then becomes:

$$\frac{x(x^2 + 4xy - 5y^2)}{x(x - y)}$$

When those values for x cancel out, then the new polynomial on top can be factored into:

$$\frac{(x - y)(x + 5y)}{x - y}$$

The two equivalent binomials can be canceled, and the simplified expression becomes $x + 5y$.

4. A: Solving an equation for another variable involved manipulating each part. It requires performing inverse operations to move variables across the equal sign. The first step in solving for r is dividing by P. Then the equation becomes:

$$\frac{A}{P} = 1 + rt$$

Then, the 1 can be subtracted to move it to the left side: $\frac{A}{P} - 1 = rt$. The final step is dividing by t, which makes the new equation:

$$\frac{A}{Pt} - \frac{1}{t} = r$$

5. C: One form for an equation of a straight line is $y = mx + b$, where the m is the slope and the b is the y-intercept. To first solve for slope, the change in y over the change in x, the following equation is used:

$$\frac{8 - 3}{4 - 0} = \frac{5}{4}$$

When this slope is substituted into the equation and one other point is used, the value for the y-intercept can be found. The equation becomes:

$$8 = \frac{5}{4}(4) + b$$

Solving for b yields a value of 3, so the linear equation becomes:

$$y = \frac{5}{4}x + 3$$

Reading

Information and Ideas

Topic, Main Idea, and Supporting Details

The **topic** of a text is the general subject matter. Text topics can usually be expressed in one word, or a few words at most. Additionally, readers should ask themselves what point the author is trying to make. This point is the **main idea** or **primary purpose** of the text, the one thing the author wants readers to know concerning the topic. Once the author has established the main idea, they will support the main idea by supporting details. Supporting details are evidence that support the main idea and include personal testimonies, examples, or statistics.

One analogy for these components and their relationships is that a text is like a well-designed house. The topic is the roof, covering all rooms. The main idea is the frame. The supporting details are the various rooms. To identify the topic of a text, readers can ask themselves what or who the author is writing about in the paragraph. To locate the main idea, readers can ask themselves what one idea the author wants readers to know about the topic. To identify supporting details, readers can put the main idea into question form and ask, "what does the author use to prove or explain their main idea?"

Let's look at an example. An author is writing an essay about the Amazon rainforest and trying to convince the audience that more funding should go into protecting the area from deforestation. The author makes the argument stronger by including evidence of the benefits of the rainforest: it provides habitats to a variety of species, it provides much of the earth's oxygen which in turn cleans the atmosphere, and it is the home to medicinal plants that may be the answer to some of the world's deadliest diseases. Here is an outline of the essay looking at topic, main idea, and supporting details:

Topic: Amazon rainforest

Main Idea: The Amazon rainforest should receive more funding in order to protect it from deforestation.

Supporting Details:

1. It provides habitats to a variety of species

2. It provides much of the earth's oxygen which in turn cleans the atmosphere

3. It is home to medicinal plants that may be the answer to some of the world's deadliest diseases.

Notice that the topic of the essay is listed in a few key words: "Amazon rainforest." The main idea tells us what about the topic is important: that the topic should be funded in order to prevent deforestation. Finally, the supporting details are what the author relies on to convince the audience to act or to believe in the truth of the main idea.

Comparing and Contrasting Themes from Print and Other Sources

The **theme** of a piece of text is the central idea the author communicates. Whereas the **topic** of a passage of text may be concrete in nature, by contrast, the theme is always conceptual. For example, while the topic of Mark Twain's novel *The Adventures of Huckleberry Finn* might be described as something like the coming-of-age experiences of a poor, illiterate, functionally-orphaned boy around and on the Mississippi River in 19th-century Missouri, one theme of the book might be that human beings are corrupted by society. Another might be that slavery and "civilized" society itself are hypocritical. Whereas the **main idea** in a text is the most important single point that the author wants to make, the theme is the concept or view around which the author centers the text.

Throughout time, humans have told stories with similar themes. Some themes are universal across time, space, and culture. These include themes of the individual as a hero, conflicts of the individual against nature, the individual against society, change vs. tradition, the circle of life, coming-of-age, and the complexities of love. Themes involving war and peace have featured prominently in diverse works, like Homer's *Iliad*, Tolstoy's *War and Peace* (1869), Stephen Crane's *The Red Badge of Courage* (1895), Hemingway's *A Farewell to Arms* (1929), and Margaret Mitchell's *Gone with the Wind* (1936). Another universal literary theme is that of the quest. These appear in folklore from countries and cultures worldwide, including the Gilgamesh Epic, Arthurian legend's Holy Grail quest, Virgil's *Aeneid*, Homer's *Odyssey*, and the *Argonautica*. Cervantes' *Don Quixote* is a parody of chivalric quests. J.R.R. Tolkien's *The Lord of the Rings* trilogy (1954) also features a quest.

Similar themes across cultures often occur in countries that share a border or are otherwise geographically close together. For example, a folklore story of a rabbit in the moon using a mortar and pestle is shared among China, Japan, Korea, and Thailand—making medicine in China, making rice cakes in Japan and Korea, and hulling rice in Thailand. Another instance is when cultures are more distant geographically, but their languages are related. For example, East Turkestan's Uighurs and people in Turkey share tales of folk hero Effendi Nasreddin Hodja. Another instance, which may either be called cultural diffusion or simply reflect commonalities in the human imagination, involves shared themes among geographically- and linguistically-different cultures: both Cameroon's and Greece's folklore tell of centaurs; Cameroon, India, Malaysia, Thailand, and Japan, of mermaids; Brazil, Peru, China, Japan, Malaysia, Indonesia, and Cameroon, of underwater civilizations; and China, Japan, Thailand, Vietnam, Malaysia, Brazil, and Peru, of shape-shifters.

Two prevalent literary themes are love and friendship, which can end happily, sadly, or both. William Shakespeare's *Romeo and Juliet*, Emily Brontë's *Wuthering Heights*, Leo Tolstoy's *Anna Karenina*, and both *Pride and Prejudice* and *Sense and Sensibility* by Jane Austen are famous examples. Another theme recurring in popular literature is of revenge, an old theme in dramatic literature, e.g. Elizabethans Thomas Kyd's *The Spanish Tragedy* and Thomas Middleton's *The Revenger's Tragedy*. Some more well-known instances include Shakespeare's tragedies *Hamlet* and *Macbeth*, Alexandre Dumas' *The Count of Monte Cristo*, John Grisham's *A Time to Kill*, and Stieg Larsson's *The Girl Who Kicked the Hornet's Nest*.

Themes are underlying meanings in literature. For example, if a story's main idea is a character succeeding against all odds, the theme is overcoming obstacles. If a story's main idea is one character wanting what another character has, the theme is jealousy. If a story's main idea is a character doing something they were afraid to do, the theme is courage. Themes differ from topics in that a topic is a subject matter; a theme is the author's opinion about it. For example, a work could have a topic of war and a theme that war is a curse. Authors present themes through characters' feelings, thoughts, experiences, dialogue, plot actions, and events. Themes function as "glue" holding other essential story elements together. They offer readers insights into characters' experiences, the author's philosophy, and how the world works.

Summarizing a Complex Text

An important skill is the ability to read a complex text and then reduce its length and complexity by focusing on the key events and details. A **summary** is a shortened version of the original text, written by the reader in their own words. The summary should be shorter than the original text, and it must include the most critical points.

In order to effectively summarize a complex text, it's necessary to understand the original source and identify the major points covered. It may be helpful to outline the original text to get the big picture and avoid getting bogged down in the minor details. For example, a summary wouldn't include a statistic from the original source unless it was the major focus of the text. It's also important for readers to use their own words yet retain the original meaning of the passage. The key to a good summary is emphasizing the main idea without changing the focus of the original information.

Complex texts will likely be more difficult to summarize. Readers must evaluate all points from the original source, filter out the unnecessary details, and maintain only the essential ideas. The summary often mirrors the original text's organizational structure. For example, in a problem-solution text structure, the author typically presents readers with a problem and then develops solutions through the course of the text. An effective summary would likely retain this general structure, rephrasing the problem and then reporting the most useful or plausible solutions.

Paraphrasing is somewhat similar to summarizing. It calls for the reader to take a small part of the passage and list or describe its main points. Paraphrasing is more than rewording the original passage, though. As with summary, a paraphrase should be written in the reader's own words, while still retaining the meaning of the original source. The main difference between summarizing and paraphrasing is that a summary would be appropriate for a much larger text, while paraphrase might focus on just a few lines of text. Effective paraphrasing will indicate an understanding of the original source, yet still help the reader expand on their interpretation. A paraphrase should neither add new information nor remove essential facts that change the meaning of the source.

Information that is Explicitly Stated

In the Reading section, test takers will be asked questions based on their direct knowledge of the passage. The information explicitly stated in the passage leaves the reader no room for confusion. The sections below allow test takers to determine what type of information is explicitly stated in the passage. Is the information an author's opinion or an objective fact? Does the information contain bias or stereotype? And within the information stated, what words are directly stated and what words leave room for a connotative interpretation? Being cautious of the author's presentation of information will aid the test taker in determining the correct answer choice for the question stem.

Facts and Opinions

A fact is a statement that is true empirically or an event that has actually occurred in reality and can be proven or supported by evidence; it is generally objective. In contrast, an opinion is subjective, representing something that someone believes rather than something that exists in the absolute. People's individual understandings, feelings, and perspectives contribute to variations in opinion. Though facts are typically objective in nature, in some instances, a statement of fact may be both factual and yet also

138

subjective. For example, emotions are individual subjective experiences. If an individual says that they feel happy or sad, the feeling is subjective, but the statement is factual; hence, it is a subjective fact. In contrast, if one person tells another that the other is feeling happy or sad—whether this is true or not—that is an assumption or an opinion.

Biases

Biases usually occur when someone allows their personal preferences or ideologies to interfere with what should be an objective decision. In personal situations, someone is biased towards someone if they favor them in an unfair way. In academic writing, being biased in your sources means leaving out objective information that would turn the argument one way or the other. The evidence of bias in academic writing makes the text less credible, so be sure to present all viewpoints when writing, not just your own, so to avoid coming off as biased. Being objective when presenting information or dealing with people usually allows the author to gain more credibility.

Stereotypes

Stereotypes are preconceived notions that place a particular rule or characteristics on an entire group of people. Stereotypes are usually offensive to the group they refer to or allies of that group and often have negative connotations. The reinforcement of stereotypes isn't always obvious. Sometimes stereotypes can be very subtle and are still widely used in order for people to understand categories within the world. For example, saying that women are more intuitive or nurturing than men is a stereotype, although this is still an assumption used by many in order to understand differences between one another.

Reading Critically

One technique authors often use to make their fictional stories more interesting is not giving away too much information by providing hints and descriptions. It is then up to the reader to draw a conclusion about the author's meaning by connecting textual clues with the reader's own pre-existing experiences and knowledge. Critical readers are able to draw conclusions and garner a deeper understanding of a text. Rather than directly stating who, what, where, when, or why, authors often describe story elements. Then, readers must draw conclusions to understand significant story components. As they go through a text, readers can think about the setting, characters, plot, problem, and solution; whether the author provided any clues for consideration; and combine any story clues with their existing knowledge and experiences to draw conclusions about what occurs in the text.

Making Predictions

Before and during reading, readers can apply the strategy of making predictions about what they think may happen next. For example, what plot and character developments will occur in fiction? What points will the author discuss in nonfiction? Making predictions about portions of text they have not yet read prepares readers mentally, and also gives them a purpose for reading. To inform and make predictions about text, the reader can do the following:

- Consider the title of the text and what it implies
- Look at the cover of the book
- Look at any illustrations or diagrams for additional visual information
- Analyze the structure of the text
- Apply outside experience and knowledge to the text

Readers may adjust their predictions as they read. Reader predictions may or may not come true in text.

Making Inferences

Authors describe settings, characters, character emotions, and events. Readers must infer to understand the text fully. Inferring enables readers to figure out meanings of unfamiliar words, make predictions about upcoming text, draw conclusions, and reflect on reading. Readers can infer about text before, during, and after reading. In everyday life, we use sensory information to infer. Readers can do the same with text. When authors do not answer all readers' questions, readers must infer by looking at illustrations, considering characters' behaviors, and asking questions during reading. Taking clues from text and connecting text to prior knowledge help to draw conclusions. Readers can infer word meanings, settings, reasons for occurrences, character emotions, pronoun referents, author messages, and answers to questions unstated in text.

Making inferences and drawing conclusions involve skills that are quite similar: both require readers to fill in information the author has omitted. Authors may omit information as a technique for inducing readers to discover the outcomes themselves; or they may consider certain information unimportant; or they may assume their reading audience already knows certain information. To make an inference or draw a conclusion about text, readers should observe all facts and arguments the author has presented and consider what they already know from their own personal experiences. Reading students taking multiple-choice tests that refer to text passages can determine correct and incorrect choices based on the information in the passage. For example, from a text passage describing an individual's signs of anxiety while unloading groceries and nervously clutching their wallet at a grocery store checkout, readers can infer or conclude that the individual may not have enough money to pay for everything.

The test may include multiple-choice questions asking about the logical conclusion that can be drawn from reading a text, and you will have to identify the choice that unavoidably leads to that conclusion. In order to eliminate the incorrect choices, the test-taker should come up with a hypothetical situation wherein an answer choice is true, but the conclusion is not true. Here is an example:

> Fred purchased the newest PC available on the market. Therefore, he purchased the most expensive PC in the computer store.
>
> What can one assume for this conclusion to follow logically?

a. Fred enjoys purchasing expensive items.
b. PCs are some of the most expensive personal technology products available.
c. The newest PC is the most expensive one.

The premise of the text is the first sentence: Fred purchased the newest PC. The conclusion is the second sentence: Fred purchased the most expensive PC. Recent release and price are two different factors; the difference between them is the logical gap. To eliminate the gap, one must connect the new information from the conclusion with the pertinent information from the premise. In this example, there must be a connection between product recency and product price. Therefore, a possible bridge to the logical gap could be a sentence stating that the newest PCs always cost the most.

Rhetoric

Evaluating an Argument and its Specific Claims

When authors write with the purpose of persuading others to agree with them, they assume a **position** with the subject matter about which they are writing. Rather than presenting information objectively, the author treats the subject matter subjectively so that the information presented supports their position. In their argumentation, the author presents information that refutes or weakens opposing positions. Another technique authors use in persuasive writing is to anticipate arguments against the position. When students learn to read subjectively, they gain experience with the concept of persuasion in writing, and learn to identify positions taken by authors. This enhances their reading comprehension and develops their skills for identifying pro and con arguments and biases.

There are five main parts of the classical argument that writers employ in a well-designed stance:

- **Introduction:** In the introduction to a classical argument, the author establishes goodwill and rapport with the reading audience, warms up the readers, and states the thesis or general theme of the argument.

- **Narration:** In the narration portion, the author gives a summary of pertinent background information, informs the readers of anything they need to know regarding the circumstances and environment surrounding and/or stimulating the argument, and establishes what is at risk or the stakes in the issue or topic. Literature reviews are common examples of narrations in academic writing.

- **Confirmation:** The confirmation states all claims that the thesis and furnishes evidence for each claim, arranging this material in a logical order—e.g. from most obvious to most subtle or strongest to weakest.

- **Refutation and Concession:** The refutation and concession discuss opposing views and anticipate reader objections without weakening the thesis, yet permitting as many oppositions as possible.

- **Summation:** The summation strengthens the argument while summarizing it, supplying a strong conclusion, and showing readers the superiority of the author's solution.

Introduction

A classical argument's **introduction** must pique reader interest, get readers to perceive the author as a writer, and establish the author's position. Shocking statistics, new ways of restating issues, or quotations or anecdotes focusing the text can pique reader interest. Personal statements, parallel instances, or analogies can also begin introductions—so can bold thesis statements if the author believes readers will agree. Word choice is also important for establishing author image with readers.

The introduction should typically narrow down to a clear, sound thesis statement. If readers cannot locate one sentence in the introduction explicitly stating the writer's position or the point they support, the writer probably has not refined the introduction sufficiently.

Narration and Confirmation

The **narration** part of a classical argument should create a context for the argument by explaining the issue to which the argument is responding, and by supplying any background information that influences the issue. Readers should understand the issues, alternatives, and stakes in the argument by the end of the narration to enable them to evaluate the author's claims equitably. The **confirmation** part of the classical argument enables the author to explain why he or she believes in the argument's thesis. The author builds a chain of reasoning by developing several individual supporting claims and explaining why that evidence supports each claim, and also supports the overall thesis of the argument.

Refutation and Concession and Summation

The classical argument is the model for argumentative/persuasive writing, so authors often use it to establish, promote, and defend their positions. In the **refutation** aspect of the refutation and concession part of the argument, authors disarm readers' opposition by anticipating and answering their possible objections, which helps persuade them to accept the author's viewpoint. In the **concession** aspect, authors can concede those opposing viewpoints with which they agree. This can avoid weakening the author's thesis while establishing reader respect and goodwill for the author: all refutation and no concession can antagonize readers who disagree with the author's position. In the conclusion part of the classical argument, a less skilled writer might simply summarize or restate the thesis and related claims; however, this does not provide the argument with either momentum or closure. More skilled authors revisit the issues and the narration part of the argument, which helps reminds readers of what is at stake.

Evaluating the Author's Purpose in a Given Text

Authors may have many purposes for writing a specific text. They could be imparting information, entertaining their audience, expressing their own feelings, or trying to persuade their readers of a particular position. Authors' purposes are their reasons for writing something. A single author may have one overriding purpose for writing or multiple reasons. An author may explicitly state their intention in the text, or the reader may need to infer that intention. When readers can identify the author's purpose, they are better able to analyze information in the text. By knowing why the author wrote the text, readers can glean ideas for how to approach it. The following is a list of questions readers can ask in order to discern an author's purpose for writing a text:

- Does the title of the text give you any clues about its purpose?
- Was the purpose of the text to give information to readers?
- Did the author want to describe an event, issue, or individual?
- Was it written to express emotions and thoughts?
- Did the author want to convince readers to consider a particular issue?
- Do you think the author's primary purpose was to entertain?
- Why do you think the author wrote this text from a certain point of view?
- What is your response to the text as a reader?
- Did the author state their purpose for writing it?

Rather than simply consuming the text, readers should attempt to interpret the information being presented. Being able to identify an author's purpose efficiently improves reading comprehension, develops critical thinking, and makes students more likely to consider issues in depth before accepting writer viewpoints. Authors of fiction frequently write to entertain readers. Another purpose for writing fiction is making a political statement; for example, Jonathan Swift wrote "A Modest Proposal" (1729) as a political satire. Another purpose for writing fiction as well as nonfiction is to persuade readers to take some action or further a particular cause. Fiction authors and poets both frequently write to evoke certain moods; for example, Edgar Allan Poe wrote novels, short stories, and poems that evoke moods of gloom, guilt, terror, and dread. Another purpose of poets is evoking certain emotions: love is popular, as in

Shakespeare's sonnets and numerous others. In "The Waste Land" (1922), T.S. Eliot evokes society's alienation, disaffection, sterility, and fragmentation.

Authors seldom directly state their purposes in texts. Some students may be confronted with nonfiction texts such as biographies, histories, magazine and newspaper articles, and instruction manuals, among others. To identify the purpose in nonfiction texts, students can ask the following questions:

- Is the author trying to teach something?
- Is the author trying to persuade the reader?
- Is the author imparting factual information only?
- Is this a reliable source?
- Does the author have some kind of hidden agenda?

To apply author purpose in nonfictional passages, students can also analyze sentence structure, word choice, and transitions to answer the aforementioned questions and to make inferences. For example, authors wanting to convince readers to view a topic negatively often choose words with negative connotations.

Narrative Writing

Narrative writing tells a story. The most prominent type of narrative writing is the fictional novel. Here are some examples:

- Mark Twain's *The Adventures of Tom Sawyer* and *The Adventures of Huckleberry Finn*
- Victor Hugo's *Les Misérables*
- Charles Dickens' *Great Expectations, David Copperfield,* and *A Tale of Two Cities*
- Jane Austen's *Northanger Abbey, Mansfield Park, Pride and Prejudice*, and *Sense and Sensibility*
- Toni Morrison's *Beloved, The Bluest Eye*, and *Song of Solomon*
- Gabriel García Márquez's *One Hundred Years of Solitude* and *Love in the Time of Cholera*

Nonfiction works can also appear in narrative form. For example, some authors choose a narrative style to convey factual information about a topic, such as a specific animal, country, geographic region, and scientific or natural phenomenon.

Narrative writing tells a story, and the one telling the story is called the narrator. The narrator may be a fictional character telling the story from their own viewpoint. This narrator uses the first person (*I, me, my, mine* and *we, us, our,* and *ours*). The narrator may also be the author; for example, when Louisa May Alcott writes "Dear reader" in *Little Women*, she (the author) addresses us as readers. In this case, the novel is typically told in third person, referring to the characters as he, she, they, or them. Another more common technique is the omniscient narrator; in other words, the story is told by an unidentified individual who sees and knows everything about the events and characters—not only their externalized actions, but also their internalized feelings and thoughts. Second person narration, which addresses readers as you throughout the text, is more uncommon than the first and third person options.

Expository Writing

Expository writing is also known as **informational writing**. Its purpose is not to tell a story as in narrative writing, to paint a picture as in descriptive writing, or to persuade readers to agree with something as in argumentative writing. Rather, its point is to communicate information to the reader. As such, the point of view of the author will be more objective. Whereas other types of writing appeal to the reader's emotions, appeal to the reader's reason by using logic, or use subjective descriptions to sway the reader's opinion or thinking, expository writing seeks simply to provide facts, evidence, observations, and objective descriptions of the subject matter instead. Some examples of expository writing include research reports, journal articles, books about history, academic textbooks, essays, how-to articles, user instruction manuals, news articles, and other factual journalistic reports.

Technical Writing

Technical writing is similar to expository writing because it provides factual and objective information. Indeed, it may even be considered a subcategory of expository writing. However, technical writing differs from expository writing in two ways: (1) it is specific to a particular field, discipline, or subject, and (2) it uses technical terminology that belongs only to that area. Writing that uses technical terms is intended only for an audience familiar with those terms. An example of technical writing would be a manual on computer programming and use.

Persuasive Writing

Persuasive writing, or **argumentative writing**, attempts to convince the reader to agree with the author's position. Some writers may respond to other writers' arguments by making reference to those authors or texts and then disagreeing with them. However, another common technique is for the author to anticipate opposing viewpoints, both from other authors and from readers. The author brings up these opposing viewpoints, and then refutes them before they can even be raised, strengthening the author's argument. Writers persuade readers by appealing to the readers' reason and emotion, as well as to their own character and credibility. Aristotle called these appeals **logos**, **pathos**, and **ethos**, respectively.

Evaluating the Author's Point of View in a Given Text

When a writer tells a story using the first person, readers can identify this by the use of first-person pronouns, like *I, me, we, us,* etc. However, first-person narratives can be told by different people or from different points of view. For example, some authors write in the first person to tell the story from the main character's viewpoint, as Charles Dickens did in his novels *David Copperfield* and *Great Expectations*. Some authors write in the first person from the viewpoint of a fictional character in the story, but not necessarily the main character. For example, F. Scott Fitzgerald wrote *The Great Gatsby* as narrated by Nick Carraway, a character in the story, about the main characters, Jay Gatsby and Daisy Buchanan. Other authors write in the first person, but as the omniscient narrator—an often unnamed person who knows all of the characters' inner thoughts and feelings. Writing in first person as oneself is more common in nonfiction.

Third Person

The third-person narrative is probably the most prevalent voice used in fictional literature. While some authors tell stories from the point of view and in the voice of a fictional character using the first person, it is a more common practice to describe the actions, thoughts, and feelings of fictional characters in the third person using *he, him, she, her, they, them,* etc.

Although plot and character development are both necessary and possible when writing narrative texts from a first-person point of view, they are also more difficult, particularly for new writers and those who find it unnatural or uncomfortable to write from that perspective. Therefore, writing experts advise beginning writers to start out writing in the third person. A big advantage of third-person narration is that the writer can describe the thoughts, feelings, and motivations of every character in a story, which is not possible for the first-person narrator. Third-person narrative can impart information to readers that the characters do not know. On the other hand, beginning writers often regard using the third-person point

144

of view as more difficult because they must write about the feelings and thoughts of every character, rather than only about those of the protagonist.

Second Person

Narrative texts written in the second person address someone else as "you." In novels and other fictional works, the second person is the narrative voice most seldom used. The primary reason for this is that it often reads in an awkward manner, which prevents readers from being drawn into the fictional world of the novel. The second person is more often used in informational text, especially in how-to manuals, guides, and other instructions.

First Person

First person uses pronouns such as *I, me, we, my, us, and our.* Some writers naturally find it easier to tell stories from their own points of view, so writing in the first person offers advantages for them. The first-person voice is better for interpreting the world from a single viewpoint, and for enabling reader immersion in one protagonist's experiences. However, others find it difficult to use the first-person narrative voice. Its disadvantages can include overlooking the emotions of characters, forgetting to include description, producing stilted writing, using too many sentence structures involving "I did…", and not devoting enough attention to the story's "here-and-now" immediacy.

How an Author's Word Choice Shapes Meaning, Style, and Tone

Words can be very powerful. When written words are used with the intent to make an argument or support a position, the words used—and the way in which they are arranged—can have a dramatic effect on the readers. Clichés, colloquialisms, run-on sentences, and misused words are all examples of ways that word choice can negatively affect writing quality. Unless the writer carefully considers word choice, a written work stands to lose credibility.

If a writer's overall intent is to provide a clear meaning on a subject, he or she must consider not only the exact words to use, but also their placement, repetition, and suitability. Academic writing should be intentional and clear, and it should be devoid of awkward or vague descriptions that can easily lead to misunderstandings. When readers find themselves reading and rereading just to gain a clear understanding of the writer's intent, there may be an issue with word choice. Although the words used in academic writing are different from those used in a casual conversation, they shouldn't necessarily be overly academic either. It may be relevant to employ key words that are associated with the subject, but struggling to inject these words into a paper just to sound academic may defeat the purpose. If the message cannot be clearly understood the first time, word choice may be the culprit.

Word choice also conveys the author's attitude and sets a tone. Although each word in a sentence carries a specific **denotation**, it might also carry positive or negative **connotations**—and it is the connotations that set the tone and convey the author's attitude. Consider the following similar sentences:

It was the same old routine that happens every Saturday morning—eat, exercise, chores.

The Saturday morning routine went off without a hitch—eat, exercise, chores.

The first sentence carries a negative connotation with the author's "same old routine" word choice. The feelings and attitudes associated with this phrase suggest that the author is bored or annoyed at the Saturday morning routine. Although the second sentence carries the same topic—explaining the Saturday morning routine—the choice to use the expression "without a hitch" conveys a positive or cheery attitude.

An author's writing style can likewise be greatly affected by word choice. When writing for an academic audience, for example, it is necessary for the author to consider how to convey the message by carefully considering word choice. If the author interchanges between third-person formal writing and second-person informal writing, the author's writing quality and credibility are at risk. Formal writing involves complex sentences, an objective viewpoint, and the use of full words as opposed to the use of a subjective viewpoint, contractions, and first- or second-person usage commonly found in informal writing.

Content validity, the author's ability to support the argument, and the audience's ability to comprehend the written work are all affected by the author's word choice.

The Organization or Structure

Text structure is the way in which the author organizes and presents textual information so readers can follow and comprehend it. One kind of text structure is sequence. This means the author arranges the text in a logical order from beginning to middle to end. There are three types of sequences:

- Chronological: ordering events in time from earliest to latest

- Spatial: describing objects, people, or spaces according to their relationships to one another in space

- Order of Importance: addressing topics, characters, or ideas according to how important they are, from either least important to most important

Chronological sequence is the most common sequential text structure. Readers can identify sequential structure by looking for words that signal it, like *first, earlier, meanwhile, next, then, later, finally*, and specific times and dates the author includes as chronological references.

Problem-Solution Text Structure

The problem-solution text structure organizes textual information by presenting readers with a problem and then developing its solution throughout the course of the text. The author may present a variety of alternatives as possible solutions, eliminating each as they are found unsuccessful, or gradually leading up to the ultimate solution. For example, in fiction, an author might write a murder mystery novel and have the character(s) solve it through investigating various clues or character alibis until the killer is identified. In nonfiction, an author writing an essay or book on a real-world problem might discuss various alternatives and explain their disadvantages or why they would not work before identifying the best solution. For scientific research, an author reporting and discussing scientific experiment results would explain why various alternatives failed or succeeded.

Comparison-Contrast Text Structure

Comparison identifies similarities between two or more things. **Contrast** identifies differences between two or more things. Authors typically employ both to illustrate relationships between things by highlighting their commonalities and deviations. For example, a writer might compare Windows and Linux as operating systems, and contrast Linux as free and open-source vs. Windows as proprietary. When writing an essay, sometimes it is useful to create an image of the two objects or events you are comparing or contrasting. Venn diagrams are useful because they show the differences as well as the similarities between two things. Once you've seen the similarities and differences on paper, it might be helpful to create an outline of the essay with both comparison and contrast. Every outline will look different because every two or more things will have a different number of comparisons and contrasts. Say you are trying to compare and contrast carrots with sweet potatoes. Here is an example of a compare/contrast outline using those topics:

- Introduction: Talk about why you are comparing and contrasting carrots and sweet potatoes. Give the thesis statement.
- Body paragraph 1: Sweet potatoes and carrots are both root vegetables (similarity)
- Body paragraph 2: Sweet potatoes and carrots are both orange (similarity)
- Body paragraph 3: Sweet potatoes and carrots have different nutritional components (difference)
- Conclusion: Restate the purpose of your comparison/contrast essay.

Of course, if there is only one similarity between your topics and two differences, you will want to rearrange your outline. Always tailor your essay to what works best with your topic.

Descriptive Text Structure

Description can be both a type of text structure and a type of text. Some texts are descriptive throughout entire books. For example, a book may describe the geography of a certain country, state, or region, or tell readers all about dolphins by describing many of their characteristics. Many other texts are not descriptive throughout but use descriptive passages within the overall text. The following are a few examples of descriptive text:

- When the author describes a character in a novel
- When the author sets the scene for an event by describing the setting
- When a biographer describes the personality and behaviors of a real-life individual
- When a historian describes the details of a particular battle within a book about a specific war
- When a travel writer describes the climate, people, foods, and/or customs of a certain place

A hallmark of description is using sensory details, painting a vivid picture so readers can imagine it almost as if they were experiencing it personally.

Cause and Effect Text Structure

When using cause and effect to extrapolate meaning from text, readers must determine the cause when the author only communicates effects. For example, if a description of a man walking down the sidewalk includes details such as his jacket billowing or his hat nearly flying off his head, the reader can infer or conclude that it must be windy outside. A useful technique for making such decisions is wording them in "If...then" form, e.g. "If the man's jacket is billowing and his hat nearly flies off his head, then it may be a windy day." Cause and effect text structures explain why certain events or actions resulted in particular outcomes. For example, an author might describe America's historical large flocks of dodo birds, the fact that gunshots did not startle/frighten dodos, and that because dodos did not flee, settlers killed whole flocks in one hunting session, explaining how the dodo was hunted into extinction.

Recognizing Events in a Sequence

Sequence structure is the order of events in which a story or information is presented to the audience. Sometimes the text will be presented in chronological order, or sometimes it will be presented by displaying the most recent information first, then moving backwards in time. The sequence structure depends on the author, the context, and the audience. The structure of a text also depends on the genre in which the text is written. Is it literary fiction? Is it a magazine article? Is it instructions for how to complete a certain task? Different genres will have different purposes for switching up the sequence.

Narrative Structure

The structure presented in literary fiction, called **narrative structure**, is the foundation on which the text moves. The narrative structure comes from the plot and setting. The plot is the sequence of events in the narrative that move the text forward through cause and effect. The setting is the place or time period in which the story takes place. Narrative structure has two main categories: linear and nonlinear.

Linear Narrative

A narrative is linear when it is told in chronological order. Traditional linear narratives will follow the plot diagram below depicting the narrative arc. The narrative arc consists of the exposition, conflict, rising action, climax, falling action, and resolution.

- Exposition: The exposition is in the beginning of a narrative and introduces the characters, setting, and background information of the story. The exposition provides the context for the upcoming narrative. Exposition literally means "a showing forth" in Latin.

- Conflict: In a traditional narrative, the conflict appears toward the beginning of the story after the audience becomes familiar with the characters and setting. The conflict is a single instance between characters, nature, or the self, in which the central character is forced to make a decision or move forward with some kind of action. The conflict presents something for the main character, or protagonist, to overcome.

- Rising Action: The rising action is the part of the story that leads into the climax. The rising action will feature the development of characters and plot and creates the tension and suspense that eventually lead to the climax.

- Climax: The climax is the part of the story where the tension produced in the rising action comes to a culmination. The climax is the peak of the story. In a traditional structure, everything before the climax builds up to it, and everything after the climax falls from it. It is the height of the narrative and is usually either the most exciting part of the story or is marked by some turning point in the character's journey.

- Falling Action: The falling action happens as a result of the climax. Characters continue to develop, although there is a wrapping up of loose ends here. The falling action leads to the resolution.

- Resolution: The resolution is where the story comes to an end and usually leaves the reader with the satisfaction of knowing what happened within the story and why. However, stories do not always end in this fashion. Sometimes readers can be confused or frustrated at the end from lack of information or the absence of a happy ending.

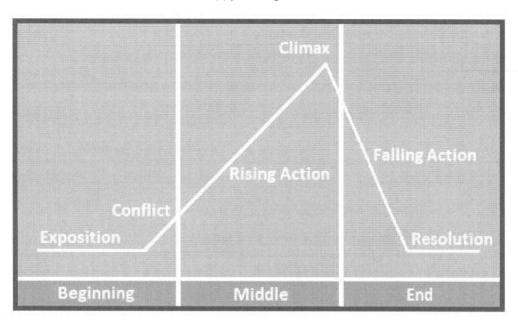

Nonlinear Narrative

A nonlinear narrative deviates from the traditional narrative because it does not always follow the traditional plot structure of the narrative arc. Nonlinear narratives may include structures that are disjointed, circular, or disruptive, in the sense that they do not follow chronological order. **In medias res** is an example of a nonlinear structure. *In medias res* is Latin for "in the middle of things," which is how many ancient texts, especially epic poems, began their story, such as Homer's *Iliad*. Instead of having a clear exposition with a full development of characters, they would begin right in the middle of the action.

Many modernist texts in the late nineteenth and early twentieth centuries experimented with disjointed narratives, moving away from traditional linear narrative. Disjointed narratives are depicted in novels like *Catch 22*, where the author, Joseph Heller, structures the narrative based on free association of ideas rather than chronology. Another nonlinear narrative can be seen in the novel *Wuthering Heights*, written by Emily Brontë; after the first chapter, the narrative progresses retrospectively instead of chronologically. There seem to be two narratives in *Wuthering Heights* working at the same time: a present narrative as well as a past narrative. Authors employ disrupting narratives for various reasons; some use it for the purpose of creating situational irony for the readers, while some use it to create a certain effect, such as excitement, discomfort, or fear.

Sequence Structure in Technical Documents

The purpose of technical documents, such as instructions manuals, cookbooks, or "user-friendly" documents, is to provide information to users as clearly and efficiently as possible. In order to do this, the sequence structure in technical documents should be as straightforward as possible. This usually involves some kind of chronological order or a direct sequence of events. For example, someone who is reading an instruction manual on how to set up their Smart TV wants directions in a clear, simple, straightforward manner that does not confuse them or leave them guessing about the proper sequence.

Sequence Structure in Informational Texts

The structure of informational texts depends on the specific genre. For example, a newspaper article may start by stating an exciting event that happened, then talk about that event in chronological order. Many informational texts also use **cause and effect structure**, which describes an event and then identifies reasons for why that event occurred. Some essays may write about their subjects by way of **comparison and contrast**, which is a structure that compares two things or contrasts them to highlight their differences. Other documents, such as proposals, will have a **problem to solution structure**, where the document highlights some kind of problem and then offers a solution. Finally, some informational texts are written with lush details and description in order to captivate the audience, allowing them to visualize the information presented to them. This type of structure is known as **descriptive**.

Synthesis

Comparing Informational Texts that Address the Same Topic

Informational texts about the same topic can include vastly different pieces of information, perceptions, or opinions. When comparing two or more informational texts that address the same topic, the first comparison to make is to determine and understand the source of each text. Based on the source, the authors may hold rather different intentions for writing the text. For example, an author of an academic textbook is likely to present information that is evidence based, instructional, and/or reviewed by peers with expert-level credentialing. A journalist who writes about the same topic may present similar information yet include a personal editorial opinion, such as the application of the information in the real world. These two authors are writing on the same topic but presenting to largely different readerships; therefore, their method of information sharing is likely to be different. Understanding the audience for whom the author is writing, the purpose of writing their text, and the author's own credentials can be useful components of a comparison analysis.

Additionally, the point of view from which an informational text is written can also be useful in understanding the different values between two pieces of text that address the same topic. For example, the first-person account of a historical event from someone who experienced it directly will likely present different information, a different perspective, and evoke different emotions from the reader than the recount of the same event by an objective researcher who is simply sharing facts about the event. In addition to focusing on where the two accounts differ, readers should note similarities between the two passages (such as factual information or similar feelings that are expressed by both authors).

Analyzing Two Arguments and Evaluating the Types of Evidence Used to Support Each Claim

Authors use arguments to persuade the reader to agree with their claim. When analyzing the strength of an argument, the reader should summarize the author's message and determine whether or not they agree or disagree with the claim and whether, overall, they believe the evidence the author presented to support it. Next the reader should identify each individual detail and examine it to determine if it supports the claim, fails to support the claim, or even distract from the author's goal.

As readers examine each piece of evidence, they should consider its type and its effectiveness in proving the author's claim both individually and in context. Readers should pay attention to details that contradict the evidence, and readers should question the way the author uses details.

150

Facts can often be interpreted in ways that mislead the reader, so they will believe a claim that is unproven or untrue. If the claim is supported by facts such as statistics or empirical evidence, the reader should examine them. The reader should question whether the facts are relevant or, if they were interpreted differently, they would lead to a different conclusion that would fail to support the argument or even contradict it. They should consider whether the scope of the data is appropriate, or if it is too broad or narrow, and they should question whether the source is credible, and whether a source has been cited at all.

If the author uses expert opinions, the reader should consider whether the expert is credible and appropriate. If a doctor offers an opinion about pediatric medicine, the reader should ask if the doctor is an expert in that field or if they practice a different form of medicine.

Finally, the reader should consider whether the author has anticipated and adequately responded to any potential counterarguments to the claim and decide if the argument overall is strong, or if the evidence fails to persuade them to accept the author's claim.

Recognizing or Predicting Ideas or Situations that are Extensions of or Similar to What Has Been Presented in a Reading Selection

In its most basic form, an analogy compares two different things. An analogy question is a situation that parallels the principles or foundations given in another situation. The source will require you to pick out the most apt target in a set of particular events.

Analogy questions may look like the following:

Based on the hypothetical situation given in paragraph 4, which of the following is most closely analogous?

The answer choices will consist of particular situations that attempt to mirror the hypothetical situation given in the passage. In order to find the correct answer, it might be helpful to know the basics of what an analogy is.

The following is a list of different types of analogies:

Analogous Relationships	
Category	**Example**
Part to whole	"All screwdrivers are considered tools." Tools is the whole, and screwdrivers is the part to that whole. Be careful of reversing this logic, though. It would be an error to say "Likewise, all tools are considered screwdrivers." In simplified terms, saying "All A are B" is not the same as saying "All B are A."
Confusing causation with correlation	"The number of traffic accidents in Florida has gone up this past summer. The temperature has also increased this summer by 10 degrees. I bet the heat is making drivers more irritable." This logic confuses causation (the heat is causing accidents) with correlation. Traffic accidents have gone up and so has the heat, but that doesn't necessarily mean that one is causing the other. A new iPhone could have been released, creating distracted drivers. Or, there could have been more rain in the summer, causing dangerous driving conditions.
Performer to related action	"A lawyer passes the bar exam after finishing law school." "A student passes the SAT after finishing high school." Performer to related action requires a test taker to make an association between actions and their performers. Here, we see a performer passing some kind of exam after they've gone through years of training. In this way, the student and their actions are analogous to the lawyer and their actions.
Cause and effect	"A restaurant was shut down because it had an infestation problem." "A company went out of business because it couldn't produce enough inventory." In the analogy above, we see something shutting down because of a problem. The cause and effect analogy presents an unequivocal effect to an action and requires no effort to make something happen.
Unintended consequence	"Two parents enter therapy with the purpose of finding help for their son, who is struggling with substance abuse and behavioral problems at school. As a result, they find that they also are dealing with unresolved issues in the past and learn ways to cope with these issues." Here, a group of people set out to do one thing, and receive another in return. In this situation, there is an unintended consequence beside an intended consequence. In some situations, the intended consequence might not happen at all, and the unintended consequence will have the opposite effect of the intended consequence, creating an ironic situation.

Let's look at an example of an analogy question. This is a passage from *Ten Great Events in History* by James Johonnot.

> Meantime, in the Church of England a spirit of criticism had grown up. Stricter thinkers disliked the imposing ceremonies which the English church still retained: some of the ministers ceased to wear gowns in preaching, performed the marriage ceremony without using a ring, and were in favor of simplifying all the church service. Unpretentious workers began to tire of the everlasting quarreling, and to long for a religion simple and quiet. These soon met trouble, for the rulers had decided that salvation was by the Church of England, as the sovereign, its head, should order. Dissent was the two-fold guilt of heresy and revolution—sin against God and crime against the king and English law. They were forbidden to preach at all if they would not wear a gown during service, and the people who went to hear them were punished. This treatment caused serious thought among the "non-conformists," as they were called, and, once thinking, they soon concluded that the king had no such supreme right to order the church, and the church had over its ministers no such right of absolute dictation.

Given Johonnot's account of the criticism of the Church of England in the Middle Ages, which one of the following is most analogous to the situation of the ministers' refusal to wear gowns and the workers' resistance of fighting leading to problems with the church?
  a. A church body meets resistance from an outside secular entity for issues related to social injustice.
  b. Three members of a sorority refuse to do the hazing ritual, so they are kicked out of the sorority by the other members.
  c. A group of kids at school who create an exclusive club that says anyone can join as long as they are in second grade and live on Magnolia Street.
  d. A book club that finds it is no longer useful to its members, and thus attempts to change the group to a film club instead.

What we have in the original source are members part of a group refusing to participate in a tradition, so as a result, they are punished by the group. The ministers and workers are refusing to participate in church traditions, so they are punished or banished by the church.

Choice *B* is the correct answer to this analogy question. We have members of a group refusing to participate in a tradition (a hazing ritual), so they are punished by the other members of the group. This target fits the original analogy source the closest.

Choice *A* is incorrect. Although we are dealing with a church, the structure of the analogy is not the same. In this situation, the group is experiencing external problems rather than internal problems depicted in the original source.

Choice *C* is incorrect because this analogy depicts a creation of a group and the rules for joining it. In the original analogy, the group is already established with its laws and traditions.

Choice *D* is incorrect because this group is able to adapt to dissent as a whole, and is not in disagreement about traditions that are no longer working.

Applying Ideas Presented in a Reading Selection to Other Situations

There may be questions that give a scenario with a general conclusion and ask you to apply that general conclusion to a new context. Skills for making inferences and drawing conclusions will be helpful in the first portion of this question type. Reading the initial scenario carefully and finding the general concept, or the bigger picture, is necessary for when the test taker attempts to apply this general concept to the new context the question provides. Here is an example of a test question that asks the test taker to apply information in a selection to a new context:

> The placebo effect is a phenomenon used in clinical trial studies to test the effectiveness of new medications. A group of people are given either the new medication or the placebo but are not told which. Interestingly, about one-third of people who are given the placebo in clinical trials will report a cessation of their symptoms. In one trial in 1925, a group of people were given sugar pills and told their migraines should dissipate as a result of the pills. Forty-two percent noticed that in the following six months, their weekly migraines evaporated. Researchers believe that human belief and expectation might be a reason that the placebo will work in some patients.

Considering the phenomenon of the placebo effect, what would probably happen to someone who is given a shot with no medication and told their arm should go numb from it?

> a. The patient might experience some burning in their arm, but then they would feel nothing.
> b. The patient would feel their arm going numb, as the placebo effect is certain to work.
> c. Nothing would happen because the shot does not actually have any medication in it.
> d. The individual might actually experience a numbing sensation in their arm, as the placebo works on some people by simply being told the placebo will have certain effects.

The answer is Choice *D*. The individual might actually experience a numbing sensation in their arm, as the placebo works on some people by simply being told the placebo will have certain effects. Choices *B* and *C* are too absolute to be considered correct—watch out for words like "never" or "always" in the answer choices so you can rule them out if possible. Choice *A* is incorrect because we don't know what the initial sensation of the shot would feel like for this individual. The placebo effect would have a chance of working with the shot, just like it would have a chance of working in the above example with the pill. The patient's belief in an effect is what can possibly manifest the desired result of the placebo.

Integrating Data from Multiple Sources in Various Formats, Including Media

Books as Resources

When a student has an assignment to research and write a paper, one of the first steps after determining the topic is to select research sources. The student may begin by conducting an Internet or library search of the topic, refer to a reading list provided by the instructor, or use an annotated bibliography of works related to the topic. To evaluate the worth of the book for the research paper, the student first considers the book's title to get an idea of its content. Then the student can scan the book's table of contents for chapter titles and topics to get further ideas of their applicability to the topic. The student may also turn to the end of the book to look for an alphabetized index. Most academic textbooks and scholarly works have these; students can look up key terms regarding their topic to see how many are included and how many pages are devoted to them.

Journal Articles

Like books, journal articles are primary or secondary sources the student may need to use for researching any topic. To assess whether a journal article will be a useful source for a particular paper topic, a student can first get some idea about the content of the article by reading its title and subtitle, if any exists. Many journal articles, particularly scientific ones, include abstracts. These are brief summaries of the content. The student should read the abstract to get a more specific idea of whether the experiment, literature

154

review, or other work documented is applicable to the paper topic. Students should also check the references at the end of the article, which today often contain links to related works for exploring the topic further online.

Encyclopedias and Dictionaries

Dictionaries and encyclopedias are both reference books for looking up information alphabetically. **Dictionaries** are more exclusively focused on vocabulary words. They include each word's correct spelling, pronunciation, variants, part(s) of speech, definitions of one or more meanings, and examples used in a sentence. Some dictionaries provide illustrations of certain words when these inform the meaning. Some dictionaries also offer synonyms, antonyms, and related words under a word's entry. **Encyclopedias,** like dictionaries, often provide word pronunciations and definitions. However, they have broader scopes: one can look up entire subjects in encyclopedias, not just words, and find comprehensive, detailed information about historical events, famous people, countries, disciplines of study, and many other things. Dictionaries are for finding meanings, pronunciations, and spellings of words; encyclopedias are for finding breadth and depth of information on a variety of topics.

Card Catalogs

A **card catalog** is a means of organizing, classifying, and locating the large numbers of books found in libraries. Without being able to look up books in library card catalogs, it would be virtually impossible to find them on library shelves. Card catalogs may be on traditional paper cards filed in drawers, or electronic catalogs accessible online; some libraries combine both. Books are shelved by subject area; subjects are coded using formal **classification systems**—standardized sets of rules for identifying and labeling books by subject and author. These assign each book a **call number**, which is a code indicating the classification system, subject, author, and title. Call numbers also function as bookshelf "addresses" where books can be located. Most public libraries use the Dewey Decimal Classification System. Most university, college, and research libraries use the Library of Congress Classification. Nursing students will also encounter the National Institute of Health's National Library of Medicine Classification System, which major collections of health sciences publications utilize.

Databases

A **database** is a collection of digital information organized for easy access, updating, and management. Users can sort and search databases for information. One way of classifying databases is by content, i.e. full-text, numerical, bibliographical, or images. Another classification method used in computing is by organizational approach. The most common approach is a relational database, which is tabular and defines data so they can be accessed and reorganized in various ways. A distributed database can be reproduced or interspersed among different locations within a network. An object-oriented database is organized to be aligned with object classes and subclasses defining the data. Databases usually collect files like product inventories, catalogs, customer profiles, sales transactions, student bodies, and resources. An associated set of application programs is a database management system or database manager. It enables users to specify which reports to generate, control access to reading and writing data, and analyze database usage. Structured Query Language (SQL) is a standard computer language for updating, querying, and otherwise interfacing with databases.

Identifying Information from a Graphic Representation of Information

Line Graphs

Line graphs are useful for visually representing data that vary continuously over time, like an individual student's test scores. The horizontal or x-axis shows dates/times; the vertical or y-axis shows point values.

A dot is plotted on the point where each horizontal date line intersects each vertical number line, and then these dots are connected, forming a line. Line graphs show whether changes in values over time exhibit trends like ascending, descending, flat, or more variable, like going up and down at different times. For example, suppose a student's scores on the same type of reading test were 75% in October, 80% in November, 78% in December, 82% in January, 85% in February, 88% in March, and 90% in April.

A line graph of these scores, which helps visualize the trends, would look like this:

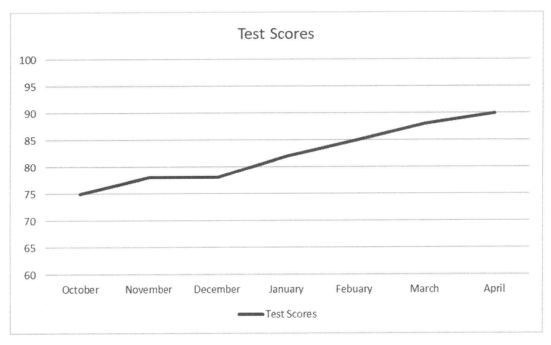

Bar Graphs

Bar graphs feature equally spaced, horizontal or vertical rectangular bars representing numerical values. They can show changes over time as line graphs do, but unlike line graphs, bar graphs can also show differences and similarities among values at a single point in time. Bar graphs are also helpful for visually representing data from different categories, especially when the horizontal axis displays some value that is not numerical, like various countries with inches of annual rainfall. From the following is a bar graph that compares different classes and how many books they read, it can be seen that the fewest books were read by the students in Class D:

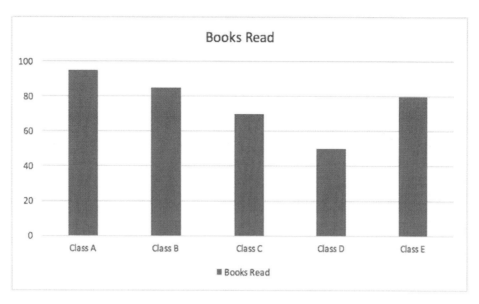

Pie Charts

Pie charts, also called **circle graphs**, are good for representing percentages or proportions of a whole quantity because they represent the whole as a circle or "pie," with the various proportion values shown as "slices" or wedges of the pie. This gives viewers a clear idea of how much of a total each item occupies. To calculate central angles to make each portion the correct size, each percentage is multiplied by 3.6 (because this is 360/100). For example, biologists may have information that 60% of Americans have brown eyes, 20% have hazel eyes, 15% have blue eyes, and 5% have green eyes. A pie chart of these distributions would look like this:

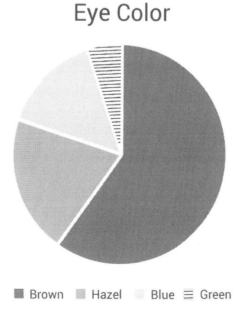

Eye Color

■ Brown ■ Hazel ■ Blue ≡ Green

Line Plots

Rather than showing trends or changes over time like line graphs, **line plots** show the frequency with which a value occurs in a group. Line plots are used for visually representing data sets that total 50 or fewer values. They make visible features like gaps between some data points, clusters of certain numbers/number ranges, and outliers (data points with significantly smaller or larger values than others). For example, the age ranges in a class of nursing students might appear like this in a line plot:

xxxxxxxxx	xxxxx	xx	x	xxx	xx	x
18	23	28	33	38	43	48

Pictograms

Magazines, newspapers, and other similar publications designed for consumption by the general public often use **pictograms** to represent data. Pictograms feature icons or symbols that look like whatever category of data is being counted, such as little silhouettes shaped like human beings commonly used to represent people. If the data involve large numbers, like populations, one person symbol might represent one million people, or one thousand, etc. For smaller values, such as how many individuals out of ten fit a given description, one symbol might equal one person. Male and female silhouettes are used to differentiate gender, and child shapes for children. Little clock symbols are used to represent amounts of time, such as a given number of hours; calendar pages might depict months; suns and moons could show days and nights; hourglasses might represent minutes. While pictogram symbols are easily recognizable and appealing to general viewers, one disadvantage is that it is difficult to precisely display and interpret partial symbols for in-between quantities.

Identifying Primary Sources in Various Media

A **primary source** is a piece of original work. This can include books, musical compositions, recordings, movies, works of visual art (paintings, drawings, photographs), jewelry, pottery, clothing, furniture, and other artifacts. Within books, primary sources may be of any genre. Whether nonfiction based on actual events or a fictional creation, the primary source relates the author's firsthand view of some specific event, phenomenon, character, place, process, ideas, field of study or discipline, or other subject matter. Whereas primary sources are original treatments of their subjects, **secondary sources** are a step removed from the original subjects; they analyze and interpret primary sources. These include journal articles, newspaper or magazine articles, works of literary criticism, political commentaries, and academic textbooks.

In the field of history, primary sources frequently include documents that were created around the same time period that they were describing, and most often produced by someone who had direct experience or knowledge of the subject matter. In contrast, secondary sources present the ideas and viewpoints of other authors about the primary sources; in history, for example, these can include books and other written works about the particular historical periods or eras in which the primary sources were produced. Primary sources pertinent in history include diaries, letters, statistics, government information, and original journal articles and books. In literature, a primary source might be a literary novel, a poem or book of poems, or a play. Secondary sources addressing primary sources may be criticism, dissertations, theses, and journal articles. **Tertiary sources**, typically reference works referring to primary and secondary sources, include encyclopedias, bibliographies, handbooks, abstracts, and periodical indexes.

In scientific fields, when scientists conduct laboratory experiments to answer specific research questions and test hypotheses, lab reports and reports of research results constitute examples of primary sources. When researchers produce statistics to support or refute hypotheses, those statistics are primary sources. When a scientist is studying some subject longitudinally or conducting a case study, they may keep a journal or diary. For example, Charles Darwin kept diaries of extensive notes on his studies during sea voyages on the *Beagle*, visits to the Galápagos Islands, etc.; Jean Piaget kept journals of observational notes for case studies of children's learning behaviors. Many scientists, particularly in past centuries, shared and discussed discoveries, questions, and ideas with colleagues through letters, which also constitute primary sources. When a scientist seeks to replicate another's experiment, the reported results, analysis, and commentary on the original work is a secondary source, as is a student's dissertation if it analyzes or discusses others' work rather than reporting original research or ideas.

Vocabulary

Analyzing Word Parts

Readers can learn some etymologies, or origins, of words and their parts, making it easier to break down new words into components and analyze their combined meanings. For example, the root word soph is Greek for "wise" or "knowledge." Knowing this informs the meanings of English words including *sophomore, sophisticated,* and *philosophy.* Those who also know that phil is Greek for "love" will realize that philosophy means "love of knowledge." They can then extend this knowledge of *phil* to understand *philanthropist* (one who loves people), *bibliophile* (book lover), *philharmonic* (loving harmony), *hydrophilic* (water-loving), and so on. In addition, *phob* derives from the Greek *phobos*, meaning "fear." Words with this root indicate fear of various things *acrophobia* (fear of heights), *arachnophobia* (fear of spiders), *claustrophobia* (fear of enclosed spaces), *ergophobia* (fear of work), and *hydrophobia* (fear of water), among others.

Some English word origins from other languages, like ancient Greek, are found in large numbers and varieties of English words. An advantage of the shared ancestry of these words is that once readers recognize the meanings of some Greek words or word roots, they can determine or at least get an idea of what many different English words mean. As an example, the Greek word *métron* means to measure, a measure, or something used to measure; the English word meter derives from it. Knowing this informs many other English words, including *altimeter, barometer, diameter, hexameter, isometric,* and *metric.* While readers must know the meanings of the other parts of these words to decipher their meaning fully, they already have an idea that they are all related in some way to measures or measuring.

While all English words ultimately derive from a proto-language known as Indo-European, many of them historically came into the developing English vocabulary later, from sources like the ancient Greeks, the Latin used throughout Europe and much of the Middle East during the reign of the Roman Empire, and the Anglo-Saxon languages used by England's early tribes. In addition to classic revivals and native foundations, by the Renaissance era other influences included French, German, Italian, and Spanish. Today we can often discern English word meanings by knowing common roots and affixes, particularly from Greek and Latin.

The following is a list of common prefixes and their meanings:

Prefix	Definition	Examples
a-	without	atheist, agnostic
ad-	to, toward	advance
ante-	before	antecedent, antedate
anti-	opposing	antipathy, antidote
auto-	self	autonomy, autobiography
bene-	well, good	benefit, benefactor
bi-	two	bisect, biennial
bio-	life	biology, biosphere
chron-	time	chronometer, synchronize
circum-	around	circumspect, circumference
com-	with, together	commotion, complicate
contra-	against, opposing	contradict, contravene
cred-	belief, trust	credible, credit
de-	from	depart
dem-	people	demographics, democracy
dis-	away, off, down, not	dissent, disappear
equi-	equal, equally	equivalent
ex-	from, out of	extract
for-	away, off, from	forget, forswear
fore-	before, previous	foretell, forefathers
homo-	same, equal	homogenized
hyper-	excessive, over	hypercritical, hypertension
in-	in, into	intrude, invade
inter-	among, between	intercede, interrupt
mal-	bad, poorly, not	malfunction
micr(o)-	small	microbe, microscope
mis-	bad, poorly, not	misspell, misfire
mono-	one, single	monogamy, monologue
mor-	die, death	mortality, mortuary
neo-	new	neolithic, neoconservative
non-	not	nonentity, nonsense
omni-	all, everywhere	omniscient
over-	above	overbearing
pan-	all, entire	panorama, pandemonium
para-	beside, beyond	parallel, paradox
phil-	love, affection	philosophy, philanthropic
poly-	many	polymorphous, polygamous
pre-	before, previous	prevent, preclude
prim-	first, early	primitive, primary
pro-	forward, in place of	propel, pronoun
re-	back, backward, again	revoke, recur

Prefix	Definition	Examples
sub-	under, beneath	subjugate, substitute
super-	above, extra	supersede, supernumerary
trans-	across, beyond, over	transact, transport
ultra-	beyond, excessively	ultramodern, ultrasonic, ultraviolet
un-	not, reverse of	unhappy, unlock
vis-	to see	visage, visible

The following is a list of common suffixes and their meanings:

Suffix	Definition	Examples
-able	likely, able to	capable, tolerable
-ance	act, condition	acceptance, vigilance
-ard	one that does excessively	drunkard, wizard
-ation	action, state	occupation, starvation
-cy	state, condition	accuracy, captaincy
-er	one who does	teacher
-esce	become, grow, continue	convalesce, acquiesce
-esque	in the style of, like	picturesque, grotesque
-ess	feminine	waitress, lioness
-ful	full of, marked by	thankful, zestful
-ible	able, fit	edible, possible, divisible
-ion	action, result, state	union, fusion
-ish	suggesting, like	churlish, childish
-ism	act, manner, doctrine	barbarism, socialism
-ist	doer, believer	monopolist, socialist
-ition	action, result, state,	sedition, expedition
-ity	quality, condition	acidity, civility
-ize	cause to be, treat with	sterilize, mechanize, criticize
-less	lacking, without	hopeless, countless
-like	like, similar	childlike, dreamlike
-ly	like, of the nature of	friendly, positively
-ment	means, result, action	refreshment, disappointment
-ness	quality, state	greatness, tallness
-or	doer, office, action	juror, elevator, honor
-ous	marked by, given to	religious, riotous
-some	apt to, showing	tiresome, lonesome
-th	act, state, quality	warmth, width
-ty	quality, state	enmity, activity

Using Context Clues to Understand the Meaning of Unfamiliar Words

Readers can often figure out what unfamiliar words mean without interrupting their reading to look them up in dictionaries by examining context. Context includes the other words or sentences in a passage. One

161

common context clue is the root word and any affixes (prefixes/suffixes). Another common context clue is a synonym or definition included in the sentence. Sometimes both exist in the same sentence. Here's an example:

Scientists who study birds are *ornithologists*.

Many readers may not know the word *ornithologist*. However, the example contains a definition (scientists who study birds). The reader may also have the ability to analyze the suffix (*-logy*, meaning the study of) and root (*ornitho-*, meaning bird).

Another common context clue is a sentence that shows differences. Here's an example:

Birds *incubate* their eggs outside of their bodies, unlike mammals.

Some readers may be unfamiliar with the word *incubate*. However, since the sentence includes the phrase "unlike mammals," the reader can infer that incubate relates to an aspect of prenatal development that mammals and birds do not have in common, such as the way they keep the embryo at a temperature suitable for development.

In addition to analyzing the etymology of a word's root and affixes and extrapolating word meaning from sentences that contrast an unknown word with an antonym, readers can also determine word meanings from sentence context clues based on logic. Here's an example:

Birds are always looking out for predators that could attack their young.

The reader who is unfamiliar with the word *predator* could determine from the context of the sentence that predators usually prey upon baby birds and possibly other young animals. Readers might also use the context clue of etymology here, as *predator* and *prey* have the same root.

When readers encounter an unfamiliar word in text, they can use the surrounding context to help determine the word's meaning. The text's overall subject matter, the specific chapter or section, and the immediate sentence context can all provide clues to help the reader understand the word. Among others, one category of context clues is grammar. For example, the position of a word in a sentence and its relationship to the other words can help the reader establish whether the unfamiliar word is a verb, a noun, an adjective, an adverb, etc. This narrows down the possible meanings of the word to one part of speech. However, this may be insufficient. In a sentence that many birds *migrate* twice yearly, the reader can determine the word is a verb, and probably does not mean eat or drink; but it could mean travel, mate, lay eggs, hatch, or molt.

Some words can have a number of different meanings depending on how they are used. For example, the word *fly* has a different meaning in each of the following sentences:

- "His trousers have a fly on them."
- "He swatted the fly on his trousers."
- "Those are some fly trousers."
- "They went fly fishing."
- "She hates to fly."
- "If humans were meant to fly, they would have wings."

As strategies, readers can try substituting a familiar word for an unfamiliar one and see whether it makes sense in the sentence. They can also identify other words in a sentence, offering clues to an unfamiliar word's meaning.

Different Interpretations That Can Be Made of the Same Word or Phrase

Language can function differently depending on its context. The same words can convey meaning in nuanced ways depending on the surrounding context and the style and tone of the composition. Just as how people can speak with a variety of tones and inflections that can alter the meaning of the same sentence, so too can writers insert tone into written words. Punctuation choice is one example of how the same sentence can be interpreted slightly differently.

Consider the following three sentences:

Camille hates dogs.

Camille hates dogs!

Camille hates dogs?

Although the wording is identical in these three simple sentences, the end punctuation affects the tone, and each option allows for a slightly different interpretation. The first sentence is simply stating that Camille hates dogs; the period at the end of the sentence elicits no significant emotional response. The exclamation point at the end of the second sentence could evoke surprise, exasperation, or urgency/alarm. Perhaps, for example, someone was about to introduce a large mastiff to Camille who had her back turned to the dog. One of Camille's friends who saw what was about to happen may have shouted that sentence in caution to prevent a terrified Camille. The last sentence is obviously a question, but that doesn't mean it's affectless. It could have been asked simply out of desire for clarification or confirmation, or it could have been asked in an incredulous or surprised tone because the speaker found it hard to believe that Camille could hate dogs.

The writer could further display tone by italicizing one of the words to indicate emphasis. Consider the difference between the following three examples:

Camille hates dogs?

Camille *hates* dogs?

Camille hates *dogs*?

The first example places the emphasis on Camille. The speaker could be surprised that Camille, not another person, supposedly hates dogs. In the second example, the speaker's focus is on the word *hate*. He or she is seeking clarity or confirmation that Camille actually hates dogs (as opposed to simply being annoyed by them, allergic to them, afraid of them, etc.). The italicized *dogs* in the last sentence indicates the speaker is verifying or expressing shock that Camille hates dogs in particular (rather than cats, spiders, rats, etc.). Other punctuation marks, especially commas, can also shape the way a sentence is read and interpreted.

In addition to punctuation and emphasis indicators, a word's connotation can also determine its interpretation. Denotation, a word's explicit definition, is often set in comparison to connotation, the emotional, cultural, social, or personal implications associated with a word. Denotation is more of an objective definition, whereas connotation can be more subjective, although many connotative meanings of words are similar for certain cultures. The denotative meanings of words are usually based on facts, and the connotative meanings of words are usually based on emotion. Here are some examples of words and their denotative and connotative meanings in Western culture:

Word	Denotative Meaning	Connotative Meaning
Home	A permanent place where one lives, usually as a member of a family.	A place of warmth; a place of familiarity; comforting; a place of safety and security. "Home" usually has a positive connotation.
Snake	A long reptile with no limbs and strong jaws that moves along the ground; some snakes have a poisonous bite.	An evil omen; a slithery creature (human or nonhuman) that is deceitful or unwelcome. "Snake" usually has a negative connotation.
Winter	A season of the year that is the coldest, usually from December to February in the northern hemisphere and from June to August in the southern hemisphere.	Circle of life, especially that of death and dying; cold or icy; dark and gloomy; hibernation, sleep, or rest. Winter can have a negative connotation, although many who have access to heat may enjoy the snowy season from their homes.

For one final example, consider how the word *fly* has a different meaning in each of the following sentences:

- "His trousers have a fly on them."
- "He swatted the fly on his trousers."
- "Those are some fly trousers."
- "They went fly fishing."
- "She hates to fly."
- "If humans were meant to fly, they would have wings."

As strategies, readers can try substituting a familiar word for an unfamiliar one and see whether it makes sense in the sentence. They can also identify other words in a sentence, offering clues to an unfamiliar word's meaning.

Interpreting Nonliteral Language

Authors of a text use language with multiple levels of meaning for many different reasons. When the meaning of a text requires directness, the author will use literal language to provide clarity. On the other hand, an author will use figurative language to produce an emotional effect or facilitate a deeper understanding of a word or passage. For example, a set of instructions on how to use a computer would require literal language. However, a commentary on the social implications of immigration bans might contain a wide range of figurative language to elicit an empathetic response. A single text can have a mixture of both literal and figurative language.

Literal Language

Literal language uses words in accordance with their actual definition. Many informational texts employ literal language because it is straightforward and precise. Documents such as instructions, proposals, technical documents, and workplace documents use literal language for the majority of their writing, so there is no confusion or complexity of meaning for readers to decipher. The information is best communicated through clear and precise language. The following are brief examples of literal language:

- I cook with olive oil.
- There are 365 days in a year.
- My grandma's name is Barbara.
- Yesterday we had some scattered thunderstorms.
- World War II began in 1939.
- Blue whales are the largest species of whale.

Figurative Language

Not meant to be taken literal, **figurative language** is useful when the author of a text wants to produce an emotional effect in the reader or add a heightened complexity to the meaning of the text. Figurative language is used more heavily in texts such as literary fiction, poetry, critical theory, and speeches. It goes beyond literal language, allowing readers to form associations they wouldn't normally form. Using language in a figurative sense appeals to the imagination of the reader. It is important to remember that words themselves are signifiers of objects and ideas and not the objects and ideas themselves. Figurative language can highlight this detachment by creating multiple associations but it also points to the fact that language is fluid and capable of creating a world full of linguistic possibilities. It can be argued that figurative language is the heart of communication even outside of fiction and poetry. People connect through humor, metaphors, cultural allusions, puns, and symbolism in their everyday rhetoric. The following are terms associated with figurative language:

Simile

A **simile** is a comparison of two things using *like*, *than*, or *as*. A simile usually takes objects that have no apparent connection, such as a mind and an orchid, and compares them:

> His mind was as complex and rare as a field of ghost orchids.

Similes encourage new, fresh perspectives on objects or ideas that wouldn't otherwise occur. Unlike similes, metaphors are comparisons that do not use *like*, *than*, or *as*. So, a metaphor from the above example would be:

> His mind was a field of ghost orchids.

Similes highlight the comparison by focusing on the figurative side of the language, elucidating more the author's intent: a field of ghost orchids is something complex and rare, like the mind of a genius. Metaphors, however, provide a beautiful yet somewhat equivocal comparison.

Metaphor

A popular use of figurative language, **metaphors** compare objects or ideas directly, asserting that something *is* a certain thing, even if it isn't. The following is an example of a metaphor used by author Virginia Woolf:

> Books are the mirrors of the soul.

165

Metaphors have a *vehicle* and a *tenor*. The tenor is "books" and the vehicle is "mirrors of the soul." That is, the tenor is what is meant to be described, and the vehicle is that which carries the weight of the comparison. In this metaphor, perhaps the author means to say that written language (books) reflect a person's most inner thoughts and desires.

Dead metaphors are phrases that have been overused to the point where the figurative language has taken on a literal meaning, like "crystal clear." This phrase is in such popular use that the meaning seems literal ("perfectly clear") even when it is not.

Finally, an extended metaphor is one that goes on for several paragraphs,, or even an entire text. "On First Looking into Chapman's Homer," a poem by John Keats, begins, "Much have I travell'd in the realms of gold," and goes on to explain the first time he hears Chapman's translation of Homer's writing. We see the extended metaphor begin in the first line. Keats is comparing travelling into "realms of gold" and exploration of new lands to the act of hearing a certain kind of literature for the first time. The extended metaphor goes on until the end of the poem where Keats stands "Silent, upon a peak in Darien," having heard the end of Chapman's translation. Keats has gained insight into new lands (new text) and is the richer for it.

The following are brief definitions and examples of popular figurative language:

- **Onomatopoeia**: A word that, when spoken, imitates the sound to which it refers. Ex: "We heard a loud *boom* while driving to the beach yesterday."

- **Personification**: When human characteristics are given to animals, inanimate objects, or abstractions. An example would be in William Wordsworth's poem "Daffodils" where he sees a "crowd... / of golden daffodils... / Fluttering and dancing in the breeze." Dancing is usually a characteristic attributed solely to humans, but Wordsworth personifies the daffodils here as a crowd of people dancing.

- **Hyperbole**: A hyperbole is an exaggeration. Ex: "I'm so tired I could sleep for centuries."

- **Pun**: Puns are used in popular culture to invoke humor by exploiting the meanings of words. They can also be used in literature to give hints of meaning in unexpected places. In "Romeo and Juliet," Mercutio makes a pun after he is stabbed by Tybalt: "look for me tomorrow and you will find me a grave man."

- **Imagery**: This is a collection of images given to the reader by the author. If a text is rich in imagery, it is easier for the reader to imagine themselves in the author's world. One example of a poem that relies on imagery is William Carlos Williams' "The Red Wheelbarrow":

> so much depends
> upon
> a red wheel
> barrow
> glazed with rain
> water
> beside the white
> chickens

The starkness of the imagery and the placement of the words in this poem bring to life the images of a purely simple world. Through its imagery, this poem tells a story in just sixteen words.

- **Symbolism**: A symbol is used to represent an idea or belief system. For example, poets in Western civilization have been using the symbol of a rose for hundreds of years to represent love. In Japan, poets have used the firefly to symbolize passionate love, and sometimes even spirits of those who have died. Symbols can also express powerful political commentary and can be used in propaganda.

Denotation and Connotation

Denotation, a word's explicit definition, is often set in comparison to connotation, the emotional, cultural, social, or personal implications associated with a word. Denotation is more of an objective definition, whereas connotation can be more subjective, although many connotative meanings of words are similar for certain cultures. The denotative meanings of words are usually based on facts, and the connotative meanings of words are usually based on emotion.

Here are some examples of words and their denotative and connotative meanings in Western culture:

Word	Denotative Meaning	Connotative Meaning
Home	A permanent place where one lives, usually as a member of a family.	A place of warmth; a place of familiarity; comforting; a place of safety and security. "Home" usually has a positive connotation.
Snake	A long reptile with no limbs and strong jaws that moves along the ground; some snakes have a poisonous bite.	An evil omen; a slithery creature (human or nonhuman) that is deceitful or unwelcome. "Snake" usually has a negative connotation.
Winter	A season of the year that is the coldest, usually from December to February in the northern hemisphere and from June to August in the southern hemisphere.	Circle of life, especially that of death and dying; cold or icy; dark and gloomy; hibernation, sleep, or rest. "Winter" can have a negative connotation, although many who have access to heat may enjoy the snowy season from their homes.

Practice Quiz

1. Ecologist: If we do not act now, more than one hundred animal species will be extinct by the end of the decade. The best way to save them is to sell hunting licenses for endangered species. Hunters can pay for the right to kill old and lame animals. Otherwise, there's no way to fund our conservation efforts.

Which one of the following assumptions does the ecologist's argument rely upon?
    a.   Hunting licenses for non-endangered species aren't profitable.
    b.   All one hundred animal species must be saved.
    c.   The new hunting license revenue will fund conservation efforts.
    d.   Conservation efforts should have begun last decade.
    e.   It is physically impossible for old and lame animals to reproduce.

2. Politician: Every cigarette smoked costs the city more than $1,000. Smokers are bankrupting our healthcare system. Discarded filters pollute our waterways, and second-hand smoke poisons our airways, threatening all pedestrians. The city must ban tobacco smoking immediately.

Which one of the following, if true, would most strengthen the politician's argument?
    a.   Placing a high tax on tobacco hasn't reduced smoking at all.
    b.   Smoking cigarettes is already banned in bars and restaurants.
    c.   The city's waterways and airways also suffer from heavy industrial pollution.
    d.   Many tobacco substitutes are readily available.
    e.   The state government is also considering a ban on tobacco.

The next question is based on the following passage, which is a preface for Poems by Alexander Pushkin *by Ivan Panin.*

> I do not believe there are as many as five examples of deviation from the literalness of the text. Once only, I believe, have I transposed two lines for convenience of translation; the other deviations are (*if* they are such) a substitution of an *and* for a comma in order to make now and then the reading of a line musical. With these exceptions, I have sacrificed *everything* to faithfulness of rendering. My object was to make Pushkin himself, without a prompter, speak to English readers. To make him thus speak in a foreign tongue was indeed to place him at a disadvantage; and music and rhythm and harmony are indeed fine things, but truth is finer still. I wished to present not what Pushkin would have said, or should have said, if he had written in English, but what he does say in Russian. That, stripped from all ornament of his wonderful melody and grace of form, as he is in a translation, he still, even in the hard English tongue, soothes and stirs, is in itself a sign that through the individual soul of Pushkin sings that universal soul whose strains appeal forever to man, in whatever clime, under whatever sky.

3. According to the author, _____ is the most important aim of translation work.
   a. to retain the beauty of the work
   b. to retain the truth of the work
   c. to retain the melody of the work
   d. to retain the form of the work

4. Journalist: Our newspaper should only consider the truth in its reporting. When a party is clearly in the wrong, like if he or she is spreading a pernicious, false narrative, their position should never be presented alongside the truth without comment. The purpose of journalism is to deliver facts and context. Both sides of an issue should be called for comment, but their responses should be framed appropriately, especially when there's a potential conflict of interest or source of bias at play. Our editorial board needs to seriously consider how our newspaper isn't currently meeting these basic standards, exposing us to charges of bias from all sides.

The primary purpose of the journalist's argument is to _____
   a. persuade the newspaper to adopt a more rigorous approach to journalism.
   b. defend the newspaper against charges of bias in its reporting.
   c. argue for the newspaper to hire more journalists with the appropriate skills.
   d. define the professional responsibilities of a journalist.

The next question is based on the passage entitled Architecture and Democracy *by Claude Bragdon.*

The world war represents not the triumph, but the birth of democracy. The true ideal of democracy—the rule of a people by the *demos*, or group soul—is a thing unrealized. How then is it possible to consider or discuss an architecture of democracy—the shadow of a shade? It is not possible to do so with any degree of finality, but by an intention of consciousness upon this juxtaposition of ideas—architecture and democracy—signs of the times may yield new meanings, relations may emerge between things apparently unrelated, and the future, always existent in every present moment, may be evoked by that strange magic which resides in the human mind.

Architecture, at its worst as at its best, reflects always a true image of the thing that produced it; a building is revealing even though it is false, just as the face of a liar tells the thing his words endeavor to conceal. This being so, let us make such architecture as is ours declare to us our true estate.

The architecture of the United States, from the period of the Civil War, up to the beginning of the present crisis, everywhere reflects a struggle to be free of a vicious and depraved form of feudalism, grown strong under the very ægis of democracy. The qualities that made feudalism endeared and enduring; qualities written in beauty on the cathedral cities of mediaeval Europe—faith, worship, loyalty, magnanimity—were either vanished or banished from this pseudo-democratic, aridly scientific feudalism, leaving an inheritance of strife and tyranny—a strife grown mean, a tyranny grown prudent, but full of sinister power the weight of which we have by no means ceased to feel.

Power, strangely mingled with timidity; ingenuity, frequently misdirected; ugliness, the result of a false ideal of beauty—these in general characterize the architecture of our immediate past; an architecture "without ancestry or hope of posterity," an architecture devoid of coherence or conviction; willing to lie, willing to steal. What impression such a city as Chicago or Pittsburgh might have made upon some denizen of those cathedral-crowned feudal cities of the past we do not know. He would certainly have been amazed at its giant energy, and probably revolted at its grimy dreariness. We are wont to pity the mediaeval man for the dirt he lived in, even while smoke greys our sky and dirt permeates the

169

very air we breathe: we think of castles as grim and cathedrals as dim, but they were beautiful and gay with color compared with the grim, dim canyons of our city streets.

5. The author's attitude toward modern architecture can best be characterized as:
   a.   Narcissistic
   b.   Aggrieved
   c.   Virtuous
   d.   Sarcastic

See answers on next page.

Answer Explanations

1. C: Choice *C* correctly identifies a necessary assumption in the argument. The argument is that hunting licenses for endangered species should be sold to support conservation efforts. If the revenue from those licenses isn't funding conservation efforts, then the ecologist's entire argument falls apart.

Choice *A* is incorrect. Hunting licenses for non-endangered species could be profitable, and the ecologist's argument wouldn't be impacted one way or another. The ecologist could still argue that hunting licenses should be expanded to further increase funding for species that are still endangered.

Choice *B* is incorrect. The ecologist would definitely agree that all one hundred animal species should be saved, but it isn't a necessary assumption. The argument would function the same if the ultimate goal were to save ten endangered animal species.

Choice *D* is incorrect. Like Choice *B*, the ecologist would agree that conservation efforts should've begun earlier, but it isn't a necessary assumption.

Choice *E* is incorrect. The ecologist likely supports hunting licenses for endangered species due to old and lame animals' diminished capacity to reproduce. But reproduction being physically impossible isn't a necessary assumption. The argument would be the same even if those animals were reproducing on a limited basis.

2. A: Choice *A* correctly identifies the statement that most strengthens the argument. The argument is that the city must ban smoking, because every cigarette that's smoked costs the city $1,000. Choice *A* eliminates a possible counterargument for a less extreme measure—taxing tobacco. Since the tax didn't work, the city would be more likely to pursue a total ban.

Choice *B* is incorrect. If smoking cigarettes was already banned in bars and restaurants, it might strengthen the argument by laying the foundation for a total ban. However, a total ban is much more extreme, and Choice *A* is stronger since it eliminates a primary counterargument against changing the law.

Choice *C* is incorrect. Non-smoking related pollution in the waterways and airways might increase the need to avoid additional pollutants, but it's not as strong as Choice *A*.

Choice *D* is incorrect. The existence of tobacco substitutes doesn't justify banning tobacco. It also doesn't necessarily mean that they'll be better for the healthcare system and environment.

Choice *E* is incorrect. The state government's decision to ban tobacco could encourage the city government to do the same, but Choice *A* has a more direct impact on that debate as it pertains to the city.

3. B:. The author says that "music and rhythm and harmony are indeed fine things, but truth is finer still," which means that the author stuck to a literal translation instead of changing up any words that might make the English language translation sound better.

4. A: Choice *A* correctly identifies the argument's primary purpose. The purpose is clearly persuasive, and the focus is on the newspaper's approach to journalism. According to the conclusion, the newspaper isn't currently meeting basic editorial standards, and the journalist wants the newspaper to adopt the best practices described in the argument.

Choice *B* is incorrect. The journalist mentions that the newspaper is currently exposed to charges of bias from all sides, but the argument isn't defending the newspaper. It's calling for a change in editorial policy.

Choice *C* is incorrect. Although the journalist might agree that the newspaper needs to shake up its staff, the primary focus is on the newspaper's approach to journalism.

Choice *D* is incorrect. The journalist touches on the professional responsibilities of a journalist, but it's in the context of the newspaper's failings, which Choice *D* doesn't reference.

5. B: Considering the strong, negative language used throughout the passage, such as "power, strangely mingled with timidity," "ingenuity, frequently misdirected," and "grim, dim canyons of our city streets," one can assume that the author is annoyed, offended, and disgruntled by modern architecture. Therefore, Choice *B*, aggrieved, is the most likely choice. None of the other answer choices accurately match the author's attitude.

Writing

Expression of Ideas

Development

Producing an Argumentative Essay to Support a Claim Using Relevant and Sufficient Evidence

An argumentative essay is written for the purpose of persuading readers to agree with the author's position with the subject matter about which he or she is writing. Rather than presenting information objectively, the author treats the subject matter subjectively so that the information presented supports their position. In their argumentation, the author presents information that refutes or weakens opposing positions.

An argumentative essay typically includes the following five main elements:

- Introduction: In the introduction, the writer should draw readers in, encourage readers to perceive him or her as a trustworthy authority on the subject, and establish the purpose or thesis. Shocking statistics, new ways of restating issues, or quotations or anecdotes focusing the text can pique readers' interest. Personal statements, parallel instances, or analogies can also begin introductions—so can bold thesis statements if the author believes readers will agree. The introduction should typically narrow down to a clear, sound thesis statement. If readers cannot locate one sentence in the introduction explicitly stating the writer's position or the point the writer supports, the writer probably has not refined the introduction sufficiently.

- Narration: In the narration portion, the writer summarizes pertinent background information, informs the readers of anything they need to know regarding the circumstances and environment surrounding and/or stimulating the argument, and establishes what is at risk or at stake in the issue or topic. Literature reviews are common examples of narrations in academic writing.

- Confirmation: The confirmation states all claims supporting the thesis and furnishes evidence for each claim, arranging this material in logical order—e.g. from most obvious to most subtle or strongest to weakest. It is where the writer explains why he or she believes the stated thesis. The writer builds a chain of reasoning by developing several individual supporting claims and explaining why that evidence supports each claim and also supports the overall thesis of the argument.

- Refutation and Concession: The refutation and concession discuss opposing views and anticipate readers' objections without weakening the thesis, yet permitting as many oppositions as possible. In the refutation, writers disarm reader opposition by anticipating and answering their possible objections, persuading them to accept the author's viewpoint. In the concession, writers can concede those opposing viewpoints with which they agree.

- Summation: The summation strengthens the argument while summarizing it, supplying a strong conclusion and showing readers the superiority of the author's solution. Writers should revisit the issues and the narration part of the argument, reminding readers of what is at stake.

Addressing the Assigned Task Appropriately

One consideration when planning and writing an essay—whether argumentative, informative, or otherwise—is the intended audience of readers. Writers should tailor their language, reasoning, and inclusion or exclusion of relevant background information depending on the perceived expertise, education, and age of the majority of anticipated readers. For example, if writing a persuasive essay about the need to increase our country's reliance on renewable energy resources for power, the author must decide how much background information to provide about the types, availability, pros and cons, cost, etc. of renewable resources as well as those of more conventional finite resources such as coal and oil.

If the writer is intending their work to be read by an audience of adults reasonably informed about the subject matter, the need for significant background information is unnecessary and may even detract from the strength of the argument by bogging down the text with extensive data, statistics, and textbook-like information dumping. In contrast, if the essay is intended for a less informed population with little knowledge about energy and resources, such as a class of middle school students, background information would be important so that readers could follow the logic of the argument and understand the factors involved in the issue. Moreover, the language and vocabulary used for these two populations should also differ somewhat. Even greater contrast would exist between educated adults and young children.

While it's not always possible to accurately predict the entire audience for a written piece of work (and there's likely too much variety within the audience to sufficiently tailor the writing to each subset), writers should do their best to consider the likely audience or write for a specific audience in mind to facilitate their readers' comprehension and reception of the essay. On the Praxis Core Writing test, essays should be geared toward an audience of educated adults. Language, reasoning, structure, and information should be expressed accordingly.

Providing and Sustaining a Clear Focus or Thesis

The **thesis statement** typically appears near the end of the first paragraph of the introduction. It should clearly state the writer's position on the subject matter in a single sentence. It should be easy for readers to quickly identify the thesis statement. The thesis itself should be stated clearly in language that avoids ambiguity. It should be concise, while still providing ample verbiage to express the crux of the writer's main idea.

The thesis should provide a road map for the entire essay in that the writer should then use the subsequent body paragraphs of the essay to provide supporting details and reasons that he or she believes whatever is stated in the thesis. The thesis statement should be used to focus the entire essay. Writers should be mindful that whatever details, examples, and explanations they provide stay on topic with their thesis and/or the main idea of the essay. The strength of an argument is decreased if readers are taken on irrelevant tangents or provided superfluous information that veers off topic.

While it may be appealing to pad an essay with some of the inevitably large amount of research obtained while working on it or demonstrate one's command and expertise on the subject by inserting lots of facts and information, doing so actually detracts from the quality of the essay and the degree to which it logically flows. When choosing to include a given example, reason, or idea, writers should ask themselves if that item is unique (in that it hasn't already been stated elsewhere in the essay), if it is relevant to the main idea or thesis, if it adds anything to the argument, and if it will enhance readers' comprehension and support of the essay as a whole. Points or sentences that fail to accomplish one of these goals should be omitted.

174

Using Supporting Reasons, Examples, and Details

Arguments need supporting reasons and examples to support the points the author is trying to make. Unsubstantiated claims can weaken an argument because they give reason to question the credibility and accuracy of the writer's ideas and points. Tangible details and relatable examples also help readers connect with the ideas and "buy in" to the author's ideas. They help bring the ideas to life and provide evidence of their validity. It's particularly important to provide details that facilitate the ability of readers follow the logic of an argument and connect the points made and their implications. Writers should use a variety of credible primary and secondary sources to substantiate their points. It is important to credit the source and cite it appropriately to give the original author due credit and so that readers can locate the source of their own, should they be interested in further information.

Organization

Organizing and Developing Ideas Logically

An essay is only successful if readers can understand its reasoning, follow its logic, determine its focus or thesis, and understand the included points that support the main idea. Readers must have confidence that the writer is presenting the full gamut of evidence and presenting the ideas without bias. If readers cannot follow the chain of reasoning or easily and decisively identify the thesis, they are likely to stop reading or walk away without being convinced of the point that the author intended to support. Likewise, a reader will not be persuaded to adopt the author's opinion (if it is different from their own) if the essay is disjointed, if the ideas don't flow or follow logically, if conflicting points are argued such that the thesis is not consistent throughout, and if the language and writing style is not coherent. It is the writer's responsibility to guide readers through the essay and through its reasoning.

The former involves producing writing that is clear, coherent, grammatically correct, and understandable. The use of transitional words and phrases that help link ideas with the appropriate connection will remove the guesswork for readers. Words like *thus, consequently, therefore, as such, however, besides*, and *accordingly* are helpful in this regard. It is also useful to include words that insinuate or shepherd readers toward a particular interpretation of statements that the writer wants the reader to adopt after reading the statement. Words like *fortunately, unfortunately*, and *thankfully* are examples of these types of qualifiers. The takeaway of a sentence, or it's emotional impact, can vary significantly by the tacking on of one of these words. As such, such words can be useful tools for a writer when crafting an argumentative piece to persuade readers to side with the writer's opinion. Consider the following example and notice how the meaning of the same sentence varies significantly when the sole qualifying word changes:

> Fortunately, her role as hall monitor has changed.

> Unfortunately, her role as hall monitor has changed.

While this sentence is short and it is difficult to get a sense of who "she" is and why her role as hall monitor has changed because there's no surrounding context, it is possible to see how the two sentences carry opposite meanings. In the first, it's a good thing that her role has changed. Perhaps she was bad at her role as hall monitor, disliked it, or now has a better job. Although we don't know why it's a favorable change, we are left with the takeaway that this change is a positive thing. The opposite can be said for the second sentence. Here, we see that regardless of the reason she's no longer acting as hall monitor, it's a negative change.

Lastly, writers can include temporal words like *first, next*, and *finally* to help readers follow along in the list of evidence or points made. For example, if the writer asserts that there are four reasons why renewable energy sources are actually the most energy-efficient choices these days, he or she could use *firstly...,* *secondly...,* *thirdly...,* *lastly....* Writers will increase the effectiveness of their arguments and the ease with which they can be followed by using language that helps guide the reader.

Transitional Words and Phrases

In writing, some sentences naturally lead to others, whereas in other cases, a new sentence expresses a new idea. Transitional phrases connect sentences and the ideas they convey, which makes the writing coherent. Transitional language also guides the reader from one thought to the next. For example, when pointing out an objection to the previous idea, starting a sentence with "However," "But," or "On the other hand" is transitional. When adding another idea or detail, writers use "Also," "In addition," "Furthermore," "Further," "Moreover," "Not only," etc. Readers have difficulty perceiving connections between ideas without such transitional wording.

Sentence Fluency

For fluent composition, writers must use a variety of sentence types and structures, and also ensure that they smoothly flow together when they are read. To accomplish this, they must first be able to identify fluent writing when they read it. This includes being able to distinguish among simple, compound, complex, and compound-complex sentences in text; to observe variations among sentence types, lengths, and beginnings; and to notice figurative language and understand how it augments sentence length and imparts musicality. Once students/writers recognize superior fluency, they should revise their own writing to be more readable and fluent. They must be able to apply acquired skills to revisions before being able to apply them to new drafts.

One strategy for revising writing to increase its sentence fluency is flipping sentences. This involves rearranging the word order in a sentence without deleting, changing, or adding any words. For example, the student or other writer who has written the sentence, "We went bicycling on Saturday" can revise it to, "On Saturday, we went bicycling." Another technique is using appositives. An appositive is a phrase or word that renames or identifies another adjacent word or phrase. Writers can revise for sentence fluency by inserting main phrases/words from one shorter sentence into another shorter sentence, combining them into one longer sentence, e.g. from "My cat Peanut is a gray and brown tabby. He loves hunting rats." to "My cat Peanut, a gray and brown tabby, loves hunting rats." Revisions can also connect shorter sentences by using conjunctions and commas and removing repeated words: "Scott likes eggs. Scott is allergic to eggs" becomes "Scott likes eggs, but he is allergic to them."

One technique for revising writing to increase sentence fluency is "padding" short, simple sentences by adding phrases that provide more details specifying why, how, when, and/or where something took place. For example, a writer might have these two simple sentences: "I went to the market. I purchased a cake." To revise these, the writer can add the following informative dependent and independent clauses and prepositional phrases, respectively: "Before my mother woke up, I sneaked out of the house and went to the supermarket. As a birthday surprise, I purchased a cake for her." When revising sentences to make them longer, writers must also punctuate them correctly to change them from simple sentences to compound, complex, or compound-complex sentences.

One way writers can increase fluency is by varying the beginnings of sentences. Writers do this by starting most of their sentences with different words and phrases rather than monotonously repeating the same ones across multiple sentences. Another way writers can increase fluency is by varying the lengths of sentences. Since run-on sentences are incorrect, writers make sentences longer by also converting them from simple to compound, complex, and compound-complex sentences. The coordination and subordination involved in these also give the text more variation and interest, hence more fluency.

Here are a few more ways writers can increase fluency:

- Varying the transitional language and conjunctions used makes sentences more fluent.
- Writing sentences with a variety of rhythms by using prepositional phrases.
- Varying sentence structure adds fluency.

Effective Language Use

<u>Word Choice</u>
Idiomatic Expressions
An **idiomatic expression** is a phrase that has an understood meaning that is entirely different from the meaning of the individual words within the phrase. For example, consider the following sentence that includes a common idiomatic phrase:

> I know Phil is coming to visit this weekend because I heard it straight from the horse's mouth.

The speaker of this sentence did not consult a horse nor hear anything uttered from a horse in relation to Phil's visit. Instead, "straight from the horse's mouth" is an idiom that means the information came directly from an original or reliable source. As in the sentence above, it often means whatever said should be taken as truth because it was spoken by the person to which it pertains (in this case, Phil). The phrase is derived from the fact that sellers of horses at auctions would sometimes try to lie about the age of the horse. However, the size and shape of a horse's teeth can provide a fairly accurate estimate of the horse's true age. Therefore, the truth regarding the horse's age essentially comes straight from their mouth. The idiomatic expression came to mean getting the truth in any situation.

Finding errors in idiomatic expressions can be difficult because it requires familiarity with the idiom. Because there are more than one thousand idioms in the English language, memorizing all of them is impractical. However, it is helpful to review the most common ones. There are many webpages dedicated to listing and explaining frequently used idioms.

Errors in the idiomatic expressions are typically one of two types. The idiomatic expression may be stated improperly, or it may be used in an incorrect context. In the first type of issue, the prepositions used are often incorrect. For example, it might say "straight in the horse's mouth" or "straight with the horse's mouth." In the second error type, the idiomatic expression is used improperly because the meaning it carries does not make sense in the context in which it appears. Consider the following:

> He was looking straight from the horse's mouth when he complained about the phone his father bought him.

Here, the writer has confused the idiom "straight from the horse's mouth" with "looking a gift horse in the mouth," which means to find fault in a gift or favor.

Either type of error can be difficult to detect and correct without prior knowledge of the idiomatic phrase. Practicing usage of idioms and studying their origins can help you remember their meanings and precise wordings, which will then help you identify and correct errors in their usage.

Frequently Confused Words

The English language can be confusing and it is common for students to make mistakes in word choice, meaning, or spelling. **Homophones** are words that sound the same in speech, but have different spellings and meanings. For example, *to, too,* and *two* all sound alike, but have three different spellings and meanings. Homophones with different spellings are also called *heterographs. Homographs* are words that are spelled identically, but have different meanings. If they also have different pronunciations, they are heteronyms. For instance, *tear* pronounced one way means a drop of liquid formed by the eye; pronounced another way, it means to rip. Homophones that are also homographs are **homonyms**. For example, *bark* can mean the outside of a tree or a dog's vocalization; both meanings have the same spelling. *Stalk* can mean a plant stem or to pursue and/or harass somebody; these are spelled and pronounced the same. *Rose* can mean a flower or the past tense of *rise.* Many non-linguists confuse things by using "homonym" to mean sets of words that are homophones but not homographs, and also those that are homographs but not homophones.

The word *row* can mean to use oars to propel a boat; a linear arrangement of objects or print; or an argument. It is pronounced the same with the first two meanings, but differently with the third. Because it is spelled identically regardless, all three meanings are homographs. However, the two meanings pronounced the same are homophones, whereas the one with the different pronunciation is a *heteronym.* By contrast, the word *read* means to peruse language, whereas the word *reed* refers to a marsh plant. Because these are pronounced the same way, they are homophones; because they are spelled differently, they are heterographs. Homonyms are both homophones and *homographs*—pronounced and spelled identically, but with different meanings. One distinction between homonyms is of those with separate, unrelated etymologies, called "true" homonyms, e.g. *skate* meaning a fish or *skate* meaning to glide over ice/water. Those with common origins are called *polysemes* or *polysemous homonyms,* e.g. the *mouth* of an animal/human or of a river.

There are some words that do not abide by the typical rules when turning them into their plural form, and it's common for students to struggle forming and using these irregular plurals. While many words in English can become plural by adding –s or –es to the end, there are some words that have irregular plural forms. One type includes words that are spelled the same whether they are singular or plural, such as deer, fish, salmon, trout, sheep, moose, offspring, species, aircraft, etc. The spelling rule for making these words plural is simple: they do not change. Other irregular English plurals change form based on vowel shifts, linguistic mutations, or grammatical and spelling conventions from their languages of origin, like Latin or German. Some examples include *tooth* and *teeth, man* and *men, child* and *children,* and *person* and *people.*

Wrong Word Usage

One of the most common reasons that a writer chooses the wrong word for a given application is if the word has multiple meanings and spellings. Words that have different meanings and spellings but sound the same are called **homophones**. Whereas listeners must rely entirely on context to differentiate spoken homophone meanings, readers with good spelling knowledge have a distinct advantage since homophones are spelled differently. For instance, *their* means belonging to them; *there* indicates location; and *they're* is a contraction of *they are,* despite different meanings, they all sound the same. *Lacks* can be a plural noun or a present-tense, third-person singular verb; either way it refers to absence—*deficiencies* as a plural noun, and *is deficient in* as a verb. But *lax* is an adjective that means loose, slack, relaxed, uncontrolled, or negligent. These two spellings, derivations, and meanings are completely different. With speech, listeners cannot know spelling and must use context; but with print, readers with spelling knowledge can differentiate them with or without context.

178

One other issue that students may make is misspelling certain difficult words. Spelling errors not only negatively affect the polished feel of an essay, but they can result in confusion, particularly if the spelling mistake results in the formation of a different, unintended word. One source of spelling errors is not knowing whether to drop the final letter *e* from a word when its form is changed; some words retain the final *e* when another syllable is added while others lose it. For example, *true* becomes *truly; argue* becomes *arguing; come* becomes *coming; write* becomes *writing;* and *judge* becomes *judging.* In these examples, the final *e* is dropped before adding the ending. But *severe* becomes *severely; complete* becomes *completely; sincere* becomes *sincerely; argue* becomes *argued;* and *care* becomes *careful.* In these instances, the final *e* is retained before adding the ending. Note that some words, like argue in these examples, drops the final e when the –ing ending is added to indicate the participial form, but the regular past tense form keeps the e and adds a –d to make it argued.

Other commonly misspelled English words are those containing the vowel combinations ei and ie. Many people confuse these two. Some examples of words with the ei combination include:

> *ceiling, conceive, leisure, receive, weird, their, either, foreign, sovereign, neither, neighbors, seize, forfeit, counterfeit, height, weight, protein,* and *freight*

Words with *ie* include *piece, believe, chief, field, friend, grief, relief, mischief, siege, niece, priest, fierce, pierce, achieve, retrieve, hygiene, science,* and *diesel.* A rule that also functions as a mnemonic device is "I before E except after C, or when sounded like A as in 'neighbor' or 'weigh'." However, it is obvious from the list above that many exceptions exist.

People often misspell certain words by confusing whether they have the vowel a, e, or i. For example, in the following correctly spelled words, the vowel in boldface is the one people typically get wrong by substituting one of the others for it:

> cem**e**tery, quant**i**ties, ben**e**fit, priv**i**lege, unpleas**a**nt, sep**a**rate, independ**e**nt, excell**e**nt, cat**e**gories, indispens**a**ble, and irrelev**a**nt

Some words with final syllables that sound the same when spoken but are spelled differently include *unpleasant, independent, excellent,* and *irrelevant.* Another source of misspelling is whether or not to double consonants when adding suffixes. For example, double the last consonant before –ed and –ing endings in controlled, beginning, forgetting, admitted, occurred, referred, and hopping; but do not double before the suffix in *shining, poured, sweating, loving, hating, smiling,* and *hoping.*

One final example of common misspellings involves either the failure to include silent letters or the converse of adding extraneous letters. If a letter is not pronounced in speech, it is easy to leave it out in writing. For example, some people omit the silent *u* in *g**u**arantee,* overlook the first *r* in *su**r**prise,* leave out the *z* in *reali**z**e,* fail to double the *m* in *reco**mm**end,* leave out the middle *i* from *asp**i**rin,* and exclude the *p* from *tem**p**erature.* The converse error, adding extra letters, is common in words like *until* by adding a second *l* at the end; or by inserting a superfluous syllabic *a* or *e* in the middle of *athletic,* reproducing a common mispronunciation.

Redundancy

Redundancy, in terms of word choice, refers to repeating the same words or phrases or using different words to restate the same thing. Writers should strive to be concise in stating their points and backing them up with adequate and relevant examples. Wordiness detracts from the overall takeaways from an essay and redundancy can bore readers. State the point and move forward. It only makes sense to reword it and reiterate the point if it needs explicit emphasis.

An example of wordiness can be seen in the following sentence:

In spite of the fact that I stayed home from school today, I still feel sick.

In spite of the fact is wordy. The five-word phrase can be replaced by the single word *although*.

Although I stayed home from school today, I still feel sick.

The following sentence demonstrates redundancy:

We often shop there most days .

Instead, one of the following two options is preferable:

We often shop there.

We shop there most days.

Contractions

Contractions are formed by joining two words together, omitting one or more letters from one of the component words, and replacing the omitted letter(s) with an apostrophe. An obvious yet often forgotten rule for spelling contractions is to place the apostrophe where the letters were omitted. For example, didn't is a contraction of did not; therefore, the apostrophe replaces the "o" that is omitted from the "not." Another common error is confusing contractions with *possessives* because both include apostrophes, e.g. spelling the possessive *its* as "it's," which is a contraction of "it is"; spelling the possessive *their* as "they're," a contraction of "they are"; spelling the possessive *whose* as "who's," a contraction of "who is"; or spelling the possessive *your* as "you're," a contraction of "you are."

Style, Tone, and Mood

Choosing Words and Phrases for Effect

Skillful writers are artists. They breathe life into the words they've written by choosing language that provides details that enable their readers to visualize what they have read and that makes the writing more exciting and engaging. Adjectives, adverbs, and more descriptive noun and verb choices can all help animate a piece of writing and make it more memorable. More specific words can also be used instead of vague or general ones. For example, instead of *I walked to the steps and slowly got in the water,* the sentence could be *I gingerly walked to the steps, and slowly eased myself into the water.* This second variation paints a clearer picture that the speaker is hesitant to swim. Writers should try to vary the words they choose to use as well to reduce the monotony of repetitiveness.

Choosing Words and Phrases to Convey Ideas Precisely

Writers communicate their ideas through their word choice and the way they structure the chosen words into sentences and paragraphs. The best way for writers to ensure that readers interpret a piece of writing appropriately is to be as precise as possible with word choice. **Synonyms** are words with similar meanings, like *happy* and *glad* or *arrogant* and *pompous*. While a piece of writing that uses a variety of vocabulary words is often more interesting to read and less monotonous, it's important for writers to ensure that the specific words chosen best convey the intended meaning. Even synonyms have nuances between them and just because a certain word sounds more impressive or novel, it does not mean it's necessarily the best choice in the context of the piece of writing.

Maintaining Consistency in Style and Tone

The style and tone of a piece of writing should match the intended audience and purpose. The **style** of a piece of writing refers to the way the writer has composed it. It entails the specific words chosen, the selection and arrangement of sentence structures, and the paragraph structure. The **tone** of a piece relates to the how the writer has conveyed their ideas. A tone, for example, might be serious, humorous, or somber. The tone of most formal pieces is impersonal or authoritative because the purpose is to inform and demonstrate a command of a topic or idea. Argumentative essays tend to be more emotional and passionate, as they usually attempt to evoke an emotional reaction in the reader.

Writers should strive to maintain consistency in the style and tone used in a given essay. For example, if the essay uses formal writing, it should be free from informal language, slang, and grammatical rule bending that is somewhat more permissible in conversational or informal writing. If the tone of a piece is authoritative and the writer is striving to assert himself or herself as an expert, the writer should not switch to a silly or playful tone. Writers can help ensure that style and tone remain consistent by maintaining the same "voice" in a given essay and remembering to write in a way that reflects the purpose and audience of the piece.

Standard English Conventions

Sentence Structure

Sentence Structures

All complete sentences contain the same two basic components: a subject and a predicate. The **subject** is who or what is doing the action or being described in the sentence. The **predicate** is everything else in the sentence; the predicate includes the **verb**, which describes the action the subject is doing or the condition of the subject. The predicate, therefore, describes what the subject does or is.

Although all sentences contain these same two basic elements, there are different ways that the subject and predicate can be combined. There are four general sentence structures used in the English language.

Simple sentences contain one subject and one verb, but still express a complete thought:

> The mouse ate cheese.

The subject is *the mouse*. The verb is *ate*.

A sentence can still be considered a simple sentence if it has a compound subject or compound verb. A **compound noun** or verb consists of more than one elements. The following sentence contains a compound subject:

> *The mouse and the gerbil* ate cheese.

When two or more simple sentences are joined together to form a single sentence with more than one subject-verb combinations, it is considered a **compound sentence:**

> *The mouse ate cheese,* and *the boy built him a maze.*

This structure contains two independent clauses: (1) *the mouse ate cheese* and (2) *the boy built him a maze*. These two clauses are independent because they can stand on their own. However, they are combined with a comma and a coordinating conjunction *(and)* to form a compound sentence. Other coordinating conjunctions, such as *but* and *so* can also be used to form compound sentences.

> Jenny read for two hours, *but* she did not finish her reading assignment.

> The book was dense, *so* she was unable to understand it.

Complex sentences are formed from an independent clause and at least one dependent clause. Subordinating conjunctions, such as *although, because, unless, while, as soon as, since, if,* and *when*, are used to connect the dependent clause to the sentence.

> Pablo bought a new bike helmet *because* his old one was cracked.

> *Unless* you plan to renew your library books, they must be returned in two weeks.

The necessary punctuation in a complex sentence depends on the order of the clauses. When the dependent clause begins the sentence, a comma is used after it to separate it from the independent clause. However, if a dependent clause comes after an independent clause, a comma is not necessary.

Lastly, a **compound-complex sentence** consists of at least two independent clauses and at least one dependent clause:

> Before you go home, please recycle your scrap paper, and stack your chair on your desk.

The first independent clause in the compound sentence structure includes a subordinating clause—*before you go home*. Therefore, the sentence structure is both complex and compound.

Structural Relationships
The Placement of Phrases and Clauses Within a Sentence

Clauses contain a subject and a predicate, while **phrases** only contain a noun with no verb or a verb with no noun, and they do not have a predicate. Clauses can be independent or dependent. **Independent clauses** can stand on their own as simple sentences. For example:

> She collects stamps.

Dependent clauses need independent clauses to form a complete sentence; they cannot stand alone. For example:

> Although she collects stamps...

Phrases can take on many forms including prepositional phrases, gerund phrases, noun phrases, infinitive phrases, verb phrases, etc. Regardless of the type, phrases cannot stand alone as complete sentence.

Phrases and clauses must be appropriately placed in a sentence such that it is clear to readers what they are modifying.

Consider the following misplaced prepositional phrase:

> At the bottom of the pile, Lila found her scarf.

182

In the above sentence, the phrase *at the bottom of the pile* is intended to modify the noun phrase *the scarf* by providing details about where the scarf was found. However, as written, the prepositional phrase is next to the subject, Lila, so it is modifying Lila. This is incorrect because presumably Lila herself wasn't at the bottom of a pile, her scarf was.

Misplaced and Dangling Modifiers

Modifiers are optional elements that can clarify or add details about a phrase or another element of a sentence. They are a dependent phrase and removing them usually does not change the grammatical correctness of the sentence; however, the meaning will be changed because, as their name implies, modifiers modify another element in the sentence. Consider the following:

> Nico loves sardines.

> Nico, who is three years old, loves sardines.

The first simple sentence is grammatically correct; however, we learn a lot more from the second sentence, which contains the modifier *who is three years old*. Sardines tend to be a food that young children don't like, so adding the modifier helps readers see why Nico loving sardines is noteworthy.

Beginning writers sometimes place modifiers incorrectly. Then, instead of enhancing comprehension and providing helpful description for the reader, the modifier causes more confusion. A **misplaced modifier** is located incorrectly in relation to the phrase or word it modifies. Consider the following sentence:

> Because it is salty, Nico loves fish.

The modifier in this sentence is "because they are salty," and the noun it is intended to modify is "fish." However, due to the erroneous placement of the modifier next to the subject, Nico, the sentence is actually saying that Nico is salty.

> Nico loves fish because it is salty.

The modifier is now adjacent to the appropriate noun, clarifying which of the two elements is salty.

Dangling modifiers are so named because they modify a phrase or word that is not clearly found in the sentence, making them rather unattached. They are not intended to modify the word or phrase they are placed next to. Consider the following:

> Walking home from school, the sky opened and Bruce got drenched.

The modifier here, "walking home from school," should modify who was walking (Bruce). Instead, the noun immediately after the modifier is "the sky"—but the sky was not walking home from school. Although not always the case, dangling modifiers are often found at the beginning of a sentence.

Coordinating and Subordinating Conjunctions

Conjunctions connect or coordinate words, phrases, clauses, or sentences together, typically as a way to demonstrate a relationship.

> Tony has a cat *and* a rabbit.

> Tony likes animals, *but* he is afraid of snakes.

Coordinating conjunctions join words or phrases that have equal rank or emphasis. There are seven coordinating conjunctions, all short words, that can be remembered by the mnemonic FANBOYS: *for, and, nor, but, or, yet, so*. They can join two words that are of the same part of speech (two verbs, two adjectives, two adverbs, or two nouns). They can also connect two phrases or two independent clauses.

Subordinating conjunctions help transition and connect two elements in the sentence, but in a way that diminishes the importance of the one it introduces, known as the dependent, or subordinate, clause. They include words like *because, since, unless, before, after, whereas, if*, and *while*.

Fragments and Run-Ons

Every sentence must have a subject and a verb to be complete. As mentioned, **sentence fragments** are caused by absent subjects, absent verbs, or dangling/uncompleted dependent clauses. An example of a fragment is "Raining all night long," because there is no subject present. "It was raining all night long" is one correction. Another example of a sentence fragment is the second part in "Many scientists think in unusual ways. Einstein, for instance." The second phrase is a fragment because it has no verb. One correction is "Many scientists, like Einstein, think in unusual ways." Finally, look for "cliffhanger" words like *if, when, because*, or *although* that introduce dependent clauses, which cannot stand alone without an independent clause. For example, to correct the sentence fragment "If you get home early," add an independent clause: "If you get home early, we can go dancing."

A **run-on sentence** combines two or more complete sentences without punctuating them correctly or separating them. For example, a run-on sentence caused by a lack of punctuation is the following:

> There are too many people here for the number of available seats however there is nobody around who has access to the room with additional chairs.

One correction is, "There is a malfunction in the computer system; however, there is nobody available right now who knows how to troubleshoot it." Another is, "There is a malfunction in the computer system. However, there is nobody available right now who knows how to troubleshoot it."

An example of a *comma splice* of two sentences is the following:

> Xavier decided to buy the chicken, he had enough money.

Replacing the comma with a period or a semicolon corrects this. Commas that try and separate two independent clauses without a contraction are considered comma splices.

Correlative Conjunctions

Correlative conjunctions are pairs of conjunctions that must both be used in the sentence, though in different spots, to make the sentence grammatically sound. They help relate one aspect of the sentence to another. Examples of correlative conjunctions pairs are *neither/nor, both/and, not/but, either/or, as/as, such/that* and *rather/than*. They tend to be more like coordinating conjunctions rather than subordinating conjunctions in that they typically connect two words or phrases of equal weight in the sentence.

Parallel Structure

As mentioned, **parallel structure** in a sentence matches the forms of sentence components. Any sentence containing more than one description or phrase should keep them consistent in wording and form. Readers can easily follow writers' ideas when they are written in parallel structure, making it an important element of correct sentence construction. For example, this sentence lacks parallelism: "Our coach is a skilled manager, a clever strategist, and works hard." The first two phrases are parallel, but the third is not.

184

Correction: "Our coach is a skilled manager, a clever strategist, and a hard worker." Now all three phrases match in form. Here is another example:

> Fred intercepted the ball, escaped tacklers, and a touchdown was scored.

This is also non-parallel. Here is the sentence corrected:

> Fred intercepted the ball, escaped tacklers, and scored a touchdown.

Usage

Parts of Speech

Possessives

Possessive forms indicate possession, i.e. that something belongs to or is owned by someone or something. As such, the most common parts of speech to be used in possessive form are adjectives, nouns, and pronouns. The rule for correctly spelling/punctuating possessive nouns and proper nouns is with -*'s*, like "the woman's briefcase" or "Frank's hat." With possessive adjectives, however, apostrophes are not used: these include *my, your, his, her, its, our,* and *their,* like "my book," "your friend," "his car," "her house," "its contents," "our family," or "their property." Possessive pronouns include *mine, yours, his, hers, its, ours,* and *theirs.* These also have no apostrophes. The difference is that possessive adjectives take direct objects, whereas possessive pronouns replace them. For example, instead of using two possessive adjectives in a row, as in "I forgot my book, so Blanca let me use her book," which reads monotonously, replacing the second one with a possessive pronoun reads better: "I forgot my book, so Blanca let me use hers."

Pronouns

There are three pronoun cases: subjective case, objective case, and possessive case. Pronouns as subjects are pronouns that replace the subject of the sentence, such as *I, you, he, she, it, we, they* and *who.* Pronouns as objects replace the object of the sentence, such as *me, you, him, her, it, us, them,* and *whom.* Pronouns that show possession are *mine, yours, hers, its, ours, theirs,* and *whose.* The following are examples of different pronoun cases:

- Subject pronoun: *She* ate the cake for her birthday. *I* saw the movie.
- Object pronoun: You gave *me* the card last weekend. She gave the picture to *him.*
- Possessive pronoun: That bracelet you found yesterday is *mine. His* name was Casey.

Adjectives

Adjectives are descriptive words that modify nouns or pronouns. They may occur before or after the nouns or pronouns they modify in sentences. For example, in "This is a big house," *big* is an adjective modifying or describing the noun *house.* In "This house is big," the adjective is at the end of the sentence rather than preceding the noun it modifies.

A rule of punctuation that applies to adjectives is to separate a series of adjectives with commas. For example, "Their home was a large, rambling, old, white, two-story house." A comma should never separate the last adjective from the noun, though.

Adverbs

Whereas adjectives modify and describe nouns or pronouns, adverbs modify and describe adjectives, verbs, or other adverbs. Adverbs can be thought of as answers to questions in that they describe when, where, how, how often, how much, or to what extent.

Many (but not all) adjectives can be converted to adverbs by adding *–ly*. For example, in "She is a quick learner," *quick* is an adjective modifying *learner*. In "She learns quickly," *quickly* is an adverb modifying *learns*. One exception is *fast*. *Fast* is an adjective in "She is a fast learner." However, *–ly* is never added to the word *fast*; it retains the same form as an adverb in "She learns fast."

Verbs

A verb is a word or phrase that expresses action, feeling, or state of being. Verbs explain what their subject is *doing*. Three different types of verbs used in a sentence are action verbs, linking verbs, and helping verbs.

Action verbs show a physical or mental action. Some examples of action verbs are *play, type, jump, write, examine, study, invent, develop,* and *taste*. The following example uses an action verb:

Kat *imagines* that she is a mermaid in the ocean.

The verb *imagines* explains what Kat is doing: she is imagining being a mermaid.

Linking verbs connect the subject to the predicate without expressing an action. The following sentence shows an example of a linking verb:

The mango *tastes* sweet.

The verb *tastes* is a linking verb. The mango doesn't *do* the tasting, but the word *taste* links the mango to its predicate, sweet. Most linking verbs can also be used as action verbs, such as *smell, taste, look, seem, grow,* and *sound*. Saying something *is* something else is also an example of a linking verb. For example, if we were to say, "Peaches is a dog," the verb *is* would be a linking verb in this sentence, since it links the subject to its predicate.

Helping verbs assist the main verb in a sentence. Examples of helping verbs are *be, am, is, was, have, has, do, did, can, could, may, might, should,* and *must,* among others. The following are examples of helping verbs:

Jessica *is* planning a trip to Hawaii.

Brenda *does* not like camping.

Xavier *should* go to the dance tonight.

Notice that after each of these helping verbs is the main verb of the sentence: *planning, like,* and *go*. Helping verbs usually show an aspect of time.

Common Grammatical Errors

Subject-Verb Agreement

Lack of subject-verb agreement is a very common grammatical error. One of the most common instances is when people use a series of nouns as a compound subject with a singular instead of a plural verb. Here is an example:

> Identifying the best books, locating the sellers with the lowest prices, and paying for them *is* difficult

instead of saying "*are* difficult." Additionally, when a sentence subject is compound, the verb is plural:

> He and his cousins *were* at the reunion.

However, if the conjunction connecting two or more singular nouns or pronouns is "or" or "nor," the verb must be singular to agree:

> That pen or another one like it is in the desk drawer.

If a compound subject includes both a singular noun and a plural one, and they are connected by "or" or "nor," the verb must agree with the subject closest to the verb: "Sally or her sisters go jogging daily"; but "Her sisters or Sally goes jogging daily."

Simply put, singular subjects require singular verbs and plural subjects require plural verbs. A common source of agreement errors is not identifying the sentence subject correctly. For example, people often write sentences incorrectly like, "The group of students *were* complaining about the test." The subject is not the plural "students" but the singular "group." Therefore, the correct sentence should read, "The group of students *was* complaining about the test." The converse also applies, for example, in this incorrect sentence: "The facts in that complicated court case *is* open to question." The subject of the sentence is not the singular "case" but the plural "facts." Hence the sentence would correctly be written: "The facts in that complicated court case *are* open to question." New writers should not be misled by the distance between the subject and verb, especially when another noun with a different number intervenes as in these examples. The verb must agree with the subject, not the noun closest to it.

Inappropriate Shifts in Verb Tense

Verb tense helps indicate when an action or a state existed occurred or existed.

Simple present tense is used to indicate that the action or state of being is currently happening or happens regularly:

> He *plays* guitar.

Present continuous tense is used to indicate that the action or state of being is in progress. It is formed by the proper to be + verb + *-ing*.

> Unfortunately, I can't go to the park right now. I *am fixing* my bicycle.

Past tense is used to indicate that the action or state of being occurred previously. It should be noted, however, that in conversational English, speakers frequently use a mix of present and past tense, or simply present tense when describing events in the past. With that said, it is important for writers (and speakers in formal situations) to be consistent and grammatically correct in their verb tenses to avoid confusing readers. Consider the following passage:

I scored a goal in our soccer game last Saturday. At the start of the first half, Billy kicked me the ball. I run toward it and strike it directly toward the goal. It goes in and we won the game!

The passage above inappropriately switches from past tense—*scored, kicked*—to present tense—*run, strike, goes*—and then back to past tense—*won*. Instead, past tense should be carried throughout the passage:

I *scored* a goal in our soccer game last Saturday. At the start of the first half, Billy *kicked* me the ball. I *ran* toward it and strike it directly toward the goal. It *went* in and we *won* the game!

Noun-Noun Agreement

When multiple nouns are included in the same sentence and are related to one another in that sentence, they need to agree in number. This means that if one noun is singular, all other related nouns in the sentence must be singular as well. Similarly, if one noun is plural, the rest should follow in form and be plural as well. Consider the following sentence with an error in noun-noun agreement:

Mary and Sharon both have jobs as a teacher.

Because the noun *jobs* is plural, the noun *teachers*, which is also plural, must be used in place of *teacher*, which is singular.

Mary and Sharon both have jobs as teachers.

Pronoun-Antecedent Agreement

Pronouns within a sentence must refer specifically to one noun, known as the **antecedent**. Sometimes, if there are multiple nouns within a sentence, it may be difficult to ascertain which noun belongs to the pronoun. It's important that the pronouns always clearly reference the nouns in the sentence so as not to confuse the reader. Here's an example of an unclear pronoun reference:

After Catherine cut Libby's hair, David bought her some lunch.

The pronoun in the examples above is *her*. The pronoun could either be referring to *Catherine* or *Libby*. Here are some ways to write the above sentence with a clear pronoun reference:

After Catherine cut Libby's hair, David bought Libby some lunch.

David bought Libby some lunch after Catherine cut Libby's hair.

But many times the pronoun will clearly refer to its antecedent, like the following:

After David cut Catherine's hair, he bought her some lunch.

Pronoun Case

There are three **pronoun cases**: subjective case, objective case, and possessive case. Pronouns as subjects are pronouns that replace the subject of the sentence, such as *I, you, he, she, it, we, they* and *who*. Pronouns as objects replace the object of the sentence, such as *me, you, him, her, it, us, them,* and *whom*.

Pronouns that show possession are *mine, yours, hers, its, ours, theirs,* and *whose.* The following are examples of different pronoun cases:

- Subject pronoun: *She* ate the cake for her birthday. *I* saw the movie.
- Object pronoun: You gave *me* the card last weekend. She gave the picture to *him.*
- Possessive pronoun: That bracelet you found yesterday is *mine. His* name was Casey.

Intensive Pronoun Errors

An **intensive pronoun** ends in "self" or "selves" and adds emphasis to the sentence's subject or antecedent. Like reflexive pronouns, intensive pronouns include the singular pronouns *myself, yourself, himself, herself,* and *itself,* and the plural pronouns *ourselves, yourselves,* and *themselves.* However, intensive and reflexive pronouns differ in that removing a reflexive pronoun will cause the sentence to no longer make sense, whereas intensive pronouns can be removed because they only add emphasis; they are not mandatory. An example of a sentence with an intensive pronoun is the following:

We want to hear the author herself read the story.

The intensive pronoun *herself* adds emphasis that the speakers want to specifically hear the author read the story, rather than anyone else.

The most common error in the use of intensive pronouns is choosing the wrong pronoun; for example, using the plural pronoun when the singular one is needed, or using a singular pronoun when a plural one is needed. Using the same example from above, an error in agreement occurs in the following sentence:

We want to hear the author themselves read the story.

Author is singular and *themselves* is plural, so there is an error in number agreement.

Pronoun Number and Person Errors

Pronouns must agree in number and person. However, it is common, unfortunately, for writers to shift between persons or numbers when using pronouns. For example, a sentence might start with third person pronouns (*he, she, it, they,* etc.), but then switch to second person. Or, a sentence might start in second person and switch to first or third person. The following sentence contains a pronoun shift in person:

If you drink more water, most people see improvements in their skin and body composition.

This example begins with second person (using the pronoun *you*), but switches to third person (*their*). Consistency in person is needed. Therefore, the sentence should be one of the following two options:

If you drink more water, you will likely see improvements in your skin and body composition.

If they drink more water, most people see improvements in their skin and body composition.

Inappropriate pronoun shifts also occur when writers switch from using singular pronouns to plural ones, or vice versa. Sometimes, sentences will have errors in pronoun number and person.

Everyone should keep a journal about their life because you will want to pass the stories of your life along.

These sentences are usually easier to spot because the errors are two-fold and more apparent.

Vague Pronouns

A **pronoun** replaces a noun in a sentence, which is called the **antecedent**. It should be clear which noun the pronoun is replacing. Vague pronouns are unclear, cause ambiguity and confusion, may refer to more than one antecedent, and disturb the meaning of the sentence. Consider the following example:

> Tommy gave Greg a gift card, and he blushed.

In the above sentence, *he* is the pronoun, but it isn't readily apparent who *he* refers to. Did Tommy blush or did Greg blush? It's plausible that either person blushed. Instead, the name of the person, the antecedent, needs to be used instead:

> Tommy gave Greg a gift card, and Greg blushed.

The pronoun *it* is often the culprit in cases of a vague pronoun. Consider the following:

> Grandma dropped the glass frame on her hand and it broke.

Did the frame break or did grandma's hand break? The pronoun *it* should be replaced with the proper antecedent to clarify the intended meaning.

Other times, there is no clear antecedent, which also causes ambiguity and confusion:

> Mom called the store, but they didn't answer the phone.

Why is *they?* The store cannot answer the phone. A person answers a phone. Therefore, this sentence is incorrect. Instead, it should be amended in some way, such as the following:

> Mom called the store, but no employees answered the phone.

Punctuation

Ellipses

Ellipses (...) signal omitted text when quoting. Some writers also use them to show a thought trailing off, but this should not be overused outside of dialogue. An example of an ellipsis would be if someone is quoting a phrase out of a professional source but wants to omit part of the phrase that isn't needed: "Dr. Skim's analysis of pollen inside the body is clearly a myth... that speaks to the environmental guilt of our society."

Commas

Commas separate words or phrases in a series of three or more. The Oxford comma is the last comma in a series. Many people omit this last comma, but many times it causes confusion. Here is an example:

> I love my sisters, the Queen of England and Madonna.

This example without the comma implies that the "Queen of England and Madonna" are the speaker's sisters. However, if the speaker was trying to say that they love their sisters, the Queen of England, as well as Madonna, there should be a comma after "Queen of England" to signify this.

Commas also separate two coordinate adjectives ("big, heavy dog") but not cumulative ones, which should be arranged in a particular order for them to make sense ("beautiful ancient ruins").

190

A comma ends the first of two independent clauses connected by conjunctions. Here is an example:

I ate a bowl of tomato soup, and I was hungry very shortly after.

Here are some brief rules for commas:

- Commas follow introductory words like *however, furthermore, well, why,* and *actually,* among others.
- Commas go between city and state: Houston, Texas.
- If using a comma between a surname and Jr. or Sr. or a degree like M.D., also follow the whole name with a comma: "Martin Luther King, Jr., wrote that."
- A comma follows a dependent clause beginning a sentence: "Although she was very small,..."
- Nonessential modifying words/phrases/clauses are enclosed by commas: "Wendy, who is Peter's sister, closed the window."
- Commas introduce or interrupt direct quotations: "She said, 'I hate him.' 'Why,' I asked, 'do you hate him?'"

Semicolons

Semicolons are used to connect two independent clauses but should never be used in the place of a comma. They can replace periods between two closely connected sentences: "Call back tomorrow; it can wait until then." When writing items in a series and one or more of them contains internal commas, separate them with semicolons, like the following:

People came from Springfield, Illinois; Alamo, Tennessee; Moscow, Idaho; and other locations.

Hyphens

Here are some rules concerning hyphens:

- Compound adjectives like state-of-the-art or off-campus are hyphenated.
- Original compound verbs and nouns are often hyphenated, like "throne-sat," "video-gamed," "no-meater."
- Adjectives ending in *–ly* are often hyphenated, like "family-owned" or "friendly-looking."
- "Five years old" is not hyphenated, but singular ages like "five-year-old" are.
- Hyphens can clarify. For example, in "stolen vehicle report," "stolen-vehicle report" clarifies that "stolen" modifies "vehicle," not "report."
- Compound numbers twenty-one through ninety-nine are spelled with hyphens.
- Prefixes before proper nouns/adjectives are hyphenated, like "mid-September" and "trans-Pacific."

Parentheses

Parentheses enclose information such as an aside or more clarifying information: "She ultimately replied (after deliberating for an hour) that she was undecided." They are also used to insert short, in-text definitions or acronyms: "His FBS (fasting blood sugar) was higher than normal." When parenthetical information ends the sentence, the period follows the parentheses: "We received new funds ($25,000)." Only put periods within parentheses if the whole sentence is inside them: "Look at this. (You'll be astonished.)" However, this can also be acceptable as a clause: "Look at this (you'll be astonished)." Although parentheses appear to be part of the sentence subject, they are not, and do not change subject-verb agreement: "Will (and his dog) was there."

Quotation Marks

Quotation marks are typically used when someone is quoting a direct word or phrase someone else writes or says. Additionally, quotation marks should be used for the titles of poems, short stories, songs, articles, chapters, and other shorter works. When quotations include punctuation, periods and commas should *always* be placed inside of the quotation marks.

If a quotation contains another quotation within it, the inner quotation should have single quotation marks around it, while the outer quotation should have double quotation marks around it. For example: "Timmy was begging, 'Don't go! Don't leave!'" When using both double and single quotation marks, writers will find that many word-processing programs may automatically insert enough space between the single and double quotation marks to be visible for clearer reading. But if this is not the case, the writer should write/type them with enough space between to keep them from looking like three single quotation marks. Additionally, non-standard usages, terms used in an unusual fashion, and technical terms are often clarified by quotation marks. Here are some examples:

My "friend," Dr. Sims, has been micromanaging me again.

This way of extracting oil has been dubbed "fracking."

Apostrophes

One use of the apostrophe is followed by an *s* to indicate possession, like *Mrs. White's home* or *our neighbor's dog*. When using the *'s* after names or nouns that also end in the letter *s*, no single rule applies: some experts advise adding both the apostrophe and the *s*, like "the Jones's house," while others prefer using only the apostrophe and omitting the additional *s*, like "the Jones' house." The wisest expert advice is to pick one formula or the other and then apply it consistently. One common way of using apostrophes this way is by using *'s* after common nouns ending with *s*, but using just an apostrophe after proper nouns or names ending with *s*. One common error is to place the apostrophe before a name's final *s* instead of after it: "Ms. Hasting's book" is incorrect if the name is Ms. Hastings.

Plural nouns should not include apostrophes (e.g. "apostrophe's"). Exceptions are to clarify atypical plurals, like verbs used as nouns: "These are the do's and don'ts." Irregular plurals that do not end in *s* always take apostrophe-*s*, not *s*-apostrophe—a common error, as in "childrens' toys," which should be "children's toys." Compound nouns like mother-in-law, when they are singular and possessive, are followed by apostrophe-*s*, like "your mother-in-law's coat." When a compound noun is plural and possessive, the plural is formed before the apostrophe-*s*, like "your sisters-in-laws' coats." When two people named possess the same thing, use apostrophe-*s* after the second name only, like "Dennis and Pam's house."

Irregular Plurals

While many words in English can become plural by adding –s or –es to the end, there are some words that have irregular plural forms. One type includes words that are spelled the same whether they are singular or plural, such as deer, fish, salmon, trout, sheep, moose, offspring, species, aircraft, etc. The spelling rule for making these words plural is simple: they do not change. Other irregular English plurals change form based on vowel shifts, linguistic mutations, or grammatical and spelling conventions from their languages of origin, like Latin or German. Some examples include *tooth* and *teeth; man* and *men; child* and *children;* and *person* and *people*.

Rules of Capitalization

The first word of any document, and of each new sentence, is capitalized. Proper nouns, like names and adjectives derived from proper nouns, should also be capitalized. Here are some examples:

- Grand Canyon
- Pacific Palisades
- Golden Gate Bridge
- Freudian slip
- Shakespearian, Spenserian, or Petrarchan sonnet
- Irish song

Some exceptions are adjectives, originally derived from proper nouns, which through time and usage are no longer capitalized, like *quixotic, herculean*, or *draconian*. Capitals draw attention to specific instances of people, places, and things. Some categories that should be capitalized include the following:

- Brand names
- Companies
- Months
- Governmental divisions or agencies
- Historical eras
- Major historical events
- Holidays
- Institutions
- Famous buildings
- Ships and other manmade constructions
- Natural and manmade landmarks
- Territories
- Nicknames
- Organizations
- Planets
- Nationalities
- Tribes
- Religions
- Names of religious deities
- Roads
- Special occasions, like the Cannes Film Festival or the Olympic Games

Exceptions

Related to American government, capitalize the noun Congress but not the related adjective congressional. Capitalize the noun U.S. Constitution, but not the related adjective constitutional. Many experts advise leaving the adjectives federal and state in lowercase, as in federal regulations or state water board, and only capitalizing these when they are parts of official titles or names, like Federal Communications Commission or State Water Resources Control Board. While the names of the other planets in the solar system are capitalized as names, Earth is more often capitalized only when being described specifically as a planet, like Earth's orbit, but lowercase otherwise since it is used not only as a proper noun but also to mean *land, ground, soil*, etc.

Names of animal species or breeds are not capitalized unless they include a proper noun. Then, only the proper noun is capitalized. Antelope, black bear, and yellow-bellied sapsucker are not capitalized. However, Bengal tiger, German shepherd, Australian shepherd, French poodle, and Russian blue cat are capitalized.

Stars, moons, and suns are not capitalized, but planets specific names and the Sun and the Moon, when referring to the Earth's specific sun and moon, are capitalized as proper nouns. Medical conditions like tuberculosis or diabetes are lowercase; again, exceptions are proper nouns, like Epstein-Barr syndrome, Alzheimer's disease, and Down syndrome. Seasons and related terms like winter solstice or autumnal equinox are lowercase. Plants, including fruits and vegetables, like poinsettia, celery, or avocados, are not capitalized unless they include proper names, like Douglas fir, Jerusalem artichoke, Damson plums, or Golden Delicious apples.

Titles and Names

When official titles precede names, they should be capitalized, except when there is a comma between the title and name. But if a title follows or replaces a name, it should not be capitalized. For example, "the president" without a name is not capitalized, as in "The president addressed Congress." But with a name it is capitalized, like "President Obama addressed Congress." Or, "Chair of the Board Janet Yellen was appointed by President Obama." One exception is that some publishers and writers nevertheless capitalize President, Queen, Pope, etc., when these are not accompanied by names to show respect for these high offices. However, many writers in America object to this practice for violating democratic principles of equality. Occupations before full names are not capitalized, like owner Mark Cuban, director Martin Scorsese, or coach Roger McDowell.

Some universal rules for capitalization in composition titles include capitalizing the following:

- The first and last words of the title
- Forms of the verb *to be* and all other verbs
- Pronouns
- The word *not*

Universal rules for NOT capitalizing in titles include the articles *the, a,* or *an;* the conjunctions *and, or,* or *nor,* and the preposition *to,* or *to* as part of the infinitive form of a verb. The exception to all of these is UNLESS any of them is the first or last word in the title, in which case they are capitalized. Other words are subject to differences of opinion and differences among various stylebooks or methods. These include *as, but, if,* and *or,* which some capitalize and others do not. Some authorities say no preposition should ever be capitalized; some say prepositions five or more letters long should be capitalized. The *Associated Press Stylebook* advises capitalizing prepositions longer than three letters (like *about, across,* or *with*).

Practice Quiz

The next five questions are based on the following passage:

(1) Café Adriatico was the best place in town to go for authentic Italian cuisine. (2) The entire restaurant consisted of the kitchen in the far back of the restaurant, one small bathroom, and a quaint dining area that comfortably held ten tables. (3) There was always Italian classical music playing in the background, and the atmosphere always put me in mind of being in my own grandparents home.

(4) Angela, the sole owner and head chef, was a unique character. (5) She loved her guests and treated them like her extended family. (6) She would saunter around from table to table, talking with the diners and occasionally pulling up a chair to gab a little longer. (7) One famous story she used to tell was of her younger years in Italy, and how once she won a national beauty contest. (8) She wouldn't tell the story in an arrogant way. (9) She would just matter-of-factly tell us what it was like when she was honored with this award. (10) She was reminiscing about the good old days, I guess, and who doesn't like to do that?

(11) People didn't expect to be fed right away at Café Adriatico. (12) Everything was cooked from scratch and made from the freshest and highest-quality of ingredients. (13) Going to Café Adriatico was the equivalent of going out for the evening. (14) Boy, was Angela something else! It wasn't the least bit uncommon to see her walking around the restaurant with a cigarette hanging out of her mouth and her tiny poodle walking along at her ankles. (15) This doesn't seem to bother any of the locals though. (16) Angela was too well-liked. (17) People went there for the comradery, the excellent cuisine, and the reminder of what it was like to be served an authentic Italian meal in the comfort of one's home. (18) If you ever visit Hamilton, Ontario, Canada, be sure to visit Café Adriatico. (19) And if Angela is still sauntering from table to table, please tell her I say hello!

1. Which is the best version of the underlined portion of Sentence 3 (reproduced below)?

   There was always Italian classical music playing in the background, and the atmosphere always put me in mind of being in my own <u>grandparents</u> home.

   a. Leave it as is
   b. grandparent's
   c. grandparents'
   d. grandparents's

2. Which is the best version of the underlined portion of Sentence 6 (reproduced below)?

   She <u>would saunter</u> around from table to table, talking with the diners and occasionally pulling up a chair to gab a little longer.

   a. Leave it as is
   b. sauntered
   c. was sauntering
   d. had sauntered

3. Which is the best version of the underlined portion of Sentence 7 (reproduced below)?

One famous story she used to tell was of her younger years in Italy, and how once she won a <u>national beauty contest</u>.

a. Leave it as is
b. National Beauty Contest
c. National beauty contest
d. national Beauty contest

4. Which is the best version of the underlined portion of Sentence 15 (reproduced below)?

This <u>doesn't</u> seem to bother any of the locals though.

a. Leave it as is
b. hadn't
c. didn't
d. never

5. Which is the best version of the underlined portion of Sentence 16 (reproduced below)?

Angela was too <u>well-liked</u>.

a. Leave it as is
b. well liked
c. much liked
d. liked

See answers on next page.

Answer Explanations

1. C: The best answer is Choice *C*, which is grandparents'. To show possession of a plural noun that ends in an "s," the apostrophe is placed directly after the final "s."

2. A: The original choice is the best answer here. Sauntering is not something Angela did just one time; she did it often. When referring to repeated past actions, the word "would" is used with the present tense verb, in this case "saunter."

3. A: The best answer is Choice *A*. There is no need to use any uppercase letters in the name because the specific name of a contest is not being used. The words in a proper noun would be capitalized.

4. C: Choice *C* is the best answer: "didn't." The entire story is written in the past tense, and the verbs must reflect this tense in order to keep the passage coherent.

5. B: The best answer is Choice *B*: "well liked." The phrase "well liked" when it appears before the verb: "The well-liked hostess sauntered around the room." In this sentence, "well liked" appears after the verb, so no hyphen is needed.

Write Placer

Argument Structure and Organization

When authors write text for the purpose of persuading others to agree with them, they assume a position with the subject matter about which they are writing. Rather than presenting information objectively, the author treats the subject matter subjectively so that the information presented supports their position. In their argumentation, the author presents information that refutes or weakens opposing positions. Another technique authors use in persuasive writing is to anticipate arguments against the position. When students learn to read subjectively, they gain experience with the concept of persuasion in writing and learn to identify positions taken by authors. This enhances their reading comprehension and develops their skills for identifying pro and con arguments and biases.

There are five main parts of the classical argument that writers employ in a well-designed stance:

- Introduction: In the introduction to a classical argument, the author establishes goodwill and rapport with the reading audience, warms up the readers, and states the thesis or general theme of the argument.

- Narration: In the narration portion, the author gives a summary of pertinent background information, informs the readers of anything they need to know regarding the circumstances and environment surrounding and/or stimulating the argument, and establishes what is at risk or the stakes in the issue or topic. Literature reviews are common examples of narrations in academic writing.

- Confirmation: The confirmation states all claims supporting the thesis and furnishes evidence for each claim, arranging this material in logical order—e.g. from most obvious to most subtle or strongest to weakest.

- Refutation and Concession: The refutation and concession discuss opposing views and anticipate reader objections without weakening the thesis, yet permitting as many oppositions as possible.

- Summation: The summation strengthens the argument while summarizing it, supplying a strong conclusion and showing readers the superiority of the author's solution.

Introduction
A classical argument's introduction must pique reader interest, get readers to perceive the author as a writer, and establish the author's position. Shocking statistics, new ways of restating issues, or quotations or anecdotes focusing the text can pique reader interest. Personal statements, parallel instances, or analogies can also begin introductions—so can bold thesis statements if the author believes readers will agree. Word choice is also important for establishing author image with readers.

The introduction should typically narrow down to a clear, sound thesis statement. If readers cannot locate one sentence in the introduction explicitly stating the writer's position or the point they support, the writer probably has not refined the introduction sufficiently.

Narration and Confirmation
The narration part of a classical argument should create a context for the argument by explaining the issue to which the argument is responding, and by supplying any background information that influences

the issue. Readers should understand the issues, alternatives, and stakes in the argument by the end of the narration to enable them to evaluate the author's claims equitably. The confirmation part of the classical argument enables the author to explain why they believe in the argument's thesis. The author builds a chain of reasoning by developing several individual supporting claims and explaining why that evidence supports each claim and also supports the overall thesis of the argument.

Refutation and Concession and Summation

The classical argument is the model for argumentative/persuasive writing, so authors often use it to establish, promote, and defend their positions. In the refutation aspect of the refutation and concession part of the argument, authors disarm reader opposition by anticipating and answering their possible objections, persuading them to accept the author's viewpoint. In the concession aspect, authors can concede those opposing viewpoints with which they agree. This can avoid weakening the author's thesis while establishing reader respect and goodwill for the author: all refutation and no concession can antagonize readers who disagree with the author's position. In the conclusion part of the classical argument, a less skilled writer might simply summarize or restate the thesis and related claims; however, this does not provide the argument with either momentum or closure. More skilled authors revisit the issues and the narration part of the argument, reminding readers of what is at stake.

Formal and Informal Language

Formal language is more impersonal than informal language. It is more "buttoned-up" and business-like, adhering to proper grammatical rules. It is used in professional or academic contexts, to convey respect or authority. For example, one would use formal language to write an informative or argumentative essay for school or to address a superior. Formal language avoids contractions, slang, colloquialisms, and first-person pronouns. Formal language uses sentences that are usually more complex and often in passive voice. Punctuation can differ as well. For example, **exclamation points (!)** are used to show strong emotion or can be used as an **interjection** but should be used sparingly in formal writing situations.

Informal language is often used when communicating with family members, friends, peers, and those known more personally. It is more casual, spontaneous, and forgiving in its conformity to grammatical rules and conventions. Informal language is used for personal emails and correspondence between coworkers or other familial relationships. The tone is more relaxed. In informal writing, slang, contractions, clichés, and the first- and second-person are often used.

Elements of the Writing Process

Skilled writers undergo a series of steps that comprise the writing process. The purpose of adhering to a structured approach to writing is to develop clear, meaningful, coherent work.

The stages are pre-writing or planning, organizing, drafting/writing, revising, and editing. Not every writer will necessarily follow all five stages for every project but will judiciously employ the crucial components of the stages for most formal or important work. For example, a brief informal response to a short reading passage may not necessitate the need for significant organization after idea generation, but larger assignments and essays will likely mandate use of the full process.

Pre-Writing/Planning

Brainstorming

Before beginning the essay, read the prompt thoroughly and make sure you understand its expectations. Brainstorm as many ideas as you can think of that relate to the topic and list them or put them into a graphic organizer. Refer to this list as you organize your essay outline.

Freewriting

Like brainstorming, freewriting is another prewriting activity to help the writer generate ideas. This method involves setting a timer for two or three minutes and writing down all ideas that come to mind about the topic using complete sentences. Once time is up, writers should review the sentences to see what observations have been made and how these ideas might translate into a more unified direction for the topic. Even if sentences lack sense as a whole, freewriting is an excellent way to get ideas onto the page in the very beginning stages of writing. Using complete sentences can make this a bit more challenging than brainstorming, but overall, it is a worthwhile exercise, as it may force the writer to come up with more complete thoughts about the topic.

Take the ideas you generated during pre-writing and organize them in the form of an outline.

Organizing

Although sometimes it is difficult to get going on the brainstorming or prewriting phase, once ideas start flowing, writers often find that they have amassed too many thoughts that will not make for a cohesive and unified essay. During the organization stage, writers should examine the generated ideas, hone in on the important ones central to their main idea, and arrange the points in a logical and effective manner. Writers may also determine that some of the ideas generated in the planning process need further elaboration, potentially necessitating the need for research to gather information to fill the gaps.

Once a writer has chosen their thesis and main argument, selected the most applicable details and evidence, and eliminated the "clutter," it is time to strategically organize the ideas. This is often accomplished with an outline.

Outlining

An *outline* is a system used to organize writing. When composing essays, outlining is important because it helps writers organize important information in a logical pattern using Roman numerals. Usually, outlines start out with the main ideas and then branch out into subgroups or subsidiary thoughts or subjects. Not only do outlines provide a visual tool for writers to reflect on how events, ideas, evidence, or other key parts of the argument relate to one another, but they can also lead writers to a stronger conclusion.

The sample below demonstrates what a general outline looks like:

I. Introduction
    1. Background
    2. Thesis statement
II. Body
    1. Point A
        a. Supporting evidence
        b. Supporting evidence
    2. Point B
        a. Supporting evidence
        b. Supporting evidence
    3. Point C
        a. Supporting evidence
        b. Supporting evidence
III. Conclusion
    1. Restatement of main points.
    2. Memorable ending.

Drafting/Writing

Now it comes time to actually write the essay. In this stage, writers should follow the outline they developed in the brainstorming process and try to incorporate the useful sentences penned in the freewriting exercise. The main goal of this phase is to put all the thoughts together in cohesive sentences and paragraphs.

It is helpful for writers to remember that their work here does not have to be perfect. This process is often referred to as **drafting** because writers are just creating a rough draft of their work. Because of this, writers should avoid getting bogged down on the small details.

Referencing Sources

Anytime a writer quotes or paraphrases another text, they will need to include a citation. A citation is a short description of the work that a quote or information came from. The style manual your teacher wants you to follow will dictate exactly how to format that citation. For example, this is how one would cite a book according to the APA manual of style:

- *Format*: Last name, First initial, Middle initial. (Year Published) *Book Title*. City, State: Publisher.
- *Example*: Sampson, M. R. (1989). *Diaries from an Alien Invasion*. *Springfield, IL*: Campbell Press.

Revising

Revising involves going back over a piece of writing and improving it. Try to read your essay from the perspective of a potential reader to ensure that it makes sense. When revising, check that the main points are clearly stated, logically organized, and directly supported by the sub-points. Remove unnecessary details that do not contribute to the argument.

The main goal of the revision phase is to improve the essay's flow, cohesiveness, readability, and focus. For example, an essay will make a less persuasive argument if the various pieces of evidence are scattered and presented illogically or clouded with unnecessary thought. Therefore, writers should consider their essay's structure and organization, ensuring that there are smooth transitions between sentences and paragraphs. There should be a discernable introduction and conclusion as well, as these crucial components of an essay provide readers with a blueprint to follow.

Additionally, if the writer includes copious details that do little to enhance the argument, they may actually distract readers from focusing on the main ideas and detract from the strength of their work. The ultimate goal is to retain the purpose or focus of the essay and provide a reader-friendly experience. Because of this, writers often need to delete parts of their essay to improve its flow and focus. Removing sentences, entire paragraphs, or large chunks of writing can be one of the toughest parts of the writing process because it is difficult to part with work one has done. However, ultimately, these types of cuts can significantly improve one's essay.

Lastly, writers should consider their voice and word choice. The voice should be consistent throughout and maintain a balance between an authoritative and warm style, to both inform and engage readers. One way to alter voice is through word choice. Writers should consider changing weak verbs to stronger ones and selecting more precise language in areas where wording is vague. In some cases, it is useful to modify sentence beginnings or to combine or split up sentences to provide a more varied sentence structure.

Editing

Rather than focusing on content (as is the aim in the revising stage), the editing phase is all about the mechanics of the essay: the syntax, word choice, and grammar. This can be considered the proofreading stage. Successful editing is what sets apart a messy essay from a polished document.

Look for the following types of errors when checking over your work:

1. Spelling

2. Tense usage

3. Punctuation and capitalization

4. Unclear, confusing, or incomplete sentences

5. Subject/verb and noun/pronoun agreement

One of the most effective ways of identifying grammatical errors, awkward phrases, or unclear sentences is to read the essay out loud. Listening to one's own work can help move the writer from simply the author to the reader.

During the editing phase, it's also important to ensure the essay follows the correct formatting and citation rules as dictated by the assignment.

Recursive Writing Process

While the writing process may have specific steps, the good news is that the process is recursive, meaning the steps need not be completed in a particular order. Many writers find that they complete steps at the same time such as drafting and revising, where the writing and rearranging of ideas occur simultaneously or in very close order. Similarly, a writer may find that a particular section of a draft needs more development and will go back to the prewriting stage to generate new ideas. The steps can be repeated at any time, and the more these steps of the recursive writing process are employed, the better the final product will be.

Practice Makes Prepared Writers

Like any other useful skill, writing only improves with practice. While writing may come more easily to some than others, it is still a skill to be honed and improved. Regardless of a person's natural abilities, there is always room for growth in writing. Practicing the basic skills of writing can aid in preparations for the exam.

One way to build vocabulary and enhance exposure to the written word is through reading. This can be through reading books, but reading of any materials such as newspapers, magazines, and even social media count towards practice with the written word. This also helps to enhance critical reading and thinking skills, through analysis of the ideas and concepts read. Think of each new reading experience as a chance to sharpen these skills.

Developing a Well-Organized Paragraph

A paragraph is a series of connected and related sentences addressing one topic. Writing good paragraphs benefits writers by helping them to stay on target while drafting and revising their work. It benefits readers by helping them to follow the writing more easily. Regardless of how brilliant their ideas may be, writers who do not present them in organized ways will fail to engage readers—and fail to accomplish their writing goals. A fundamental rule for paragraphing is to confine each paragraph to a single idea. When writers find themselves transitioning to a new idea, they should start a new paragraph. However, a paragraph can include several pieces of evidence supporting its single idea; and it can include several points if they are all related to the overall paragraph topic. When writers find each point becoming lengthy, they may choose instead to devote a separate paragraph to every point and elaborate upon each more fully.

An effective paragraph should have these elements:

- Unity: One major discussion point or focus should occupy the whole paragraph from beginning to end.

- Coherence: For readers to understand a paragraph, it must be coherent. Two components of coherence are logical and verbal bridges. In logical bridges, the writer may write consecutive sentences with parallel structure or carry an idea over across sentences. In verbal bridges, writers may repeat key words across sentences.

- A topic sentence: The paragraph should have a sentence that generally identifies the paragraph's thesis or main idea.

- Sufficient development: To develop a paragraph, writers can use the following techniques after stating their topic sentence:

  - Define terms
  - Cite data
  - Use illustrations, anecdotes, and examples
  - Evaluate causes and effects
  - Analyze the topic
  - Explain the topic using chronological order

A topic sentence identifies the main idea of the paragraph. Some are explicit, some implicit. The topic sentence can appear anywhere in the paragraph. However, many experts advise beginning writers to place

203

each paragraph topic sentence at or near the beginning of its paragraph to ensure that their readers understand what the topic of each paragraph is. Even without having written an explicit topic sentence, the writer should still be able to summarize readily what subject matter each paragraph addresses. The writer must then fully develop the topic that is introduced or identified in the topic sentence. Depending on what the writer's purpose is, they may use different methods for developing each paragraph.

Two main steps in the process of organizing paragraphs and essays should both be completed after determining the writing's main point, while the writer is planning or outlining the work. The initial step is to give an order to the topics addressed in each paragraph. Writers must have logical reasons for putting one paragraph first, another second, etc. The second step is to sequence the sentences in each paragraph. As with the first step, writers must have logical reasons for the order of sentences. Sometimes the work's main point obviously indicates a specific order.

Topic Sentences

To be effective, a topic sentence should be concise so that readers get its point without losing the meaning among too many words. As an example, in *Only Yesterday: An Informal History of the 1920s* (1931), author Frederick Lewis Allen's topic sentence introduces his paragraph describing the 1929 stock market crash: "The Bull Market was dead." This example illustrates the criteria of conciseness and brevity. It is also a strong sentence, expressed clearly and unambiguously. The topic sentence also introduces the paragraph, alerting the reader's attention to the main idea of the paragraph and the subject matter that follows the topic sentence.

Experts often recommend opening a paragraph with the topic sentences to enable the reader to realize the main point of the paragraph immediately. Application letters for jobs and university admissions also benefit from opening with topic sentences. However, positioning the topic sentence at the end of a paragraph is more logical when the paragraph identifies a number of specific details that accumulate evidence and then culminates with a generalization. While paragraphs with extremely obvious main ideas need no topic sentences, more often—and particularly for students learning to write—the topic sentence is the most important sentence in the paragraph. It not only communicates the main idea quickly to readers; it also helps writers produce and control information.

Writing Prompt

In response to the following prompt, write a 300- to 600-word essay.

Substance abuse recovery centers in Florida have doubled in the past two years. Additionally, the centers that already existed are filled to the maximum occupancy. In order to accommodate the patients, some recovery centers are expanding their residencies and adding more staff. The reason for this rise in recovery centers speaks to the state of our nation with the abuse of drugs and alcohol. The substance abuse problem is worse than ever before and will only continue to grow if we allow the trafficking and consumption of drugs to go unpunished.

Write a response in which you identify your stance on the argument above. Once you've identified your stance, use concrete evidence to support your argument.

Practice Test #1

Arithmetic

1. What is $\frac{12}{60}$ converted to a percentage?
    a. 0.20
    b. 20%
    c. 25%
    d. 12%

2. Which of the following is the correct decimal form of the fraction $\frac{14}{33}$ rounded to the nearest hundredth place?
    a. 0.420
    b. 0.420
    c. 0.424
    d. 0.140

3. Which of the following represents the correct sum of $\frac{14}{15}$ and $\frac{2}{5}$, in lowest possible terms?

    a. $\frac{20}{15}$

    b. $\frac{4}{3}$

    c. $\frac{16}{20}$

    d. $\frac{4}{5}$

4. What is the product of $\frac{5}{14}$ and $\frac{7}{20}$, in lowest possible terms?

    a. $\frac{1}{8}$

    b. $\frac{35}{280}$

    c. $\frac{12}{34}$

    d. $\frac{1}{2}$

5. What is the result of dividing 24 by $\frac{8}{5}$, in lowest possible terms?

    a. $\frac{5}{3}$

    b. $\frac{3}{5}$

    c. $\frac{120}{8}$

    d. 15

6. Subtract $\frac{5}{14}$ from $\frac{5}{24}$. Which of the following is the correct result?

    a. $\frac{25}{168}$

    b. 0

    c. $-\frac{25}{168}$

    d. $\frac{1}{10}$

7. Which of the following is a correct mathematical statement?

    a. $\frac{1}{3} < -\frac{4}{3}$

    b. $-\frac{1}{3} > \frac{4}{3}$

    c. $\frac{1}{3} > -\frac{4}{3}$

    d. $-\frac{1}{3} \geq \frac{4}{3}$

8. Which of the following is INCORRECT?

    a. $-\frac{1}{5} < \frac{4}{5}$

    b. $\frac{4}{5} > -\frac{1}{5}$

    c. $-\frac{1}{5} > \frac{4}{5}$

    d. $\frac{1}{5} > -\frac{4}{5}$

9. In a neighborhood, 15 out of 80 of the households have children under the age of 18. What percentage of the households have children under 18?

    a. 0.1875%

    b. 18.75%

    c. 1.875%

    d. 15%

10. Gina took an algebra test last Friday. There were 35 questions, and she answered 60% of them correctly. How many correct answers did she have?

    a. 35

    b. 20

    c. 21

    d. 25

11. Paul took a written driving test, and he got 12 of the questions correct. If he answered 75% of the total questions correctly, how many questions were on the test?
    a. 25
    b. 16
    c. 20
    d. 18

12. If a car is purchased for $15,395 with a 7.25% sales tax, how much is the total price?
    a. $15,395.07
    b. $16,511.14
    c. $16,411.13
    d. $15,402

13. A car manufacturer usually makes 15,412 SUVs, 25,815 station wagons, 50,412 sedans, 8,123 trucks, and 18,312 hybrids a month. About how many cars are manufactured each month?
    a. 120,000
    b. 200,000
    c. 300,000
    d. 12,000

14. A family goes to the grocery store every week and spends $105. About how much does the family spend annually on groceries?
    a. $10,000
    b. $50,000
    c. $500
    d. $5,000

15. Bindee is having a barbeque on Sunday and needs 12 packets of ketchup for every 5 guests. If 60 guests are coming, how many packets of ketchup should she buy?
    a. 100
    b. 12
    c. 144
    d. 60

16. A grocery store sold 48 bags of apples in one day. If 9 of the bags contained Granny Smith apples and the rest contained Red Delicious apples, what is the ratio of bags of Granny Smith to bags of Red Delicious that were sold?
    a. 48:9
    b. 39:9
    c. 9:48
    d. 9:39

17. If Oscar's bank account totaled $4,000 in March and $4,900 in June, what was the rate of change in his bank account total over those three months?
    a. $900 a month
    b. $300 a month
    c. $4,900 a month
    d. $100 a month

18. The percentage of smokers above the age of 18 in 2000 was 23.2%. The percentage of smokers above the age of 18 in 2015 was 15.1%. Find the average rate of change in the percent of smokers above the age of 18 from 2000 to 2015.

    a. −0.54%

    b. −54%

    c. −5.4%

    d. −15%

19. In order to estimate deer population in a forest, biologists obtained a sample of deer in that forest and tagged each one of them. The sample had 300 deer in total. They returned a week later, harmlessly captured 400 deer, and found that 5 were tagged. Use this information to estimate how many total deer were in the forest.

    a. 24,000 deer

    b. 30,000 deer

    c. 40,000 deer

    d. 80,000 deer

20. The number of members of the House of Representatives varies directly with the total population in a state. If the state of New York has 20,000,000 residents and has 27 total representatives, how many should Ohio have with a population of 11,600,000?

    a. 10

    b. 16

    c. 11

    d. 5

Quantitative Reasoning, Algebra, and Statistics

1. What is the solution to the equation $3(x + 2) = 14x − 5$?

    a. $x = 1$

    b. No solution

    c. $x = 0$

    d. All real numbers

2. What is the solution to the equation $10 − 5x + 2 = 7x + 12 − 12x$?

    a. $x = 12$

    b. No solution

    c. $x = 0$

    d. All real numbers

3. Which of the following is the result when solving the equation $4(x + 5) + 6 = 2(2x + 3)$?

    a. Any real number is a solution.

    b. There is no solution.

    c. $x = 6$ is the solution.

    d. $x = 26$ is the solution.

4. How many cases of cola can Lexi purchase if each case is $3.50 and she has $40?
   a. 10
   b. 12
   c. 11.4
   d. 11

5. Two consecutive integers exist such that the sum of three times the first and two less than the second is equal to 411. What are those integers?
   a. 103 and 104
   b. 104 and 105
   c. 102 and 103
   d. 100 and 101

6. Erin and Katie work at the same ice cream shop. Together, they always work less than 21 hours a week. In a week, if Katie worked two times as many hours as Erin, how many hours could Erin work?
   a. Less than 7 hours
   b. Less than or equal to 7 hours
   c. More than 7 hours
   d. Less than 8 hours

7. Which expression is equivalent to $\sqrt[4]{x^6} - \frac{x}{x^3} + x - 2$?

   a. $x^{\frac{3}{2}} - x^2 + x - 2$

   b. $x^{\frac{2}{3}} - x^{-2} + x - 2$

   c. $x^{\frac{3}{2}} - \frac{1}{x^2} + x - 2$

   d. $x^{\frac{2}{3}} - \frac{1}{x^2} + x - 2$

8. How many possible positive zeros does the polynomial function $f(x) = x^4 - 3x^3 + 2x + x - 3$ have?
   a. 4
   b. 3
   c. 2
   d. 1

9. What is the solution to the following linear inequality?

$$7 - \frac{4}{5}x < \frac{3}{5}$$

   a. $(-\infty, 8)$
   b. $(8, \infty)$
   c. $[8, \infty)$
   d. $(-\infty, 8]$

10. Triple the difference of five and a number is equal to the sum of that number and 5. What is the number?
    a. 5
    b. 2
    c. 5.5
    d. 2.5

11. What is an equivalent form of the rational expression $\sqrt{200x^6y^7z^2}$? Assume all variables represent positive real numbers.
    a. $20x^3y^3z\sqrt{y}$

    b. $10x^3y^3z\sqrt{2y}$

    c. $10xyz\sqrt{2xyz}$

    d. $10x^2y^3z\sqrt{2z}$

12. What is the simplified form of $(4y^3)^4(3y^7)^2$?
    a. $12y^{26}$
    b. $2,304y^{16}$
    c. $12y^{14}$
    d. $2,304y^{26}$

13. Which equation correctly shows how to find the surface area of a cylinder?

    a. $SA = 2\pi \times 5 \times 10 + 2\pi \times 5^2$
    b. $SA = 5 \times 2\pi \times 5$
    c. $SA = 2\pi \times 5^2$
    d. $SA = 2\pi \times 10 + \pi \times 5^2$

14. A study of adult drivers finds that it is likely that an adult driver wears his seatbelt. Which of the following could be the probability that an adult driver wears his seat belt?

    a. 0.90
    b. 0.05
    c. 0.25
    d. 0

15. What is the area of the shaded region?

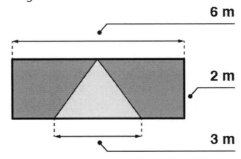

    a. 9 m^2
    b. 12 m^2
    c. 6 m^2
    d. 8 m^2

16. What is the volume of the cylinder below? Use 3.14 for π.

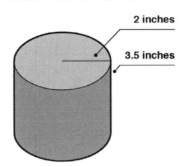

    a. 18.84 in^3
    b. 45.00 in^3
    c. 70.43 in^3
    d. 43.96 in^3

17. What is the solution to the following system of linear equations?

$$2x + y = 14$$

$$4x + 2y = -28$$

    a. $(14, -28)$
    b. $(2, -4)$
    c. All real numbers
    d. There is no solution

18. Which of the following is perpendicular to the line $4x + 7y = 23$?

    a. $y = -\frac{4}{7}x + 23$

    b. $y = \frac{7}{4}x - 12$

    c. $4x + 7y = 14$

    d. $y = -\frac{7}{4}x + 11$

19. What is the solution to the following system of equations?

$$2x - y = 6$$

$$y = 8x$$

    a. $(1, 8)$
    b. $(-1, 8)$
    c. $(-1, -8)$
    d. All real numbers

20. What is the missing length x?

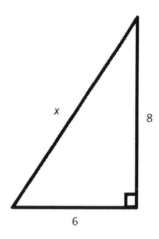

    a. 6
    b. −10
    c. 10
    d. 100

Advanced Algebra and Functions

1. Which of the following relations is a function?

    a. $\{(1, 4), (1, 3), (2, 4), (5, 6)\}$
    b. $\{(-1, -1), (-2, -2), (-3, -3), (-4, -4)\}$
    c. $\{(0, 0), (1, 0), (2, 0), (1, 1)\}$
    d. $\{(1, 0), (1, 2), (1, 3), (1, 4)\}$

2. Find the indicated function value: $f(5)$ for $f(x) = x^2 - 2x + 1$.
    a. 16
    b. 1
    c. 5
    d. -8

3. What is the domain of $f(x) = 4x^2 + 2x - 1$?
    a. $(0, \infty)$
    b. $(-\infty, 0)$
    c. $(-\infty, \infty)$
    d. $(-1, 4)$

4. The function $f(x) = 3.1x + 240$ models the total U.S. population, in millions, x years after the year 1980. Use this function to answer the following question: What is the total U.S. population in 2011? Round to the nearest million.
    a. 336 people
    b. 336 million people
    c. 6,474 people
    d. 647 million people

5. What is the domain of the logarithmic function $f(x) = \log_2(x - 2)$?
    a. 2
    b. $(-\infty, \infty)$
    c. $(0, \infty)$
    d. $(2, \infty)$

6. The function $f(t) = \frac{20,000}{1 + 10e^{-2t}}$ represents the number of people who catch a disease t weeks after its initial outbreak in a population of 20,000 people. How many people initially had the disease at the time of the initial outbreak? Round to the nearest whole number.
    a. 20,000
    b. 1,818
    c. 2,000
    d. 0

7. What are the zeros of the following quadratic function?

$$f(x) = 2x^2 - 12x + 16$$

    a. $x = 2$ and $x = 4$
    b. $x = 8$ and $x = 2$
    c. $x = 2$ and $x = 0$
    d. $x = 0$ and $x = 4$

8. What is the equivalent exponential form of the following logarithmic function?

$$f(x) = \log_5(x + 3)$$

    a. $3^y = x$
    b. $5^y = x$
    c. $5^y = x + 3$
    d. $3^y = x + 5$

9. What is the range of the polynomial function $f(x) = 2x^2 + 5$?
    a. $(-\infty, \infty)$
    b. $(2, \infty)$
    c. $(0, \infty)$
    d. $[5, \infty)$

10. What is an equivalent logarithmic form of the following exponential function?

$$f(x) = 10^{x+3}$$

    a. $x = 3 + \log y$
    b. $-3 + \log y = x$
    c. $\log(x - 3) = y$
    d. $\log_3 x = y$

11. For which two values of x are the following functions equal?
$$f(x) = 4x + 4$$
$$g(x) = x^2 + 3x + 2$$

    a. 1, 0
    b. −2, −1
    c. −1, 2
    d. 1, 2

12. The population of coyotes in the local national forest has been declining since 2000. The population can be modeled by the function $y = -(x - 2)^2 + 1{,}600$, where y represents number of coyotes and x represents the number of years past 2000. When will there be no more coyotes?
    a. 2020
    b. 2040
    c. 2012
    d. 2042

13. Given the linear function $g(x) = \frac{1}{4}x - 2$, which domain value corresponds to a range value of $\frac{1}{8}$?
    a. $\frac{17}{2}$

    b. $-\frac{63}{32}$

    c. 0

    d. $\frac{2}{17}$

14. A ball is thrown up from a building that is 800 feet high. Its position s in feet above the ground is given by the function $s = -32t^2 + 90t + 800$, where t is the number of seconds since the ball was thrown. How long will it take for the ball to come back to its starting point? Round your answer to the nearest tenth of a second.

    a. 0.0 seconds
    b. 2.8 seconds
    c. 3.0 seconds
    d. 8.0 seconds

15. What are the zeros of the following cubic function?

$$g(x) = x^3 - 2x^2 - 9x + 18$$

    a. 2, 3
    b. 2, 3, -2
    c. 2, 3, -3
    d. 2, -2

16. What is the domain of the following rational function?

$$f(x) = \frac{x^3 + 2x + 1}{2 - x}$$

    a. $(-\infty, -2) \cup (-2, \infty)$
    b. $(-\infty, 2) \cup (2, \infty)$
    c. $(2, \infty)$
    d. $(-2, \infty)$

17. Given the function $f(x) = 4x - 2$, what is the correct form of the simplified difference quotient:
$$\frac{f(x + h) - f(x)}{h}$$

    a. $4x - 1$
    b. $4x$
    c. 4
    d. $4x + h$

18. Is the function $g(x) = 7x^3 + 5x - 2$ odd, even, both even and odd, or neither even nor odd?

    a. Odd
    b. Even
    c. Both
    d. Neither

19. The mass of the Moon is about 7.348×10^{22} kilograms and the mass of Earth is 5.972×10^{24} kilograms. How many times greater is Earth's mass than the Moon's mass?

    a. 8.127×10^1
    b. 8.127
    c. 812.7
    d. 8.127×10^{-1}

20. What is the equation of the line that passes through the two points $(-3, 7)$ and $(-1, -5)$?
   a. $y = -6x + 11$
   b. $y = 6x$
   c. $y = -6x - 11$
   d. $y = -6x$

Reading

Directions for the next 18 questions: After reading the passage, choose the best answer to the question based on what is expressed or suggested in the passage.

1. Rehabilitation, rather than punitive justice, is becoming much more popular in prisons around the world. Prisons in America, especially, where the recidivism rate is 67 percent, would benefit from mimicking prison tactics in Norway, which has a recidivism rate of only 20 percent. In Norway, the idea is that a rehabilitated prisoner is much less likely to offend than one harshly punished. Rehabilitation includes proper treatment for substance abuse, psychotherapy, healthcare and dental care, and education programs.

Which of the following best captures the author's purpose?
   a. To show the audience one of the effects of criminal rehabilitation by comparison
   b. To persuade the audience to donate to American prisons for education programs
   c. To convince the audience of the harsh conditions of American prisons
   d. To inform the audience of the incredibly lax system of Norwegian prisons

2. What a lark! What a plunge! For so it had always seemed to her, when, with a little squeak of the hinges, which she could hear now, she had burst open the French windows and plunged at Bourton into the open air. How fresh, how calm, stiller than this of course, the air was in the early morning; like the flap of a wave; the kiss of a wave; chill and sharp and yet (for a girl of eighteen as she then was) solemn, feeling as she did, standing there at the open window, that something awful was about to happen; looking at the flowers, at the trees with the smoke winding off them and the rooks rising, falling; standing and looking until Peter Walsh said, "Musing among the vegetables?"—was that it?—"I prefer men to cauliflowers"—was that it? He must have said it at breakfast one morning when she had gone out on to the terrace—Peter Walsh. He would be back from India one of these days, June or July, she forgot which, for his letters were awfully dull; it was his sayings one remembered; his eyes, his pocket-knife, his smile, his grumpiness and, when millions of things had utterly vanished—how strange it was!—a few sayings like this about cabbages.

From *Mrs. Dalloway* by Virginia Woolf

What was the narrator feeling right before Peter Walsh's voice distracted her?
   a. A spark of excitement for the morning
   b. Anger at the larks
   c. A sense of foreboding
   d. Confusion at the weather

3. According to the plan of the convention, all judges who may be appointed by the United States are to hold their offices *during good behavior,* which is conformable to the most approved of the State constitutions and among the rest, to that of this State. Its propriety having been drawn into question by the adversaries of that plan, is no light symptom of the rage for objection, which disorders their imaginations and judgments. The standard of good behavior for the continuance in office of the judicial magistracy, is certainly one of the most valuable of the modern improvements in the practice of government. In a monarchy it is an excellent barrier to the despotism of the prince; in a republic it is a no less excellent barrier to the encroachments and oppressions of the representative body. And it is the best expedient which can be devised in any government, to secure a steady, upright, and impartial administration of the laws.

From *The Federalist No. 78* by Alexander Hamilton

What is Hamilton's point in this excerpt?
   a. To show the audience that despotism within a monarchy is no longer the standard practice in the states
   b. To convince the audience that judges holding their positions based on good behavior is a practical way to avoid corruption
   c. To persuade the audience that having good behavior should be the primary characteristic of a person in a government body and that their voting habits should reflect this
   d. To convey the position that judges who serve for a lifetime will not be perfect and, therefore, we must forgive them for their bad behavior when it arises

4. There was a man named Webster who lived in a town of twenty-five thousand people in the state of Wisconsin. He had a wife named Mary and a daughter named Jane and he was himself a fairly prosperous manufacturer of washing machines. When the thing happened of which I am about to write, he was thirty-seven or thirty-eight years old and his one child, the daughter, was seventeen. Of the details of his life up to the time a certain revolution happened within him it will be unnecessary to speak. He was however a rather quiet man inclined to have dreams which he tried to crush out of himself in order that he function as a washing machine manufacturer; and no doubt, at odd moments, when he was on a train going some place or perhaps on Sunday afternoons in the summer when he went alone to the deserted office of the factory and sat several hours looking out at a window and along a railroad track, he gave way to dreams.

From *Many Marriages* by Sherwood Anderson

What does the author mean by the following sentence?

Of the details of his life up to the time a certain revolution happened within him it will be unnecessary to speak.

   a. The details of his external life don't matter; only the details of his internal life matter.
   b. Whatever happened in his life before he had a certain internal change is irrelevant.
   c. He had a traumatic experience earlier in his life which rendered it impossible for him to speak.
   d. Before the revolution, he was a lighthearted man who always wished to speak to others no matter who they were.

The next seven questions are based on the following passage from The Story of Germ Life *by Herbert William Conn:*

The first and most universal change effected in milk is its souring. So universal is this phenomenon that it is generally regarded as an inevitable change that cannot be avoided, and, as already pointed out, has in the past been regarded as a normal property of milk. To-day, however, the phenomenon is well understood. It is due to the action of certain of the milk bacteria upon the milk sugar which converts it into lactic acid, and this acid gives the sour taste and curdles the milk. After this acid is produced in small quantity its presence proves deleterious to the growth of the bacteria, and further bacterial growth is checked. After souring, therefore, the milk for some time does not ordinarily undergo any further changes.

Milk souring has been commonly regarded as a single phenomenon, alike in all cases. When it was first studied by bacteriologists it was thought to be due in all cases to a single species of micro-organism which was discovered to be commonly present and named *Bacillus acidi lactici*. This bacterium has certainly the power of souring milk rapidly, and is found to be very common in dairies in Europe. As soon as bacteriologists turned their attention more closely to the subject it was found that the spontaneous souring of milk was not always caused by the same species of bacterium. Instead of finding this *Bacillus acidi lactici* always present, they found that quite a number of different species of bacteria have the power of souring milk, and are found in different specimens of soured milk.

The number of species of bacteria that have been found to sour milk has increased until something over a hundred are known to have this power. These different species do not affect the milk in the same way. All produce some acid, but they differ in the kind and the amount of acid, and especially in the other changes which are effected at the same time that the milk is soured, so that the resulting soured milk is quite variable. In spite of this variety, however, the most recent work tends to show that the majority of cases of spontaneous souring of milk are produced by bacteria which, though somewhat variable, probably constitute a single species, and are identical with the *Bacillus acidi lactici*. This species, found common in the dairies of Europe, according to recent investigations occurs in this country as well. We may say, then, that while there are many species of bacteria infesting the dairy which can sour the milk, there is one that is more common and more universally found than others, and this is the ordinary cause of milk souring.

When we study more carefully the effect upon the milk of the different species of bacteria found in the dairy, we find that there is a great variety of changes they produce when they are allowed to grow in milk. The dairyman experiences many troubles with his milk. It sometimes curdles without becoming acid. Sometimes it becomes bitter, or acquires an unpleasant "tainted" taste, or, again, a "soapy" taste. Occasionally, a dairyman finds his milk becoming slimy, instead of souring and curdling in the normal fashion. At such times, after a number of hours, the milk becomes so slimy that it can be drawn into long threads. Such an infection proves very troublesome, for many a time it persists in spite of all attempts made to remedy it. Again, in other cases the milk will turn blue, acquiring about the time it becomes sour a beautiful sky-blue colour. Or it may become red, or occasionally yellow. All of these troubles the dairyman owes to the presence in his milk of unusual species of bacteria which grow there abundantly.

5. What is the tone of this passage?
   a. Excitement
   b. Anger
   c. Neutral
   d. Sorrowful

6. The word *deleterious* in the first paragraph can be best interpreted as meaning which one of the following?
   a. Amicable
   b. Smoldering
   c. Luminous
   d. Ruinous
   e. Virtuous

7. Which of the following best explains how the passage is organized?
   a. The author begins by presenting the effects of a phenomenon, then explains the process of this phenomenon, and then ends by giving the history of the study of this phenomenon.
   b. The author begins by explaining a process or phenomenon, then gives the history of the study of this phenomenon, then ends by presenting the effects of this phenomenon.
   c. The author begins by giving the history of the study of a certain phenomenon, then explains the process of this phenomenon, then ends by presenting the effects of this phenomenon.
   d. The author begins by giving a broad definition of a subject, then presents more specific cases of the subject, then ends by contrasting two different viewpoints on the subject.
   e. The author begins by contrasting two different viewpoints, then gives a short explanation of a subject, then ends by summarizing what was previously stated in the passage.

8. What is the primary purpose of the passage?
   a. To inform the reader of the phenomenon, investigation, and consequences of milk souring
   b. To persuade the reader that milk souring is due to *Bacillus acidi lactici*, which is commonly found in the dairies of Europe
   c. To describe the accounts and findings of researchers studying the phenomenon of milk souring
   d. To discount the former researchers' opinions on milk souring and bring light to new investigations
   e. To narrate the story of one researcher who discovered the phenomenon of milk souring and its subsequent effects

9. What does the author say about the ordinary cause of milk souring?
   a. Milk souring is caused mostly by a species of bacteria called *Bacillus acidi lactici*, although former research asserted that it was caused by a variety of bacteria.
   b. The ordinary cause of milk souring is unknown to current researchers, although former researchers thought it was due to a species of bacteria called *Bacillus acidi lactici*.
   c. Milk souring is caused mostly by a species of bacteria identical to that of *Bacillus acidi lactici*, although there are a variety of other bacteria that cause milk souring as well.
   d. Soured milk will sometimes curdle without becoming acidic, and sometimes it will turn colors other than white, or have strange smells or tastes.
   e. The ordinary cause of milk souring is from bacteria with a strange, "soapy" smell, usually the color of sky blue.

10. The author of the passage would most likely agree most with which of the following?
    a. Milk researchers in the past have been incompetent and have sent us on a wild goose chase when determining what causes milk souring.
    b. Dairymen are considered more expert in the field of milk souring than milk researchers.
    c. The study of milk souring has improved throughout the years, as we now understand more of what causes milk souring and what happens afterward.
    d. Any type of bacteria will turn milk sour, so it's best to keep milk in an airtight container while it is being used.
    e. The effects of milk souring is a natural occurrence of milk, so it should not be dangerous to consume.

11. Given the author's account of the consequences of milk souring, which of the following is most closely analogous to the author's description of what happens after milk becomes slimy?
    a. The chemical change that occurs when a firework explodes
    b. A rainstorm that overwaters a succulent plant
    c. Mercury inside of a thermometer that leaks out
    d. A child who swallows flea medication
    e. A large block of ice that melts into a liquid

12. What type of paragraph would most likely come after the third?
    a. A paragraph depicting the general effects of bacteria on milk
    b. A paragraph explaining a broad history of what researchers have found in regard to milk souring
    c. A paragraph outlining the properties of milk souring and the way in which it occurs
    d. A paragraph showing the ways bacteria infiltrate milk and ways to avoid this infiltration
    e. A paragraph naming all the bacteria in alphabetical order with a brief definition of what each does to milk

The next 6 questions are based on the following two passages, labeled "Passage A" and "Passage B":

Passage A

> In approaching this problem of interpretation, we may first put out of consideration certain obvious limitations upon the generality of all guaranties of free speech. An occasional unthinking malcontent may urge that the only meaning not fraught with danger to liberty is the literal one that no utterance may be forbidden, no matter what its intent or result; but in fact it is nowhere seriously argued by anyone whose opinion is entitled to respect that direct and intentional incitations to crime may not be forbidden by the state. If a state may properly forbid murder or robbery or treason, it may also punish those who induce or counsel the commission of such crimes. Any other view makes a mockery of the state's power to declare and punish offences. And what the state may do to prevent the incitement of serious crimes which are universally condemned, it may also do to prevent the incitement of lesser crimes, or of those in regard to the bad tendency of which public opinion is divided. That is, if the state may punish John for burning straw in an alley, it may also constitutionally punish Frank for inciting John to do it, though Frank did so by speech or writing. And if, in 1857, the United States could punish John for helping a fugitive slave to escape, it could also punish Frank for inducing John to do this, even though a large section of public opinion might applaud John and condemn the Fugitive Slave Law.

Free Speech in War Time by James Parker Hall

221

Passage B

The true boundary line of the First Amendment can be fixed only when Congress and the courts realize that the principle on which speech is classified as lawful or unlawful involves the balancing against each other of two very important social interests, in public safety and in the search for truth. Every reasonable attempt should be made to maintain both interests unimpaired, and the great interest in free speech should be sacrificed only when the interest in public safety is really imperiled, and not, as most men believe, when it is barely conceivable that it may be slightly affected. In war time, therefore, speech should be unrestricted by the censorship or by punishment, unless it is clearly liable to cause direct and dangerous interference with the conduct of the war.

Thus our problem of locating the boundary line of free speech is solved. It is fixed close to the point where words will give rise to unlawful acts. We cannot define the right of free speech with the precision of the Rule against Perpetuities or the Rule in Shelley's Case, because it involves national policies which are much more flexible than private property, but we can establish a workable principle of classification in this method of balancing and this broad test of certain danger. There is a similar balancing in the determination of what is "due process of law." And we can with certitude declare that the First Amendment forbids the punishment of words merely for their injurious tendencies. The history of the Amendment and the political function of free speech corroborate each other and make this conclusion plain.

Freedom of Speech in War Time by Zechariah Chafee, Jr.

13. Which one of the following questions is central to both passages?
    a. What is the interpretation of the First Amendment and its limitations?
    b. Do people want absolute liberty, or do they only want liberty for a certain purpose?
    c. What is the true definition of freedom of speech in a democracy?
    d. How can we find an appropriate boundary for freedom of speech during wartime?

14. The authors of the two passages would be most likely to DISAGREE over which of the following?
    a. Throwing a man in jail due to his provocation of violence in Washington, D.C. during a riot
    b. Releasing a man from jail after he steals bread for his starving family
    c. Throwing a man in jail for encouraging a riot against the U.S. government for its wartime tactics, although no violence ensued
    d. Throwing a man in jail because he is caught as a German spy working within the U.S. army

15. The relationship between Passage *A* and Passage *B* is most analogous to the relationship between the documents described in which of the following?

   a. A journal article in the Netherlands about the law of euthanasia that cites evidence to support only the act of passive euthanasia as an appropriate way to die; a journal article in the Netherlands about the law of euthanasia that cites evidence to support voluntary euthanasia in any aspect

   b. An article detailing the effects of radiation in Fukushima; a research report describing the deaths and birth defects as a result of the hazardous waste dumped on the Somali Coast

   c. An article that suggests that labor laws during times of war should be left up to the states; an article that showcases labor laws during the past that have been altered due to the current crisis of war

   d. A research report arguing that the leading cause of methane emissions in the world is from agriculture practices; an article stating that the leading cause of methane emissions in the world is the transportation of coal, oil, and natural gas

16. The author uses the examples in the last lines of Passage *A* in order to do what?

   a. To compare different types of crimes to see by which one the principle of freedom of speech would become objectionable

   b. To demonstrate that anyone who incites a crime, despite the severity or magnitude of the crime, should be held accountable for that crime in some degree

   c. To prove that the definition of "freedom of speech" is altered depending on what kind of crime is being committed

   d. To show that some crimes are in the best interest of a nation and should not be punishable if they are proven to prevent harm to others

17. Which of the following, if true, would most seriously undermine the claim proposed by the author in Passage *A* that if the state can punish a crime, then it can punish the incitement of that crime?

   a. The idea that human beings are able and likely to change their minds between the utterance and execution of an event that may harm others

   b. The idea that human beings will always choose what they think is right based on their cultural upbringing

   c. The idea that the limitation of free speech by the government during wartime will protect the country from any group that causes a threat to that country's freedom

   d. The idea that those who support freedom of speech probably have intentions of subverting the government

18. What is the primary purpose of the second passage?

   a. To analyze the First Amendment in historical situations in order to make an analogy to the current war at hand in the nation

   b. To demonstrate that the boundaries set during wartime are different from those set when the country is at peace, and that we should change our laws accordingly

   c. To offer the idea that during wartime, the principle of freedom of speech should be limited to exclude even minor utterances in relation to a crime

   d. To claim the interpretation of freedom of speech is already evident in the First Amendment and to offer a clear perimeter of the principle during wartime

Directions for the next two questions: The following sentence has a blank where something has been left out. Beneath the sentence are four words or phrases. Choose the word or phrase that, when inserted in the sentence, best fits the meaning of the sentence as a whole.

223

19. The publishers purposely kept a(n) _____ mood surrounding the novel; they knew that its secrecy would enchant its potential readers.
    a. Demonstrative
    b. Reticent
    c. Apathetic
    d. Buoyant

20. She seemed to _____ in him a new sensation, probably what others would consider a taste of first love.
    a. Galvanize
    b. Placate
    c. Quell
    d. Relinquish

Writing

The next five questions are based on the following passage from The Life, Crime, and Capture of John Wilkes Booth *by George Alfred Townsend:*

(1) The box in which the President sat consisted of two boxes turned into one. As on all occasions when a state party visited the theater, the middle partition was removed. (2) The box was on a level with the dress circle; about twelve feet above the stage. (3) There were two entrances—the door nearest to the wall having been closed and locked; the door nearest the balustrades of the dress circle, and at right angles with it, being open and left open, after the visitors had entered. (4) The interior was carpeted, lined with crimson paper, and furnished with a sofa covered with crimson velvet, three arm chairs similarly covered, and six cane-bottomed chairs.

(5) President Lincoln took one of the arm-chairs and seated himself in the front of the box, in the angle nearest the audience, where, partially screened from observation, he had the best view of what was transpiring on the stage. (6) Mrs. Lincoln sat next to him, and Miss Harris in the opposite angle nearest the stage. (7) Major Rathbone sat just behind Mrs. Lincoln and Miss Harris. (8) These four were the only persons in the box.

(9) The play proceeded, although "Our American Cousin," without Mr. Sothern, has, since that gentleman's departure from this country, been justly esteemed a very dull affair. (10) The audience at Ford's Theater including Mrs. Lincoln seemed to enjoy it very much. (11) The worthy wife of the President leaned forward, her hand upon her husband's knee, watching every scene in the drama with amused attention.

1. In context, which of the following is the best way to revise and combine Sentences 1 & 2 (reproduced below)?

> The box in which the President sat consisted of two boxes turned into one. As on all occasions when a state party visited the theater, the middle partition was removed.

    a. The box in which the President sat consisted of two boxes turned into one, the middle partition was removed, as on all occasions when a state party visited the theater.

    b. The middle partition being removed due to the state party visiting the theater, the box in which the President sat two boxes turned into one.

    c. The box in which the President sat consisted of two boxes turned into one, the middle partition being removed, as on all occasions when a state party visited the theater.

    d. As on all occasions when a state party visited the theater, the middle partition as in the box in which the President sat consisted of two boxes turned into one.

2. In context, where would the following sentence best be placed?

> Even across the President's face at intervals swept a smile, robbing it of its habitual sadness.

    a. After Sentence 11

    b. After Sentence 9

    c. After Sentence 6

    d. After Sentence 2

3. In context, which of the following phrases is best to insert at the beginning of Sentence 8 (reproduced below)?

> These four were the only persons in the box.

    a. Next,

    b. After the fact,

    c. Immediately following,

    d. All in all,

4. In context, which of the following sentences would best be inserted at the end of Paragraph 1?

    a. It is presumed that she was saddled and bridled with exquisite care.

    b. Booth who was even more fashionably and richly dressed than usual, walked thence around to the front of the theater, and went in.

    c. Mr. Ford casually noticed this as a slightly extraordinary symptom of interest on the part of an actor so familiar with the routine of the theater and the play.

    d. Festoons of flags hung before the front of the box against a background of lace.

5. In context, which is the best revision to Sentence 10 (reproduced below)?

> The audience at Ford's Theatre including Mrs. Lincoln seemed to enjoy it very much.

    a. The audience at Ford's Theater; including Mrs. Lincoln; seemed to enjoy it very much.

    b. The audience at Ford's Theater, including Mrs. Lincoln, seemed to enjoy it very much.

    c. The audience at Fords Theater, including Mrs. Lincoln, seemed to enjoy it very much.

    d. The audience at Fords Theater including Mrs. Lincoln seemed to enjoy it very much.

The next five questions are based on the following passage from The Story of Germ Life *by Herbert William Conn:*

(1) The first and most universal change effected in milk is its souring. (2) So universal is this phenomenon that it is generally regarded as an inevitable change which cannot be avoided, and, as already pointed out, has in the past been regarded as a normal property of milk. (3) It is due to the action of certain of the milk bacteria upon the milk sugar which converts it into lactic acid, and this acid gives the sour taste and curdles the milk. (4) After this acid is produced in small quantity its presence proves deleterious to the growth of the bacteria, and further bacterial growth is checked. (5) After souring, the milk for some time does not ordinarily undergo any further changes.

(6) Milk souring has been commonly regarded as a single phenomenon, alike in all cases. (7) When it was first studied by bacteriologists it was thought to be due in all cases to a single species of micro-organism which was discovered to be commonly present and named *Bacillus acidi lactici.* (8) This bacterium has certainly the power of souring milk rapidly, and is found to be very common in dairies in Europe. (9) As soon as bacteriologists turned their attention more closely to the subject it was found that the spontaneous souring of milk was not always caused by the same species of bacterium. (10) The number of species of bacteria which have been found to sour milk has increased until something over a hundred are known to have this power. (11) These different species do not affect the milk in the same way. (12) All produce some acid, but they differ in the kind and the amount of acid, and especially in the other changes which are affected at the same time that the milk is soured, so that the resulting soured milk is quite variable.

6. In context, which of the following phrases is best to insert at the beginning of Sentence 5 (reproduced below)?

After souring, the milk for some time does not ordinarily undergo any further changes.

- a. Furthermore,
- b. Additionally,
- c. However,
- d. Therefore,

7. In context, where would the following sentence best be placed?

Instead of finding this *Bacillus acidi lactici* always present, they found that quite a number of different species of bacteria have the power of souring milk, and are found in different specimens of soured milk.

- a. After Sentence 2
- b. After Sentence 9
- c. After Sentence 10
- d. After Sentence 12

8. In context, which of the following is the best way to revise and combine Sentences 10 & 11 (reproduced below)?

> The number of species of bacteria which have been found to sour milk has increased until something over a hundred are known to have this power. These different species do not affect the milk in the same way.

a. The number of species of bacteria which have been found to sour milk has increased until something over a hundred are known to have this power, and these different species do not affect the milk in the same way.

b. The number of species of bacteria which have been found to sour milk has increased until something over a hundred are known to have this power, or these different species do not affect the milk in the same way.

c. The number of species of bacteria which have been found to sour milk has increased until something over a hundred are known to have this power, but these different species do not affect the milk in the same way.

d. The number of species of bacteria which have been found to sour milk has increased until something over a hundred are known to have this power, so these different species do not affect the milk in the same way.

9. In context, which is the best revision to Sentence 8 (reproduced below)?

> This bacterium has certainly the power of souring milk rapidly, and is found to be very common in dairies in Europe.

a. This bacterium has certainly the power of souring milk rapidly; and is found to be very common in dairies in Europe.

b. This bacterium has certainly the power of souring milk rapidly finding to be very common in dairies in Europe.

c. This bacterium has certainly the power of souring milk rapidly and is found to be very common in dairies in Europe.

d. This bacterium has certainly the power of souring milk rapidly, and is found to be very common in dairies in Europe.

10. In context, which of the following sentences would best be inserted after Sentence 2 (reproduced below)?

> So universal is this phenomenon that it is generally regarded as an inevitable change which cannot be avoided, and, as already pointed out, has in the past been regarded as a normal property of milk.

a. Today, however, the phenomenon is well understood.

b. However, today the phenomenon is not well understood.

c. Flowers also have unusual properties which undergo transformation.

d. The properties in milk are the same as any other product that undergoes souring.

The next five questions are from Rhetoric and Poetry in the Renaissance: A Study of Rhetorical Terms in English Renaissance Literary Criticism *by D.L. Clark:*

(1) To the Greeks and Romans rhetoric meant the theory of oratory. (2) As a pedagogical mechanism it endavored to teach students to persuade an audience. (3) The content of rhetoric included all that the ancients had learned to be of value in persuasive public speech. (4) It taught how to work up a case by drawing valid inferences from sound evidence, how to organize this material in the most persuasive order, how to compose in clear and harmonious sentences.

(5) In both these respects the ancients felt that poetics the theory of poetry was different from rhetoric. (6) As the critical theorists believed that the poets were inspired, they endeavored less to teach men to be poets than to point out the excellences which the poets had attained. (7) Although these critics generally, with the exceptions of Aristotle and Eratosthenes, believed the greatest value of poetry to be in the teaching of morality, no one of them endeavored to define poetry, as they did rhetoric, by its purpose. (8) To Aristotle, and centuries later to Plutarch, the distinguishing mark of poetry was imitation. (9) Not until the renaissance did critics define poetry as an art of imitation endeavoring to inculcate morality...

(10) The same essential difference between classical rhetoric and poetics appears in the content of classical poetics. (11) It is a commonplace that classical literary critics paid little attention to the lyric. (12) It is less frequently realized that they devoted almost as little space to discussion of metrics. (13) By far the greater bulk of classical treatises on poetics is devoted to characterization and to the technique of plot construction, involving as it does narrative and dramatic unity and movement as distinct from logical unity and movement.

11. In context, which is the best revision to Sentence 5 (reproduced below)?

In both these respects the ancients felt that poetics the theory of poetry was different from rhetoric.

a. In both these respects the ancients felt that poetics; the theory of poetry, was different from rhetoric.
b. In both these respects the ancients felt that poetics, the theory of poetry, was different from rhetoric.
c. In both these respects the ancients felt that poetics the theory of poetry, was different from rhetoric.
d. In both these respects the ancients felt that poetics the theory of poetry was different from rhetoric.

12. In context, which of the following is the best way to revise and combine Sentences 11 & 12 (reproduced below)?

It is a commonplace that classical literary critics paid little attention to the lyric. It is less frequently realized that they devoted almost as little space to discussion of metrics.

a. Because it is a commonplace, that classical literary critics paid little attention to the lyric, and, it is less frequently realized that they devoted almost as little space to discussion of metrics.
b. Less frequently realized is that they devoted almost as little space to discussion of metrics, but literary critics paid little attention to the lyric.
c. Although it is a commonplace that classical literary critics paid little attention to the lyric, it is less frequently realized that they devoted almost as little space to discussion of metrics.
d. Literary critics paid little attention to the lyric, everybody knows that, but what everyone doesn't know is that they paid way less attention to the discussion of metrics.

228

13. In context, which of the following sentences would best be inserted after Sentence 4 (reproduced below)?

> It taught how to work up a case by drawing valid inferences from sound evidence, how to organize this material in the most persuasive order, how to compose in clear and harmonious sentences.

a. Thus to the Greeks and Romans rhetoric was defined by its function of discovering means to persuasion and was taught in the schools as something that every free-born man could and should learn.
b. Many modern critics have found the classical distinction between rhetoric and poetic very suggestive.
c. A survey of what Aristotle includes in his *Poetics*, what he excludes, and what he ignores, will be a helpful initial step in an investigation of what he meant by poetic.
d. The first quoted passage is indeed not only "embroidery," but mere talk about shipwrecks, and the terrors of the deep.

14. In context, which is the best spelling of the underlined word in Sentence 2 (reproduced below)?

> As a pedagogical mechanism it <u>endavored</u> to teach students to persuade an audience.

a. Endaevored
b. Endevored
c. Endeavored
d. Endavored

15. In context, where would the following sentence best be placed?

> Whereas classical rhetoric deals with speeches which might be delivered to convict or acquit a defendant in the law court, or to secure a certain action by the deliberative assembly, or to adorn an occasion, classical poetics deals with lyric, epic, and drama.

a. After Sentence 2
b. After Sentence 4
c. After Sentence 7
d. After Sentence 10

The next five questions are based on the following passage:

> (1) The vast industrialization of Europe which took place between 1760 and 1840 was perhaps the most significant watershed period in the history of Europe. (2) It was a time of astronomical growth and progress for Europeans as a whole, yet it was simultaneously a wretched and dehumanizing period for the majority of European individuals. (3) Many problems—economic, social, and political—were either created or magnified by the Industrial Revolution: problems that threatened European society not with annihilation but with massive change in the form of a social revolution that would shift the distribution of political might and change class structure.
>
> (4) The Industrial Revolution touched and altered almost every aspect of the economic and political life of pre–1760 Europe, which, in turn, changed the existing social order. (5)

With roots digging as deeply into the past as the thirteenth century, when capitalism and commerce began to develop, industrialization slowly became inevitable. (6) It was aided by a gradual expansion of the market, a demand for more goods by an increasing number of consumers, and the step-by-step liberation of private enterprise from government control. (7) Industrialization began in earnest in the textile industry of Great Britain, and, due to progress in the field of technological innovations, caused a huge upswing in the amount of money necessary to establish a factory. (8) Industry became the new source of wealth, which had formerly been land, but the power remained concentrated within a small group of rich men—the capitalists. (9) The existence of this wealthy class directly contrasted with that of the impoverished working class (people who had once worked the land, until they were forced by industrialization to undertake factory labor in order to survive). (10) The juxtaposition of a small (17) number of people, who held great wealth, with a population for whom extreme and widespread poverty was inescapable was one of the greatest problems the Industrial Revolution created.

16. Which is the best version of the underlined portion of Sentence 1 (reproduced below)?

The vast <u>industrialization of Europe which took place between 1760 and 1840 was perhaps the most significant watershed</u> period in the history of Europe.

 a. Leave it as is
 b. industrialization of Europe, which took place between 1760 and 1840 was perhaps the most significant watershed
 c. industrialization of Europe, which took place between 1760 and 1840, was perhaps the most significant watershed
 d. industrialization of Europe which took place, between 1760 and 1840, was perhaps the most significant watershed

17. In the context of the essay as a whole, which of the following words is the most accurate substitution for the underlined portion of Sentence 4?

The Industrial Revolution touched and altered almost every aspect of the economic and political life of Europe prior to 1760, which, in turn, <u>changed</u> the existing social order.

 a. transfigured
 b. disrupted
 c. destroyed
 d. transformed

18. Which is the best version of the underlined portion of Sentence 5 (reproduced below)?

<u>With roots digging deeply into the past as the thirteenth century</u>, when capitalism and commerce began to develop, industrialization slowly became inevitable.

 a. Leave it as
 b. With roots, digging deeply into the past as the thirteenth century
 c. With roots digging as deeply into the past as the thirteenth century
 d. With roots that were digging deeply into the past as the thirteenth century

19. A transition sentence is needed to improve the flow from Sentence 7 to Sentence 8. Which of the following sentences best accomplishes the transition?
   a. The demand for large amounts of capital was met by a small group of wealthy investors.
   b. Therefore, the need of large capitalists was predominant.
   c. Capitalists, with their deep pockets, came to the rescue.
   d. The economic theory of supply and demand was born.

20. Sentence 8 Which option best rephrases the underlined sentence
   a. Land, formerly the source of wealth, was overshadowed by industry, dominated by rich capitalists.
   b. Capitalists invested in industry, which replaced land as the primary source of wealth. As a result, power remained concentrated in the hands of the capitalists.
   c. By investing their capital in industry, the capitalists changed the source of wealth from land to industry and retained most of the power.
   d. Formerly the major source of wealth, land was replaced by industry, and the capitalists held all the power.

The next five questions are based on the following passage:

(1) The two main types of stroke are ischemic and hemorrhagic. Ischemic stroke occurs when a blood clot blocks an artery in the central nervous system (CNS). (2) The blockage disrupts the flow of oxygen-rich blood to CNS tissue and to the brain to the extent that the supply of oxygen and glucose is insufficient to support ongoing metabolism. (3) Thrombotic stroke and embolic stroke are two subtypes of ischemic stroke. (4) In thrombotic stroke, a blood clot or atherosclerotic plaque develops locally to create blockage. (5) In embolic stroke, a blood clot or atherosclerotic plaque develops elsewhere, such as in the heart, breaks apart, and travels in the bloodstream without blocking blood flow until it reaches a central nervous system artery, then it travels through the artery up to the brain, lodging there.

(6) Headache, nausea, vomiting, numbness, and loss of consciousness are all warning signs of a possible stroke these symptoms require immediate medical attention to prevent damage to—or complete loss of—brain cells. (7) The three most common symptoms of stroke are varying degrees of facial drooping, unilateral limb weakness, and speech difficulty. (8) Noncontrast computed tomography (CT) scans can detect mass lesions, such as a tumor or an abscess, and an acute hemorrhage. (9) Strokes can also cause depression and a loss of the ability to control emotions.

(10) Hemorrhagic stroke is caused when a blood vessel ruptures, sending blood into the surrounding brain tissue. (11) Intracerebral hemorrhage is one subtype of hemorrhagic stroke and is characterized by bleeding within brain tissue. (12) Subarachnoid hemorrhage is a second subtype and occurs when bleeding is within the space between the arachnoid and pia mater membranes of the meninges, the connective tissue around the brain. (13) Bleeding within the brain is a serious condition, as the blood leaked can destroy brain tissue and impairment can happen within a matter of minutes.

(14) With both ischemic stroke and hemorrhagic stroke, structural damage in the central nervous system can disrupt connecting pathways, leading to significant loss of neurologic function and disability. (15) The development of neurological disease may be a consequence of stroke-associated disruption of certain neuronal pathways.

21. Which of the following is the best form of Sentence 2?
    a. The punctuation is correct as is.
    b. The blockage disrupts the flow of oxygen-rich blood to CNS tissue and to the brain, to the extent that the supply of oxygen and glucose is insufficient to support ongoing metabolism.
    c. The blockage disrupts the flow of oxygen-rich blood to CNS tissue, and to the brain to the extent that the supply of oxygen and glucose is insufficient to support ongoing metabolism.
    d. The blockage disrupts the flow of oxygen-rich blood, to CNS tissue and to the brain to the extent that the supply of oxygen and glucose is insufficient to support ongoing metabolism.

22. There is a semicolon missing from Sentence 5. What is the correct position for it?
    a. In embolic stroke, a blood clot or atherosclerotic plaque develops elsewhere, such as in the heart; breaks apart, and travels in the bloodstream without blocking blood flow until it reaches a central nervous system artery, then it travels through the artery up to the brain, lodging there.

    b. In embolic stroke, a blood clot or atherosclerotic plaque develops elsewhere, such as in the heart, breaks apart, and travels in the bloodstream without blocking blood flow until it reaches a central nervous system artery; then it travels through the artery up to the brain, lodging there.

    c. In embolic stroke, a blood clot or atherosclerotic plaque develops elsewhere; such as in the heart, breaks apart, and travels in the bloodstream without blocking blood flow until it reaches a central nervous system artery, then it travels through the artery up to the brain, lodging there.

    d. In embolic stroke, a blood clot or atherosclerotic plaque develops elsewhere, such as in the heart, breaks apart; and travels in the bloodstream without blocking blood flow until it reaches a central nervous system artery, then it travels through the artery up to the brain, lodging there.

23. Which punctuation mark is the correct one to place between "stroke" and "these" as is?
    a. Slash (/)
    b. Dash (—)
    c. Semicolon (;)
    d. Period (.)

24. Which sentence, if any, interrupts the flow of the discussion in Paragraph 2?
    a. None
    b. Sentence 7
    c. Sentence 8
    d. Sentence 9

25. Which is the best version of the underlined portion of Sentence 13 (reproduced below)?

Bleeding within the brain is a serious condition, <u>as the blood leaked can destroy brain tissue</u> and impairment can happen within a matter of minutes.

    a. Leave it as is
    b. as the blood is leaked can destroy brain tissue
    c. as the blood is leaked, can destroy brain tissue
    d. because as blood leaked, it can destroy brain tissue

Write Placer Prompt

Read the passage below then answer in an essay format.

> According to the plan of the convention, all judges who may be appointed by the United States are to hold their offices *during good behavior*, which is conformable to the most approved of the State constitutions and among the rest, to that of this State. Its propriety having been drawn into question by the adversaries of that plan, is no light symptom of the rage for objection, which disorders their imaginations and judgments. The standard of good behavior for the continuance in office of the judicial magistracy is certainly one of the most valuable of the modern improvements in the practice of government. In a monarchy, it is an excellent barrier to the despotism of the prince; in a republic, it is a no less excellent barrier to the encroachments and oppressions of the representative body. And it is the best expedient which can be devised in any government, to secure a steady, upright, and impartial administration of the laws.

Write an essay and explain what the author means by the passage above. Then, choose a side on the issue and argue why you agree or disagree. Give specific examples to support the argument.

Answer Explanations #1

Arithmetic

1. B: The fraction $\frac{12}{60}$ can be reduced to $\frac{1}{5}$, in lowest terms. First, it must be converted to a decimal. Dividing 1 by 5 results in 0.2. Then, to convert to a percentage, move the decimal point two units to the right and add the percentage symbol. The result is 20%.

2. B: If a calculator is used, divide 33 into 14 and keep two decimal places. If a calculator is not used, multiply both the numerator and denominator by 3. This results in the fraction $\frac{42}{99}$, and hence a decimal of 0.42.

3. B: Common denominators must be used. The LCD is 15, and $\frac{2}{5} = \frac{6}{15}$. Therefore, $\frac{14}{15} + \frac{6}{15} = \frac{20}{15}$, and in lowest terms the answer is $\frac{4}{3}$. A common factor of 5 was divided out of both the numerator and denominator.

4. A: A product is found by multiplication. Multiplying two fractions together is easier when common factors are canceled first to avoid working with larger numbers.

$$\frac{5}{14} \times \frac{7}{20} = \frac{5}{2 \times 7} \times \frac{7}{5 \times 4} = \frac{1}{2} \times \frac{1}{4} = \frac{1}{8}$$

5. D: Division is completed by multiplying by the reciprocal:

$$24 \div \frac{8}{5} = \frac{24}{1} \times \frac{5}{8} = \frac{3 \times 8}{1} \times \frac{5}{8} = \frac{15}{1} = 15$$

6. C: A common denominator must be used to subtract fractions. Remember that in order to find the least common denominator, the least common multiple of both of the denominators must be determined. The smallest multiple that 24 and 14 share is 168, which is 24×7 and 14×12. The LCD is 168, which can be found by finding the LCM of 14 and 24, so each fraction must be converted to have 168 as the denominator.

$$\frac{5}{24} - \frac{5}{14} = \frac{5}{24} \times \frac{7}{7} - \frac{5}{14} \times \frac{12}{12} = \frac{35}{168} - \frac{60}{168} = -\frac{25}{168}$$

7. C: The correct mathematical statement is the one in which the number to the left on the number line is less than the number to the right on the number line. It is written in Choice C that $\frac{1}{3} > -\frac{4}{3}$, which is the same as $-\frac{4}{3} < \frac{1}{3}$, a correct statement.

8. C: $-\frac{1}{5} > \frac{4}{5}$ is an incorrect statement. The expression on the left is negative, which means that it is smaller than the expression on the right. As it is written, the inequality states that the expression on the left is greater than the expression on the right, which is not true.

9. B: First, the information is translated into the ratio $\frac{15}{80}$. To find the percentage, translate this fraction into a decimal by dividing 15 by 80. The corresponding decimal is 0.1875. Move the decimal point two places to the right to obtain the percentage 18.75%.

10. C: Gina answered 60% of 35 questions correctly; 60% can be expressed as the decimal 0.60. Therefore, she answered $0.60 \times 35 = 21$ questions correctly.

11. B: The unknown quantity is the number of total questions on the test. Let x be equal to this unknown quantity. Since 75% is equal to $\frac{3}{4}$ as a fraction, $\frac{3}{4}x = 12$. To solve for x, multiply both sides by $\frac{4}{3}$. Therefore,

$$x = 12 \times \frac{4}{3} = \frac{48}{3} = 16$$

12. B: If sales tax is 7.25%, the price of the car must be multiplied by 1.0725 to account for the additional sales tax. This is the same as multiplying the initial price by 0.0725 (the tax) and adding that to the initial cost. Therefore:

$$15,395 \times 1.0725 = 16,511.1375$$

This amount is rounded to the nearest cent, which is $16,511.14.

13. A: Rounding can be used to find the best approximation. All of the values can be rounded to the nearest thousand. 15,412 SUVs can be rounded to 15,000. 25,815 station wagons can be rounded to 26,000. 50,412 sedans can be rounded to 50,000. 8,123 trucks can be rounded to 8,000. Finally, 18,312 hybrids can be rounded to 18,000. The sum of the rounded values is 117,000, which is closest to 120,000.

14. D: There are 52 weeks in a year, and if the family spends $105 each week, that amount is close to $100. A good approximation is $100 a week for 50 weeks, which is found through the product:

$$50 \times \$100 = \$5,000$$

15. C: This problem involves ratios and proportions. If 12 packets are needed for every 5 people, this statement is equivalent to the ratio $\frac{12}{5}$. The unknown amount x is the number of ketchup packets needed for 60 people. The proportion $\frac{12}{5} = \frac{x}{60}$ must be solved. Cross-multiply to obtain $12 \times 60 = 5x$. Therefore, $720 = 5x$. Divide each side by 5 to obtain $x = 144$.

16. D: There were 48 total bags of apples sold. If 9 bags were Granny Smith and the rest were Red Delicious, then $48 - 9 = 39$ bags were Red Delicious. Therefore, the ratio of Granny Smith to Red Delicious is $9 : 39$.

17. B: The average rate of change is found by calculating the difference in dollars over the elapsed time. Therefore, the rate of change is equal to $(\$4,900 - \$4,000) \div 3$ months, which is equal to $\$900 \div 3$, or $300 per month.

18. A: The formula for the rate of change is the same as slope: change in y over change in x. The y-value in this case is percentage of smokers and the x-value is year. The change in percentage of smokers from 2000 to 2015 was 8.1%. The change in x was $2000 - 2015 = -15$. Therefore, $\frac{8.1\%}{-15} = -0.54\%$. The percentage of smokers decreased 0.54% each year.

19. A: A proportion should be used to solve this problem. The ratio of tagged to total deer in each instance is set equal to one another, and the unknown quantity is a variable x. The proportion is:

$$\frac{300}{x} = \frac{5}{400}$$

Cross-multiplying gives $120{,}000 = 5x$, and dividing through by 5 results in 24,000.

20. B: The number of representatives varies directly with the population, so the equation necessary is $N = k \times P$, where N is number of representatives, k is the variation constant, and P is total population in millions. Plugging in the information for New York allows k to be solved for. This process gives $27 = k \times 20$, so $k \approx 1.35$. Therefore, the formula for number of representatives given total population in millions is:

$$N = 1.35 \times P$$

Plugging in $P = 11.6$ for Ohio results in $N \approx 15.66$, which rounds up to 16 total representatives.

Quantitative Reasoning, Algebra, and Statistics

1. A: First, the distributive property must be used on the left side. This results in:

$$3x + 6 = 14x - 5$$

The addition principle is then used to add 5 to both sides, and then to subtract $3x$ from both sides, resulting in $11 = 11x$. Finally, the multiplication principle is used to divide each side by 11. Therefore, $x = 1$ is the solution.

2. D: First, like terms are collected to obtain $12 - 5x = -5x + 12$. Then, if the addition principle is used to move the terms with the variable, $5x$ is added to both sides and the mathematical statement $12 = 12$ is obtained. This is always true; therefore, all real numbers satisfy the original equation.

3. B: The distributive property is used on both sides to obtain $4x + 20 + 6 = 4x + 6$. Then, like terms are collected on the left, resulting in $4x + 26 = 4x + 6$. Next, the addition principle is used to subtract $4x$ from both sides, and this results in the false statement $26 = 6$. Therefore, there is no solution.

4. D: This is a one-step, real-world application problem. The unknown quantity is the number of cases of cola to be purchased. Let x be equal to this amount. Because each case costs $3.50, the total number of cases multiplied by $3.50 must equal $40. This translates to the mathematical equation $3.5x = 40$. Divide both sides by 3.5 to obtain $x = 11.4286$, which has been rounded to four decimal places. Because cases are sold whole, and there is not enough money to purchase 12 cases, 11 cases is the correct answer.

5. A: First, the variables have to be defined. Let x be the first integer; therefore, $x + 1$ is the second integer. This is a two-step problem. The sum of three times the first and two less than the second is translated into the following expression:

$$3x + (x + 1 - 2)$$

Set this expression equal to 411 to obtain:

$$3x + (x + 1 - 2) = 411$$

The left-hand side is simplified to obtain $4x - 1 = 411$. To solve for x, first add 1 to both sides and then divide both sides by 4 to obtain $x = 103$. The next consecutive integer is 104.

236

6. A: Let x be the unknown, the number of hours Erin can work. We know Katie works $2x$, and the sum of all hours is less than 21. Therefore, $x + 2x < 21$, which simplifies into $3x < 21$. Solving this results in the inequality $x < 7$ after dividing both sides by 3. Therefore, Erin can work less than 7 hours.

7. C: By switching from a radical expression to rational exponents:

$$\sqrt[4]{x^6} = x^{\frac{6}{4}} = x^{\frac{3}{2}}$$

Also, properties of exponents can be used to simplify $\frac{x}{x^3}$ into:

$$x^{1-3} = x^{-2} = \frac{1}{x^2}$$

The other terms can be left alone, resulting in an equivalent expression:

$$x^{\frac{3}{2}} - \frac{1}{x^2} + x - 2$$

8. B: Using Descartes' Rule of Signs, count the number of sign changes in coefficients in the polynomial. This results in the number of possible positive zeros. The coefficients are 1, -3, 2, 1, and -3, so the sign changes from 1 to -3, -3 to 2, and 1 to -3, a total of 3 times. Therefore, there are at most 3 positive zeros.

9. B: The goal is to first isolate the variable. The fractions can easily be cleared by multiplying the entire inequality by 5, resulting in $35 - 4x < 3$. Then, subtract 35 from both sides and divide by -4. This results in $x > 8$. Notice the inequality symbol has been flipped because both sides were divided by a negative number. The solution set, all real numbers greater than 8, is written in interval notation as $(8, \infty)$. A parenthesis shows that 8 is not included in the solution set.

10. D: Let x be the unknown number. Difference indicates subtraction, and sum represents addition. To triple the difference, it is multiplied by 3. The problem can be expressed as the following equation:

$$3(5 - x) = x + 5$$

Distributing the 3 results in:

$$15 - 3x = x + 5$$

Subtract 5 from both sides, add $3x$ to both sides, and then divide both sides by 4. This results in:

$$x = \frac{10}{4} = \frac{5}{2} = 2.5$$

11. B: The expression under the radical can be factored into perfect squares as such:

$$\sqrt{100 \times 2 \times x^6 \times y^6 \times y \times z^2}$$

Using rational exponents, this is the same as

$$(100 \times 2 \times x^6 \times y^6 \times y \times z^2)^{\frac{1}{2}}$$

$$100^{\frac{1}{2}} \times 2^{\frac{1}{2}} \times x^{\frac{6}{2}} \times y^{\frac{6}{2}} \times y^{\frac{1}{2}} \times z^{\frac{2}{2}}$$

$$\sqrt{100} \times \sqrt{2} \times x^3 \times y^3 \times \sqrt{y} \times z$$

$$10x^3y^3z\sqrt{2y}$$

12. D: The exponential rules $(ab)^m = a^m b^m$ and $(a^m)^n = a^{mn}$ can be used to rewrite the expression as:

$$4^4y^{12} \times 3^2y^{14}$$

The coefficients are multiplied together and the exponential rule $a^m a^n = a^{m+n}$ is then used to obtain the simplified form $2{,}304y^{26}$.

13. A: The surface area for a cylinder is the sum of the two circle bases and the rectangle formed on the side. This is easily seen in the net of a cylinder.

The Net of a Cylinder

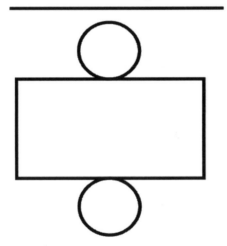

The area of a circle is found by multiplying π times the radius squared. The rectangle's area is found by multiplying the circumference of the circle by the height. The equation $SA = 2\pi \times 5 \times 10 + 2\pi \times 5^2$ shows the area of the rectangle as $2\pi \times 5 \times 10$, which yields 314. The area of the bases is found by $\pi \times 5^2$, which yields 78.5, and then is multiplied by 2 for the two bases. Adding these together gives 471.

14. A: The probability of 0.9 is closer to 1 than any of the other answers. The closer a probability is to 1, the greater the likelihood that the event will occur. The probability of 0.05 shows that it is very unlikely that an adult driver will wear their seatbelt because it is close to zero. A zero probability means that it will not occur. The probability of 0.25 is closer to zero than to one, so it shows that it is unlikely an adult will wear their seatbelt.

15. A: The area of the shaded region is calculated in a few steps. First, the area of the rectangle is found using the formula:

$$A = length \times width = 6 \text{ m} \times 2 \text{ m} = 12 \text{ m}^2$$

Second, the area of the triangle is found using the formula:

$$A = \frac{1}{2} \times base \times height = \frac{1}{2} \times 3 \text{ m} \times 2 \text{ m} = 3 \text{ m}^2$$

The last step is to take the rectangle area and subtract the triangle area. The area of the shaded region is:

$$A = 12 \text{ m}^2 - 3 \text{ m}^2 = 9 \text{ m}^2$$

16. D: The volume for a cylinder is found by using the formula:

$$V = \pi r^2 h = (3.14)(2 \text{ in})^2 \times 3.5 \text{ in} = 43.96 \text{ in}^3$$

17. D: This system can be solved using the method of substitution. Solving the first equation for y results in $y = 14 - 2x$. Plugging this into the second equation gives $4x + 2(14 - 2x) = -28$, which simplifies to $28 = -28$, an untrue statement. Therefore, this system has no solution because no x-value will satisfy the system.

18. B: The slopes of perpendicular lines are negative reciprocals, meaning their product is equal to -1. The slope of the line given needs to be found. Its equivalent form in slope-intercept form is $y = -\frac{4}{7}x + \frac{23}{7}$, so its slope is $-\frac{4}{7}$. The negative reciprocal of this number is $\frac{7}{4}$. The only line in the options given with this same slope is $y = \frac{7}{4}x - 12$.

19. C: This system can be solved using substitution. Plug the second equation in for y in the first equation to obtain $2x - 8x = 6$, which simplifies to $-6x = 6$. Divide both sides by 6 to get $x = -1$, which is then substituted back into either original equation to obtain $y = -8$.

20. C: The Pythagorean theorem can be used to find the missing length x because it is a right triangle. The theorem states that $6^2 + 8^2 = x^2$, which simplifies into $100 = x^2$. Taking the positive square root of both sides results in the missing value $x = 10$.

Advanced Algebra and Functions

1. B: The only relation in which every x-value corresponds to exactly one y-value is the relation given in Choice *B*, making it a function. The other relations have the same x-value paired up to different y-values, which goes against the definition of functions.

2. A: To find a function value, plug in the number given for the variable and evaluate the expression using the order of operations (parentheses, exponents, multiplication, division, addition, subtraction):

$$f(5) = 5^2 - 2 \times 5 + 1$$

$$f(5) = 25 - 10 + 1 = 16$$

3. C: The function given is a polynomial function. Anything can be plugged into a polynomial function to get an output. Therefore, its domain is all real numbers, which is expressed in interval notation as $(-\infty, \infty)$.

4. B: The variable x represents the number of years after 1980. The year 2011 was 31 years after 1980, so plug 31 into the function to obtain:

$$f(31) = 3.1 \times 31 + 240 = 336.1$$

This value rounds to 336 and represents 336 million people.

5. D: The argument of a logarithmic function has to be greater than 0. Basically, one cannot take the logarithm of a negative number or 0. Therefore, to find the domain, set the argument greater than 0 and solve the inequality. This results in $x - 2 > 0$, or $x > 2$. Therefore, in order to obtain an output of the function, the number plugged into the function must be greater than 2. This domain is represented as $(2, \infty)$.

6. B: The time of the initial outbreak corresponds to $t = 0$. Therefore, 0 must be plugged into the function. This results in $\frac{20,000}{1+10e^0} = \frac{20,000}{1+10} = \frac{20,000}{11} = 1,818.182$, which rounds to 1,818. Therefore, there were 1,818 people in the population that initially had the disease.

7. A: The zeros of a polynomial function are the x-values where the graph crosses the x-axis, or where $y = 0$. Therefore, set y equal to 0 and solve the polynomial equation. This quadratic can be solved using factoring, as follows:

$$0 = 2x^2 - 12x + 16$$

$$2(x^2 - 6x + 8) = 2(x - 4)(x - 2)$$

Setting both factors equal to 0 results in the two solutions $x = 4$ and $x = 2$, which are the zeros of the original function.

8. C: Given a logarithmic function $f(x) = \log_b x$, its base is b and it can be written as $y = \log_b x$ with equivalent exponential equation $b^y = x$. In this problem, the base is 5, so its equivalent exponential equation is:

$$5^y = x + 3$$

9. D: This is a parabola that opens up, as the coefficient on the x^2-term is positive. The smallest number in its range occurs when plugging 0 into the function $f(0) = 5$. Any other output is a number larger than 5, even when a negative number is plugged in. When a negative number gets plugged into the function, the output is positive, and same with a positive number. Therefore, the domain is written as $[5, \infty)$ in interval notation.

10. B: The equivalent equation form of the function is $y = 10^{x+3}$. The expression can be written in logarithmic form as:

$$\log_{10} y = x + 3$$

A logarithm with base 10 is known as the common logarithm and is written without the base. Adding -3 to both sides results in:

$$-3 + \log y = x$$

11. C: First, set the functions equal to one another, resulting in:

$$x^2 + 3x + 2 = 4x + 4$$

This is a quadratic equation, so the best way to find the answer is to convert it to standard form by subtracting $4x + 4$ from both sides of the equation, setting it equal to 0:

$$x^2 - x - 2 = 0$$

Then, factor the equation:

$$(x - 2)(x + 1) = 0$$

Setting both factors equal to zero results in $x = 2$ and $x = -1$.

12. D: There will be no more coyotes when the population is 0, so set y equal to 0 and solve the quadratic equation:

$$0 = -(x - 2)^2 + 1600$$

Subtract 1600 from both sides and divide through by -1. This results in:

$$1600 = (x - 2)^2$$

Then, take the square root of both sides. This process results in the following equation: $\pm 40 = x - 2$. Adding 2 to both sides results in two solutions: $x = 42$ and $x = -38$. Because the problem involves years after 2000, the only solution that makes sense is 42. Add 42 to 2000, so therefore in the year 2042 there will be no more coyotes.

13. A: The range value is given, and this is the output of the function. Therefore, the function must be set equal to $\frac{1}{8}$ and solved for x. Thus, $\frac{1}{8} = \frac{1}{4}x - 2$ needs to be solved. The fractions can be cleared by multiplying times the LCD 8. This results in $1 = 2x - 16$. Add 16 to both sides and divide by 2 to obtain $x = \frac{17}{2}$.

14. B: The ball is back at the starting point when the function is equal to 800 feet. Therefore, this results in solving the equation:

$$800 = -32t^2 + 90t + 800$$

Subtract 800 off of both sides and factor the remaining terms to obtain:

$$0 = 2t(-16t + 45)$$

Setting both factors equal to 0 results in $t = 0$, which is when the ball was thrown up initially, and $t = \frac{45}{16} = 2.8$ seconds. Therefore, it will take the ball 2.8 seconds to come back down to its starting point.

15. C: To find the zeros, set the function equal to 0 and factor the polynomial. Because there are four terms, it should be factored by grouping. Factor a common factor out of the first set of two terms, and then find a shared binomial factor in the second set of two terms. This results in:

$$x^2(x-2) - 9(x-2) = 0$$

The binomial can then be factored out of each set to get:

$$(x^2 - 9)(x-2) = 0$$

This can be factored further as:

$$(x+3)(x-3)(x-2) = 0$$

Setting each factor equal to zero and solving results in the three zeros -3, 3, and 2.

16. B: Given a rational function, the expression in the denominator can never be equal to 0. To find the domain, set the denominator equal to 0 and solve for x. This results in $2 - x = 0$, and its solution is $x = 2$. This value needs to be excluded from the set of all real numbers, and therefore the domain written in interval notation is $(-\infty, 2) \cup (2, \infty)$.

17. C: Plugging the function into the formula results in:

$$\frac{4(x+h) - 2 - (4x - 2)}{h}$$

Which is simplified to:

$$\frac{4x + 4h - 2 - 4x + 2}{h} = \frac{4h}{h} = 4$$

This value is also equal to the derivative of the given function. The derivative of a linear function is its slope.

18. D: To determine whether a function is even or odd, plug $-x$ into the function. If the result is $g(x)$ the function is even, and if the result is $-g(x)$ the function is odd.

$$g(-x) = 7(-x)^3 + 5(-x) - 2 = -7x^3 - 5x - 2$$

This function is neither $g(x)$ nor $-g(x)$, so the given function is neither even nor odd.

19. A: Division can be used to solve this problem. The division necessary is:

$$\frac{5.972 \times 10^{24}}{7.348 \times 10^{22}}$$

To compute this division, divide the constants first then use algebraic laws of exponents to divide the exponential expression. This results in about 0.8127×10^2, which, written in scientific notation, is 8.127×10^1.

20. C: First, the slope of the line must be found. This is equal to the change in y over the change in x, given the two points. Therefore, the slope is -6. The slope and one of the points are then plugged into the point-slope form of a line:

$$y - y_1 = m(x - x_1)$$

This results in:

$$y - 7 = -6(x + 3)$$

The –6 is distributed and the equation is solved for y to obtain $y = -6x - 11$.

Reading

1. A: Choice *B* is incorrect because although it is obvious the author favors rehabilitation, the author never asks for donations from the audience. Choices *C* and *D* are also incorrect. We can infer from the passage that American prisons are probably harsher than Norwegian prisons. However, the best answer that captures the author's purpose is choice *A*, because the author compares Norwegian and American prison recidivism rates.

2. C: The narrator, after feeling excitement for the morning, feels "that something awful was about to happen," which is considered foreboding. The narrator mentions larks and weather in the passage, but there is no proof of anger or confusion at either of them.

3. B: To convince the audience that judges holding their positions based on good behavior is a practical way to avoid corruption. Choice *A* is incorrect because although he mentions the condition of good behavior as a barrier to despotism, he does not discuss it as a practice in the states. Choice *C* is incorrect because the author does not argue that the audience should vote based on judges' behavior, but rather that good behavior should be the condition for holding their office. Choice *D* is not represented in the passage, so it is incorrect.

4. B: Whatever happened in his life before he had a certain internal change is irrelevant. Choices *A*, *C*, and *D* use some of the same language as the original passage, like "revolution," "speak," and "details," but they are incorrect. The narrator is not concerned with the character's life before his epiphany and has no intention of talking about it.

5. C: The tone of this passage is neutral since it is written in an academic/informative voice. It is important to look at the author's word choice to determine what the tone of a passage is. We have no indication that the author is excited, angry, or sorrowful at the effects of bacteria on milk, so Choices *A*, *B*, and *D* are incorrect.

6. D: The word *deleterious* can be best interpreted as referring to the word *ruinous*. The first paragraph attempts to explain the process of milk souring, so the "acid" would probably prove "ruinous" to the growth of bacteria and cause souring. Choice *A*, *amicable*, means friendly, so this does not make sense in context. Choice *B*, *smoldering*, means to boil or simmer, so this is also incorrect. Choices *C* and *E*, *luminous* and *virtuous*, have positive connotations and don't make sense in the context of the passage. Luminous means shining or brilliant, and virtuous means to be honest or ethical.

7. B: The author begins by explaining a process or phenomenon, then gives the history of the study of this phenomenon, and ends by presenting the effects of this phenomenon. The author explains the process of souring in the first paragraph by informing the reader that "it is due to the action of certain of the milk bacteria upon the milk sugar which converts it into lactic acid, and this acid gives the sour taste and curdles the milk." In the second paragraph, we see how the phenomenon of milk souring was viewed when it was "first studied," and then we proceed to gain insight into "recent investigations" toward the end of the paragraph. Finally, the passage ends by presenting the effects of the phenomenon of milk souring. We see the milk curdling, becoming bitter, tasting soapy, turning blue, or becoming thread-like. All of the other answer choices are incorrect.

8. A: The primary purpose is to inform the reader of the phenomenon, investigation, and consequences of milk souring. Choice *B* is incorrect because the passage states that *Bacillus acidi lactici* is not the only cause of milk souring. Choice *C* is incorrect because, although the author mentions the findings of researchers, the main purpose of the text does not seek to describe their accounts and findings, as we are not even told the names of any of the researchers. Choice *D* is tricky. We do see the author present us with new findings in contrast to the first cases studied by researchers. However, this information is only in the second paragraph, so it is not the primary purpose of the *entire passage*. Finally, Choice *E* is incorrect because the genre of the passage is more informative than narrative, although the author does talk about the phenomenon of milk souring and its subsequent effects.

9. C: Milk souring is caused mostly by a species of bacteria identical to that of *Bacillus acidi lactici* although there are a variety of other bacteria that cause milk souring as well. Choice *A* is incorrect because it contradicts the assertion that the souring is still caused by a variety of bacteria. Choice *B* is incorrect because the ordinary cause of milk souring *is known* to current researchers. Choice *D* is incorrect because this names mostly the effects of milk souring, not the cause. Choice *E* is incorrect because the bacteria itself doesn't have a strange soapy smell or is a different color, but it eventually will cause the milk to produce these effects.

10. C: The study of milk souring has improved throughout the years, as we now understand more of what causes milk souring and what happens afterward. None of the choices here are explicitly stated, so we have to rely on our ability to make inferences. Choice *A* is incorrect because there is no indication from the author that milk researchers in the past have been incompetent—only that recent research has done a better job of studying the phenomenon of milk souring. Choice *B* is incorrect because the author refers to dairymen in relation to the effects of milk souring and their "troubles" surrounding milk souring, and does not compare them to milk researchers.

Choice *D* is incorrect because we are told in the second paragraph that only certain types of bacteria are able to sour milk. Choice *E* is incorrect; although we are told that milk souring is a natural occurrence, the author makes no implication that soured milk is safe to consume. Choice C is the best answer choice here because although the author does not directly state that the study of milk souring has improved, we can see this might be true due to the comparison of old studies to newer studies and the fact that the newer studies are being used as a reference in the passage.

11. A: It is most analogous to the chemical change that occurs when a firework explodes. The author tells us that after milk becomes slimy, "it persists in spite of all attempts made to remedy it," which means the milk has gone through a chemical change. It has changed its state from milk to sour milk by changing its odor, color, and material. After a firework explodes, there is little one can do to change the substance of a firework back to its original form—the original substance has combusted and released its energy as heat and light. Choice B is incorrect because, although the rain overwatered the plant, the plant did not become a different type of substance. Choice *C* is incorrect because although mercury leaking out may be dangerous, the actual substance itself stays the same and does not alter into something else. Choice *D* is incorrect; this situation is not analogous to the alteration of a substance. Choice *E* is also incorrect. Ice

244

melting into a liquid is a physical change, which means it can be undone. Milk turning sour, as the author asserts, cannot be undone.

12. D: It would most likely be a paragraph showing the ways bacteria infiltrate milk and ways to avoid this infiltration. Choices *A, B,* and *C* are incorrect because these are already represented in the third, second, and first paragraphs. Choice E is incorrect, although this choice isn't impossible. There could be a glossary right after the third paragraph, but this would be an awkward place for a glossary. Choice *D* is the best answer because it follows a sort of problem/solution structure in writing.

13. A: Choice *B* is incorrect; a quote mentions this at the end of the first passage, but this question is not found in the second passage. Choice *C* is incorrect, as the passages are not concerned with the definition of freedom of speech, but with how to interpret the concept. Choice *D* is incorrect; this is a question for the second passage, but is not found in the first passage.

14. C: The author of Passage A says that "If a state may properly forbid murder or robbery or treason, it may also punish those who induce or counsel the commission of such crimes." This statement tells us that the author of Passage *A* would support throwing the man in jail for encouraging a riot, although no violence ensued. The author of Passage B states, "And we can with certitude declare that the First Amendment forbids the punishment of words merely for their injurious tendencies."

15. A: To figure out the correct answer choice we must find out the relationship between To figure out the correct answer choice we must find out the relationship between Passage *A* and Passage *B*. Between the two passages, we have a general principle (freedom of speech) that is questioned on the basis of interpretation. In Choice *A*, we see that we have a general principle (right to die, or euthanasia) that is questioned on the basis of interpretation as well. Should euthanasia only include passive euthanasia, or euthanasia in any aspect? Choice *B* is incorrect because it does not question the interpretation of a principle, but rather describes the effects of two events that happened in the past involving contamination by radioactive substances. Choice *C* begins with a principle—that of labor laws during wartime—but in the second document, the interpretation isn't questioned. The second document looks at the historical precedent of labor laws in the past during wartime. Choice *D* is incorrect because the two texts disagree over the cause of something rather than the interpretation of it.

16. B: This is the best answer choice because the author is trying to demonstrate by the examples that anyone who incites a crime, despite the severity or magnitude of the crime, should be held accountable for that crime in some degree. Choice *A* is incorrect because the crimes mentioned are not being compared to each other, but they are being used to demonstrate a point. Choice *C* is incorrect because the author makes the same point using both of the examples and does not question the definition of freedom of speech but its ability to be limited. Choice *D* is incorrect because this sentiment goes against what the author has been arguing throughout the passage.

17. A: The idea that human beings are able and likely to change their minds between the encouragement and execution of an event that may harm others. The idea in Choice A most seriously undermines the claim because it brings into question the tendency to commit a crime and points out the difference between utterance and action in moral situations. Choice *B* is incorrect; this idea does not undermine the claim at hand, but introduces an observation irrelevant to the claim. Choices *C* and *D* are incorrect because they would actually strengthen the author's claim rather than undermine it.

18. D: Choice *A* is incorrect; the passage calls upon no historical situations as precedent. Choice *B* is incorrect; we can infer that the author would not agree with this, because they state that "In war time, therefore, speech should be unrestricted... by punishment." Choice *C* is incorrect; this is more consistent with the main idea of the first passage.

19. B: *Reticent* is the best choices for this sentence because it means reserved, secretive, or quiet. *Demonstrative* means expressive, so this is the opposite of what we are looking for. *Apathetic* is incorrect because it means disinterested or uncaring. *Buoyant* means resilient or light in weight and does not fit within the context of the sentence.

20. A *Galvanize* is the best answer here because it means to awaken or arouse something. *Placate* is incorrect because it means to soothe or pacify. *Quell* means to suppress, so this is the opposite of the correct answer. Finally, *relinquish* is incorrect because it denotes giving up or letting go.

Writing

1. C: Choice *C* is the best answer: "The box in which the President sat consisted of two boxes turned into one, the middle partition being removed, as on all occasions when a state party visited the theater." Choice *A* is incorrect because the first comma is a comma splice. A comma splice incorrectly joins two independent clauses with a comma rather than a period or semicolon. Choice *B* is incorrect; the phrase "the box in which the President sat two boxes turned into one" is missing a verb between the words "sat" and "two." Choice *D* is incorrect because the meaning is changed; the middle partition is not said to have been removed as in the original sentence.

2. A: The sentence is best placed after Sentence 11. The passage is at a point where it is describing the President's wife, even going so far to describe the emotion on her face. The next sentence describing the President's facial features would be the most logical.

3. D: The phrase "All in all" is the best fit here because it means taking everything in mind, or in sum, there were 4 people gathered. The other phrases don't quite fit the context and are meant for more of a transitional phrase.

4. D: Choice *D* is the best answer. The first paragraph is dedicated to describing the box in which the President and his party sat. Choice *D* concludes by describing the last area of the box to be described—the "background of lace." The other choices deviate from the topic of the paragraph and do not mention a description of the box.

5. B: Choice *B* is the best answer. The interrupting phrase "including Mrs. Lincoln" should be separated by commas. If we take out this phrase, the sentence would stand as an independent clause by itself, so the commas are needed. Choice *A* is incorrect; semicolons should only be used to separate independent clauses, not interrupting phrases. Choice *C* is incorrect; the word "Ford's" is possessive because it's known as "Ford's theater," not Fords plural. Choice *D* is incorrect; again, the "Fords" is plural instead of possessive, and there are no commas separating the interrupting phrase.

6. D: Choice *D*, *therefore*, is the correct answer. The word *therefore* indicates a result of something. We see that in the sentence before, the acid is deleterious to growth. As a result of this, "the milk does not undergo any further changes." The other transition words indicate an addition of information, and this is more of a result of the previous information.

7. B: This sentence is best placed after Sentence 9. The sentence in question logically fits after Sentence 9 because it explains that there was a variety of bacteria besides "the same species of bacterium" in Sentence 9 that was found to be the cause of milk souring.

8. C: The correct answer is the following sentence: "The number of species of bacteria which have been found to sour milk has increased until something over a hundred are known to have this power, but these different species do not affect the milk in the same way." The conjunction "but" is the best choice for this sentence because it indicates a contrast; although one might think all bacteria would affect milk the same way, they do not.

9. C: Choice *C* is the best answer. Simple sentences with a conjunction don't require a comma. Choice *A* is incorrect because semicolons require independent clauses (complete sentences) on either side of them. Choice *B* is incorrect; the gerund "finding" coupled with "to be" is not proper verb usage. Choice *D* is incorrect because, like the original, simple sentences with a conjunction don't require a comma.

10. A: Choice *A* is the best answer. One must look at the surrounding context to choose the right answer choice. A "phenomenon" is seen as a wonder or miracle, not something that logically follows something else. Assuring the reader that this "phenomenon" is well understood today would appropriately follow Sentence 2. Sentence 3 then goes on to explain how this property is "well understood," so we have two surrounding sentences that work well with Choice *A*. Choice *B* is incorrect because the following sentence goes on to explain how we understand this happening, and Choice *B* says that it is *not* well understood. Choices *C* and *D* should be ruled out because they do not fall between Sentences 2 & 3 in a logical way; they deviate from the topic.

11. B: Choice *B* is the correct answer. The sentence includes an interrupting phrase which acts as a short definition for the word "poetics." Choice *A* is incorrect; a semicolon should have an independent clause on either side, and the second clause is not independent because it does not have a subject. Choice *C* is incorrect because it's missing a comma after the word "poetics." Choice *D*, the original sentence, is incorrect because it lacks the commas necessary to set aside the definition phrase.

12. C: Choice *C* is the most straightforward combination of the two sentences. Choices *A*, *B*, and *D* are less direct, have unnecessary commas, and contain an awkward combination of sentences.

13. A: Choice *A* is the best sentence to insert after Sentence 4 because it acts as a summary or concluding sentence of the first paragraph by explaining the function of rhetoric and describing who was expected to learn the concept. The other answer choices are off topic and do not act as an appropriate concluding sentence to the first paragraph. Choices *B*, *C*, and *D* act as an introduction to new concepts.

14. C: The correct spelling of the word is *endeavored*.

15. D: After sentence 10. Sentence 10 is vital to the paragraph because it describes the "essential difference between classical rhetoric and poetics" mentioned in Sentence 10.

16. C: The correct answer is Choice *C* because the phrase "which took place between 1760 and 1840" is set off with commas. Choice *B* is incorrect because it lacks a comma after "1840," and Choice *D* is incorrect because the comma after "place" interrupts the phrase "took place between 1760 and 1840."

17. D: Choice *D*, "transformed," is the most accurate substitution because the essay describes the dramatic demographic changes that happened to European society during the Industrial Revolution. Choice *A* ("transfigured") suggests a radical change in figure or appearance, and as such is less exact than "transformed." Choice *B* ("disrupted") does not convey the idea of change, and Choice *C* ("destroyed") is inaccurate because the existing social order was not destroyed.

18. C: The correct answer is Choice *C* because it includes the missing word "as" ("digging *as* deeply"). Choices *A*, *B*, and *D* are incorrect because they do not include the missing word.

19. A: Choice *A* is the best selection, because it provides the link from the expense of building factories to the capitalists, which led to industry becoming the new source of wealth. Choice *B* is awkwardly worded, and although it correctly states the need for capitalists, it does not put them into action. Choice *C* is factually correct, but it is not the best choice because the tone is more casual than that of the rest of the essay. Choice *D* is factually incorrect and does not logically link the two sentences.

20. B: Choice *B* is the clearest rewrite. Forming two sentences allows for linear sequencing of the activities. Choice *A* loses information by not including that land was dominated by rich capitalists. Choice *C* is less clear because it refers to the capitalists by "their" before introducing them. Choice *D* is incorrect because it halts the flow from the previous sentence.

21. B: Choice *B* is correct because the comma separates the main clause in the sentence from the subordinating clause. Choice *A* is incorrect because it leaves out a necessary comma after "to the brain." Choice *C* would be correct if there was a comma after "brain" as well. Choice *D* is incorrect because the comma interrupts the prepositional phrase "to CNS tissue."

22. B: A semicolon separates main clauses that are not joined by a coordinating conjunction, such as "and." Choice *B* breaks this long sentence into two main clauses, each of which can stand on its own as a complete sentence.

23. C: The correct answer is Choice *C*, the semicolon. Because there is a set of dashes later in the sentence, Choice *B* ("dash") won't work because dashes should be used sparingly and there's already a pair in the sentence. Choice *A* ("slash") is used to separate two options, not two parts of a sentence. A period, Choice *D*, would be appropriate only if the lowercase "t" in "there" appeared as a capital "T" in the sentence.

24. C: Sentence 8, the sentence beginning, "Noncontrast computed tomography...", disrupts the flow of the paragraph by inserting a comment about imaging technology into a discussion of stroke symptoms.

25. A: The sentence is correct as written. Choice *B* would be correct only if a comma and the word "it" were inserted after "leaked" ("as the blood is leaked, it can destroy brain tissue"). Choice *C* ("as the blood is leaked, can destroy brain tissue") is incorrect because the pronoun "it" is missing before "can." Choice *D* is incorrect because the tense changes mid-sentence.

Practice Test #2

Arithmetic

1. Determine the missing subtotal in gray:

Location	Type of Clothing	Sales
High St.	Men's	$591
High St.	Men's	$879
	Men's Total	**$1,470**
High St.	Women's	$522
High St.	Women's	$788
	Women's	
High St. Total		$2,780
Main St.	Men's	$607
Main St.	Men's	$981
	Men's Total	**$1,588**
Main St.	Women's	$342
Main St.	Women's	$287
	Women's	$629
Main St. Total		**$2,217**

    a. $1,310
    b. $2,780
    c. $1,470
    d. $788
    e. $266

2. Ms. Katy is wrapping end-of-the-year gifts for her class. There are 27 students in the class and each gift needs 2 feet, 4 inches of ribbon to tie around the package. What is the total length of ribbon that she needs to wrap all the gifts?
    a.   63 inches
    b.   63 feet
    c.   54 inches
    d.   65 feet
    e.   54 feet

3. Determine the missing subtotal:

Trees	Plants Sold
Maple	12
Oak	45
Pine	33
Subtotal	**90**
Flowers	
Magnolia	45
Marigold	75
Daffodils	22
Subtotal	
Total	**232**

    a. 90
    b. 322
    c. 142
    d. 92
    e. 374

4. Use the ruler shown below to answer the question regarding the piano:

If the actual piano is 3.5 meters long, what is the scale of the picture of the piano?

    a.   1 unit = 1 meter
    b.   1 unit = 0.5 meter
    c.   1 unit = 2 meters
    d.   1 unit = 20 centimeters
    e.   1 unit = 10 centimeters

5. What is the area of the following figure?

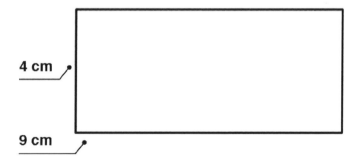

    a.   26 cm
    b.   36 cm
    c.   13 cm^2
    d.   36 cm^2
    e.   65 cm^2

6. What is the volume of the given figure?

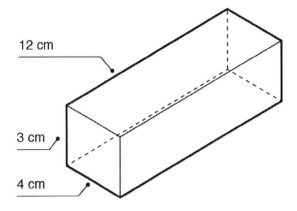

12 cm

3 cm

4 cm

  a. 36 cm^2
  b. 144 cm^3
  c. 72 cm^3
  d. 36 cm^3
  e. 144 cm^2

7. If a new monitor cost $300 with a 40% discount, what was its original price?
  a. $420
  b. $500
  c. $460
  d. $340
  e. $560

8. Which of the following is equivalent to $16^{\frac{1}{4}} \times 16^{\frac{1}{2}}$?
  a. 8
  b. 16
  c. 4
  d. 4,096
  e. 64

9. What is $\frac{15}{60}$ converted to a percentage?

  a. 0.25
  b. 2.5%
  c. 25%
  d. 0.25%

10. What is the product of $\frac{5}{9}$ and $\frac{7}{15}$, in lowest possible terms?

    a. $\frac{7}{27}$

    b. $\frac{35}{135}$

    c. $\frac{5}{27}$

    d. $\frac{13}{45}$

11. What is the result of dividing 2 by $\frac{8}{5}$?

    a. $1\frac{1}{8}$

    b. $1\frac{2}{5}$

    c. $1\frac{1}{5}$

    d. $1\frac{1}{4}$

12. Which of the following decimal values is equal to $\frac{7}{100}$?

    a. 0.7

    b. 0.07

    c. 0.007

    d. 7

13. A library had 4,536 books at the end of the day on Friday. On Saturday, 100 books were returned, but 54 were checked out. How many books were left in the library at the end of the day on Saturday?

    a. 4,582

    b. 4,690

    c. 4,382

    d. 4,536

14. Round 5.6783 to the nearest hundredth.

    a. 5.67

    b. 5.678

    c. 5.68

    d. 5.7

15. Kevin has $200 and donates 25% to a charity of his choice. How much did he donate?

    a. $25

    b. $50

    c. $12.50

    d. $100

16. A centipede measured 1.25 inches long, but by the time it was full grown, it measured 1.726 inches long. By how much did the centipede grow?
    a.   2.976 inches
    b.   0.51 inches
    c.   0.5 inches
    d.   0.476 inches

17. Order the following numbers from least to greatest:
$$\frac{1}{2}\%, 0.5, 0.05\%$$

    a. $\frac{1}{2}\%, 0.5, 0.05\%$

    b. $0.5, 0.05\%, \frac{1}{2}\%$

    c. $0.05\%, \frac{1}{2}\%, 0.5$

    d. $\frac{1}{2}\%, 0.05\%, 0.5$

18. Consider the following inequalities. Which one is false?
    a. $\frac{1}{4} < \frac{3}{16}$
    b. $\frac{3}{8} < \frac{1}{2}$
    c. $\frac{2}{5} < \frac{2}{3}$
    d. $\frac{4}{5} < \frac{7}{8}$

19. Determine which number is 52% of 156.
    a.   81
    b.   300
    c.   152
    d.   400

20. Calculate the following: $0.542 + 0.004 + 0.021$.
    a.   0.567
    b.   0.603
    c.   0.756
    d.   0.548

Quantitative Reasoning, Algebra, and Statistics

1. Using the graph below, what is the mean number of visitors for the first 4 hours?

Museum Visitors

a. 12
b. 13
c. 14
d. 15
e. 16

2. What is the mode for the grades shown in the chart below?

Science Grades	
Jerry	65
Bill	95
Anna	80
Beth	95
Sara	85
Ben	72
Jordan	98

a. 65
b. 33
c. 95
d. 90
e. 84.3

3. The following set represents the test scores from a university class: {35, 79, 80, 87, 87, 90, 92, 95, 95, 98, 99}. If the outlier is removed from this set, which of the following is TRUE?
- a. The mean and the median will decrease.
- b. The mean and the median will increase.
- c. The mean and the mode will increase.
- d. The mean and the mode will decrease.
- e. The mean, median, and mode will increase.

4. Which of the statements below is a statistical question?
- a. What was your grade on the last test?
- b. What were the grades of the students in your class on the last test?
- c. What kind of car do you drive?
- d. What was Sam's time in the marathon?
- e. What textbooks does Marty use this semester?

Use the following information to answer the next three questions, rounding to the closest minute. Eva Jane is practicing for an upcoming 5K run. She has recorded the following times (in minutes):

> 25, 18, 23, 28, 30, 22.5, 23, 33, 20

5. What is Eva Jane's mean time rounded to the nearest minute?
- a. 26 minutes
- b. 19 minutes
- c. 24 minutes
- d. 23 minutes
- e. 25 minutes

6. What is the mode of Eva Jane's times?
- a. 16 minutes
- b. 20 minutes
- c. 23 minutes
- d. 33 minutes
- e. 25 minutes

7. What is Eva Jane's median time?
- a. 23 minutes
- b. 17 minutes
- c. 28 minutes
- d. 19 minutes
- e. 25 minutes

8. What is the perimeter of the following figure?

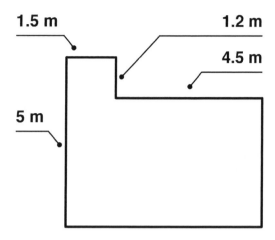

a. 13.4 m
b. 22 m
c. 12.2 m
d. 22.5 m
e. 24.4 m

9. Which of the following measures always corresponds to the 50th percentile on a standardized test?
a. The mean
b. The median
c. The mode
d. The minimum
e. The maximum

10. Which of these percentiles falls within a standardized test score range that would have a stanine score of 5?
a. 75th percentile
b. 35th percentile
c. 10th percentile
d. 55th percentile
e. 85th percentile

11. A taxi costs a flat rate of $4.00 plus $2.25 per mile in New York City. If Tal has $21, what is the maximum number of miles he can ride in this taxi?
a. 5
b. 6
c. 7
d. 8
e. 9

12. From the chart below, which two are preferred by more men than women?

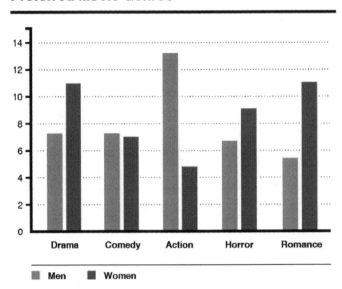

Preferred Movie Genres

Men   Women

a. Comedy and Action
b. Drama and Comedy
c. Action and Horror
d. Action and Romance
e. Romance and Comedy

13. Which type of graph best represents a continuous change over a period of time?
a. Stacked bar graph
b. Bar graph
c. Pie graph
d. Histogram
e. Line graph

14. What type of relationship is there between age and attention span as represented in the graph below?

Attention Span

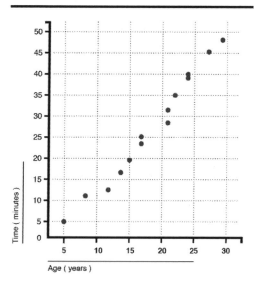

a. No correlation
b. Positive correlation
c. Negative correlation
d. Weak correlation
e. Inverse correlation

15. How many centimeters are in 3 feet? (Note: 2.54 cm = 1 in)
    a. 0.635
    b. 1.1811
    c. 14.17
    d. 7.62
    e. 91.44

16. What is the missing length x?

a. 6
b. 12
c. 10
d. 100
e. 14

17. The sides of a triangle have the following lengths: 4 inches, 4 inches, and 7.5 inches. If the smallest angle within the triangle has a measurement of 20°, what is the measure of the largest angle?

    a. 100°
    b. 140°
    c. 120°
    d. 160°

18. On the first four tests this semester, a student received the following scores out of 100: 74, 76, 82, and 84. The student must earn at least what score on the fifth test to receive a B in the class? Assume that the final test is also out of 100 points and that to receive a B in the class, he must have at least an 80% average.

    a. 80
    b. 84
    c. 82
    d. 78

19. Evaluate the expression: $5b^2 - 3ab + 10a$, when $a = 3$ and $b = -1$.

    a. 84
    b. 26
    c. 44
    d. 30

20. Solve: $5(x - 2) - 3x = 20 + x$.

    a. 22
    b. 15
    c. 30
    d. 10

Advanced Algebra and Functions

1. For which values of x is the following function undefined?

$$f(x) = \frac{x^2 + 3x + 1}{-3x + x^2}$$

    a. 2, 3
    b. 0, 3
    c. 1, 2
    d. 0, 1

2. If $h(x) = -6x + 11$, what is $h(-2)$?

    a. 1
    b. -1
    c. 23
    d. -23

3. For which of the following values of x is the following function undefined?
$$f(x) = \frac{-10}{x^2 - 10x + 25}$$
   a. −5
   b. 5
   c. −10
   d. 0

4. Given the following functions, what is the value of $g(2)$?
$$f(x) = -9x + 2$$
$$g(x) = f(x) - 4$$
   a. −16
   b. −20
   c. −2
   d. −4

5. Given that $m = 2\sqrt{5}$ and $3m = \sqrt{4n}$, which is the correct value of n?
   a. 45
   b. $\sqrt{45}$
   c. 36
   d. 145

6. Given the equation $6\sqrt{x-2} = 5\sqrt{x}$, what is the value of x?
   a. 72
   b. $\frac{72}{11}$
   c. $\frac{6}{11}$
   d. 44

7. Which are the values of x that satisfy the equation $2x^2 - 10x + 3 = 0$?
   a. $5 \pm \frac{\sqrt{19}}{2}$
   b. $5 \pm \sqrt{19}$
   c. $\frac{5}{2} \pm \frac{\sqrt{19}}{2}$
   d. $-\frac{5}{2} \pm \sqrt{19}$

8. What is the value of the constant b in the following equation?
$$-4x(x-9) + 8(x-3) = ax^2 + bx + c$$
   a. −4
   b. −44
   c. −24
   d. 44

9. A circle has a radius of 8 and the y-coordinate of the center in the xy-plane is –6. Two points on the circumference of the circle are (4, 2) and (–4, –6). Which of the following is the x-coordinate of the center?

    a. 4
    b. –4
    c. 6
    d. 11

10. What is the correct result when rationalizing the denominator of $\frac{49}{x-\sqrt{7}}$?

    a. $\frac{49}{x^2-7}$

    b. $\frac{49x+49\sqrt{7}}{x^2-7}$

    c. $\frac{x}{x^2-49}$

    d. $\frac{49}{x}$

11. Given the function $h(x) = -5x - 7$, what is the value of $h(-5x)$?

    a. $-25x - 7$
    b. $25x - 7$
    c. $25x^2 - 7$
    d. 18

12. Consider the function $g(x) = ax^2 + 4x + 9$. It is true that $g(2) = -7$ and a is a constant. What is the value of a?

    a. –6
    b. 6
    c. –7
    d. 12

13. Which is equivalent to the following expression?

$$\frac{4x - 2}{x + 5} - \frac{2x - 1}{x - 5}$$

    a. $\frac{6x^2-12x+5}{x^2-25}$

    b. $\frac{2x-1}{x^2-25}$

    c. $\frac{2x-1}{x+5}$

    d. $\frac{2x^2-31x+15}{x^2-25}$

14. If $M = 5x^2 - 4x + 2$ and $N = -2x^2 - 6x + 1$, which of the following is $3M - \frac{3}{4}N$?

    a. $\frac{33}{2}x^2 - \frac{15}{2}x + \frac{21}{4}$

    b. $\frac{27}{2}x^2 - \frac{21}{2}x + \frac{27}{4}$

    c. $\frac{33}{2}x^2 - 18x + 7$

    d. $\frac{27}{2}x^2 + \frac{21}{x} + \frac{27}{4}$

15. Which of the expressions is equal to B for the equation below?

$$B + \frac{4}{9x + 2} = \frac{81x^2}{9x + 2}$$

    a. $9x + 2$
    b. $81x^2$
    c. $9x - 2$
    d. $81x^2 - 4$

16. Which of the following is the equation of a vertical line that runs through the point (1, 4)?
    a. $x = 1$
    b. $y = 1$
    c. $x = 4$
    d. $y = 4$

17. What is the correct factorization of the following binomial?
$$2y^3 - 128$$

    a. $2(y + 8)(y - 8)$
    b. $2(y + 4)(y^2 + 4y + 16)$
    c. $2(y + 4)(y - 4)^2$
    d. $2(y - 4)^3$
    e. $2(y - 4)(y^2 + 4y + 16)$

18. What is the domain of the function: $f(x) = \frac{x+4}{x^2-1}$?
    a. $x \neq -1$
    b. All real numbers
    c. $x \neq 1$
    d. $x \neq 1, -1$

19. Solve: $24 = e^{x-3}$.
    a. 3
    b. $\ln(24) + 3$
    c. $\ln(24) - 3$
    d. -3

20. What is vertex of the function $f(x) = x^2 - 4x + 10$?
    a. $(2, 6)$
    b. $(2, 22)$
    c. $(-2, 22)$
    d. $(-2, 8)$

Reading

Directions for the next 18 questions: After reading the passage, choose the best answer to the question based on what is expressed or suggested in the passage.

1. Director: Movies require the audience to suspend their disbelief. As such, directors need to create a universe with consistent internal logic. When the subject matter is based on real events and communities, the director must closely mirror reality. For example, characters should talk like people from that specific region and historical period.

Critic: Movies hold immense power in our culture in defining what is and isn't socially acceptable. Consequently, directors have a responsibility not to use language that offends various groups, especially people in vulnerable positions. Censoring hate speech and racial slurs won't break the audience's disbelief.

Which one of the following best describes the main point in dispute between the director and critic?
    a. Movie audiences suspend their disbelief.
    b. Hate speech and racial slurs offend people.
    c. Movies should avoid offending people.
    d. Directors enjoy full creative control over their work.
    e. Movies have enormous cultural relevancy.

2. The other of the minor deities at Nemi was Virbius. Legend had it that Virbius was the young Greek hero Hippolytus, chaste and fair, who learned the art of venery from the centaur Chiron, and spent all his days in the greenwood chasing wild beasts with the virgin huntress Artemis (the Greek counterpart of Diana) for his only comrade.

From *The Golden Bough* by Sir James George Frazer

Based on a prior knowledge of literature, the reader can infer this passage is taken from which of the following?
    a. A eulogy
    b. A myth
    c. A historical document
    d. A technical document

3. When I wrote the following passages, or rather the bulk of them, I lived alone, in the woods, a mile from any neighbor, in a house which I had built myself on the shore of Walden Pond, in Concord, Massachusetts, and earned my living by the labor of my hands only. I lived there two years and two months. At present I am a sojourner in civilized life again.

From *Walden* by Henry David Thoreau

What does the word *sojourner* most likely mean at the end of the passage?
  a. Illegal immigrant
  b. Temporary resident
  c. Lifetime partner
  d. Farm crop

4. The old castle soon proved to be too small for the family, and in September 1853 the foundation-stone of a new house was laid. After the ceremony the workmen were entertained at dinner, which was followed by Highland games and dancing in the ballroom.

Two years later they entered the new castle, which the Queen described as "charming; the rooms delightful; the furniture, papers, everything perfection."

The Prince was untiring in planning improvements, and in 1856 the Queen wrote: "Every year my heart becomes more fixed in this dear Paradise, and so much more so now, that *all* has become my dearest Albert's *own* creation, own work, own building, own laying out as at Osborne; and his great taste, and the impress of his dear hand, have been stamped everywhere. He was very busy today, settling and arranging many things for next year."

From the biography *Queen Victoria* by E. Gordon Browne, M.A.

What does the word *impress* mean in the third paragraph?
  a. To affect strongly in feeling
  b. To urge something to be done
  c. A certain characteristic or quality imposed upon something else
  d. To press a thing onto something else

The next six questions are based on the following passage from The Life, Crime, and Capture of John Wilkes Booth *by George Alfred Townsend:*

> The box in which the President sat consisted of two boxes turned into one, the middle partition being removed, as on all occasions when a state party visited the theater. The box was on a level with the dress circle; about twelve feet above the stage. There were two entrances—the door nearest to the wall having been closed and locked; the door nearest the balustrades of the dress circle, and at right angles with it, being open and left open, after the visitors had entered. The interior was carpeted, lined with crimson paper, and furnished with a sofa covered with crimson velvet, three arm chairs similarly covered, and six cane-bottomed chairs. Festoons of flags hung before the front of the box against a background of lace.

> President Lincoln took one of the arm-chairs and seated himself in the front of the box, in the angle nearest the audience, where, partially screened from observation, he had the best view of what was transpiring on the stage. Mrs. Lincoln sat next to him, and Miss Harris in the opposite

angle nearest the stage. Major Rathbone sat just behind Mrs. Lincoln and Miss Harris. These four were the only persons in the box.

The play proceeded, although "Our American Cousin," without Mr. Sothern, has, since that gentleman's departure from this country, been justly esteemed a very dull affair. The audience at Ford's, including Mrs. Lincoln, seemed to enjoy it very much. The worthy wife of the President leaned forward, her hand upon her husband's knee, watching every scene in the drama with amused attention. Even across the President's face at intervals swept a smile, robbing it of its habitual sadness.

About the beginning of the second act, the mare, standing in the stable in the rear of the theater, was disturbed in the midst of her meal by the entrance of the young man who had quitted her in the afternoon. It is presumed that she was saddled and bridled with exquisite care.

Having completed these preparations, Mr. Booth entered the theater by the stage door; summoned one of the scene shifters, Mr. John Spangler, emerged through the same door with that individual, leaving the door open, and left the mare in his hands to be held until he (Booth) should return. Booth who was even more fashionably and richly dressed than usual, walked thence around to the front of the theater, and went in. Ascending to the dress circle, he stood for a little time gazing around upon the audience and occasionally upon the stage in his usual graceful manner. He was subsequently observed by Mr. Ford, the proprietor of the theater, to be slowly elbowing his way through the crowd that packed the rear of the dress circle toward the right side, at the extremity of which was the box where Mr. and Mrs. Lincoln and their companions were seated. Mr. Ford casually noticed this as a slightly extraordinary symptom of interest on the part of an actor so familiar with the routine of the theater and the play.

5. Which of the following best describes the author's attitude toward the events leading up to the assassination of President Lincoln?
   a. Excitement, due to the setting and its people
   b. Sadness, due to the death of a beloved president
   c. Anger, due to the impending violence
   d. Neutrality, due to the style of the report
   e. Apprehension, due to the crowd and their ignorance

6. What does the author mean by the last sentence in the passage?
   a. Mr. Ford was suspicious of Booth and assumed he was making his way to Mr. Lincoln's box.
   b. Mr. Ford assumed Booth's movement throughout the theater was due to being familiar with the theater.
   c. Mr. Ford thought that Booth was making his way to the theater lounge to find his companions.
   d. Mr. Ford thought that Booth was elbowing his way to the dressing room to get ready for the play.
   e. Mr. Ford thought that Booth was coming down with an illness due to the strange symptoms he displayed.

7. Given the author's description of the play "Our American Cousin," which one of the following is most analogous to Mr. Sothern's departure from the theater?
   a. A ballet dancer leaves the New York City Ballet just before they go on to their final performance.
   b. A basketball player leaves an NBA team, and the next year they make it to the championship but lose.
   c. A lead singer leaves their band to begin a solo career, and the band's sales on their next album drop by 50 percent.
   d. A movie actor dies in the middle of making a movie, and the movie is made anyway by an actor who resembles the deceased.
   e. A professor who switches to the top-rated university in his field only to find the university he left behind has surpassed his new department's rating.

8. Which of the following texts most closely relates to the organizational structure of the passage?
   a. A chronological account in a novel of a woman and a man meeting for the first time
   b. A cause-and-effect text ruminating on the causes of global warming
   c. An autobiography that begins with the subject's death and culminates in his birth
   d. A text focusing on finding a solution to the problem of the Higgs boson particle
   e. A text contrasting the realities of life on Mars versus life on Earth

9. Which of the following words, if substituted for the word *festoons* in the first paragraph, would LEAST change the meaning of the sentence?
   a. Feathers
   b. Armies
   c. Adornments
   d. Buckets
   e. Boats

10. What is the primary purpose of the passage?
   a. To persuade the audience that John Wilkes Booth killed Abraham Lincoln
   b. To inform the audience of the setting wherein Lincoln was shot
   c. To narrate the bravery of Lincoln and his last days as president
   d. To recount in detail the events that led up to Abraham Lincoln's death
   e. To disprove the popular opinion that John Wilkes Booth is the person who killed Abraham Lincoln

The next two questions are based on the excerpt from Variation of Animals and Plants under Domestication *by Charles Darwin.*

> Peach (*Amygdalus persica*).—In the last chapter I gave two cases of a peach-almond and a double-flowered almond which suddenly produced fruit closely resembling true peaches. I have also recorded many cases of peach-trees producing buds, which, when developed into branches, have yielded nectarines. We have seen that no less than six named and several unnamed varieties of the peach have thus produced several varieties of nectarine. I have shown that it is highly improbable that all these peach-trees, some of which are old varieties, and have been propagated by the million, are hybrids from the peach and nectarine, and that it is opposed to all analogy to attribute the occasional production of nectarines on peach-trees to the direct action of pollen from some neighbouring nectarine-tree. Several of the cases are highly remarkable, because, firstly, the fruit thus produced has sometimes been in part a nectarine and in part a peach; secondly, because nectarines thus suddenly produced have reproduced themselves by seed; and thirdly, because nectarines are produced from peach-trees from seed as well as from buds. The

seed of the nectarine, on the other hand, occasionally produces peaches; and we have seen in one instance that a nectarine-tree yielded peaches by bud-variation. As the peach is certainly the oldest or primary variety, the production of peaches from nectarines, either by seeds or buds, may perhaps be considered as a case of reversion. Certain trees have also been described as indifferently bearing peaches or nectarines, and this may be considered as bud-variation carried to an extreme degree.

11. Which of the following statements is NOT a detail from the passage?
    a. At least six named varieties of the peach have produced several varieties of nectarine.
    b. It is not probable that all of the peach-trees mentioned are hybrids from the peach and nectarine.
    c. An unremarkable case is the fact that nectarines are produced from peach-trees from seed as well as from buds.
    d. The production of peaches from nectarines might be considered a case of reversion.

12. Which of the following is an accurate paraphrasing of the following phrase?

Certain trees have also been described as indifferently bearing peaches or nectarines, and this may be considered as bud-variation carried to an extreme degree.

    a. Some trees are described as bearing peaches and some trees have been described as bearing nectarines, but individually the buds are extreme examples of variation.
    b. One way in which bud-variation is said to be carried to an extreme degree is when specific trees have been shown to casually produce peaches or nectarines.
    c. Certain trees are indifferent to bud-variation, as recently shown in the trees that produce both peaches and nectarines in the same season.
    d. Nectarines and peaches are known to have cross-variation in their buds, which indifferently bears other sorts of fruit to an extreme degree.

The next 3 questions are based on the book On the Trail *by Lina Beard and Adelia Belle Beard:*

For any journey, by rail or by boat, one has a general idea of the direction to be taken, the character of the land or water to be crossed, and of what one will find at the end. So it should be in striking the trail. Learn all you can about the path you are to follow. Whether it is plain or obscure, wet or dry; where it leads; and its length, measured more by time than by actual miles. A smooth, even trail of five miles will not consume the time and strength that must be expended upon a trail of half that length which leads over uneven ground, varied by bogs and obstructed by rocks and fallen trees, or a trail that is all up-hill climbing. If you are a novice and accustomed to walking only over smooth and level ground, you must allow more time for covering the distance than an experienced person would require and must count upon the expenditure of more strength, because your feet are not trained to the wilderness paths with their pitfalls and traps for the unwary, and every nerve and muscle will be strained to secure a safe foothold amid the tangled roots, on the slippery, moss-covered logs, over precipitous rocks that lie in your path. It will take time to pick your way over boggy places where the water oozes up through the thin, loamy soil as through a sponge; and experience alone will teach you which hummock of grass or moss will make a safe stepping-place and will not sink beneath your weight and soak your feet with hidden water. Do not scorn to learn all you can about the trail you are to take... It is not that you hesitate to encounter difficulties, but that you may prepare for them. In unknown regions take a responsible guide with you, unless the trail is short, easily followed, and a frequented one.

Do not go alone through lonely places; and, being on the trail, keep it and try no explorations of your own, at least not until you are quite familiar with the country and the ways of the wild.

Blazing the Trail

A woodsman usually blazes his trail by chipping with his axe the trees he passes, leaving white scars on their trunks, and to follow such a trail you stand at your first tree until you see the blaze on the next, then go to that and look for the one farther on; going in this way from tree to tree you keep the trail though it may, underfoot, be overgrown and indistinguishable.

If you must make a trail of your own, blaze it as you go by bending down and breaking branches of trees, underbrush, and bushes. Let the broken branches be on the side of bush or tree in the direction you are going, but bent down away from that side, or toward the bush, so that the lighter underside of the leaves will show and make a plain trail. Make these signs conspicuous and close together, for in returning, a dozen feet without the broken branch will sometimes confuse you, especially as everything has a different look when seen from the opposite side. By this same token it is a wise precaution to look back frequently as you go and impress the homeward-bound landmarks on your memory. If in your wanderings you have branched off and made ineffectual or blind trails which lead nowhere, and, in returning to camp, you are led astray by one of them, do not leave the false trail and strike out to make a new one, but turn back and follow the false trail to its beginning, for it must lead to the true trail again. Don't lose sight of your broken branches.

13. According to the passage, what does the author say about unknown regions?
    a. You should try and explore unknown regions in order to learn the land better.
    b. Unless the trail is short or frequented, you should take a responsible guide with you.
    c. All unknown regions will contain pitfalls, traps, and boggy places.
    d. It's better to travel unknown regions by rail rather than by foot.
    e. It's wise to leave a false trail that you yourself know is false to deceive potential unwelcome people.

14. Which statement is NOT a detail from the passage?
    a. Learning about the trail beforehand is imperative.
    b. Time will differ depending on the land.
    c. Once you are familiar with the outdoors you can go places on your own.
    d. Be careful of wild animals on the trail you are on.
    e. Break branches on the side of bush or tree in the direction you are going.

15. In the last paragraph, which of the following does the author suggest when being led astray by a false trail?
    a. Bend down and break the branches off trees, underbrush, and bushes.
    b. Ignore the false trail and strike out to make a new one.
    c. Follow the false trail back to its beginning so that you can rediscover the real trail.
    d. Make the signs conspicuous so that you won't be confused when you turn around.
    e. Conceal the trail by bending the lighter side of the leaves downward to cover it.

The next three questions are based on the excerpt from A Christmas Carol *by Charles Dickens:*

Meanwhile the fog and darkness thickened so, that people ran about with flaring links, proffering their services to go before horses in carriages, and conduct them on their way. The ancient tower of a church, whose gruff old bell was always peeping slyly down at Scrooge out of a Gothic window in the wall, became invisible, and struck the hours and quarters in the clouds, with tremulous vibrations afterwards as if its teeth were chattering in its frozen head up there. The cold became intense. In the main street, at the corner of the court, some labourers were repairing the gas-pipes, and had lighted a great fire in a brazier, round which a party of ragged men and boys were gathered: warming their hands and winking their eyes before the blaze in rapture. The water-plug being left in solitude, its overflowings sullenly congealed, and turned to misanthropic ice. The brightness of the shops where holly sprigs and berries crackled in the lamp heat of the windows, made pale faces ruddy as they passed. Poulterers' and grocers' trades became a splendid joke; a glorious pageant, with which it was next to impossible to believe that such dull principles as bargain and sale had anything to do. The Lord Mayor, in the stronghold of the mighty Mansion House, gave orders to his fifty cooks and butlers to keep Christmas as a Lord Mayor's household should; and even the little tailor, whom he had fined five shillings on the previous Monday for being drunk and bloodthirsty in the streets, stirred up to-morrow's pudding in his garret, while his lean wife and the baby sallied out to buy the beef.

Foggier yet, and colder. Piercing, searching, biting cold. If the good Saint Dunstan had but nipped the Evil Spirit's nose with a touch of such weather as that, instead of using his familiar weapons, then indeed he would have roared to lusty purpose. The owner of one scant young nose, gnawed and mumbled by the hungry cold as bones are gnawed by dogs, stopped down at Scrooge's keyhole to regale him with a Christmas carol: but at the first sound of

"God bless you, merry gentleman! May nothing you dismay!"

Scrooge seized the ruler with such energy of action, that the singer fled in terror, leaving the keyhole to the fog and even more congenial frost.

16. Which of the following can NOT be inferred from the passage?
    a. The narrative takes place during winter.
    b. The majority of the narrative is located in a bustling city street.
    c. This passage takes place during the night time.
    d. The Lord Mayor is a wealthy person within the narrative.
    e. Scrooge was not kind and receptive to the caroler.

17. According to the passage, which of the following regarding the poulterers and grocers is true?
    a. They were so poor in the quality of their products that customers saw them as a joke
    b. They put on a pageant in the streets every year for Christmas to entice their customers
    c. They did not believe in Christmas, so they refused to participate in the town parade
    d. They worked tirelessly to convert non-believers and spread the Christmas spirit
    e. They set their shops up to be entertaining public spectacles rather than a dull trade exchange

18. The author's depiction of the scene in the last few paragraphs does all EXCEPT which of the following?
    a. Offer an allusion to religious affiliation in England
    b. Attempt to evoke empathy for the character of Scrooge
    c. Provide a palpable experience through the use of imagery and diction
    d. Depict Scrooge as an uncaring, terrifying character to his fellows
    e. Help readers visualize the setting and the adverse personality of Scrooge

Directions for the next two questions: The following sentence has a blank where something has been left out. Beneath the sentence are four words or phrases. Choose the word or phrase that, when inserted in the sentence, best fits the meaning of the sentence as a whole.

19. The job description requires candidates to be _____ in English and Spanish so that they can easily communicate with native speakers of both languages.
    a. Notorious
    b. Inept
    c. Proficient
    d. Unassuming

20. The organization revised their policies and procedures since the former ones were _____ and many no longer applied.
    a. Resuscitated
    b. Obsolete
    c. Ostentatious
    d. Contemporary

Writing

The next five questions are based on the following passage.

Nobody knew where she went. She wasn't in the living room, the dining room, or the kitchen. She wasn't underneath the staircase, and she certainly wasn't in her bedroom. The bathroom was thoroughly checked, and the closets were emptied. Where could she have possibly gone? Outside was dark, cold, and damp. Each person took a turn calling for her. "Eva! Eva!" (1) they'd each cry out, but not a sound was heard in return. The littlest sister in the house began to cry. "Where could my cat have gone?" Everyone just looked at each other (2) in utter silence. Lulu was only five years old and brought this kitten home only six weeks ago and she was so fond of her. (3) Every morning, Lulu would comb her fur, feed her, and play a cat-and-mouse game with her before she left for school. At night, Eva would curl up on the pillow next to Lulu and stay with her across the night (4). They were already becoming best friends. But this evening, right after dinner, Eva snuck outside when Lulu's brother came in from the yard. It was already dark out and Eva ran so quickly that nobody could see where she went.

It was really starting to feel hopeless when all of a sudden Lulu had an idea. She remembered how much Eva loved the cat-and-mouse game, so she decided to go outside and pretend that she was playing with Eva. Out she went. She curled up on the grass and began to play cat and mouse. Within seconds, Lulu could see shining eyes in the distance. The eyes got closer, and closer, and closer. Lulu continued to play in order that (5) she wouldn't scare the kitten away. In less than five minutes, her beautiful kitten had crawled right up to her lap as if asking to join in the game. Eva was back, and Lulu couldn't have been more thrilled! Gently, she scooped up her kitten, grabbed the cat-and-mouse game, and headed back inside, grinning from ear to ear. That night, Eva and Lulu snuggled right back down again, side by side, and had a very restful sleep.

1. Choose the best replacement punctuation.
   a. NO CHANGE
   b. 'Eva! Eva!'
   c. 'Eva, Eva'!
   d. "Eva, Eva"!

2. Choose the best replacement word or phrase.
   a. NO CHANGE
   b. one another
   c. themselves
   d. each one

3. Choose the best replacement sentence.
   a. NO CHANGE
   b. Lulu brought this kitten home only six weeks ago and she was so fond of her
   c. Lulu brought this kitten home only six weeks ago, and she was so fond of her
   d. Lulu was only five years old, and brought this kitten home only six weeks ago, and she was so fond of her

4. Choose the best replacement word or phrase.
   a. NO CHANGE
   b. below the night
   c. through the night
   d. amidst the night

5. Choose the best replacement word or phrase.
   a. NO CHANGE
   b. so,
   c. so that
   d. so that,

The next five questions are based on the following passage.

In our busy family, there are chores that each member must do every day. There are chores for our daughter, for me, and for my husband. There is always so much going on in our family and so many scheduled events every week that without a set list of <u>chores and</u> (6) without ensuring the chores are completed, our household would be utterly chaotic.

I work days, from home. My husband works evenings about a half-hour away, and our <u>13-year-old</u> (7) daughter, Niamh, attends a homeschooling program. She is an avid hockey player and the third-highest scorer on the team. She simply lives for hockey. Three times a week, she has hockey practice, and <u>once, approximately, a week</u> (8), she has a hockey game. Niamh is responsible for washing her jerseys and her hockey pants and making sure all her gear is properly stored after every practice and game in the garage. Occasionally she forgets and leaves it all in the middle of the dining room floor. Niamh must also clean the kitchen every evening after dinner, empty the dishwasher, and feed her two guinea pigs and her cat. Every Saturday, we also give Niamh an allowance for doing extra chores. She sweeps and washes our floors, cleans windows, vacuums, and tidies up the bathrooms.

272

As for me, I am responsible for walking and feeding the dogs, preparing the lunches and dinners, and keeping up with the laundry. My husband takes out the trash and recycling, keeps up with the yard work, and pays all the bills. Both my husband and <u>myself</u> (9) drive our daughter to friends' houses, school, the arena, the grocery store, medical appointments, and more.

We very rarely seem to get a break, but we are always happy and healthy, and that's what really matters. So, now that you know the breakdown of chores between our daughter, my husband, and me, who do you think has <u>more</u> (10) chores?

6. Choose the best replacement.
   a. NO CHANGE
   b. chores, and,
   c. chores and,
   d. chores, and

7. Choose the best replacement.
   a. NO CHANGE
   b. 13 year old
   c. 13-year old
   d. 13 year-old

8. Choose the best replacement.
   a. NO CHANGE
   b. approximately once a week
   c. approximately bi-weekly
   d. once a week

9. Choose the best replacement.
   a. NO CHANGE
   b. I
   c. me
   d. myself,

10. Choose the best replacement.
   a. NO CHANGE
   b. the most
   c. lesser
   d. less

The next five questions are based on the following passage.

Imagine yourself in a secluded room. There is no one to talk to. The room has a bed, a desk, and a computer, and its one window faces the yard. Every day, you must work in this isolated room, away from everyone. There isn't a sound heard <u>accept</u> (11) for the <u>birds outside</u> (12) and your own hands tapping on the computer keyboard. Imagine having to work in that somber environment every day. The only breaks you receive are to go to the bathroom or grab a quick bite to eat. It feels like solitary confinement, and you start to feel yourself slipping <u>ever-so</u> (13) slowly into a depressed state. What should you do? If you don't get the work done, you won't get paid.

Suddenly, you have an idea. You decide that at least two days a week, you can pack up and work at the library. Although it is quiet at the library, there are people coming and going. You will be able to hear the librarians helping students and visitors, and you can people-watch. Feeling optimistic, <u>the day suddenly makes you smile</u>. (14) When the morning arrives, you pack up your computer, notebooks, calendar, phone, and you head out the door. You arrive at the library just as the doors are opening. You find a quiet place to <u>set up and</u> (15) you settle down into your work day. At first, you are thrilled with the new scenery and you love the extra space you have to work with. But before long, you realize your work isn't getting done. You spent so much time watching the different people coming and going and daydreaming about what it would be like to casually read a book that you stopped working altogether! Perhaps the library wasn't the ideal spot for your after all.

You pack up your computer, your notebooks, your calendar, and your phone, and you head back out the door, back to the solitary room with the bed, the desk, the computer, and the window, and you settle down once again, into your work day.

11. Choose the best replacement.
    a. NO CHANGE
    b. exceptionally
    c. except
    d. expect

12. Choose the best replacement.
    a. NO CHANGE
    b. birds chirping outside
    c. birds, outside
    d. birds, chirping outside

13. Choose the best replacement.
    a. NO CHANGE
    b. ever-so,
    c. ever so
    d. everso

14. Choose the best replacement word or phrase.
    a. NO CHANGE
    b. the day no longer seems so sad.
    c. the day brightens your mood.
    d. you smile for the rest of the day.

15. Choose the best replacement.
    a. NO CHANGE
    b. set up, and
    c. set up; and
    d. set up. And

The next five questions are based on the following passage.

Why must I always be last? I'm the last one in line at the cafeteria, I'm the last one to my locker, and I'm always <u>last</u> (16) one to class. For once, I'd really like to be first. I would even be happy being right smack dab in the middle!

Having also been the last of all the siblings, <u>my older sisters always teased me</u>. (17) I was the last to be potty-trained, the last to get a big girl's bed, and the last to start school. When we entered the teenage years, I was the last to get my driver's license and the last to dye my hair—I went with purple. My older sisters did spoil me, though. When they got their driver's licenses, they would take me out for ice cream or to the movies, and I even got to tag along from time to time when they went out on dates. I guess they thought I was cute or something. Each time I would complain about being last, my mother would say, "Don't ever worry about being last. That means you're the best!" I never quite knew what that meant. My father's famous line was, <u>'Last, but not least'</u>! (18) and I'm still trying to figure *that* one out too.

Of course, I'm not being completely honest with you <u>and</u> (19) I've never been the last in my class. In fact, I always seem to score in the top tenth percentile which isn't too bad at all. I have come in first, second, and even third in different swimming events, and when it comes to dinner, I am usually the *first* to finish my plate. And now that I think about it, maybe being last doesn't really matter anyway. <u>After all</u> (20), being the youngest in my family means that I get away with a lot too. I don't have to do a lot of the chores my older sisters have to do. Yes, come to think of it, maybe being last isn't so bad after all.

16. Choose the best replacement.
   a. NO CHANGE
   b. the last
   c. late
   d. the last,

17. Choose the best replacement.
   a. NO CHANGE
   b. my older sisters would always tease me.
   c. I was always teased by my older sisters.
   d. my older sisters, always, teased me.

18. Choose the best replacement.
   a. NO CHANGE
   b. 'Last but not least!'
   c. "Last, but not least"!
   d. "Last but not least!"

19. Choose the best replacement.
   a. NO CHANGE
   b. ;
   c. even though
   d. but

20. Choose the best replacement.
    a. NO CHANGE
    b. Therefore
    c. However
    d. On the contrary

The next five questions are based on the following passage.

The school bell was about to ring at Juniper High, but Matt wasn't ready. He wasn't ready because he hadn't studied for today's science test in Mr. <u>Jones</u> (26) class. He planned on studying. He brought his textbook, notebook, and study guide home, but something unexpected happened last night that changed his plans. About an hour after he arrived home from school, Matt's dad walked in the door with a brand-new synthesizer, and that was the end of studying before it even began.

Ever since Matt was five years old, he was obsessed with music—any kind of music. He would listen to his parents' kitchen radio for hours, <u>play</u> (27) their records and singing away to all the classics. When he was a teenager, he started collecting CDs, and within no time at all he had an impressive collection of artists. <u>Therefore</u> (28) what he really wanted was his very own synthesizer so he could create his own music—and that day had finally come! Matt forgot all about his science test <u>and had begun</u> (29) to experiment with his new toy immediately. He played for hours and tested every button on his synthesizer. Before he knew it, the clock struck midnight, and he fell into a deep sleep with music playing in his head.

The bell rang. Matt slowly walked into school, wondering how he was going to pass this test. It was the last test of the semester, and it was the one that was supposed to bring up his average. If he failed this test, he <u>failed</u> (30) the semester. He went to his locker, grabbed what he needed, and headed off to class. Within minutes, Matt knew this was his lucky day. The classroom door opened, and a substitute teacher walked in—the test would be delayed by a day! Now all Matt had to do was go home and study, even though that synthesizer would be tempting him all night.

21. Choose the best replacement.
    a. NO CHANGE
    b. Jones's
    c. Jones'
    d. Jone's

22. Choose the best replacement.
    a. NO CHANGE
    b. playing
    c. played
    d. would be playing

23. Choose the best replacement.
    a. NO CHANGE
    b. However
    c. However,
    d. Nonetheless,

276

24. Choose the best replacement word or phrase.
    a. NO CHANGE
    b. was beginning
    c. begins
    d. began

25. Choose the best replacement phrase.
    a. NO CHANGE
    b. had failed
    c. was going to fail
    d. would fail

Write Placer Prompt

Read the passage below then answer in an essay format.

> Substance abuse recovery centers in Florida have doubled in the past two years. Additionally, the centers that already existed are filled to the maximum occupancy. In order to accommodate the patients, some recovery centers are expanding their residencies and adding more staff. The reason for this rise in recovery centers speaks to the state of our nation with the abuse of drugs and alcohol. The substance abuse problem is worse than ever before and will only continue to grow if we allow the trafficking and consumption of drugs to go unpunished.

Write a response in which you identify and explain your stance on the argument above. Once you've identified your stance, use concrete evidence to support your argument.

Answer Explanations #2

Arithmetic

1. A: The missing entry is a subtotal for the sales in women's clothing at the High St. location: $522 + $788 = $1,310.

2. B: Each package needs 2 feet, 4 inches, which is equal to:

$$2\frac{1}{3} = \frac{7}{3} \text{ ft of ribbon}$$

Because there are 27 students in the class, Ms. Kay needs 63 ft of ribbon to wrap all of the gifts:

$$27 \times \frac{7}{3} = 63$$

3. C: To determine the missing subtotal, which is the total number of flowers sold, either add up the three types of flowers or subtract the tree subtotal from the overall total. Either way results in 142.

4. B: The picture of the piano is 7 units long. The actual piano is 3.5 meters long. That means that one unit is equal to $\frac{3.5}{7} = \frac{1}{2}$ of a meter.

5. D: The area for a rectangle is found by multiplying the length by the width. The area is also measured in square units, so the correct answer is Choice *D*. The number 26 in Choice *A* is incorrect because it is the perimeter. Choice *B* is incorrect because the answer must be in centimeters squared. The number 13 in Choice *C* is incorrect because it is the sum of the two dimensions rather than the product of them.

6. B: The volume of a rectangular prism is found by multiplying the length by the width by the height. This formula yields an answer of 144 cubic centimeters. The answer must be in cubic units because volume involves all three dimensions.

7. B: If the discount is 40%, the price of the monitor must be multiplied times 1.40 to account for the discount. Since subtracting 40% from 100% is 60%, and 60% is $\frac{3}{5}$ of 100%, this can be restated as multiplying $300 by $\frac{5}{3}$:

$$\$300 \times \frac{5}{3}$$

$$\$100 \times 5$$

$$\$500$$

8. A: The first step is to simplify the expression. The second term, $16^{\frac{1}{2}}$, can be rewritten as $\sqrt{16}$, since fractional exponents represent roots. This can then be simplified to 4, because $4^2 = 16$. The first term can be evaluated using the power rule for exponents: when an exponent is raised to another exponent, simply multiply the exponents together. The first term can thus be rewritten as:

$$16^{\frac{1}{4}} = \left(16^{\frac{1}{2}}\right)^{\frac{1}{2}} = 4^{\frac{1}{2}} = 2$$

Combining these terms, the expression is evaluated as follows:

$$16^{\frac{1}{4}} \times 16^{\frac{1}{2}} = 2 \times 4 = 8$$

9. C: The fraction $\frac{15}{60}$ can be reduced to $\frac{1}{4}$, which puts the fraction in lowest terms. First, it must be converted to a decimal. Dividing 1 by 4 results in 0.25. Then, to convert to a percentage, move the decimal point two units to the right and add the percentage symbol. The result is 25%.

10. A: A product is found by multiplying.

$$\frac{5}{9} \times \frac{7}{15}$$

$$\frac{35}{135}$$

Simplify by dividing 5 out of the numerator and denominator:

$$\frac{7}{27}$$

11. D: Division is completed by multiplying by the reciprocal. Therefore,

$$2 \div \frac{8}{5} = \frac{2}{1} \times \frac{5}{8}$$

$$\frac{10}{8} = 1\frac{1}{4}$$

12. B: This fraction can be expressed as seven-hundredths. When writing a decimal, the first place value to the right of the decimal point is the tenths place, and the second place value to the right of the decimal point is the hundredths place. Choice *B* is the correct answer since the 7 is in the hundredths place.

13. A: The library started with 4,536 and then 100 were returned. Adding 4,536 to 100 results in 4,636 books. Then, 54 were checked out. This value needs to be subtracted from 4,636 to find the total number of books left in the library that evening. This amount is $4,636 - 54 = 4,582$. Therefore, Choice *A* is the correct answer.

14. C: The 7 is in the hundredths place. Looking at the digit to its right, which is 8, one can see that it is 5 or greater. Therefore, the 7 gets rounded up and the rest of the value to its right becomes zeros. The correct answer is 5.68, which is Choice *C*.

15. B: Kevin donated 25% of $200 to charity. To find this amount, convert 25% to a decimal and multiply by $200. Therefore, he donated $0.25(\$200) = \$50$, which is equal to Choice *B*.

16. D: To find how much the centipede grew, take the difference between the full-grown length and the original length. Therefore, the centipede grew $1.726 - 1.25 = 0.476$ inches. The correct option is Choice D.

17. C: To rank the values, convert them to decimals. $\frac{1}{2}\% = 0.5\% = 0.005$ and $0.05\% = 0.0005$. Therefore, the correct order is $0.0005, 0.005, 0.5$ — which is equivalent to $0.05\%, \frac{1}{2}\%, 0.5$. The correct option is Choice C.

18. A: To determine which one is false, convert each fraction to a decimal and then compare to see if the fraction on the left is less than the fraction on the right. Choice A is $\frac{1}{4} < \frac{3}{16}$, which converts to $0.25 < 0.1875$. This is a false statement, so Choice A is the correct option.

19. C: To determine the correct answer, first convert 52% to a decimal. 52% is equal to 0.52. In this problem, the whole is missing. Percent times whole equals part. Therefore, divide the part by the percent to find the whole. The part in this case is 156. The answer is $\frac{156}{0.52} = 300$, which is equal to Choice C.

20. A: To add decimals, stack them vertically, aligning the decimals. Then, add each place value, working from right to left.

$$
\begin{array}{r}
0.542 \\
0.004 \\
+0.021 \\
\hline
0.567
\end{array}
$$

The correct option is Choice A, which is 0.567.

Quantitative Reasoning, Algebra, and Statistics

1. C: The mean for the number of visitors during the first 4 hours is 14. The mean is found by calculating the average for the four hours. Adding up the total number of visitors during those hours gives:

$$12 + 10 + 18 + 16 = 56$$

Dividing total number of visitors by four hours gives the average number of visitors per hour:

$$56 \div 4 = 14$$

2. C: The mode for a set of data is the value that occurs the most frequently. The grade that appears the most is 95. It's the only value that repeats in the set. The mean is around 84.3.

3. B: The outlier is 35. When a small outlier is removed from a data set, the mean and the median increase. The first step in this process is to identify the outlier, which is the number that lies away from the given set. Once the outlier is identified, the mean and median can be recalculated. The mean will be affected because it is the average of all of the numbers. The median will be affected because it finds the middle number, which is subject to change because a number is lost. The mode will most likely not change because it is the number that occurs the most, which will not be the outlier if there is only one outlier.

4. B: "What were the grades of the students in your class on the last test?" is a statistical question because to determine this answer one would need to collect data from each person in the class and it is expected the answers would vary. The other answers do not require data to be collected from multiple sources; therefore, the answers will not vary.

5. E: The mean is found by adding all the times together and dividing by the number of times recorded.

$$25 + 18 + 23 + 28 + 30 + 22.5 + 23 + 33 + 20 = 222.5$$

$$\frac{222.5}{9} = 24.722$$

Rounding to the nearest minute, the mean is 25 minutes.

6. C: The mode is the time from the data set that occurs most often. The number 23 occurs twice in the data set, while all others occur only once, so the mode is 23 minutes.

7. A: To find the median of a data set, you must first list the numbers from smallest to largest, and then find the number in the middle. If there are two numbers in the middle, add the two numbers together and divide by 2. Putting this list in order from smallest to greatest yields 18, 20, 22.5, 23, 23, 25, 28, 30, and 33, where 23 is the middle number, so 23 minutes is the median.

8. B: The perimeter is found by adding the length of all the exterior sides. When the given dimensions are added, the perimeter is 22 meters. Start off by adding the listed lengths:

$$5 + 1.5 + 1.2 + 4.5$$

The right side can be calculated by subtracting 1.2 from 5 to get 3.8. The bottom can be calculated by adding 1.5 to 4.5 to get 6. That gives us:

$$P = 5 + 1.5 + 1.2 + 4.5 + 3.8 + 6 = 22 \text{ m}$$

9. B: The median is the value that is located halfway between the minimum and the maximum value of the scores. Therefore, fifty percent of the scores lie below it and fifty percent of the scores lie above it. It corresponds to the 50th percentile.

10. D: A stanine score of 5 has a value that falls in the middle twenty percent of the scores, which means between the 40th percentile and the 60th percentile. The 55th percentile is located within this region.

11. C: There are a few ways in which this problem can be answered. A trial and error method can be used. Second, a direct mathematical expression could be used. Subtract the flat rate $4 from $21 and divide by $2.25 to obtain 7.56 miles. Finally, the algebraic equation $2.25m + 4 = 21$ can be solved to obtain $m = 7.56$ miles. Since the question asks for whole miles, this answer rounds down to 7 miles, because 8 miles would be too expensive.

12. A: The chart is a bar chart showing how many men and women prefer each genre of movies. The dark gray bars represent the number of women, while the light gray bars represent the number of men. The light gray bars are higher and represent more men than women for the genres of Comedy and Action.

13. E: A line graph represents continuous change over time. The line on the graph is continuous and not broken, as on a scatter plot. Stacked bar graphs are used when comparing multiple variables at one time.

They combine some elements of both pie charts and bar graphs, using the organization of bar graphs and the proportionality aspect of pie charts. A bar graph may show change but isn't necessarily continuous over time. A pie graph is better for representing percentages of a whole. Histograms are best used in grouping sets of data in bins to show the frequency of a certain variable.

14. B: The relationship between age and time for attention span is a positive correlation because the general trend for the data is up and to the right. As the age increases, so does attention span.

15. E: The conversion between feet and centimeters requires a middle term. Since there are 2.54 centimeters in 1 inch, the conversion between inches and feet must be used first. As there are 12 inches in a foot, the fractions can be set up as follows:

$$3 \text{ ft} \times \frac{12 \text{ in}}{1 \text{ ft}} \times \frac{2.54 \text{ cm}}{1 \text{ in}}$$

The feet and inches units cancel out to leave only centimeters as units for the answer. The numbers are calculated across the top and bottom to yield:

$$\frac{3 \times 12 \times 2.54}{1 \times 1} = 91.44$$

The number and units used together form the answer of 91.4 cm, when rounded to the nearest tenth of a centimeter.

16. C: The Pythagorean theorem can be used to find the missing length x because it is a right triangle. The theorem states that $6^2 + 8^2 = x^2$, which simplifies into $100 = x^2$. Taking the positive square root of both sides results in the missing value $x = 10$.

17. B: Because two sides are equal, this is an isosceles triangle. The smallest sides correspond to the 20° angles. The third angle has a measure of:

$$180 - 20 - 20 = 140°$$

18. B: Let x be equal to the fifth test score. Therefore, in order to receive, at minimum, a B in the class, the student must have:

$$\frac{74 + 76 + 82 + 84 + x}{5} = 80$$

Therefore,

$$\frac{316 + x}{5} = 80$$

Solving for x gives:

$$316 + x = 400$$

or

$$x = 84$$

Therefore, he must receive at least an 84 out of 100 on the fifth test to receive a B in the course.

19. C: Choice *C* is the correct simplification for the expression given. For the expression:

$$5b^2 - 3ab + 10a$$

$$a = 3 \text{ and } b = -1$$

The values for a and b can be substituted into the given expression. The new expression becomes:

$$5(-1)^2 - 3(3)(-1) + 10(3)$$

Simplifying this expression using the order of operations yields a final answer of 44.

20. C: Choice *C* simplifies the equation completely to find the value of x. The equation can be solved by working to isolate the variable. The first step in this process is to distribute the 5, which yields the equation:

$$5x - 10 - 3x = 20 + x$$

Then, the like terms can be collected on each side to form:

$$2x - 10 = 20 + x$$

Finally, the x-terms can be moved to one side and the constants can be moved to one side to find the final answer of $x = 30$.

Advanced Algebra and Functions

1. B: For rational functions, the denominator can never be equal to 0. Finding the undefined values for a function is the same as finding the zeros of the expression in the denominator. To find the undefined values, set the denominator equal to 0 and solve for x. This results in $-3x + x^2 = 0$, and its solutions are $x = 0$ and $x = 3$. Therefore, the undefined values of x are 0 and 3; Choice *B* is correct.

2. C: If $h(x) = -6x + 11$, then $h(-2)$ can be found by substituting –2 in for x in the function. Therefore:

$$h(-2) = -6(-2) + 11 = 12 + 11 = 23$$

3. B: A rational function is undefined when its denominator is equal to 0. Plugging 5 into the denominator results in:
$$5^2 - 10(5) + 25 = 25 - 50 + 25 = 0$$

The other options give non-zero results. Therefore, the function is undefined when $x = 5$.

4. B: To solve, substitute $-9x + 2$ in place of $f(x)$ for the function $g(2)$ and replace x with 2:

$$f(2) = -9(2) + 2 = -16$$

$$g(2) = f(2) - 4$$

Therefore,

$$g(2) = -16 - 4 = -20$$

5. A: Given that $m = 2\sqrt{5}$ and $3m = \sqrt{4n}$, we plug $2\sqrt{5}$ in for m in the second equation to obtain:

$$6\sqrt{5} = \sqrt{4n}$$

Squaring both sides results in:

$$36(5) = 4n$$

Dividing both sides by 4 gives:

$$n = \frac{36(5)}{4} = 9(5) = 45$$

6. B: Squaring both sides results in the equation:

$$36(x - 2) = 25x$$

This is equivalent to:

$$36x - 72 = 25x$$

Adding 72 to both sides and subtracting $25x$ from both sides results in:

$$11x = 72$$

Dividing by 11 gives $x = \frac{72}{11}$. Because this is a radical equation, the answer must be checked. Plugging the result, $x = \frac{72}{11}$, into the original equation creates a true equation. Therefore, it is the solution to the original equation.

7. C: To solve this quadratic equation, the quadratic formula with $a = 2$, $b = -10$, and $c = 3$ should be used. Therefore,

$$x = \frac{-(-10) \pm \sqrt{(-10)^2 - 4(2)(3)}}{2(2)} = \frac{10 \pm \sqrt{76}}{4}$$

$$x = \frac{10 \pm 2\sqrt{19}}{4} = \frac{5}{2} \pm \frac{\sqrt{19}}{2}$$

8. D: Distribute the expressions in front of the parentheses to obtain:

$$-4x^2 + 36x + 8x - 24$$

Collecting like terms results in:

$$-4x^2 + 44x - 24$$

The coefficient on the x-term is 44, so $b = 44$.

9. A: The equation for a circle with radius r and center (h, k) is:

$$(x - h)^2 + (y - k)^2 = r^2$$

From the information given, the equation is

$$(x - h)^2 + (y + 6)^2 = 64$$

Plugging in the point $(4, 2)$ results in:

$$(4 - h)^2 + 64 = 64$$

Therefore,

$$(4 - h)^2 = 0$$

$$h = 4$$

The x-coordinate of the center of this circle is 4.

10. B: To rationalize the denominator, the conjugate of the denominator must be multiplied by both the numerator and the denominator of the expression. This will result in a denominator without radicals. The conjugate of the denominator is $x + \sqrt{7}$. Multiplying this by both the numerator and denominator results in:

$$\frac{49(x + \sqrt{7})}{(x - \sqrt{7})(x + \sqrt{7})} = \frac{49(x + \sqrt{7})}{x^2 - 7} = \frac{49x + 49\sqrt{7}}{x^2 - 7}$$

11. B: In order to find $h(-5x)$, plug $-5x$ in for x in the given function. Therefore,

$$h(-5x) = -5(-5x) - 7 = 25x - 7$$

12. A: Plugging 2 in for x in the function results in:

$$g(2) = a(2)^2 + 4(2) + 9 = 4a + 17$$

Because this expression is equal to -7, it is true that $4a + 17 = -7$. Therefore, $4a = -24$ and $a = -6$.

13. D: In order to add the two rational expressions, a common denominator must be used. The common denominator is $(x + 5)(x - 5)$. Multiply by fractions equal to 1 to build the common denominator. Multiply the first expression times $\frac{x-5}{x-5}$ and the second times $\frac{x+5}{x+5}$, and then subtract to obtain:

$$\frac{(4x - 2)(x - 5)}{(x + 5)(x - 5)} - \frac{(2x - 1)(x + 5)}{(x - 5)(x + 5)}$$

$$\frac{4x^2 - 20x - 2x + 10}{(x + 5)(x - 5)} - \frac{2x^2 + 10x - x - 5}{(x + 5)(x - 5)}$$

$$\frac{2x^2 - 31x + 15}{x^2 - 25}$$

14. A: If $M = 5x^2 - 4x + 2$ and $N = -2x^2 - 6x + 1$, then:

$$3M - \frac{3}{4}N = 3(5x^2 - 4x + 2) - \frac{3}{4}(-2x^2 - 6x + 1)$$

Set the coefficients to a common denominator:

$$3M - \frac{3}{4}N = \frac{12}{4}(5x^2 - 4x + 2) - \frac{3}{4}(-2x^2 - 6x + 1)$$

Multiply each term of the polynomials by their coefficients and simplify:

$$3M - \frac{3}{4}N = \frac{60x^2}{4} - \frac{48x}{4} + \frac{24}{4} + \frac{6x^2}{4} + \frac{18x}{4} - \frac{3}{4}$$

$$3M - \frac{3}{4}N = \frac{66x^2}{4} - \frac{30x}{4} + \frac{21}{4}$$

$$3M - \frac{3}{4}N = \frac{33}{2}x^2 - \frac{15}{2}x + \frac{21}{4}$$

15. C: Solving the equation for B results in:

$$B = \frac{81x^2}{9x + 2} - \frac{4}{9x + 2}$$

$$B = \frac{81x^2 - 4}{9x + 2}$$

$$B = \frac{(9x + 2)(9x - 2)}{9x + 2}$$

$$B = 9x - 2$$

16. A: A vertical line has the same x-value for any point on the line. Other points on the line would be $(1, 3)$, $(1, 5)$, $(1, 9)$, etc. Mathematically, this is written as $x = 1$. A vertical line is always of the form $x = a$ for some constant a.

17. E: First, the common factor 2 can be factored out of both terms, resulting in:

$$2(y^3 - 64)$$

The resulting binomial is a difference of cubes that can be factored using the rule:

$$a^3 - b^3 = (a - b)(a^2 + ab + b^2)$$

$$a = y \text{ and } b = 4$$

Therefore, the result is:

$$2(y - 4)(y^2 + 4y + 16)$$

286

18. D: The domain of a function is the possible values of x for that equation. For the given function $f(x) = \frac{x+4}{x^2-1}$, all values of x are possible except for $x = -1$ and $x = 1$. These two values cannot exist for this function because they result in a denominator that is equal to zero. These points are either holes or asymptotes for this function. The answers listed in Choices A and C are both correct, but they only contain one answer, not both negative and positive one.

19. B: Solving this exponential equation requires the use of the natural log, ln. This is the opposite of raising e to a power. Once the natural log of both sides is taken, the equation becomes $\ln(24) = x - 3$. Then, it can be solved for x, which yields the equation:

$$x = \ln(24) + 3$$

20. A: The vertex of a quadratic function can be found by the equation $x = \frac{-b}{2a}$, using the standard form for a quadratic:

$$y = ax^2 + bx + c$$

For this function, the x-coordinate for the vertex is:

$$x = \frac{-(-4)}{2(1)} = \frac{4}{2} = 2$$

Then, the y-value can be found by substituting this value ($x = 2$) into the given function:

$$y = x^2 - 4x + 10$$

$$2^2 - 4(2) + 10 = 6$$

The vertex for the quadratic equation is $(2, 6)$.

Reading

1. C: Choice C correctly identifies the main point in dispute. The director and critic are arguing about the director's role. The director argues that directors should be allowed to offend people, if that would accurately reflect reality, so the audience can maintain its suspension of disbelief. The critic would argue that this violates the director's social responsibility to avoid offending people.

Choice A is incorrect. Both the director and critic would agree that movie audiences suspend their disbelief. This is the director's main point, and the critic acknowledges its existence by claiming that censoring hate speech and racial slurs won't break the audience's disbelief.

Choice B is incorrect. This is the critic's main point, and the director would likely also agree. The director isn't claiming that movies aren't offensive, but that offending people is justified to protect the suspension of disbelief.

Choice D is incorrect. This isn't the main point in dispute. In addition, both the director and critic imply that they believe this to be true. For the director, creative control is required to structure a universe where an audience can suspend its disbelief. For the critic, the director would need creative control to censor what the critic deems inappropriate.

Choice *E* is incorrect. The critic would agree that movies have enormous cultural relevancy—that's why the critic is calling for self-censorship—but it's unclear whether the director would agree or disagree.

2. B: Look for the key words that give away the type of passage this is, such as "deities," "Greek hero," "centaur," and the names of Greek deities like Artemis. A eulogy is typically a speech given at a funeral, making Choice *A* incorrect. Choices *C* and *D* are incorrect, as "virgin huntresses" and "centaurs" are typically not found in historical or professional documents.

3. B: Although we don't have much context to go off of, this person is probably not a "lifetime partner" or "farm crop" of civilized life. These two do not make sense, so Choices *C* and *D* are incorrect. Choice *A* is also a bit strange. To be an "illegal immigrant" of civilized life is not a used phrase, making Choice *A* incorrect.

4. C: A certain characteristic or quality imposed upon something else. The sentence states that "the impress of his dear hand [has] been stamped everywhere." Choice *A* is one definition of *impress*, but this definition is used more as a verb than a noun: "She impressed us as a songwriter." Choice *B* is incorrect because it is also used as a verb: "He impressed the need for something to be done." Choice *D* is incorrect because it is part of a physical act: "the businessman impressed his mark upon the envelope." The phrase in the passage is meant as figurative, since the workmen did most of the physical labor, not the prince.

5. D: Neutrality, due to the style of the report. The report is mostly objective; we see very little language that entails any strong emotion whatsoever. The story is told almost as an objective documentation of a sequence of actions—we see the president sitting in his box with his wife, their enjoyment of the show, Booth's walk through the crowd to the box, and Ford's consideration of Booth's movements. There is perhaps a small amount of bias when the author mentions the president's "worthy wife." However, the word choice and style show no signs of excitement, sadness, anger, or apprehension from the author's perspective, so the best answer is Choice *D*.

6. B: Mr. Ford assumed Booth's movement throughout the theater was due to being familiar with the theater. Choice *A* is incorrect; although Booth does eventually make his way to Lincoln's box, Mr. Ford does not make this distinction in this part of the passage. Choice *C* is incorrect; although the passage mentions "companions," it mentions Lincoln's companions rather than Booth's companions. Choice *D* is incorrect; the passage mentions "dress circle," which means the first level of the theater, but this is different from a "dressing room." Finally, Choice *E* is incorrect; the passage mentions a "symptom" but does not signify a symptom from an illness.

7. C: A lead singer leaves their band to begin a solo career, and the band's sales on their next album drop by 50 percent. The original source of the analogy displays someone significant to an event who leaves, and then the event becomes worse for it. We see Mr. Sothern leaving the theater company, and then the play becoming a "very dull affair." Choice *A* depicts a dancer who backs out of an event before the final performance, so this is incorrect. Choice *B* shows a basketball player leaving an event, and then the team makes it to the championship but then loses.

This choice could be a contestant for the right answer; however, we don't know if the team has become worse because of his departure or better. We simply do not have enough information here. Choice *D* is incorrect. The actor departs an event, but there is no assessment of the quality of the movie. It simply states that the actor who filled in resembles the deceased. Choice *E* is incorrect because the opposite of the source happens; the professor leaves the entity, and the entity becomes better. Additionally, the betterment of the entity is not due to the individual leaving. Choice *E* is not analogous to the source.

288

8. A: It's tempting to mark Choice *A* wrong because the genres are different. Choice *A* is a fiction text, and the original passage is not a fictional account. However, the question stem asks specifically for organizational structure. Choice *A* has a chronological structure just like the passage, so this is the correct answer. The passage does not have a cause and effect, problem/solution, or compare/contrast structure, making Choices *B*, *D*, and *E* incorrect. Choice *C* is tempting because it mentions an autobiography; however, the structure of this text starts at the end and works its way toward the beginning, which is the opposite structure of the original passage.

9. C: The word *adornments* would LEAST change the meaning of the sentence because it's the most closely related word to *festoons.* The other choices don't make sense in the context of the sentence. *Feathers* of flags, *armies* of flags, *buckets* of flags, and *boats* of flags are not as accurate as the phrase *adornments* of flags. The passage also talks about other décor in the setting, so the word *adornments* fits right in with the context of the paragraph.

10. D: Choice *A* is incorrect; the author makes no claims about who shot Lincoln and uses no rhetoric of persuasion towards the audience. Choice B is incorrect, though it's a tempting choice. The passage depicts the setting in exorbitant detail, but the setting itself is not the primary purpose of the passage. Choice *C* is incorrect; one could argue that this is a narrative, and the passage is about Lincoln's last few hours, but this isn't the *best* choice. The best choice is that the passage recounts the details that lead up to Lincoln's death. Finally, Choice *E* is incorrect. The author does not try to prove or disprove anything to the audience, and the passage does not even make it to when Lincoln gets shot, so this part of the story is irrelevant.

11. C: This question requires close attention to the passage. Choice *A* can be found where the passage says "no less than six named and several unnamed varieties of the peach have thus produced several varieties of nectarine," so this choice is incorrect. Choice *B* can be found where the passage says "it is highly improbable that all these peach-trees... are hybrids from the peach and nectarine." Choice *D* is incorrect because we see in the passage that "the production of peaches from nectarines, either by seeds or buds, may perhaps be considered as a case of reversion." Choice *C* is the correct answer because the word *unremarkable* should be changed to *remarkable* in order for it to be consistent with the details of the passage.

12. B: Choice *B* is the correct answer because the meaning holds true even if the words have been switched out or rearranged some. Choice *A* is incorrect because it has trees either bearing peaches or nectarines, and the trees in the original phrase bear both. Choice *C* is incorrect because the statement does not say these trees are "indifferent to bud-variation" but that they have "indifferently [bore] peaches or nectarines." Choice *D* is incorrect; the statement may use some of the same words, but the meaning is skewed in this sentence.

13. B: Choice *B* is the best answer here; the sentence states, "In unknown regions take a responsible guide with you, unless the trail is short, easily followed, and a frequented one." Choice *A* is incorrect; the passage does not state that you should try and explore unknown regions. Choice *C* is incorrect; the passage talks about trails that contain pitfalls, traps, and boggy places, but it does not say that *all* unknown regions contain these things. Choice *D* is incorrect; the passage mentions "rail" and "boat" as means of transport at the beginning, but it does not suggest it is better to travel unknown regions by rail. Choice *E* is incorrect because the passage warns against the challenges and downsides of a potential "false trail;" it does not encourage purposely creating one.

14. D: Choice *D* is correct; it may be real advice an experienced hiker would give to an inexperienced hiker. However, the question asks about details in the passage, and this is not in the passage. Choice *A* is incorrect; we do see the author encouraging the reader to learn about the trail beforehand… "wet or dry; where it leads; and its length." Choice *B* is also incorrect, because we do see the author telling us the time will lengthen with boggy or rugged places opposed to smooth places. Choice *C* is incorrect; at the end of the passage, the author tells us "do not go alone through lonely places… unless you are quite familiar with the country and the ways of the wild." Choice *E* is incorrect because the detail is found in the passage in the first sentence of the last paragraph.

15. C: The best answer here is Choice *C:* "Follow the false trail back to its beginning so that you can rediscover the real trail." Choices *A* and *D* are represented in the text; but this is advice on how to blaze a trail, not what to do when being led astray by a false trail. Choice *B* is incorrect; this is the opposite of what the text suggests doing. Choice *E* is incorrect because the author suggests bending the branches so that the light side of the leaf points upward to help make the trail clear. This advice is also in reference to blazing the main trail, not what to do should you be led astray on a false trail.

16. C: We can infer that this narrative takes place during winter. Some of the evidence here is that "the cold became intense," and people were decorating their shops with "holly sprigs,"—a Christmas tradition. It also mentions that it's Christmastime at the end of the passage. Choice *C* is correct. We cannot infer that the passage takes place during the night time. While we do have a statement that says that the darkness thickened, this is the only evidence we have. The darkness could be thickening because it is foggy outside. We don't have enough proof to infer this otherwise.

Choice *B* is incorrect; we *can* infer that the narrative is located in a bustling city street by the actions in the story. People are running around trying to sell things, the atmosphere is busy, there is a church tolling the hours, etc. The scene switches to the Mayor's house at the end of the passage, but the answer says "majority," so this is still incorrect. Choice *D* is incorrect; we *can* infer that the Lord Mayor is wealthy—he lives in the "Mansion House" and has fifty cooks. Choice *E* is incorrect because we *can* infer that Scrooge was not kind nor receptive since he scared the caroler away.

17. E: The passage tells us that the poulterers' and grocers' trades were "a glorious pageant, with which it was next to impossible to believe that such dull principles as bargain and sale had anything to do," which means they set up their shops to be entertaining public spectacles in order to increase sales. Choice *A* is incorrect; although the word "joke" is used, it is meant to be used as a source of amusement rather than something made in poor quality. Choice *B* is incorrect; that they put on a "pageant" is figurative for the public spectacle they made with their shops, not a literal play. Choice *C* is incorrect, as this is not mentioned anywhere in the passage. Finally, Choice *D* is incorrect; although it's an appealing option because the poulterers and grocers clearly aimed to spread Christmas cheer, it's not clear that they were working tirelessly to convert non-believers.

18. B: The author, at least in the last few paragraphs, does not attempt to evoke empathy for the character of Scrooge. We see Scrooge lashing out at an innocent, cold boy, with no sign of affection or feeling for his harsh conditions. We see Choice *A* when the author talks about Saint Dunstan. We see Choices *C* and *E,* providing a palpable experience and imaginable setting and character, especially with the "piercing, searching, biting cold," among other statements. Finally, we see Choice *D* when Scrooge chases the young boy away.

19. C: *Proficient* is the best choices for this sentence because it means highly skilled. *Notorious* means well-known. *Inept* means unskilled. *Unassuming* means modest.

20. B: *Obsolete* is the best choices for this sentence because it means outdated or old-fashioned. *Resuscitated* means revived. *Ostentatious* means showy or pretentious. *Contemporary* means modern or current.

Writing

1. A: Choice *A* is the best answer. To write a direct quotation, double quotation marks are placed at the beginning and ending of the quoted words. All punctuation specifically related to the quoted phrase or sentence is kept inside the quotation marks. Single quotation marks, as used in Choices *B* and *C*, are not used for dialogue in American English.

2. B: The best answer is *B*. The reciprocal pronoun "one another" generally refers to more than two people.

3. C: The best answer is *C*: "Lulu brought this kitten home only six weeks ago, and she was so fond of her." There are two independent clauses in one sentence, so separating the two clauses with a comma is the best option. The other sentences have incorrect comma placement. Additionally, the information that Lulu was only five years old is not necessary in this particular sentence—it is out of context.

4. C: Choice *C* is the best answer. We would use the preposition "through," when talking about staying with someone "through the night."

5. C: Choice *C* is the best answer here: "Lulu continued to play so that she wouldn't scare the kitten away." Usually the words "in order" are used with the word "to." Choice *A* is incorrect because the words "in order" are usually followed by the word "to" not "that." For Choice *D*, there is no need for a comma after "so that", and for Choice *B*, there is no need for a comma after "so."

6. D: The best answer is *D*: "without a set list of chores, and without ensuring the chores are completed, our household would be utterly chaotic." In this sentence, there is an interrupting phrase that must be set apart by two commas on either side of it.

7. A: Choice *A* is the best answer, no change, because "13-year-old" is correct. When an age is describing a noun and precedes the noun, hyphenation is required.

8. B: Choice *B* is the best answer, "approximately once a week." Choice *A* is not the best answer, because the adverb "approximately" interrupts the phrase "once a week," producing the awkward if grammatically correct phrase "once, approximately, a week." Choice *C* is not correct, because "bi-weekly" means twice a week or every two weeks. Choice *D* is not the best answer, because it changes the meaning to a firm "once a week."

9. B: The best answer is Choice *B*: "Both my husband and I drive our daughter." "I" is a subject pronoun, and in this sentence "I" is part of a compound subject, "my husband and I." A helpful way to answer this question is to take out the phrase "my husband" and read the sentence with each choice. Choice *A*, "myself drive our daughter" is incorrect, and so is Choice *D*, "myself, drive our daughter." Choice *C*, "me drive our daughter" is also incorrect. "I drive our daughter" is the best answer.

10. B: The best answer is Choice *B*: "who do you think has the most chores?" Since the sentence is comparing three people's chores, it is necessary to use a superlative adjective. If there were only two people, it would be correct to use the comparative adjective "more."

11. C: Choice *C* is the best answer. The words "accept" and "except" are often confused. There is no need to use the adverb "exceptionally" here, so Choice *B* is incorrect. Choice *C* is incorrect, because "expect" is a verb with a different meaning than "except."

12. B: The best answer is *B*. The word "birds" doesn't necessarily evoke a sound, but any number of actions birds make will create sound. It is best to use a qualifier here, to indicate which bird sound the person hears.

13. C: The best answer is *C*. "Ever so" is a common phrase in English. The other options are incorrectly spelled.

14. D: Choice *D* is the best answer: "you smile for the rest of the day." As the sentence is currently written, there is a dangling modifier. The sentence implies that the day, and not the person, is feeling optimistic.

15. B: The best choice is *B*. The sentence is composed of two independent clauses, and therefore requires a comma before the conjunction.

16. B: The best answer is *B*: "and I'm always the last one to class." Choice *C* changes the meaning, and Choice *D* uses an unnecessary comma. The original phrase is awkward; it is not parallel with the previous instance of the phrase "the last one." Additionally, English speakers would never omit the article "the" from the phrase "the last one."

17. C: The best answer is *C*: "I was always teased by my older sisters." The sentence in the passage demonstrates a common mistake with dangling participles. The sentence starts with the participial phrase "Having also been the last of all the siblings." That phrase can only modify the speaker, the youngest sibling. But in the original passage, the participial phrase incorrectly modifies "my older sisters." Choice *C* is the only answer that corrects this mistake.

18. D: Choice *D* is the best answer: "Last but not least!" In American English, double quotation marks are used at the beginning and ending of a quotation, and all punctuation relating specifically to the quotation must remain inside the quotation marks. There is also no need for a comma in a simple sentence containing one simple thought, making Choice *C* incorrect.

19. B: The best answer is *B*, the semicolon. The way ideas are connected is important. In this case, the second independent clause gives an example of the first. The author says she has been dishonest; the next clause shows the instance of her dishonesty. The word "and" is not grammatically wrong, but it suggests the two facts are on the same level. Choices *C* and *D* suggest different relationships between the two facts, and these relationships do not make the most sense.

20. A: Choice *A* is the best answer. The phrase "after all" means "despite earlier problems or doubts," which is the perfect transition here because the speaker is changing their mind about being the last sibling. "Therefore" denotes a conclusion, and "however" and "on the contrary" denote a counter, and the speaker is not concluding or countering here.

21. B: Choice *B* is the best answer: "Jones's class." The teacher's name is Mr. Jones, and since the name "Jones" ends in an "s," in order to show possession, it is necessary to place the apostrophe directly after the "s" in the name "Jones," followed by the possessive "s."

292

22. B: The best answer is *B*. "He would listen to his parents' kitchen radio for hours, playing their records and singing away to all the classics." In order to keep the verb tense consistent and maintain parallel structure, the verb form "playing" should match the verb form "singing."

23. C: The best answer is *C*. "However, what he really wanted…" In the choices provided, "however" as a transitional word followed by a comma is the most appropriate choice because it provides a contrast inherent in the context: that he loved music but wanted to create his own.

24. D: Choice *D* is the best answer. The two actions occur one after the other, in a sequence; first Matt forgot, then he began to play. In the original sentence, the verb "had begun" suggests Matt somehow started playing before he forgot about his test.

25. D: The best answer is *D*. This sentence is set up in the past conditional, starting with the condition "if." Therefore, the use of the conditional "would fail" is necessary.

Practice Test #3

Arithmetic

1. Which of the following numbers is the smallest?
$$0.0425, \frac{1}{8}, 0.43\%, \frac{3}{5}\%$$

    a.   0.0425

    b. $\frac{1}{8}$

    c.   0.43%

    d. $\frac{3}{5}\%$

2. Calculate the following: 4.25×2.1.
    a.   0.8925
    b.   8.5
    c.   89.25
    d.   8.925

3. When dividing 490 by 3, what is the remainder?
    a.   163
    b.   1
    c.   0.33
    d.   2

4. Calculate the following: $\frac{9}{100} + \frac{9}{10}$.

    a. $\frac{19}{100}$

    b. $\frac{99}{110}$

    c. $\frac{99}{100}$

    d. $\frac{9}{110}$

5. Which fraction is equivalent to 0.05?

    a. $\frac{5}{20}$

    b. $\frac{1}{10}$

    c. $\frac{5}{10}$

    d. $\frac{1}{20}$

6. Kristy put $150 of her $400 in her savings account. What percent of her money did this represent?
    a. 62.5%
    b. 15%
    c. 37.5%
    d. 40%

7. A car dealership had 150 cars in the morning and sold 12 cars throughout the day. What percentage of cars were left at the end of the day?
    a. 92%
    b. 8%
    c. 12%
    d. 82%

8. Round 9.9999 to the nearest tenth.
    a. 10.9
    b. 9.9
    c. 11
    d. 10

9. In Karen's recipe, each dozen of muffins calls for 2 eggs. What is the greatest number of muffins that she can make with 45 eggs?
    a. 22
    b. 23
    c. 264
    d. 276

10. Fernando works at both the library and the post office. In June, a month with 30 days, he worked 1/5 of the days of the month at the library and 1/6 of the days of the month at the post office. How many days did he not work?
    a. 11
    b. 19
    c. 5
    d. 6

11. A classroom has 22 students. If each student brings in 8 pencils on the first day of school, how many pencils come to the classroom on that first day?
    a. 30
    b. 14
    c. 176
    d. 166

12. Subtract the following mixed numbers: $7\frac{4}{5} - 5\frac{1}{2}$.

    a. $\frac{23}{10}$

    b. $\frac{11}{5}$

    c. $\frac{35}{6}$

    d. $\frac{21}{10}$

13. If 50° and 75° are the measures of two angles in a triangle, what is the measure of the third?

    a. 45°

    b. 55°

    c. 125°

    d. 90°

14. Which of the following is the largest value?

    a. 0.1101

    b. 0.1011

    c. 0.1111

    d. 0.0111

15. When evaluating 45.8×3.2, which of the following values is the closest?

    a. 135

    b. 192

    c. 184

    d. 138

16. Multiply the following: 34.2×10^{-2}.

    a. 3,400

    b. 3.42

    c. 0.342

    d. 34.2

17. Add the following mixed numbers: $1\frac{3}{4} + 2\frac{3}{5}$.

    a. $3\frac{2}{3}$

    b. 5

    c. $3\frac{3}{20}$

    d. $8\frac{2}{11}$

18. Which of the following is not a way to write 50 percent of X?

    a. $.5X$

    b. $\frac{50}{100}X$

    c. $50X$

    d. $\frac{1}{2}X$

19. Three numbers have a sum of 21. When adding an additional number, the average of the four numbers is 7. What is the value of the fourth number?

    a. 28

    b. 6

    c. 8

    d. 7

20. Jackie had $4\frac{1}{2}$ pounds of sugar, and she used $\frac{1}{3}$ of that amount in a recipe for cookies. How much did she use?

    a. $\frac{2}{3}$ lb

    b. 1 lb

    c. $\frac{3}{2}$ lb

    d. $2\frac{1}{3}$ lb

Quantitative Reasoning, Algebra, and Statistics

1. A local candy store reports that of the 100 customers that bought suckers, 35 of them bought cherry. What is the probability of selecting 2 customers simultaneously at random that both purchased a cherry sucker?

    a. $\frac{119}{990}$

    b. $\frac{35}{100}$

    c. $\frac{49}{400}$

    d. $\frac{69}{99}$

2. The table below shows tickets purchased during the week for entry to the local zoo. What is the mean of adult tickets sold for the week?

Day of the Week	Age	Tickets Sold
Monday	Adult	22
Monday	Child	30
Tuesday	Adult	16
Tuesday	Child	15
Wednesday	Adult	24
Wednesday	Child	23
Thursday	Adult	19
Thursday	Child	26
Friday	Adult	29
Friday	Child	38

 a. 24.2
 b. 21
 c. 22
 d. 26.4

3. Solve the inequality: $|3 - x| > 7$.
 a. $x < -4 \ and \ x > -10$
 b. $x > 4 \ and \ x < 10$
 c. $x < 4 \ and \ x > 10$
 d. $x > -4 \ and \ x > -10$

4. Simplify $\sqrt{16x^3y^6z^5}$.
 a. $16xy^3z$

 b. $4xy^3z^2\sqrt{xz}$

 c. $4x^2y^{3z}$

 d. $4xyz\sqrt{z}$

5. How many kiloliters are in 6 liters?
 a. 6,000
 b. 600
 c. 0.006
 d. 0.0006

6. In order to get a B in a class, Mark needs to have an 80 average on his 5 tests. He received the following grades on his first 4 tests: 85, 76, 56, and 88. What is the lowest score he would need to receive on the fifth test to get a B in the class?
 a. 90
 b. 95
 c. 85
 d. 80
 e. 100

7. Which of the following values could NOT represent a probability?
   a. 0.0123
   b. 0.99999
   c. $\frac{1}{10}$
   d. $\frac{3}{2}$

8. Which of the following is the result of the expression $\frac{14x}{y^2} - \frac{10y}{x^2}$ evaluated for $x = -2$ and $y = -3$?
   a. $\frac{79}{18}$
   b. $\frac{191}{18}$
   c. $-\frac{191}{18}$
   d. $-\frac{79}{18}$

9. If x is directly proportional to y and if $x = 8$ when $y = \frac{1}{12}$, then which of the following describes an equation that relates x and y?
   a. $x = 96y$
   b. $y = 96x$
   c. $x = 12y$
   d. $y = 1.5x$

10. In a class of 3 girls and 5 boys, the average score for boys was an 82 and the average for girls was 84. What was the class average?
   a. 82
   b. 82.75
   c. 83
   d. 83.75

11. How many 5-letter orderings of the word FRANCHISE can be made if no letters are repeated?
   a. 3,024
   b. 504
   c. 72
   d. 15,120

12. At a school raffle, 1,000 tickets are sold for $1 each with the possibility of winning a $200 or a $50 prize. What is the expected value of the gain?
   a. $0.75
   b. $1
   c. -$0.75
   d. $1.25

13. Which of the following pairs of angles could NOT be the smaller and larger interior angles of a parallelogram?
   a. 120°, 60°
   b. 125°, 55°
   c. 110°, 60°
   d. 20°, 160°

14. Use the graph below entitled "Projected Temperatures for Tomorrow's Winter Storm" to answer the question.

What is the expected temperature at 3:00 p.m.?
   a. 25 degrees
   b. 22 degrees
   c. 20 degrees
   d. 16 degrees

15. Which expression is equal to 4 less than 9 times the sum of x and y ?
   a. $4 - 9(x + y)$
   b. $4 + 9(x + y)$
   c. $9(x + y - 4)$
   d. $9(x + y) - 4$

16. If one kilometer is equal to 1,000 meters, how many meters are there in 650 kilometers?
   a. 0.65
   b. 650,000
   c. 65,000
   d. 6,500,000

17. In the Cartesian coordinate plane, a line passes through the points (6, 8) and (0, 4). What is the equation of the line?

    a. $y = \frac{3}{2}x + 4$

    b. $y = \frac{2}{3}x + 8$

    c. $y = \frac{2}{3}x - 8$

    d. $y = \frac{2}{3}x + 4$

18. Simplify the following:

$$\frac{(x^2 \cdot x^7)^4}{x^{-2}}$$

    a. x^{38}
    b. x^{34}
    c. x^{66}
    d. x^{15}

19. Find the point of intersection of the following two lines in the Cartesian coordinate plane:

$$4x - 7y = 9$$

$$x = 3$$

    a. $(3, 7)$

    b. $(3, 3)$

    c. $\left(3, \frac{3}{7}\right)$

    d. $\left(3, -\frac{3}{7}\right)$

20. Simplify the following expression: $7(x - 5) + 9x - 1$.
    a. $16x - 36$
    b. $16x + 36$
    c. $16x - 1$
    d. $10x - 36$

Advanced Algebra and Functions

1. Which of the following is equivalent to the equation $9^{10x} = 2$?

    a. $x = \frac{\ln 2}{10 \ln 9}$

    b. $x = \frac{10 \ln 2}{\ln 9}$

    c. $x = 10\ln\left(\frac{2}{9}\right)$

    d. $x = \frac{\ln 9}{10 \ln 2}$

2. Given the function $g(x) = x^2 - 4x + 2$, which of the following is equal to $g(x - 10)$?

    a. $x^2 - 4(x - 10) - 12$

    b. $x^2 - 4x - 12$

    c. $(x - 10)^2 - 4(x - 10) + 2$

    d. $(x - 10)^2 - 4x + 2$

3. What is the range of the graph of $y = -10x^2 + 7$?

    a.   All real numbers

    b. $y \leq -10$

    c. $y \geq 7$

    d. $y \leq 7$

4. Which of the following is an equation of a line that passes through the point (2,2) and is perpendicular to the line $y = -\frac{1}{2}x + 8$?

    a. $y = -\frac{1}{2}x + 2$

    b. $y = 2x - 2$

    c. $y = 2x - 4$

    d. $y = -\frac{1}{2}x$

5. Factor the expression $8x^2 - 24x - 224$.

    a. $(x + 4)(8x - 7)$

    b. $(x + 4)(x - 7)$

    c. $8(x + 4)(x - 7)$

    d. $(8x + 4)(x - 7)$

6. Simplify the function $f(x) = \frac{x^2 - 4x - 21}{x^2 - 49}$, assuming $x \neq 7$ and -7.

    a. $\frac{x+3}{x+7}$

    b. $\frac{x+3}{x-7}$

    c. $\frac{x-7}{x+7}$

    d. $\frac{x-3}{x-7}$

7. Solve the following equation: $(4x + \sqrt{6})(9x - \sqrt{21}) = 0$.

    a. $x = \frac{\sqrt{6}}{4}$ and $x = \frac{\sqrt{21}}{9}$

    b. $x = -\frac{\sqrt{3}}{2}$ and $x = \frac{\sqrt{7}}{3}$

    c. $x = -\frac{\sqrt{6}}{4}$ and $x = \frac{\sqrt{21}}{9}$

    d. $x = -\frac{\sqrt{6}}{4}$ and $x = -\frac{\sqrt{21}}{9}$

8. Solve the following equation: $4x^2 + 8x + 9 = 0$. Assume that $\sqrt{-1} = i$.

    a. $\dfrac{-2\pm5i}{4}$

    b. $\dfrac{-2\pm\sqrt{5}}{2}$

    c. $\dfrac{2\pm\sqrt{5}}{2}$

    d. $\dfrac{-2\pm i\sqrt{5}}{2}$

9. Which of the following statements is true about the function $g(x) = -6.43x^3 + 2.4x^2 - 1.423x + 9$?

    a.   It has an odd degree and y approaches $-\infty$ as x approaches ∞.

    b.   It has a degree of 7 and y approaches ∞ as x approaches ∞.

    c.   It has a degree of 3 and y approaches $-\infty$ as x approaches ∞.

    d.   It has an even degree and y approaches $-\infty$ as x approaches ∞.

10. What is the domain of the function $h(x) = \dfrac{x+2}{\sqrt{x-2}}$?

    a. $y > 2$

    b. $x > 2$

    c. $x \geq 2$

    d. $x < 2$

11. Which of the following is an equation of a line that passes through the point (1,4) and is parallel to the line $y = 5x + 8$?

    a. $y = 5x - 1$

    b. $y = 5x + 4$

    c. $y = -\dfrac{1}{5}x - 1$

    d. $y = 5x - 4$

12. If $f(x) = 8x^2 + 4$ and $g(x) = \dfrac{2+2x}{4}$, what is the value of $f\big(g(1)\big) + (g(2))^2 + \big(f(-1)\big)^2$?

    a.   144

    b. $\dfrac{633}{4}$

    c. $\dfrac{259}{4}$

    d.   256

13. If $h(x) = \dfrac{5}{2+6x}$, what is $h'(-3)$, where $h'(x)$ represents the inverse of the function $h(x)$?

    a. -3

    b. $-\dfrac{5}{15}$

    c. $-\dfrac{11}{18}$

    d. $-\dfrac{18}{11}$

14. Solve the following equation: $\sqrt{x-9} = \sqrt{3x+1}$.
   a. No solution
   b. 5
   c. 9
   d. −5

15. Simplify the following polynomial: $4x^3y^2\left(-9x^6y^{-1}z^2 - \frac{4}{5}x^{-3}y^{-4}\right) - 16z^{-1}\left(2xy^4z - \frac{1}{2}x^{-3}z^2\right)$.

   a. $-36x^9yz^2 - \frac{16}{5y^2} - 32xy^4 + \frac{8z}{x^3}$

   b. $-36x^9yz^2 - \frac{16}{5}y^2 - 32xy^4 + 8x^3$

   c. $-36x^9yz^2 - \frac{16}{5y^2} - 32xy^4z + \frac{8z}{x^3}$

   d. $-36x^8yz^2 - \frac{16}{5y^2} - 32xy^4z^3 + \frac{8z}{x^3}$

16. Which of the following represents the equation $\log_6 6\left(\log_5 x + \log_5 2x - 2\log_5(x+1)\right) = 8$?

   a. $5^8 = \frac{2x}{(x+1)^2}$

   b. $30x - 20(x+1) = 8$

   c. $5^8 = \frac{2x^2}{(x+1)^2}$

   d. $8^5 = \frac{2x^2}{(x+1)^2}$

17. Express the following in scientific notation: $(1.65 \times 10^{-5}) \div (2.2 \times 10^{-9})$.
   a. 0.75×10^{-3}
   b. 0.75×10^3
   c. 7.5×10^4
   d. 7.5×10^3

18. A population of bacteria has an initial amount of 1,000. The population is expected to double every 8 hours. Which of the following is the correct equation representing the total number of bacteria, x, after t days? There are 24 hours in one day.
   a. $x = 1000(6)^{3t}$
   b. $x = 1000(2)^{3t}$
   c. $x = 1000(2)^t$
   d. $x = 1000(2)^{6t}$

19. What will be the resulting equation if the graph of $y = x^2$ is shifted to the right 2 units and up 5 units?
   a. $y = (x+2)^2 + 5$
   b. $y = (x-5)^2 + 2$
   c. $y = (x-2)^2 - 5$
   d. $y = (x-2)^2 + 5$

20. If $f(x) = \sqrt{x}$ and $g(x) = -\sqrt{x+1}$, describe the translation of the graph from $f(x)$ to $g(x)$.
    a. Reflected across the x-axis and translated 1 unit to the right
    b. Reflected across the x-axis and translated 1 unit to the left
    c. Reflected across the y-axis and translated 1 unit to the right
    d. Reflected across the y-axis and translated 1 unit to the left

Reading

Directions for the next 18 questions: Read the statement or passage and then choose the best answer to the question. Answer the question based on what is stated or implied in the statement or passage.

The next 7 questions are based on the following passage from Rhetoric and Poetry in the Renaissance: A Study of Rhetorical Terms in English Renaissance Literary Criticism *by D.L. Clark:*

To the Greeks and Romans, rhetoric meant the theory of oratory. As a pedagogical mechanism, it endeavored to teach students to persuade an audience. The content of rhetoric included all that the ancients had learned to be of value in persuasive public speech. It taught how to work up a case by drawing valid inferences from sound evidence, how to organize this material in the most persuasive order, and how to compose in clear and harmonious sentences. Thus, to the Greeks and Romans, rhetoric was defined by its function of discovering means to persuasion and was taught in the schools as something that every free-born man could and should learn.

In both these respects, the ancients felt that poetics, the theory of poetry, was different from rhetoric. As the critical theorists believed that the poets were inspired, they endeavored less to teach men to be poets than to point out the excellences which the poets had attained. Although these critics generally, with the exceptions of Aristotle and Eratosthenes, believed the greatest value of poetry to be in the teaching of morality, no one of them endeavored to define poetry, as they did rhetoric, by its purpose. To Aristotle, and centuries later to Plutarch, the distinguishing mark of poetry was imitation. Not until the renaissance did critics define poetry as an art of imitation endeavoring to inculcate morality...

The same essential difference between classical rhetoric and poetics appears in the content of classical poetics. Whereas classical rhetoric deals with speeches which might be delivered to convict or acquit a defendant in the law court, or to secure a certain action by the deliberative assembly, or to adorn an occasion, classical poetics deals with lyric, epic, and drama. It is a commonplace that classical literary critics paid little attention to the lyric. It is less frequently realized that they devoted almost as little space to discussion of metrics. By far the greater bulk of classical treatises on poetics is devoted to characterization and to the technique of plot construction, involving as it does narrative and dramatic unity and movement as distinct from logical unity and movement.

1. What does the author say about one way in which the purpose of poetry changed for later philosophers?
   a. The author says that at first, poetry was not defined by its purpose but was valued for its ability to be used to teach morality. Later, some philosophers would define poetry by its ability to instill morality. Finally, during the Renaissance, poetry was believed to be an imitative art but was not necessarily believed to instill morality in its readers.
   b. The author says that the classical understanding of poetry dealt with its ability to be used to teach morality. Later, philosophers would define poetry by its ability to imitate life. Finally, during the Renaissance, poetry was believed to be an imitative art that instilled morality in its readers.
   c. The author says that at first, poetry was thought to be an imitation of reality, then later, philosophers valued poetry more for its ability to instill morality.
   d. The author says that the classical understanding of poetry was that it dealt with the search for truth through its content; later, the purpose of poetry would be through its entertainment value.
   e. The author says that the initial understanding of the purpose of poetry was its entertainment value. Then, as poetry evolved during a more religious era, the renaissance, it was valued for its ability to instill morality through its teaching.

2. What does the author of the passage say about classical literary critics in relation to poetics?
   a. That rhetoric was valued more than poetry because rhetoric had a definitive purpose to persuade an audience, and poetry's wavering purpose made it harder for critics to teach
   b. That although most poetry was written as lyric, epic, or drama, the critics were most focused on the techniques of lyric and epic and their performance of musicality and structure
   c. That although most poetry was written as lyric, epic, or drama, the critics were most focused on the techniques of the epic and drama and their performance of structure and character
   d. That the study of poetics was more pleasurable than the study of rhetoric due to its ability to assuage its audience, and the critics, therefore, focused on what poets did to create that effect
   e. That since poetics was made by the elite in Greek and Roman society, literary critics resented poetics for its obsession of material things and its superfluous linguistics

3. What is the primary purpose of this passage?
   a. To alert the readers to Greek and Roman culture regarding poetic texts and the focus on characterization and plot construction rather than lyric and meter
   b. To inform the readers of the changes in poetic critical theory throughout the years and to contrast those changes to the solidity of rhetoric
   c. To educate the audience on rhetoric by explaining the historical implications of using rhetoric in the education system
   d. To convince the audience that poetics is a subset of rhetoric as viewed by the Greek and Roman culture
   e. To contemplate the differences between classical rhetoric and poetry and to consider their purposes in a particular culture

4. The word *inculcate* in the second paragraph can be best interpreted as meaning which one of the following?
   a. Imbibe
   b. Instill
   c. Implode
   d. Inquire
   e. Idolize

5. Which of the following most closely resembles the way in which the passage is structured?

  a. The first paragraph presents an issue. The second paragraph offers a solution to the problem. The third paragraph summarizes the first two paragraphs.

  b. The first paragraph presents definitions and examples of a particular subject. The second paragraph presents a second subject in the same way. The third paragraph offers a contrast of the two subjects.

  c. The first paragraph presents an inquiry. The second paragraph explains the details of that inquiry. The last paragraph offers a solution.

  d. The first paragraph presents two subjects alongside definitions and examples. The second paragraph presents us a comparison of the two subjects. The third paragraph presents a contrast of the two subjects.

  e. The first paragraph offers a solution to a problem. The second paragraph questions the solution. The third paragraph offers a different solution.

6. Given the author's description of the content of rhetoric in the first paragraph, which one of the following is most analogous to what it taught? (The sentence is shown below.)

  It taught how to work up a case by drawing valid inferences from sound evidence, how to organize this material in the most persuasive order, how to compose in clear and harmonious sentences.

  a. As a musician, they taught me that the end product of the music is everything—what I did to get there was irrelevant, whether it was my ability to read music or the reliance on my intuition to compose.

  b. As a detective, they taught me that time meant everything when dealing with a new case, that the simplest explanation is usually the right one, and that documentation is extremely important to credibility.

  c. As a writer, they taught me the most important thing about writing was consistently showing up to the page every single day, no matter where my muse was.

  d. As a football player, they taught me how to understand the logistics of the game, how my placement on the field affected the rest of the team, and how to run and throw with a mixture of finesse and strength.

  e. As a doctor, they taught me how to show compassion towards patients and how to take care of my own physical and mental health while running my own practice.

7. Which of the following words, if substituted for the word *treatises* in paragraph three, would LEAST change the meaning of the sentence?

  a. Thesauruses

  b. Encyclopedias

  c. Sermons

  d. Anthems

  e. Commentary

The next four questions are based on the following passage from Oregon, Washington, and Alaska. Sights and Scenes for the Tourist, *written by E.L. Lomax in 1890:*

  Portland is a very beautiful city of 60,000 inhabitants, and situated on the Willamette river twelve miles from its junction with the Columbia. It is perhaps true of many of the growing cities of the West, that they do not offer the same social advantages as the older cities of the East. But this is principally the case as to what may be called boom cities, where the larger part of the population is of that floating class which follows in the line of temporary growth for the purposes of speculation, and in no sense applies to those centers of trade whose prosperity is based on the solid foundation of legitimate business. As the metropolis of a vast section of country, having broad agricultural valleys filled with improved farms, surrounded by mountains rich in mineral wealth, and boundless forests of as fine timber as the world produces, the cause of Portland's growth and prosperity is the trade which it has as the center of collection and distribution of this great wealth of natural resources, and it has attracted, not the boomer and speculator, who find their profits in the wild excitement of the boom, but the merchant, manufacturer, and investor, who seek the surer if slower channels of legitimate business and investment. These have come from the East, most of them within the last few years. They came as seeking a better and wider field to engage in the same occupations they had followed in their Eastern homes, and bringing with them all the love of polite life which they had acquired there, have established here a new society, equaling in all respects that which they left behind. Here are as fine churches, as complete a system of schools, as fine residences, as great a love of music and art, as can be found at any city of the East of equal size.

But while Portland may justly claim to be the peer of any city of its size in the United States in all that pertains to social life, in the attractions of beauty of location and surroundings it stands without its peer. The work of art is but the copy of nature. What the residents of other cities see but in the copy, or must travel half the world over to see in the original, the resident of Portland has at its very door.

The city is situated on a gently-sloping ground, with, on the one side, the river, and on the other a range of hills, which, within easy walking distance, rise to an elevation of a thousand feet above the river, affording a most picturesque building site. From the very streets of the thickly settled portion of the city, the Cascade Mountains, with the snow-capped peaks of Hood, Adams, St. Helens, and Rainier, are in plain view.

8. What is a characteristic of a "boom city," as indicated by the passage?
   a. A city that is built on a solid business foundation of mineral wealth and farming
   b. An area of land on the west coast that quickly becomes populated by residents from the east coast
   c. A city that, due to the hot weather and dry climate, catches fire frequently, resulting in a devastating population drop
   d. A city whose population is made up of people who seek quick fortunes rather than building a solid business foundation
   e. A city located on a river or river delta where the land is fertile and economic conditions are optimal

9. By stating that "they do not offer the same social advantages as the older cities of the East" in the first paragraph, the author most likely intends to suggest which of the following?
   a. Inhabitants who reside in older cities in the East are much more social than inhabitants who reside in newer cities in the West because of background and experience.
   b. Cities in the West have no culture compared to the East because the culture in the East comes from European influence.
   c. Cities in the East are older than cities in the West, and older cities always have better culture than newer cities.
   d. Since cities in the West are newly established, it takes them a longer time to develop cultural roots and societal functions than those cities that are already established in the East.
   e. The culture in boom cities is likely to outpace previously-popular cities because they offer so much more.

10. Based on the information at the end of the first paragraph, what would the author say of Portland?
    a. It has twice as much culture as the cities in the East
    b. Its amount of culture is dwindling as it becomes more business-oriented
    c. It doesn't have as much culture as cities in the East
    d. It doesn't have as much culture as cities in the West
    e. It has as much culture as the cities in the East

11. How many more inhabitants did San Francisco have than Portland in 1890?
    a. Approximately 110,000
    b. Approximately 240,000
    c. Approximately 500,000
    d. Approximately 1,000,000
    e. Approximately 1,500,000

12. Businessman: My cardinal rule is to only invest in privately-held small businesses that exclusively sell tangible goods and have no debt.

Which one of the following is the best investment opportunity according to the businessman's cardinal rule?

    a. Jose owns his own grocery store. He's looking for a partner, because he fell behind on his mortgage and owes the bank three months' worth of payments.

    b. Elizabeth is seeking a partner with business expertise to help expand her standalone store that sells niche board games. The store isn't currently profitable, but it's never been in debt.

    c. A family-owned accounting firm with no outstanding debts is looking for its first outside investor. The firm has turned a profit every year since it opened.

    d. A multinational corporation is selling high-yield bonds for the first time.

    e. A regional chain of liquor stores is selling the licensing rights for a new franchise to help repay its initial small business loan.

The following passage is taken from Chapter 6 of Sense and Sensibility by Jane Austen:

The first part of their journey was performed in too melancholy a disposition to be otherwise than tedious and unpleasant. But as they drew toward the end of it, their interest in the appearance of a country which they were to inhabit overcame their dejection, and a view of Barton Valley as they entered it gave them cheerfulness. It was a pleasant fertile spot, well wooded, and rich in pasture. After winding along it for more than a mile, they reached their own house. A small green court was the whole of its demesne in front; and a neat wicket gate admitted them into it.

As a house, Barton Cottage, though small, was comfortable and compact; but as a cottage it was defective, for the building was regular, the roof was tiled, the window shutters were not painted green, nor were the walls covered with honeysuckles. A narrow passage led directly through the house into the garden behind. On each side of the entrance was a sitting room, about sixteen feet square; and beyond them were the offices and the stairs. Four bed-rooms and two garrets formed the rest of the house. It had not been built many years and was in good repair. In comparison of Norland, it was poor and small indeed!—but the tears which recollection called forth as they entered the house were soon dried away. They were cheered by the joy of the servants on their arrival, and each for the sake of the others resolved to appear happy. It was very early in September; the season was fine, and from first seeing the place under the advantage of good weather, they received an impression in its favour which was of material service in recommending it to their lasting approbation.

The situation of the house was good. High hills rose immediately behind, and at no great distance on each side; some of which were open downs, the others cultivated and woody. The village of Barton was chiefly on one of these hills, and formed a pleasant view from the cottage windows. The prospect in front was more extensive; it commanded the whole of the valley, and reached into the country beyond. The hills which surrounded the cottage terminated the valley in that direction; under another name, and in another course, it branched out again between two of the steepest of them.

With the size and furniture of the house Mrs. Dashwood was upon the whole well satisfied; for though her former style of life rendered many additions to the latter indispensable, yet to add and improve was a delight to her; and she had at this time ready money enough to supply all that was wanted of greater elegance to the apartments. "As for the house itself, to be sure," said she, "it is too small for our family, but we will make ourselves tolerably comfortable for the present, as it is too late in the year for improvements. Perhaps in the spring, if I have plenty of money, as I dare say I shall, we may think about building. These parlors are both too small for such parties of our friends as I hope to see often collected here; and I have some thoughts of throwing the passage into one of them with perhaps a part of the other, and so leave the remainder of that other for an entrance; this, with a new drawing room which may be easily added, and a bed-chamber and garret above, will make it a very snug little cottage. I could wish the stairs were handsome. But one must not expect every thing; though I suppose it would be no difficult matter to widen them. I shall see how much I am before-hand with the world in the spring, and we will plan our improvements accordingly."

In the mean time, till all these alterations could be made from the savings of an income of five hundred a-year by a woman who never saved in her life, they were wise enough to be contented with the house as it was; and each of them was busy in arranging their particular concerns, and endeavoring, by placing around them books and other possessions, to form themselves a home. Marianne's pianoforte was unpacked and properly disposed of; and Elinor's drawings were affixed to the walls of their sitting room.

In such employments as these they were interrupted soon after breakfast the next day by the entrance of their landlord, who called to welcome them to Barton, and to offer them every accommodation from his own house and garden in which theirs might at present be deficient. Sir John Middleton was a good looking man about forty. He had formerly visited at Stanhill, but it was too long for his young cousins to remember him. His countenance was thoroughly good-humoured; and his manners were as friendly as the style of his letter. Their arrival seemed to afford him real satisfaction, and their comfort to be an object of real solicitude to him. He said much of his earnest desire of their living in the most sociable terms with his family, and pressed them so cordially to dine at Barton Park every day till they were better settled at home, that, though his entreaties were carried to a point of perseverance beyond civility, they could not give offence. His kindness was not confined to words; for within an hour after he left them, a large basket full of garden stuff and fruit arrived from the park, which was followed before the end of the day by a present of game.

13. What is the point of view in this passage?
    a. Third-person omniscient
    b. Second-person
    c. First-person
    d. Third-person objective

14. Which of the following events occurred first?
    a. Sir John Middleton stopped by for a visit.
    b. The servants joyfully cheered for the family.
    c. Mrs. Dashwood discussed improvements to the cottage.
    d. Elinor hung her drawings up in the sitting room.

15. Over the course of the passage, the Dashwoods' attitude shifts. Which statement best describes that shift?
   a. From appreciation of the family's former life of privilege to disdain for the family's new landlord
   b. From confidence in the power of the family's wealth to doubt in the family's ability to survive
   c. From melancholy about leaving Norland to excitement about reaching Barton Cottage in the English countryside
   d. From cheerfulness about the family's expedition to anxiety about the upkeep of such a big home

16. Which of the following is a theme of this passage?
   a. All-conquering love
   b. Power of wealth
   c. Wisdom of experience
   d. Reality vs. expectations

17. At the start of paragraph five, the narrator says, "... till all these alterations could be made from the savings of an income of five hundred a-year by a woman who never saved in her life, they were wise enough to be contented with the house as it was." What does the narrator mean?
   a. The family is going through a transitional phase.
   b. Mrs. Dashwood needs to obtain meaningful employment.
   c. The family is going through a growth phase.
   d. The Dashwood children need to be concerned about the future.

18. What is the relationship between the new landlord and the Dashwoods?
   a. He is a former social acquaintance.
   b. He is one of their cousins.
   c. He is Mrs. Dashwood's father.
   d. He is a long-time friend of the family.

Directions for the next two questions: The following sentence has a blank where something has been left out. Beneath the sentence are four words or phrases. Choose the word or phrase that, when inserted in the sentence, best fits the meaning of the sentence as a whole.

19. The event coordinator served as a _____ between the client and event vendors.
   a. Liaison
   b. Proviso
   c. Diplomat
   d. Contrarian

20. While the marketing initiative was a nice idea in theory, it was not _____ due to financial and logistical concerns.
   a. Idealistic
   b. Complacent
   c. Meticulous
   d. Pragmatic

312

Writing

The next five questions are based on the following passage.

Everybody has their own version of the perfect <u>peanutbutter</u> (31) and banana sandwich. Some will tell you the type of bread you must use and whether the bread should be toasted. Some will tell you that you must cut off the crust, while others will tell you to keep it intact. Crunchy or smooth is always a heated debate, along with just how much peanut butter a sandwich needs.

I'm no different; I consider myself an expert when it comes to peanut butter and banana sandwiches. My grandmother started <u>making me and my brothers peanut butter and banana sandwiches</u> (32) before we could speak. I'd watch my grandmother in the kitchen closely. She would start by setting out the slices of bread along the counter, <u>and then carefully add</u> (33) one thin layer of butter to each slice. She would then start back at the top and add one fine layer of smooth peanut butter. <u>Next was the final and best step.</u> (34) Instead of slicing the bananas, my grandmother would mash them! She would take a bowl, place the bananas inside, and mash them up with the back of a fork! Then she would spread the slices of bread with the mashed banana. <u>In the end</u> (35), grandma would cut the sandwich in two halves diagonally—the only way to go.

Those peanut butter and banana sandwiches with a glass of milk will live on in my memory forever. You can have your sliced bananas. You can have your toasted sandwiches. You can have your crunchy peanut butter. It is 40 years since I used to eat my grandma's sandwiches, but it seems like yesterday. When I got older and had children of my own, I started making peanut butter and banana sandwiches for them just like my grandmother did for me. I've seen different styles and recipes, but I'll stick to my grandma's peanut butter and mashed banana sandwiches. They were—and still are—simply the best.

1. Choose the best replacement.
    a. NO CHANGE
    b. peanut-butter
    c. peanut butter
    d. peanutbutter,

2. Choose the best replacement sentence.
    a. NO CHANGE
    b. making peanut butter and banana sandwiches my brothers and me
    c. making me peanut butter and my brothers banana sandwiches
    d. making I and my brothers peanut butter and banana sandwiches

3. Choose the best replacement.
    a. NO CHANGE
    b. then she would carefully add
    c. then carefully adding
    d. then carefully added

4. Choose the best replacement word or phrase.
   a. NO CHANGE
   b. The next step was the best
   c. The final step was the best step
   d. Next, the final step was the best

5. Choose the best replacement word or phrase.
   a. NO CHANGE
   b. Suddenly
   c. Immediately
   d. Finally

The next five questions are based on the following passage.

Writing academic papers is a skill that develops over time. From the earliest grades in school, students learn to spell correctly. They learn how to write coherent sentences with proper grammar and punctuation, and they learn the importance of beginning, middle, and end. In higher education, these skills become more nuanced.

When writing an academic paper, spelling, punctuation, and content development are key. (36) What will your paper be about? How will you introduce the subject? What information will you include in the body? How do you transition from one point to another? How will you wrap it all up so that the paper seamlessly flows from beginning to end?

Transitions are an extremely important part of writing. Without proper transitions, a paper might seem choppy and disconnected. (37) The points the author is trying to make might be less easily understood, and the paper itself risks losing credibility. Transitional phrases have to be carefully planned out and strategically placed. For example, if the paper is giving a chronological order of events or step-by-step instructions, transitional phrases that indicate what order to follow will likely be used. There are transitional words and phrases that emphasize a point, demonstrating (38) an opposing point of view, present a condition, introduce examples in support of an argument, and so much more. There are transitional phrases authors use to show a consequence or an effect following an event. There are even transitional phrases that are used to indicate a specific time or place. Transitional words act as a bridge connecting (39) ideas and strengthening a paper's coherency. Nonetheless (40), transitional words are a very important part of any academic paper, and the more skilled authors become in knowing when to use the most appropriate transitions, the stronger their papers will be.

6. Choose the best replacement phrase.
   a. NO CHANGE
   b. students should consider spelling, punctuation, and content development.
   c. spelling, punctuation, and content development, are key.
   d. the paper needs to contain proper spelling, punctuation, and convent development.

7. Choose the best replacement passage.
   a. NO CHANGE
   b. Transitions are an extremely important part of writing without which, a paper might seem choppy and disconnected.
   c. Transitions are an extremely important part of writing. Additionally, without them, a paper might seem choppy and disconnected.
   d. Transitions are an extremely important part of writing without them, a paper might seem choppy and disconnected.

8. Choose the best replacement sentence.
   a. NO CHANGE
   b. to demonstrate
   c. demonstrate
   d. for demonstrating

9. Choose the best replacement.
   a. NO CHANGE
   b. bridge of connection
   c. bridge connecting,
   d. bridge to connections

10. Choose the best replacement word or phrase.
   a. NO CHANGE
   b. Overall
   c. Additionally
   d. Next

The next five questions are based on the following passage:

When Nathaniel Hawthorne wrote *The Scarlet Letter* in 1850, he became the first American author to contribute a mature, tragic view of life (1) <u>in</u> the literature of the young United States. He developed a tragic vision that is fundamentally dark: man's inevitable moral downfall is determined by the workings of (2) <u>its own heart</u>. Yet Hawthorne's bleak vision also embraces the drama of the human heart, through which he depicts the heart as a redemptive agent, subtly affirming (3) <u>humanities</u> inherent goodness. He likens the human heart to a cavern. To a visitor, the mouth of the cavern is bright with sunlight and flowers, (4) <u>but a few feet in, the light dims and warmth turns to chill; the visitor stumbles, first in confusion, then in terror.</u> (5) <u>Further back,</u> a small gleam of light appears and the visitor hurries toward it, to find a scene much like that at the entrance of the cavern, only perfect. This, to Hawthorne, is the depth of (6) <u>human nature; the beauty that lies beyond fear and hopelessness.</u>

The novel relates the suffering of three people—Hester Prynne, Arthur Dimmesdale, and Roger Chillingworth—each possessing a proud heart that leads them to a choice (7) <u>between a natural morality (represented by the passion that derives from human love) and unnatural morality</u> (symbolized by the code of punishment the Puritan community adheres to). Studying the heart in the context of seventeenth-century Puritanism, Hawthorne focuses on the contradictions between the theological and intellectual definitions of sin, according to the Puritans, and the (8) <u>psychological affects</u> of applying them to the reality of their actions and lives. Within the (9) <u>rigid</u>

moral setting of the New England Puritan community, he concentrates upon the sin of pride, fostered in the dim, shadowy hollows of the heart and soul.

11. The best replacement for the underlined portion would be:
    a. NO CHANGE
    b. to
    c. from
    d. with

12. The best replacement for the underlined portion would be:
    a. NO CHANGE
    b. her own heart
    c. his own heart
    d. people's own heart

13. The best replacement for the underlined portion would be:
    a. NO CHANGE
    b. humanities'
    c. humanitys
    d. humanity's

14. The best replacement for the underlined portion would be:
    a. NO CHANGE
    b. but a few feet in the light, dims and warmth turns to chill, the visitor stumbles, first in confusion, then in terror
    c. but a few feet in the light dims and warmth turns to chill, the visitor stumbles first in confusion then in terror
    d. but a few feet in the light dims and warmth turns to chill: the visitor stumbles first in confusion, then in terror

15. The best replacement for the underlined portion would be:
    a. NO CHANGE
    b. In the back
    c. To the back
    d. Farther in

The next five questions are based on the following passage:

The escalating rate of obesity in the United States is a major health issue facing all healthcare providers and (19) <u>faculties</u>. Today, at Carter Cullen Medical Center, a community hospital in (20) <u>Wayland, Massachusetts,</u> a simple perioperative step—highlighting body mass index (BMI, determined by dividing weight by height) on surgery schedules and preoperative checklists—is saving lives. In 2014, events involving two patients with high (21) <u>BMI's</u> triggered eighteen months of focused teamwork and communication that resulted in the establishment of a groundbreaking early notification protocol. As a consequence, the healthcare professionals at Carter Cullen Medical Center are better equipped to care for patients who are morbidly obese.

Obesity carries many risks, one of which is sleep apnea. (22) <u>Sleep apnea, in turn, causes problems with intubation during surgery and disrupts the administration of anesthetics</u> or oxygen. Additional adipose tissue in the neck area prevents patients from hyperextending their necks properly. During intubation, the anesthesiologist cannot visualize the vocal cords (23) <u>if the patients neck</u> is not hyperextended, and a fiber-optic intubation device must be inserted. But such a device was not regularly available in Carter Cullen's operating rooms; (24) <u>the equipment was stocked only if difficulty was expected</u>. In the first event, an obese patient needed to be intubated, there was unanticipated difficulty with the intubation, and the patient died.

Another life-threatening risk of obesity is rhabdomyolysis. In the second event, an obese patient recovering from prolonged total joint replacement surgery was resting in one position for an (25) <u>unreasonable</u> amount of time. The patient's weight caused muscle fibers (26) <u>to break down, and release a pigment—harmful to the kidneys—</u>into (27) <u>their</u> circulation. Renal failure and death followed.

16. Which, if any, of the following choices is the most accurate choice to replace the underlined word?
    a. NO CHANGE
    b. facilities
    c. cardiologists
    d. the American Obesity Association

17. Which, if any, of the following choices is the most accurate choice to replace the underlined words?
    a. NO CHANGE
    b. Wayland Massachusetts
    c. Wayland, Massachusets
    d. a small Massachusetts town

18. Which, if any, of the following choices is the most accurate choice to replace the underlined word?
    a. NO CHANGE
    b. BMIs
    c. body mass indexes
    d. body mass indices

19. Which, if any, of the following choices is the most accurate choice to replace the underlined words?
    a. NO CHANGE
    b. Sleep apnea, in turn, caused problems with intubation during surgery and disrupted the administration of anesthetics
    c. Sleep apnea, in turn, can cause problems with intubation during surgery that disrupt the administration of anesthetics
    d. Sleep apnea, in turn, causes problems with intubation and the administration of anesthetics

20. Which, if any, of the following choices is the most accurate choice to replace the underlined words?
    a. NO CHANGE
    b. if the patient neck
    c. if the patient's neck
    d. if the patients' neck

The next five questions are based on the following passage:

Cerebrovascular accident, commonly known as stroke, is the fifth leading cause of death in the United States, and it (28) <u>affects</u> approximately 795,000 Americans each year. (29) <u>The risk of stroke varies by demographics and lifestyle factors such as age (fifty years or older), gender (female), race (African American, American Indian, and Alaskan native), geography (southeastern</u>

states), disease, and lifestyle components (including, but not limited to: exercise, eating habits, use of alcohol and/or illicit drugs, cigarette smoking, stress, quality of life, and perceived happiness).

(30) What exactly is a stroke? It is a sudden interruption in cerebral (brain) function that (31) lasts more than twenty-four hours. Stroke can result in death, and is caused by an acute disruption of blood flow coupled with insufficient oxygen reaching the brain. A stroke can be large and catastrophic, ending in death; mild, with the person who had the stroke eventually recovering most normal functions; or anywhere between these two (32) extremes.

The two main types of stroke are ischemic and hemorrhagic. Ischemic stroke occurs when a blood clot blocks an artery in the central nervous system (CNS). (33) The blockage disrupts the flow of oxygen-rich blood to CNS tissue and to the brain to the extent that the supply of oxygen and glucose is insufficient to support ongoing metabolism. Thrombotic stroke and embolic stroke are two subtypes of ischemic stroke. In thrombotic stroke, a blood clot or atherosclerotic plaque develops (34) locally to create blockage. (35) In embolic stroke, a blood clot or atherosclerotic plaque develops elsewhere, such as in the heart, breaks apart, and travels in the bloodstream without blocking blood flow until it reaches a central nervous system artery, then it travels through the artery up to the brain, lodging there.

(36) Headache, nausea, vomiting, numbness, and loss of consciousness are all warning signs of a possible stroke these symptoms require immediate medical attention to prevent damage to—or complete loss of—brain cells. The three most common symptoms of stroke are varying degrees of facial drooping, unilateral limb weakness, and speech difficulty. Strokes can also cause depression and a loss of the ability to control emotions.

21. Which choice, if any, would be an acceptable substitute for the underlined portion?
    a. destroys
    b. effects
    c. kills
    d. afflicts

22. Carlos is a 27-year-old Hispanic male who lives in New York, and he maintains a healthy lifestyle by eating wholesome foods, exercising regularly, and getting an average of eight hours of sleep per night. He enjoys an occasional beer or glass of wine on weekends, but he does not drink to excess and has never used illicit drugs. He does not smoke, he practices yoga and meditation to control stress, and he is generally satisfied with where he is in his life today. According to the underlined passage, how does this affect Carlos?
    a. He will never have a stroke if he continues living as he does now.
    b. He will never have a stroke because he is not a "match" in any of the categories.
    c. He will have a stroke if he stops exercising, gains weight, and starts smoking cigarettes.
    d. He might be one of the Americans who has a stroke.

23. If this sentence were added at the end of Paragraph 2, what would the effect be? "The prevalence of pseudobulbar affect among stroke survivors is estimated to be between eleven and fifty-two percent."
    a. It would be confusing because the information is irrelevant to the essay.
    b. It would be helpful because it adds information that supports the topic of the paragraph.
    c. It would be confusing because pseudobulbar affect has not been introduced previously.
    d. It would be helpful because it cites a relatively positive stroke survival statistic.

24. What is the most logical ordering of the three items in the underlined passage?
   a. NO CHANGE
   b. is caused by an acute disruption of blood flow, and lasts more than twenty-four hours, and can result in death
   c. can result in death, lasts more than twenty-four hours, and is caused by an acute disruption of blood flow
   d. can result in death, is caused by an acute disruption of blood flow, and lasts more than twenty-four hours

25. In the context of the sentence, which word is the closest synonym to the underlined word?
   a. Spectrums
   b. States
   c. Poles
   d. Positions

Write Placer Prompt

Read the passage below then answer in an essay format.

> Florentine painting between Giotto and Michelangelo contains the names of such artists as Orcagna, Masaccio, Fra Filippo, Pollaiuolo, Verrocchio, Leonardo, and Botticelli. Put beside these the greatest names in Venetian art, the Vivarini, the Bellini, Giorgione, Titian, and Tintoret. The difference is striking. The significance of the Venetian names is exhausted with their significance as painters. Not so with the Florentines. Forget that they were painters, they remain great sculptors; forget that they were sculptors, and still they remain architects, poets, and even men of science. They left no form of expression untried, and to none could they say, "This will perfectly convey my meaning." Painting, therefore, offers but a partial and not always the most adequate manifestation of their personality, and we feel the artist as greater than his work, and the man as soaring above the artist.

> From *The Florentine Painters of the Renaissance* by Bernhard Berenson

Write an essay explaining how the author of the following passage builds their argument. Examine how they use one or more of the features above to enhance the logic and persuasiveness of their claim. Remember your job isn't to agree or disagree with the author, but to analyze the way in which they build their argument.

Answer Explanations #3

Arithmetic

1. C: To find the smallest value, convert each number that isn't in decimal form to a decimal and then compare. The fraction $\frac{1}{8}$ is equal to 0.125, the percentage 0.43% is equal to 0.0043, and the percentage $\frac{3}{5}\% = 0.6\% = 0.006$. Therefore, the smallest value is 0.43%, which is equivalent to Choice *C*.

2. D: To multiply two decimals, first remove the decimals from each value and then multiply as whole numbers. $425 \times 21 = 8925$. Then, count the total number of decimal values in the original problem. There are 3 total values in decimal places. Move the decimal in 8925 three units to the left to obtain Choice *D*, which is 8.925.

3. B: Dividing 4 by 3 results in a 1. Then, multiply 3 times 1 to obtain 3 and write this under the 4. 4 minus 3 equals 1. Bring down the 9 and repeat the process with 19. When 19 is divided by 3 it results in a 6, and 6 times 3 equals 18. Subtract 19 from 18 to obtain a 1. Bring down the 0 to obtain a 10. Three goes into 10 three times. Then, multiply 3 times 3 to obtain 9. Subtracting 9 from 10 results in a 1, which is the remainder. The correct option is Choice *B*, which is a remainder of 1.

4. C: To add two fractions together, they must have a common denominator. The lowest common multiple of 10 and 100 is 100. Therefore, multiply the second fraction times $\frac{10}{10}$: $\frac{9}{10} \times \frac{10}{10} = \frac{90}{100}$. Then add $\frac{9}{100} + \frac{90}{100} = \frac{99}{100}$, which is Choice *C*.

5. D: The 5 is in the hundredths place in the given decimal. Therefore, write it in a fraction as 5/100. This fraction can be written in lowest terms by dividing a 5 out of both the numerator and the denominator to obtain $\frac{1}{20}$. The correct answer is Choice *D*.

6. C: Kristy placed $150 of her $400 in the account, which is equal to $\frac{150}{400}$. This fraction is simplified into $\frac{3}{8}$ by dividing a 50 out of both the numerator and the denominator, and $\frac{3}{8}$ is equivalent to 0.375, which is 37.5% written as a percentage. Choice *C* is the correct choice.

7. A: The car dealership started the day with 150 cars and sold 12, so it was left with $150 - 12 = 138$ cars. The fraction $\frac{138}{150}$ is equal to the decimal 0.92. This can be found by dividing 138 by 150. The number 0.92 is equal to 92%, which can be found by moving the decimal two places to the right. Therefore, Choice *A* is the correct answer.

8. D: The first place value to the right of the decimal is the tenth digit, and it is a 9. The value to the right of this digit is also 9, so the tenth place value gets rounded up to become 10. Therefore, the 9 in the ones unit increases by 1 and the rest of the digits become 0. The correct answer is 10, which is Choice *D*.

9. C: Each dozen of muffins calls for 2 eggs. Divide 45 by 2 to get 22 with a remainder of 1. Therefore, she can make 22 dozen muffins. Each dozen contains 12 muffins, and $22 \times 12 = 264$ muffins, therefore, Choice *C* is the correct answer.

10. B: Fernando worked $\frac{1}{5}$ of 30 days at the library, which is equal to $\left(\frac{1}{5}\right)30 = \frac{30}{5} = 6$ days. He worked $\frac{1}{6}$ of 30 days at the post office, which is equal to $\left(\frac{1}{6}\right)30 = \frac{30}{6} = 5$ days. Therefore, he worked $6 + 5 = 11$ days, and he did not work $30 - 11 = 19$ days. Choice *B* is the correct answer.

11. C: Each of the 22 students brought in 8 pencils, so there were $22 \times 8 = 176$ total pencils brought in on the first day. Therefore, Choice *C* is the correct answer.

12. A: To subtract two mixed numbers, convert them to improper fractions. Multiply the whole number times the denominator and add to the numerator. $7\frac{4}{5} = \frac{35+4}{5} = \frac{39}{5}$ and $5\frac{1}{2} = \frac{10+1}{2} = \frac{11}{2}$. Then, subtract by finding the common denominator. The lowest common multiple between 2 and 5 is 10. Therefore, multiply $\frac{39}{5}$ by $\frac{2}{2}$ and $\frac{11}{2}$ by $\frac{5}{5}$. The problem is rewritten as $\frac{78}{10} - \frac{55}{10}$, which is equal to $\frac{23}{10}$, or Choice *A*.

13. B: The sum of three angles in a triangle is always 180°. Add the two given angles and subtract that amount to find the missing value. $50° + 75° = 125°$, so the third angle is $180° - 125° = 55°$. Therefore, Choice *B* is the correct answer.

14. C: The largest value can be found by comparing the unit in each place value. Choices *A*, *B*, and *C* are all larger than Choice *D* since the value in the tenths digit is 1 rather than 0. Choices *A* and *C* are larger than Choice *B* since the value in the hundredths digit is 1 rather than 0. Choice *C* is larger than Choice *B* since the value in the thousandths digit is 1 rather than 0. The largest value is 0.1111, which is Choice *C*.

15. D: Determine the answer by rounding each value to the nearest whole number and then multiplying. 45.8 is rounded to 46, and 3.2 is rounded to 3.

$$46 \times 3 = 138$$

So, the correct answer is Choice *D*. The actual calculation is $45.8 \times 3.2 = 146.50$.

16. C: 10^{-2} is equivalent to $\frac{1}{10^2} = \frac{1}{100} = 0.01$. So, one must multiply 34.2×0.01. This can be done by moving the decimal place in 34.2 two units to the left. The correct answer is 0.342, which is Choice *C*.

17. B: To add two mixed numbers, convert them to improper fractions. Multiply the whole number times the denominator and add to the numerator: $1\frac{3}{4} = \frac{4+3}{7} = \frac{7}{4}$ and $2\frac{3}{5} = \frac{10+3}{5} = \frac{13}{5}$. Then, add by finding the common denominator. The lowest common multiple between 4 and 5 is 20. Therefore, multiply $\frac{7}{4}$ times $\frac{5}{5}$ and $\frac{13}{5}$ times $\frac{4}{4}$. The problem is rewritten as $\frac{35}{20} + \frac{65}{20}$, which is equal to $\frac{100}{5} = 20$, or Choice *B*.

18. C: To find 50 percent of a number, multiply 50% times that value. Numbers that are equivalent to 50% are 0.5, $\frac{50}{100}$ and $\frac{1}{2}$. $50X$ is equivalent to 50 times X, which is not the same as 50% times X. Choice *C* is the correct answer.

19. D: Because the average of the four numbers is 7, that means the sum of the four numbers divided by 4 is equal to 7. Multiplying 7 times 4 results in the sum of the four numbers. 7 times 4 is equal to 28. Because the sum of the three numbers is 21, that means that the missing number is $28 - 21 = 7$, which is equal to Choice *D*.

20. C: First, convert $4\frac{1}{2}$ to an improper fraction. $4\frac{1}{2} = \frac{8+1}{2} = \frac{9}{2}$. Therefore, she started with $\frac{9}{2}$ pounds of sugar. She used $\frac{1}{3}$ of that quantity in the recipe. $\frac{1}{3} \times \frac{9}{2} = \frac{3}{2}$. Therefore, she had $\frac{3}{2}$ pounds of sugar left, which is equal to Choice *C*.

Quantitative Reasoning, Algebra, and Statistics

1. A: The probability of choosing two customers simultaneously is the same as choosing one and then choosing a second without putting the first back into the pool of customers. This means that the probability of choosing a customer who bought cherry is $\frac{35}{100}$. Then without placing them back in the pool, it would be $\frac{34}{99}$.

So, the probability of choosing 2 customers simultaneously that both bought cherry would be:

$$\frac{35}{100} \times \frac{34}{99}$$

$$\frac{1,190}{9,900}$$

$$\frac{119}{990}$$

2. C: To find the mean, or average, of a data set, add all data values and divide by the number of data points in the set. Each day of the week has an adult ticket amount sold that must be added together. The equation is as follows:

$$\frac{22 + 16 + 24 + 19 + 29}{5} = 22$$

3. A: Solving inequalities that contain absolute values requires writing two different inequalities. For the given inequality, the two new ones are $3 - x > 7$ and $3 - x < -7$. These account for the absolute value part of the inequality. When these two are solved, the two inequalities that result from it are $x < -4$ and $x > -10$. If the two inequalities are not separated and solved in the beginning, then the answer may only contain one inequality and leave out part of the answer.

4. B: The given radical is a square root. The values under the radical can be taken out if they are perfect squares. Identifying perfect squares and removing them gives the radical:

$$4xy^3z^2\sqrt{xz}$$

If the incorrect number of variables are taken out of the radical, then the final simplified radical will be incorrect.

5. C: There are 0.006 kiloliters in 6 liters because 1 liter is 0.001 kiloliters. The conversion comes from the metric prefix kilo- which has a value of 1,000. Thus, 1 kiloliter is 1,000 liters, and 1 liter is 0.001 kiloliters.

6. B: Let x be the score on the fifth test. Therefore, to get a B in the class, $\frac{85+75+55+90+x}{5} > 80$. Therefore, $\frac{305+x}{5} > 80$. Multiplying times 5 on both sides results in $305 + x > 400$. Subtracting 305 from each side results in $x > 95$. Therefore, Mark must obtain at least a 95 on the last test to receive a B in the class.

7. D: A probability cannot be less than zero or exceed 1. Because 3/2 is equal to 1.5, this value cannot represent a probability. This value would mean something happening 150% of the time, which does not make sense.

8. A: First, substitute -2 for x and -3 for y. This results in:

$$\frac{14(-2)}{(-3)^2} - \frac{10(-3)}{(-2)^2}$$

Multiply the numerators and evaluate the exponents in the denominators to obtain:

$$-\frac{28}{9} - \left(\frac{-30}{4}\right) = -\frac{28}{9} + \frac{15}{2}$$

The common denominator is 18, and therefore, this expression is equivalent to:

$$-\frac{56}{18} + \frac{135}{18} = \frac{79}{18}$$

9. A: Because x is directly proportional to y, $x = ky$, for some constant k. Plugging in what is given yields $8 = k\left(\frac{1}{12}\right)$, which means that $k = 96$. Therefore, $x = 96y$.

10. B: First, we multiply each score times its weight (the number of boys and the number of girls, respectively). Therefore, $3 \times 84 = 252$ and $5 \times 82 = 410$. The total weighted score is $252 + 410 = 662$. The total weight is 8 because there are 8 students. Therefore, divide 662 by 8 to obtain a class average of 82.75.

11. D: The given word has 9 letters. Therefore, in a 5-letter ordering, there are 9 choices for the first letter. Because there are no repeats allowed, there are 8 choices for the second letter, 7 choices for the third letter, 6 choices for the fourth letter, and 5 choices for the fifth letter. Multiplying these values together results in:

$$(9)(8)(7)(6)(5) = 15{,}120 \text{ possible orderings}$$

12. C: Because there is one $200 winner and each ticket costs $1, the probability of winning $199 is 1/1,000. Also, because there is one $50 winner, the probability of winning $49 is $\frac{1}{1{,}000}$. The rest of the outcomes would be losing $1, which has a probability of 998/1,000. The expected value is the sum of the products of each outcome and their probabilities. Therefore,

$$\text{Expected value} = \$199\left(\frac{1}{1{,}000}\right) + \$49\left(\frac{1}{1{,}000}\right) - 1\left(\frac{998}{1{,}000}\right)$$

$$-\frac{750}{1{,}000} = -\$0.75$$

Expect to lose $0.75 for every ticket bought.

13. C: The smaller and larger interior angles in a parallelogram must add up to 180°. This pair is the only duo that does not have a sum of 180.

14. B: Look on the horizontal axis to find 3:00 p.m. Move up from 3:00 p.m. to reach the dot on the graph. Move directly left to the vertical axis between 20 and 25; the best answer choice is 22. The answer of 25 is too high above the projected time on the graph, and the answers of 20 and 16 degrees are too low.

15. D: 9 times the sum of x and y is equal to $9(x + y)$, and 4 less than this quantity is equal to $9(x + y) - 4$. Therefore, choice D is the correct option.

16. B: This is a proportional relationship since $1 \text{ km} = 1,000 \text{ m}$. Let x be the missing quantity and set up the proportion $\frac{650}{x} = \frac{1}{1000}$. Cross-multiply to obtain $650(1,000) = x$, so $x = 650,000$. There are 650,000 meters in 650 kilometers, so the correct answer is Choice B.

17. D: To calculate the slope, find the change in y values divided by the change in x values. Therefore:

$$m = \frac{4 - 8}{0 - 6} = \frac{-4}{-6} = \frac{2}{3}$$

The slope-intercept form of an equation of a line is $y = mx + b$, where m is the slope and b is the y-intercept. The problem gives a y-intercept of 4 since the equation passes through the point $(0, 4)$. Therefore, the correct answer is $y = \frac{2}{3}x + 4$, which is Choice D.

18. A: First, simplify the numerator. The exponents can be added inside the parentheses to obtain $\frac{(x^9)^4}{x^{-2}}$. Continue to simplify the numerator by multiplying the remaining exponents to obtain:

$$\frac{x^{36}}{x^{-2}}$$

It is true that $\frac{x^{36}}{x^{-2}} = x^{36-(-2)}$, so the correct answer is x^{38}, which is Choice A.

19. C: To find the point of intersection, plug in 3 for x in the first equation and solve for y. Therefore, $4(3) - 7y = 9$, so $12 - 7y = 9$. Subtract 12 from both sides and divide by -7 to obtain $y = \frac{3}{7}$. The correct ordered pair is $\left(3, \frac{3}{7}\right)$, which is Choice C.

20. A: First, distribute the 7 throughout the parentheses to obtain $7x - 35 + 9x - 1$. Then, collect like terms to obtain $16x - 36$, which is equal to Choice A.

Advanced Algebra and Functions

1. A: Take the natural logarithm of both sides of the equation to obtain $\ln 9^{10x} = \ln 2$. From properties of logarithms, the exponent can be placed in front of the expression on the left-hand side to obtain $10x \ln 9 = \ln 2$. Then, divide both sides by $10 \ln 9$ to obtain $x = \frac{\ln 2}{10 \ln 9}$, which is equal to Choice A.

2. C: To find $g(x - 10)$, wherever there is an x in the original function, replace it with the quantity $x - 10$. Therefore, the correct answer is $g(x - 10) = (x - 10)^2 - 4(x - 10) + 2$, which is Choice C.

3. D: This is a parabola that opens downward since the coefficient on the x^2 is negative. The graph also represents a shift of the original parabola $y = -10x^2$ up 7 units along the y-axis. The highest point on the graph is the ordered pair $(0, 7)$, so the range is all numbers less than or equal to 7. Therefore, the range is $y \leq 7$, which is equal to Choice *D*.

4. B: The given line is in slope-intercept form $y = mx + b$, where m is the slope. Therefore, the slope of the line given is $-\frac{1}{2}$. The slope of a line perpendicular is equal to the negative reciprocal of this value. In other words, their product is equal to -1. The slope of the line being sought is equal to 2. This slope and point $(2, 2)$ can be plugged into the point-slope form of a line to obtain $y - 2 = 2(x - 2)$, which simplifies to $y = 2x - 2$. The correct answer is Choice *B*.

5. C: There is a common factor of 8 in all three terms, so the trinomial can be written as $8(x^2 - 3x - 28)$. Then, the expression inside the parentheses can be factored as $(x + 4)(x - 7)$. The correct answer is Choice *C*, which is $8(x + 4)(x - 7)$.

6. B: The function can be factored into:

$$f(x) = \frac{x^2 - 4x - 21}{x^2 - 49} = \frac{(x + 3)(x - 7)}{(x + 7)(x - 7)}$$

Cancelling out common factors between the numerator and the denominator results in the expression $\frac{(x+3)}{(x+7)}$, which is equivalent to Choice *B*.

7. C: To solve the equation, since it is already factored, set each factor equal to zero and solve for x. Setting the first factor equal to zero results in $4x + \sqrt{6} = 0$. Subtract $\sqrt{6}$ from both sides and divide by 4 to obtain $x = -\frac{\sqrt{6}}{4}$. Setting the second factor equal to zero results in $9x - \sqrt{21} = 0$. Add $\sqrt{21}$ to both sides and divide by 9 to obtain $x = \frac{\sqrt{21}}{9}$. Therefore, the two solutions are $x = -\frac{\sqrt{6}}{4}$ and $x = \frac{\sqrt{21}}{9}$, which are both in Choice *C*.

8. D: This equation is not factorable, so the quadratic equation must be used with $a = 4$, $b = 8$, and $c = 9$. Therefore, the solutions are:

$$x = \frac{-8 \pm \sqrt{8^2 - 4(4)(9)}}{2(4)}$$

This simplifies into:

$$x = \frac{-8 \pm \sqrt{-80}}{8}$$

A $\sqrt{16} = 4$ can be pulled out of the radical, resulting in:

$$x = \frac{-8 \pm 4\sqrt{-5}}{8} = \frac{-2 \pm \sqrt{-5}}{2}$$

Because $\sqrt{-1} = i$, the solutions are equivalent to $x = \frac{-2 \pm i\sqrt{5}}{2}$, which is equal to Choice *D*.

9. A: The leading term of $g(x) = -6.43x^3 + 2.4x^2 - 1.423x + 9$ is $-6.43x^3$, which has a degree of 3. Therefore, the entire function has a degree of 3 and because 3 is odd, it is an odd degree. Also, because the leading coefficient (-6.43) is negative, the function approaches ∞ as x approaches $-\infty$ and it approaches $-\infty$ as x approaches ∞. Choice A is the correct option because it states that the function has an odd degree and the function, which is equal to y, approaches $-\infty$ as x approaches ∞.

10. B: The denominator of this function can never equal 0, and the expression under the radical must be greater than or equal to 0. Putting these two facts together, it is true that the radicand must be greater than zero. Therefore, $x - 2 > 0$, or $x > 2$. The correct domain is Choice B, which is all x values greater than 2.

11. A: A line parallel to another line has the same slope. The line $y = 5x + 8$ has a slope of 5. Plug $m = 5$ and the point $(1, 4)$ into the point-slope equation of a line to obtain $y - 4 = 5(x - 1)$, which simplifies to $y = 5x - 1$. This is equal to Choice A.

12. B: First, evaluate $g(1) = \frac{2+2(1)}{4} = 1$. Therefore, $f(g(1)) = f(1) = 8(1)^2 + 4 = 12$.

Secondly,

$$g(2) = \frac{2 + 2(2)}{4} = \frac{6}{4} = \frac{3}{2}$$

So,

$$(g(2))^2 = \left(\frac{3}{2}\right)^2 = \frac{9}{4}$$

Finally,

$$f(-1) = 8(-1)^2 + 4 = 8 + 4 = 12$$

So,

$$(f(-1))^2 = 144$$

Adding these three values together results in $f(g(1)) + (g(2))^2 + (f(-1))^2 = 12 + \frac{9}{4} + 144 = \frac{633}{4}$, which is equal to Choice B.

13. C: First, find the inverse function. Replace $h(x)$ with y and solve for x. Therefore, $y = \frac{5}{2+6x}$, so

$$y(2 + 6x) = 5$$

$$2y + 6xy = 5$$

$$6xy = 5 - 2y$$

$$x = \frac{5 - 2y}{6y}$$

Then, switch x and y again and replace y with $h'(x)$. The inverse function is $h'(x) = \frac{5-2x}{6x}$. Then, evaluate the function for $x = -3$. $h'(-3) = \frac{5-2(-3)}{6(-3)} = -\frac{11}{18}$, which is equivalent to Choice C.

14. D: Square both sides of the equation to obtain $x - 9 = 3x + 1$. Then, solve this linear equation for x:

$$-9 = 2x + 1$$

$$-10 = 2x$$

$$-5 = x$$

Substitute this value into the original equation to check to see if it is a solution.

$$\sqrt{-5 - 9} = \sqrt{3(-5) + 1}$$

Both sides are equal to $\sqrt{-14}$, so -5 is the solution to the equation. Choice *D* is the correct option.

15. A: Distribute the monomials throughout each set of parentheses to obtain:

$$-36x^9yz^2 - \frac{16}{5}y^{-2} - 32xy^4 + 8x^{-3}z$$

Then, move the variables with negative exponents into denominators to obtain $-36x^9yz^2 - \frac{16}{5y^2} - 32xy^4 + \frac{8z}{x^3}$, which is equivalent to Choice *A*.

16. C: Using properties of exponents, the equation can be simplified to:

$$\log_6 6 \left(\log_5 x + \log_5 2x - \log_5(x + 1)^2\right) = 8$$

Then, because all of the logarithmic expressions have the same base, the expressions inside the parentheses can be combined into:

$$\log_6 6 \left(\log_5 \frac{2x^2}{(x + 1)^2}\right) = 8$$

The expression $\log_6 6$ is equal to 1, so the equation simplifies to:

$$\log_5 \frac{2x^2}{(x + 1)^2} = 8$$

Rewriting in exponential form, this equation is equal to $5^8 = \frac{2x^2}{(x+1)^2}$, which is Choice *C*.

17. D: To divide numbers that are in scientific notation, first divide the decimals and then subtract the exponents on the powers of 10. $1.65 \div 2.2 = 0.75$ and $-5 - (-9) = 4$. Therefore, the result is 0.75×10^4. However, this is not in scientific form since 0.75 is less than 1. Move the decimal point over one unit to the right and subtract 1 off the exponent to obtain the answer 7.5×10^3, which is Choice *D*.

18. B: The exponential function $x = ab^t$ represents the total amount x given an initial amount a, growth factor b, and time t. In this scenario, the initial amount is 1,000 so $a = 1000$. The growth factor is 2 since the population doubles. The time must be multiplied times 3 since the population doubles every 8 hours, or 3 periods in one day. This is done because the units of time are in days. Therefore, the correct option is Choice *B*, $x = 1000(2)^{3t}$.

19. D: The standard equation for a quadratic equation is:

$$y = a(x - h)^2 + k$$

The vertex is given by (h, k). The vertex for the parent function, $y = x^2$, is at $(0, 0)$. A shift of 2 units to the right and 5 units up will result in a vertex of $(2, 5)$. Therefore, the equation for the transformed graph is:

$$y = (x - 2)^2 + 5$$

20. B: If a point, (x, y) is found on the graph of $f(x)$, then the point $(x, -y)$ is found on the graph of $-f(x)$. Note that the outputs become negative. Therefore, the graph of $-f(x)$ is a reflection of $f(x)$ across the x-axis. In an equation of the form $f(x) = \sqrt{x - a} + b$, the graph of the parent function, $f(x) = \sqrt{x}$, is translated a units to the right and b units up. For the function given by $g(x) = -\sqrt{x + 1}$, the graph of $f(x) = \sqrt{x}$ is reflected across the x-axis and translated left one unit.

Reading

1. B: The rest of the answer choices improperly interpret this explanation in the passage. Poetry was never mentioned for use in entertainment, which makes Choices D and E incorrect. Choices A and C are incorrect because they mix up the chronological order.

2. C: The author says that although most poetry was written as lyric, epic, or drama, the critics were most focused on the techniques of the epic and drama and their performance of structure and character. This is the best answer choice as portrayed by paragraph three. Choice A is incorrect because nowhere in the passage does it say rhetoric was more valued than poetry, although it did seem to have a more definitive purpose than poetry. Choice B is incorrect; this almost mirrors Choice A, but the critics were *not* focused on the lyric, as the passage indicates. Choice D is incorrect because the passage does not mention that the study of poetics was more pleasurable than the study of rhetoric. Choice E is incorrect because, again, we do not see anywhere in the passage where poetry was reserved for the most elite in society.

3. E: The purpose is to contemplate the differences between classical rhetoric and poetry and to consider their purposes in a particular culture. Choice A is incorrect; this thought is discussed in the third paragraph, but it is not the main idea of the passage. Choice B is incorrect; although changes in poetics throughout the years is mentioned, this is not the main idea of the passage. Choice C is incorrect; although this is partly true—that rhetoric within the education system is mentioned—the subject of poetics is left out of this answer choice. Choice D is incorrect; the passage makes no mention of poetics being a subset of rhetoric.

4. B: The correct answer choice is Choice B, *instill*. Choice A, *imbibe*, means to drink heavily, so this choice is incorrect. Choice C, *implode*, means to collapse inward, which does not make sense in this context. Choice D, *inquire*, means to investigate. This option is better than the other options, but it is not as accurate as *instill*. Choice E, *idolize*, means to admire, which does not make sense in this context.

5. B: The first paragraph presents definitions and examples of a particular subject. The second paragraph presents a second subject in the same way. The third paragraph offers a contrast of the two subjects. In the passage, we see the first paragraph defining rhetoric and offering examples of how the Greeks and Romans taught this subject. In the second paragraph, poetics is defined and examples of its dynamic definition are provided. In the third paragraph, the contrast between rhetoric and poetry is characterized through how each of these were studied in a classical context.

6. D: The best answer is Choice *D:* As a football player, they taught me how to understand the logistics of the game, how my placement on the field affected the rest of the team, and how to run and throw with a mixture of finesse and strength. The content of rhetoric in the passage... taught how to work up a case by drawing valid inferences from sound evidence, how to organize this material in the most persuasive order, and how to compose in clear and harmonious sentences. What we have here are three general principles. Each part parallels Choice *D* by logic, organization, and then style:

1. It taught them how to understand logic and reason (drawing inferences parallels to understanding the logistics of the game).

2. It taught them how to understand structure and organization (organization of material parallels to organization on the field).

3. It taught them how to make the end product beautiful (how to compose in harmonious sentences parallels to how to run with finesse and strength).

7. E: *Treatises* is most closely related to the word *commentary*. Choices *A* and *B* do not make sense because thesauruses and encyclopedias are not written about one single subject. Choice *C* is incorrect; sermons are usually given by religious leaders as advice or teachings. Choice *D* is incorrect; anthems are songs and do not fit within the context of this sentence.

8. D: Choice *A* is a characteristic of Portland but not of a boom city. Choice *B* is close—a boom city is one that becomes quickly populated, but it is not necessarily always populated by residents from the east coast. Choice *C* is incorrect because a boom city is not one that catches fire frequently, but one made up of people who are looking to make quick fortunes from the resources provided on the land.

9. D: Choice *D* is the best answer because of the surrounding context. We can see that the fact that Portland is a "boom city" means that the "floating class"—a group of people who only have temporary roots put down—go through. This would cause the main focus of the city to be on employment and industry, rather than society and culture; thus, Choice *E* is incorrect. Choice *A* is incorrect, as we are not told about the inhabitants being social or antisocial. Choice *B* is incorrect because the text does not talk about the culture in the East regarding European influence. Finally, Choice *C* is incorrect; this is an assumption that has no evidence in the text to back it up.

10. E: The author says that Portland has "as fine churches, as complete a system of schools, as fine residences, as great a love of music and art, as can be found at any city of the East of equal size," which proves that the culture is similar in this particular city to the cities in the East.

11. B: Approximately 240,000. We know from the graph that San Francisco has around 300,000 inhabitants at this time. From the text (and from the graph) we can see that Portland has 60,000 inhabitants. Subtract these two numbers to come up with 240,000.

12. B: Choice *B* correctly identifies the best investment opportunity. The cardinal rule has three requirements—privately held small business, sells tangible goods, and no debt. Elizabeth's store is a privately held small business (standalone and owned by her), it sells tangible goods (board games), and it has no debt. The lack of profitability is irrelevant, acting as a red herring. The cardinal rule doesn't mention it, presumably since the businessman thinks he can increase profitability as long as the business meets those three requirements.

Choice *A* is incorrect. Jose's grocery store owes the bank three months' worth of mortgage payments, so it has debt, violating the cardinal rule.

Choice *C* is incorrect. The accounting firm violates the cardinal rule, because it does not sell a tangible good.

Choice *D* is incorrect. A multinational corporation is not a small business, so it violates the cardinal rule.

Choice *E* is incorrect. The regional chain of liquor stores has debt (small business loan), so it's a worse investment than the board game store according to the businessman's cardinal rule.

13. A: The point of view of the narrator of the passage can best be described as third-person omniscient. The narrator refers to the characters in the story by third-person pronouns: *he, it,* and *they*. The narrator also comes across as "all-knowing" (omniscient) by relating the information and feelings about all the characters (instead of just those of a single character). Second-person point of view would incorporate the second-person pronoun, *you*. First-person point of view would incorporate first-person pronouns: *I* and *we*. Finally, the third-person objective point of view would also refer to the characters in the story by third-person pronouns *he, it,* and *they*. However, the narrator would stay detached, only telling the story and not expressing what the characters feel and think.

14. B: The chronological order of these four events in the passage is as follows:

1. The servants joyfully cheered for the family.
2. Mrs. Dashwood discussed improvements to the cottage.
3. Elinor hung her drawings up in the sitting room.
4. Sir John Middleton stopped by for a visit.

15. C: In the course of this passage, the Dashwoods' attitude shifts. The narrator initially describes the family's melancholy disposition at the start of their journey from Norland. However, the narrator then describes their spirits beginning to lift and becoming more upbeat as they make their way through the scenic English countryside to their new home at Barton Cottage. Although the remaining answer choices may contain some partial truths (appreciation for the family's former privileged life and fear about the family's expedition), they do not accurately depict the narrator's theme throughout the entire passage. For example, the family did not express disdain for their new landlord or doubt their future ability to survive.

16. D: Reality versus expectations is a theme of this passage. Although Mrs. Dashwood expects her new financial circumstances to be trying, and the family expects to miss their former place of residence for quite some time, the Dashwoods seem to begin to adapt well with the help of Sir John Middleton, their generous new landlord. A theme of love conquers all is typically used in literature when a character overcomes an obstacle due to their love for someone. A theme of power of wealth is used in literature to show that money either accomplishes things or is the root of evil. Finally, a theme of wisdom of experience is typically used in literature to show that improved judgment comes with age.

17. A: The statement at the start of paragraph five in this passage signifies the family is going through a transition. The Dashwoods find themselves in a time of great transition as they learn to accept their family's demotion in social standing and their reduced income. The statement is not meant to signify that Mrs. Dashwood needs to obtain meaningful employment, that the family is going through a growth phase, or that the Dashwood children need to be concerned about the future.

18. B: The new landlord is a cousin to the Dashwoods. This accurately depicts their relationship. The new landlord is not a former social acquaintance, Mrs. Dashwood's father, or a long-time friend of the family.

19. A: *Liaison* is the best choices for this sentence because it means someone who helps with communications between two parties. *Proviso* means a condition or stipulation. A *diplomat* is an ambassador or a person who represents their country in another land. *Contrarian* means someone who opposes a position.

20. D: *Pragmatic* is the best choices for this sentence because it means practical and realistic. *Idealistic* means the opposite—striving toward unrealistic perfection. *Complacent* means smug or self-satisfied. *Meticulous* means carefully detailed.

Writing

1. C: The best answer is *C*. "Peanut butter" is spelled as two separate words without a hyphen.

2. A: The best answer is *A*. The original sentence is correct. There is a joke in which a boy says to a genie, "Make me a peanut butter sandwich." The genie interprets the sentence incorrectly, and the boy is turned into a sandwich. However, there is nothing grammatically wrong with the way the boy expresses his wish, and there is nothing wrong with the original sentence. The word "sandwiches" is the direct object of the verb "make"; sandwiches are what the grandmother makes. The words "me and my brothers" are indirect objects of the verb "make"; the grandmother makes sandwiches for them. Choice *D* is incorrect, because the pronoun "I" is a subject, and the sentence requires the indirect object "me."

3. B: The best answer is *B*. To refer to repeated past actions as in this case, the word "would" is used, and in an independent clause like this one, the pronoun "she" needs to be repeated.

4. B: Choice *B* is the best answer, because it is the most coherent. The step listed in the passage is actually *not* the final step, so the word "final" is out of place. All the other choices are confusing, because they include the word "final."

5. D: The best answer is *D*. This truly is the final step in the process, when the grandmother would cut the sandwiches. "Finally" is a terminal transitional word. The original phrase "in the end" is more appropriate for an action that happened one time. The author is describing a process the grandmother did repeatedly, so "finally" is a better choice than "in the end."

6. B: Choice *B* is the best answer: "students should consider spelling, punctuation, and content development." This is an example of a dangling modifier. The writing of the paper is not done by the spelling, punctuation, or content development. The writing is done by the students, so the clause has to use "students" as the subject.

7. A: The best answer is *A*. Choice *B* is incorrect because there is a comma after "without which," and this comma interrupts the sentence. Choice *C* is incorrect because of the superfluous word "additionally." Additionally is not needed here because the second sentence acts as an explanation to the first. Choice *D*

331

is incorrect because it is a run-on sentence; there should be a semicolon or period after "writing" and before "without them."

8. C: The best answer is *C*. Each verb in the relative clause should show parallelism with the use of the third-person singular present tense. The clause is about words that demonstrate, words that emphasize, words that present, and so on. Therefore "demonstrate" should be parallel with the verbs "emphasize," "present," and "introduce." Choices *A, C,* and *D* are not parallel.

9. A: The best answer is *A*. The gerund form of the verb "to connect" is "connecting." Using this form of the verb creates a parallel structure, because the sentence also uses the gerund form of "to strengthen," which is "strengthening."

10. B: The best answer is *B*. None of the other transitional words make sense. Choice *C*, "additionally," is not a good answer because the sentence is not adding a new point. Likewise, Choice *D*, "next," is not appropriate because the sentence is not about something that comes next in a sequence. Because this is the final summation of the argument, the transitional word "overall" is the best answer.

11. B: The underlined portion of this sentence is a preposition. Prepositions connect an object to nouns, to pronouns, or to a phrase representing a noun. Here, the noun is "view," Hawthorne's tragic view, and the object is "the literature of the United States." The preposition is the word "in," which indicates the vision is already within the body of literature. But the beginning of the sentence makes it clear that Hawthorne's vision is a new addition, so the correct preposition is "to," to show possession (the literature now includes Hawthorne's vision). "From" is incorrect because it is the opposite of "to," and "with" is incorrect because it signals that Hawthorne and the literature are co-contributors.

12. C: Collective nouns denote a group as a single unit, and they typically take a singular pronoun ("Mankind had its finest hour.") In this passage, "man" is taken as the universal, collective subject. "His" agrees with "man" and in this context is grammatically correct. Choice *B* ("her") would make the valid point that traditional constructs unfairly exclude women, but that argument is irrelevant to the discussion of Hawthorne's allegory of the human heart. Choice *D*, people's, is grammatically correct, but it is not the best choice, because the sentence is already about one collective subject, "man," and does not need another collective term, "people."

13. D: Choice *D* is a singular possessive noun. The other choices do not follow correct sentence structure. Choice *A* makes no sense; "humanities" is the study of human culture, which does not possess inherent goodness. Choice *B* is the plural possessive of "humanities." Choice *C*, "humanitys," is not a word.

14. A: The highlighted portion is an example of two independent clauses held together by a semicolon. The first clause is "but a few feet in, the light dims and warmth turns to chill," and the second one is "the visitor stumbles, first in confusion, then in terror." The introductory phrase "but a few feet in" is an absolute phrase and must end with a comma. Inserting a comma after "dims" is inappropriate because the conjunction "and" connects only two actions. In the second clause, the comma after "confusion" substitutes for the conjunction "and." Choice *B* is incorrect because the comma separates the noun "light" from its verb "dims." Choice *C* is incorrect because the commas are needed to separate the phrases within the clauses. Choice *D* is incorrect because it lacks the appropriate commas and because the clause following the colon does not introduce a summary or an explanation.

15. D: "Farther" indicates additional distance, whereas "further" indicates an additional amount of something abstract, such as time. Choice *B* interrupts the sense of journey the writer is describing and therefore is not the best answer. Choice *C* is awkward; "toward" rather than "to" is correct.

332

16. B: While cardiologists, Choice *C*, and the American Obesity Association, Choice *D*, are actively dealing with the obesity epidemic in the United States, this paragraph focuses on a hospital's response. The correct answer is Choice *B*, "facilities." Choice *A* is incorrect because the closest definition of "faculties" that might fit in this context is "teachers and instructors in branches of learning in a college or university." If the writer had intended to use "faculties," they would have identified which branch, such as "medical faculties."

17. A: The spelling and punctuation are correct as written, Choice *A*. Choice *B* lacks a comma between the town and the state, as well as a comma after the state to enclose the clause. In Choice *C*, Massachusetts is misspelled, and if Choice *D* were used, the essay would then contain less factual information than the original.

18. B: "BMI's" is incorrect because it is the possessive form of "BMI." Choice *B* ("BMIs") is correct because it is the plural form of "BMI." Choices *C* and *D* are incorrect because the acronym is spelled out in full; as it has already been introduced to the reader, it should be used here, not the full term.

19. C: Choice *C* is the correct answer because it states that sleep apnea *can* cause problems; the other choices imply that it always causes problems. In addition, Choices *B* and *D* each have an additional error. Choice *B* is written in the incorrect tense—it uses past tense instead of present tense. Choice *D* omits mentioning that the problems are caused during surgery.

20. C: Choice *A* is incorrect because in the underlined phrase "patients" is plural, indicating more than one patient. Choice *B* is incorrect because "patient" is positioned as a descriptive adjective, rather than as a noun. Choice *D* is partly correct because "patients'" is possessive, but it is incorrect because the word is in the plural form. Choice *C* is correct: it is the singular, possessive form of "patient."

21. D: "Afflicts" is an acceptable substitute for "affects," in the context of this sentence. Choices *A* ("destroys") and *C* ("kills") are both incorrect choices because not everyone who is affected by a stroke is killed by it. Choice *B* ("effects") is not correct because it is a noun.

22. D: The key phrase in the underlined passage is "*risk* of stroke." The demographics show who in the population is prone to stroke, but they don't guarantee that those people will have strokes. Likewise, they don't guarantee that anyone falling outside of the categories listed will not have a stroke. The correct answer is Choice *D*. It is possible that Carlos might have a stroke in his lifetime.

23. C: Inserted at the end of the paragraph, the sentence about pseudobulbar affect is confusing because the condition has not been introduced yet, and so the reader has no context to put the comment in. The paragraph ends without any additional information that would justify the sentence being there. Choice *A* is incorrect because the information might be very relevant to the essay—but only if it is included in the correct place. Choice *B* is incorrect because the additional information does not support the topic sentence, "What exactly is a stroke?" Choice *D* is incorrect not because the statistic is relatively positive, but because stroke survival is not the topic of the sentence.

24. B: The logical order is the order in which the events occur, as presented in Choice *B*. The blood flow disruption begins, it can be disrupted for up to twenty-four hours, and death can be a result. The other choices do not represent a chronological order of events.

25. C: Choice *C*, "poles," is the closest synonym because as with extremes, poles lie at either end of the spectrum. Choice *A* ("spectrums") is incorrect because there is only one spectrum and it is the continuum of all possibilities that lie between the extremes, including the extremes. Choices *B* ("states") and *D* ("positions") do not connote the sense of opposites that "extremes" does.

Index

Greetings!

First, we would like to give a huge "thank you" for choosing us and this study guide for your ACCUPLACER exam. We hope that it will lead you to success on this exam and for your years to come.

Our team has tried to make your preparations as thorough as possible by covering all of the topics you should be expected to know. In addition, our writers attempted to create practice questions identical to what you will see on the day of your actual test. We have also included many test-taking strategies to help you learn the material, maintain the knowledge, and take the test with confidence.

We strive for excellence in our products, and if you have any comments or concerns over the quality of something in this study guide, please send us an email so that we may improve.

As you continue forward in life, we would like to remain alongside you with other books and study guides in our library. We are continually producing and updating study guides in several different subjects. If you are looking for something in particular, all of our products are available on Amazon. You may also send us an email!

Sincerely,
APEX Test Prep
info@apexprep.com

FREE

Free Study Tips Videos/DVD

In addition to this guide, we have created a FREE set of videos with helpful study tips. **These FREE videos provide you with top-notch tips to conquer your exam and reach your goals.**

Our simple request is that you give us feedback about the book in exchange for these strategy-packed videos. We would love to hear what you thought about the book, whether positive, negative, or neutral. It is our #1 goal to provide you with quality products and customer service.

To receive your **FREE Study Tips Videos**, scan the QR code or email freevideos@apexprep.com. Please put "FREE Videos" in the subject line and include the following in the email:

    a. The title of the book

    b. Your rating of the book on a scale of 1-5, with 5 being the highest score

    c. Any thoughts or feedback about the book

Thank you!

Made in the USA
Columbia, SC
13 July 2023